P9-BJR-341

Violence and Terrorism
04/05

Seventh Edition

EDITOR

Thomas J. Badey

Randolph-Macon College

Thomas J. Badey is an assistant professor of political science at Randolph-Macon College in Ashland, Virginia. He received a B.S. in sociology from the University of Maryland (University College) in 1986 and an M.A. in political science from the University of South Florida in 1987, while serving as a security policeman in the United States Air Force. In 1993 he received a Ph.D. in political science from the *Ruprecht-Karls Universitaet* in Heidelberg, Germany. He regularly teaches courses on international terrorism and has published a number of articles on the subject.

McGraw-Hill/Dushkin

530 Old Whitfield Street, Guilford, Connecticut 06437

Visit us on the Internet
http://www.dushkin.com

Credits

1. **The Concept of Terrorism**
   Unit photo—AP photo by Mario Suriani.
2. **Causes of Terrorism**
   Unit photo—United Nations photo.
3. **Strategies and Tactics of Terrorism**
   Unit photo—© 2003 by PhotoDisc, Inc.
4. **State-Sponsored Terrorism**
   Unit photo—Aramco photo.
5. **International Terrorism**
   Unit photo—Edward A. Gargan/NYT.
6. **Terrorism in America**
   Unit photo—Courtesy of Robin Gallagher.
7. **Terrorism and the Media**
   Unit photo—© 2003 by Sweet By & By/Cindy Brown.
8. **Terrorism and Religion**
   Unit photo—Aramco photo.
9. **Women and Terrorism**
   Unit photo—United Nations photo.
10. **Countering Terrorism**
    Unit photo—United Nations photo.
11. **Future Threats**
    Unit photo—United Nations photo.
12. **Trends and Projections**
    Unit photo—USS Vincennes.

Copyright

Cataloging in Publication Data
Main entry under title: Annual Editions: Violence and Terrorism. 2004/2005.
1. Violence and Terrorism—Periodicals. I. Badey, Thomas J., *comp*. II. Title: Violence and Terrorism.
ISBN 0–07–284719–0   658'.05   ISSN 1096–4274

Seventh Edition

Cover image © 2003 PhotoDisc, Inc.
Printed in the United States of America   1234567890BAHBAH54   Printed on Recycled Paper

Editors/Advisory Board

Members of the Advisory Board are instrumental in the final selection of articles for each edition of ANNUAL EDITIONS. Their review of articles for content, level, currentness, and appropriateness provides critical direction to the editor and staff. We think that you will find their careful consideration well reflected in this volume.

To the Reader

In publishing ANNUAL EDITIONS we recognize the enormous role played by the magazines, newspapers, and journals of the public press in providing current, first-rate educational information in a broad spectrum of interest areas. Many of these articles are appropriate for students, researchers, and professionals seeking accurate, current material to help bridge the gap between principles and theories and the real world. These articles, however, become more useful for study when those of lasting value are carefully collected, organized, indexed, and reproduced in a low-cost format, which provides easy and permanent access when the material is needed. That is the role played by ANNUAL EDITIONS.

The events of September 11, 2001, had a demoralizing effect on the American psyche. The vicious attacks on the World Trade Center and the Pentagon yielded scenes of unimaginable horror and devastation. While some declared war on terrorism, others decried American hegemony. As we approach the second anniversary of the attacks, much has changed. The successful overthrow of regimes in Afghanistan and Iraq has restored our confidence. Yet, already there are signs that the war on terrorism has not been won. The reemergence of the Taliban in Afghanistan and recent attacks on coalition forces in Iraq remind us that the war on terrorism is far from over. Violence and terrorism will continue to affect our lives well into the twenty-first century. Continuing political, economic, social, ethnic, and religious strife, fueled by the availability of weapons, advances in technology, and an ever-present international media, set the stage for the future of violence and terrorism. The only real defense against terrorism is to try to understand terrorism.

The selections for this seventh edition of *Annual Editions: Violence and Terrorism 04/05* were chosen to project a diversity of issues and actors. This revision incorporates many new articles that reflect some of the changes that have occurred since the previous edition was published. While clearly influenced by recent events, this volume endeavors to maintain sufficient regional and topical coverage to provide students with a broad perspective and a basis for understanding contemporary political violence. Articles for this introductory reader were chosen from a variety of sources and therefore take advantage of diverse writing styles. It is our hope that this broad selection will provide easy accessibility at various levels and will thus stimulate interest and discussion. In addition to the aforementioned considerations, elements such as timeliness and readability of the articles were important criteria used in their selection.

This anthology is organized into 12 units. Unit 1 attempts to address the complex task of defining and conceptualizing terrorism. It underlines the need to develop a common, internationally accepted definition of the problem. Unit 2 seeks to illuminate potential causes of contemporary terrorism. Unit 3 provides valuable insights into the tactics and strategies used by today's terrorists. Unit 4 examines the role of state sponsors in international terrorism. Focusing primarily on members of of so-called "rogue states," this section sheds light on the complex relationship between these states and terrorist organizations. Unit 5 provides a quick overview of some of the major actors in contemporary international terrorism. Shifting the focus to the domestic front, unit 6 examines terrorism in America. It includes a discussion of the potential impact of policies to combat terrorism on personal freedom and civil liberties. Unit 7 highlights the increasingly prominent role that the media plays in terrorism and points out the potential costs and consequences of increased terrorist-media interaction. Unit 8 examines the relationship between terrorism and religion, while unit 9 looks at the role of women in terrorism. Women continue to play an important, and increasingly active, role in contemporary terrorism. Finally, units 10, 11, and 12 focus on the problems associated with government response to terrorism.

This anthology provides a broad overview of the major issues associated with political violence and terrorism. It is our hope that *Annual Editions: Violence and Terrorism 04/05* will introduce students to the subject of terrorism and serve as a stimulus for further exploration.

I would like to thank the many scholars who submitted suggestions for articles to be included in this volume. I am also grateful to a group of undergraduate students in my International Terrorism course at Randolph-Macon College. I particularly thank William Heyer along with Erin Attkisson, Erin Doyle, Eric Smith, Rebecca Carelli, and Michael Youssef for their help in sorting through and reviewing the numerous articles that were submitted for consideration. These students provided valuable insights and above all a critical students' perspective, which made my job much easier. I hope that you, the reader, will take the time to fill out the article rating form on the last page of this book so we can continue to improve future versions.

Thomas J. Badey
Editor

Contents

UNIT 1
The Concept of Terrorism

Three articles examine the phenomenon of contemporary terrorism in the context of today's security issues.

UNIT 2
Causes of Terrorism

Three articles discuss the more prevalent lethal causes—including the modernization of the Western world and the socioeconomic differences between the developed and developing worlds—and the scope of contemporary terrorism.

The concepts in bold italics are developed in the article. For further expansion, please refer to the Topic Guide and the Index.

UNIT 3
Strategies and Tactics of Terrorism

Three unit articles examine some of the current methods employed by terrorists: tactics taught in training camps that include the hijacking of airplanes used in the 2001 attack on the World Trade Center and the Pentagon, kidnapping, and suicide bomber attacks.

UNIT 4
State-Sponsored Terrorism

The unit's three articles look at the many vicious forms of violence that are sanctioned by state sponsorship of terrorism and the extent to which a government can pressure its citizenry.

The concepts in bold italics are developed in the article. For further expansion, please refer to the Topic Guide and the Index.

UNIT 5
International Terrorism

Three unit selections review the current dynamics of the kind of terrorism that knows no boundaries.

UNIT 6
Terrorism in America

How terrorists affect U.S. domestic society is examined in the four articles in this unit.

The concepts in bold italics are developed in the article. For further expansion, please refer to the Topic Guide and the Index.

UNIT 7
Terrorism and the Media

The critical connection between terrorism, the media, and the audience is reviewed in this unit's four essays.

The concepts in bold italics are developed in the article. For further expansion, please refer to the Topic Guide and the Index.

UNIT 8
Terrorism and Religion

Two selections in this unit identify doomsday cults and focus on how religion has been used to justify terrorism.

UNIT 9
Women and Terrorism

Three selections examine how terrorism directly affects women in today's world.

UNIT 10
Countering Terrorism

Three articles examine methods used in counterterrorism, from logistics to retaliation through force.

The concepts in bold italics are developed in the article. For further expansion, please refer to the Topic Guide and the Index.

UNIT 11
Future Threats

In this unit, four selections consider some of the potential threats that could occur in the future: bioterrorism, ecoterrorism, and threats to our electronic infrastructure.

The concepts in bold italics are developed in the article. For further expansion, please refer to the Topic Guide and the Index.

UNIT 12
Trends and Projections

Three articles discuss how terrorism will become more complex, thus calling on a whole new level of counterterrism.

The concepts in bold italics are developed in the article. For further expansion, please refer to the Topic Guide and the Index.

Topic Guide

This topic guide suggests how the selections in this book relate to the subjects covered in your course. You may want to use the topics listed on these pages to search the Web more easily.

On the following pages a number of Web sites have been gathered specifically for this book. They are arranged to reflect the units of this *Annual Edition.* You can link to these sites by going to the DUSHKIN ONLINE support site at *http://www.dushkin.com/online/.*

ALL THE ARTICLES THAT RELATE TO EACH TOPIC ARE LISTED BELOW THE BOLD-FACED TERM.

World Wide Web Sites

The following World Wide Web sites have been carefully researched and selected to support the articles found in this reader. The easiest way to access these selected sites is to go to our DUSHKIN ONLINE support site at *http://www.dushkin.com/online/*.

AE: Violence and Terrorism 04/05

The following sites were available at the time of publication. Visit our Web site—we update DUSHKIN ONLINE regularly to reflect any changes.

General Sources

DefenseLINK (U.S. government)
http://www.defenselink.mil

The Department of Defense's public affairs online service provides DoD news releases and other public affairs documents. This is a gateway to other DoD agencies (i.e., Secretary of Defense, Army, Navy, Air Force, Marine Corps).

International Network Information Center at University of Texas
http://inic.utexas.edu

This gateway has many pointers to international sites, organized into African, Asian, Latin American, Middle East, and Russian and East European subsections.

Political Science RESOURCES
http://www.psr.keele.ac.uk/psr.htm

This is a link to sources available via European addresses. Listed by country name, it includes official government pages, official documents, speeches, elections, and political events.

U.S. Central Intelligence Agency Home Page
http://www.cia.gov

This site includes publications of the CIA, such as the *1996 World Fact Book; 1995 Fact Book on Intelligence; Handbook of International Economic Statistics, 1996;* and *CIA Maps.*

U.S. Department of State Country Reports 2002
http://www.state.gov/g/drl/rls/hrrpt/2002/

Organized alphabetically by country, this release from the Bureau of Democracy, Human Rights, and Labor includes the 2002 Country Reports on Human Rights Practices, words by Secretary of State Colin Powell, and selected reports that include hyperlinks.

U.S. White House
http://www.whitehouse.gov

This official Web page for the White House includes information on the President and Vice President and What's New. See especially The Virtual Library and Briefing Room (today's releases) for Hot Topics and latest Federal Statistics.

UNIT 1: The Concept of Terrorism

The Discovery Channel: War on Terror—Islam: Questions and Answers
http://dsc.discovery.com/news/features/terror/articles/islam3.html

This Web site is an excellent source for some basic understandings about Islam and its differences with Christianity.

Political Science Resources/International Relations
http://www.lib.umich.edu/govdocs/psintl.html

The Documents Center of the University of Michigan contains material relating to violence and terrorism under several headings, including Peace and Conflict and Human Rights. The site includes simulations.

The Terrorism Research Center
http://www.terrorism.com

The Terrorism Research Center is dedicated to informing the public of the phenomena of terrorism and information warfare. This site features essays and thought pieces on current issues, as well as links to other terrorism documents, research, and resources. Navigate the site by clicking on the area of interest.

The U.S. Department of State: The Network of Terrorism
http://usinfo.state.gov/products/pubs/terrornet/

This Web site offers complete coverage from the American government's viewpoint regarding the war against terrorism. It provides a wealth of first-hand documentation and evidence.

UNIT 2: Causes of Terrorism

Al Queda vs. the US—Winning the Hearts and Minds of the Islamic World
http://www.nsuc.org/sermons/al_queda.htm

A sermon delivered by Rev. Gary James on March 17, 2002, examines what motivated the attacks of September 11 and discusses the long-standing animosities between the Western powers and the Middle East.

FrontPage Magazine—Ecoterrorism and Us
http://www.frontpagemag.com/Articles/Printable.asp?ID=1277

Columnist Robert Locke examines the motivations behind modern ecoterrorism and signals a warning for possible future terrorist actions.

The Irish Republican Army
http://users.westnet.gr/~cgian/irahist.htm

This essay offers a brief history of the armed struggle in Irish politics against English rule. It also provides further links to more sites on Irish history and copies of public statements by the IRA.

Muhammad, Islam, and Terrorism
http://answering-islam.org.uk/Silas/terrorism.htm

This essay examines the basis for radical, fundamentalist Islam.

UNIT 3: Strategies and Tactics of Terrorism

JCSS Military Resources
http://www.tau.ac.il/jcss/lmas.html

The Jaffe Center for Strategic Studies at Tel-Aviv University lists five different groups of Web site Directories on low-intensity warfare and terrorism.

Security Resource Net's Counter Terrorism
http://nsi.org/terrorism.html

This site of the National Security Institute includes Terrorism Legislation and Executive Orders, Terrorism Facts, Commentary, Precautions, and other terrorism-related sites.

Terrorist Groups Profiles
http://web.nps.navy.mil/~library/tgp/tgpndx.htm

Material from the U.S. Department of State's publication *Patterns of Global Terrorism* includes information on terrorist groups and a chronology of terrorist incidents.

www.dushkin.com/online/

UNIT 4: State-Sponsored Terrorism

Arab.Net Contents
http://www.arab.net/sections/contents.html

Web links to 22 Arab countries ranging from Algeria through Yemen. It includes a search engine.

International Association for Counterterrorism and Security Professionals
http://www.iacsp.com/index.html

The International Association for Counterterrorism and Security Professionals was founded in 1992 to meet security challenges facing the world as it enters an era of globalization in the twenty-first century. The Web site includes a detailed overview of state-sponsored terrorism.

President Bush's Axis of Evil
http://wire.ap.org/APpackages/axis_flash/

This illustrated Web site by the Associated Press offers an overview of President Bush's statement that an axis of evil exists among Iran, Iraq, and North Korea.

UNIT 5: International Terrorism

The International Policy Institute for Counter-Terrorism
http://www.ict.org.il

ICT is a research institute and think tank dedicated to developing innovative public policy solutions to international terrorism. The Policy Institute applies an integrated, solutions-oriented approach built on a foundation of real-world and practical experience.

International Rescue Committee
http://www.intrescom.org

Committed to human dignity, the IRC goes to work in the aftermath of state violence to help people all over the world. Click on Resettlement Programs, IRC Fact Sheet, Emergency Preparedness and Response, and links to other sites.

ISN International Relations and Security Network
http://www.isn.ethz.ch

This is a one-stop information network for security and defense studies.

UNIT 6: Terrorism in America

America's War Against Terrorism
http://www.lib.umich.edu/govdocs/usterror.html

This Web site by the University of Michigan provides a news chronicle of the September 11, 2001, attacks and the war against terrorism.

FBI Homepage
http://www.fbi.gov

The home page for the Federal Bureau of Investigation includes up-to-date news and information and a section on terrorism.

The Hate Directory
http://www.bcpl.lib.md.us/~rfrankli/hatedir.htm

This site has a list of hate groups on the Web, groups that advocate violence against, separation from, defamation of, deception about, or hostility toward others based on race, religion, ethnicity, gender, or sexual orientation.

The Intelligence Project
http://www.splcenter.org/intelligenceproject/ip-index.html

This site, sponsored by the Southern Poverty Law Center, contains a map showing where various kinds of hate groups have chapters in the United States. The site has sections on legal action, teaching tolerance, and an active hate-group list.

The Militia Watchdog
http://www.adl.org/mwd/m1.asp

This page is devoted to monitoring U.S. right-wing extremism, including abortion clinic bombings and neo-Nazi militias.

UNIT 7: Terrorism and the Media

Institute for Media, Peace and Security
http://www.mediapeace.org

This Web page from the University for Peace is dedicated to examining interactions between media, conflict, and peace and security.

Terrorism, the Media, and the Government: Perspectives, Trends, and Options for Policymakers
http://usinfo.state.gov/topical/pol/terror/crs.htm

This is an essay by Raphael F. Perl examining media coverage of terrorist activities and state policy on such coverage.

UNIT 8: Terrorism and Religion

Coalition for International Justice
http://www.cij.org/index.cfm?fuseaction=homepage

This site provides all kinds of information about the investigation and prosecution of war crimes in the former Yugoslavia and in Rwanda, including some audio and video files.

Islam Denounces Terrorism
http://www.islamdenouncesterrorism.com

This Web site was launched to reveal that Islam does not endorse any kind of terror or barbarism and that Muslims share the sorrows of the victims of terrorism. It includes many references to the Koran that preach tolerance and peace.

UNIT 9: Women and Terrorism

Israel Ministry of Foreign Affairs—The Exploitation of Palestinian Women for Terrorism
http://www.mfa.gov.il/mfa/go.asp?MFAH0ll10

This official Web site of the Israeli government chronicles the use of women by Arab terrorists as agents of terror.

ReliefWeb
http://www.reliefweb.int

This is the UN's Department of Humanitarian Affairs clearinghouse for international humanitarian emergencies. It has daily updates.

Women, Militarism, and Violence
http://www.iwpr.org/pdf/terrorism.pdf

Dr. Amy Caiazza's paper, Why Gender Matters in Understanding September 11: Women, Militarism, and Violence, analyzes women's roles as victims, supporters, and opponents of violence, terrorism, and militarism and proposes policy recommendations.

UNIT 10: Countering Terrorism

Counter-Terrorism Page
http://counterterrorism.com

This site contains a summary of worldwide terrorism events, terrorist groups, and terrorism strategies and tactics, including articles from 1989 to the present of American and international origin, plus links to related Web sites, pictures, and histories of terrorist leaders.

www.dushkin.com/online/

Index of Heritage Library
http://www.heritage.org/index.cfm
   This National Security Intelligence and Counter-Terrorism site has full-text briefing papers on terrorism. Type the word terrorism into the Search window.

UNIT 11: Future Threats

Centers for Disease Control and Prevention—Bioterrorism
http://www.bt.cdc.gov
   The CDC Web site provides news, information, guidance, and facts regarding biochemical agents and threats.

Nuclear Terrorism
http://www.nci.org/nci/nci-nt.htm
   The Nuclear Control Institute's Web site includes a Quick Index to articles on nuclear terrorism and a bibliography.

Terrorism Files
http://www.terrorismfiles.org
   This is an up-to-date Web source for news and editorials covering terrorism and current events.

UNIT 12: Trends and Projections

The Brown Daily Herald—Future Terrorism Will Not Be Prevented by Retaliation
http://www.browndailyherald.com/
stories.asp?dbversion=2&storyID=4961
   This editorial by Ed Van Wesep hopes cool heads will prevail in solving our nation's problems. This article appeared in *The Brown Daily Herald* on Thursday, September 13, 2001.

Eliminate the Tools of Future Terrorism
http://backfromthebrink.org/newsroom/gorbachevv2.html
   Printed in the *Boston Globe* on October 28, 2001, former president of the Soviet Union Mikhail S. Gorbachev advocates solutions for combating terrorism.

We highly recommend that you review our Web site for expanded information and our other product lines. We are continually updating and adding links to our Web site in order to offer you the most usable and useful information that will support and expand the value of your Annual Editions. You can reach us at: *http://www.dushkin.com/annualeditions/.*

UNIT 1
The Concept of Terrorism

Unit Selections

1. **Inside Terrorism**, Tan Puay Seng
2. **Terror as a Strategy of Psychological Warfare**, Boaz Ganor
3. **Current and Future Trends in Domestic and International Terrorism: Implications for Democratic Government and the International Community**, Paul Wilkinson

Key Points to Consider

- What basic components or key criteria can be used to distinguish terrorism from other types of violence?

- What role does fear play in contemporary definitions of terrorism?

- How does the selection of a particular definition affect the U.S. government's response?

 **Links: www.dushkin.com/online/**
These sites are annotated in the World Wide Web pages.

The Discovery Channel: War on Terror—Islam: Questions and Answers
http://dsc.discovery.com/news/features/terror/articles/islam3.html

Political Science Resources/International Relations
http://www.lib.umich.edu/govdocs/psintl.html

The Terrorism Research Center
http://www.terrorism.com

The U.S. Department of State: The Network of Terrorism
http://usinfo.state.gov/products/pubs/terrornet/

Defining and conceptualizing terrorism is an essential first step in understanding it. Despite volumes of academic literature on the subject there is still no commonly agreed upon definition of terrorism. Former Supreme Court Justice Potter Stewart's famous maxim "I know it when I see it" has been replaced by an "I'll call it whatever I want to call it" mentality that has led to definitional anarchy. The U.S. government, in its efforts to address terrorism, has further confounded the definitional problem with myriad confusing statements and policies.

While arguments among academics and policymakers about how terrorism should be defined continue, most would agree that terrorism involves three basic components: the perpetrator, the victim, and the target of the violence. The perpetrator commits violence against the victim. The victim is used to communicate with or send a message to the intended target. The target is expected to respond to the perpetrator. Fear is used as a cat-alyst to enhance the communication and elicit the desired response.

Defining the problem is an essential first step in the accumulation of statistical data. Definitions have an impact not only on the collection and collation of data but also on their analysis and interpretation. Ultimately definitions have a profound effect on threat perceptions and policies developed to counter terrorism.

The first article in this unit distinguishes between the different motivations that drive ethno-nationalist and religious terrorism. The second article focuses on the use of terrorism as a means of psychological manipulation. The author argues that any cogent counterterrorism strategy must address its potential psychological as well as physical impact. In the third article, Paul Wilkinson identifies five major characteristics typical of terrorism. He discusses current trends and outlines "key components to an effective counterterrorism strategy."

Inside Terrorism

(New York: Columbia University Press, 1998)
by Bruce Hoffman

Reviewed by Mr Tan Puay Seng

Bruce Hoffman, currently director of the RAND Corporation's Washington, D.C. office and head of its terrorism research unit, presents an in-depth account of the trends and key historical themes of terrorism. The book is well researched, providing valuable insights into the difficulties of defining terrorism, the dominance of ethno-nationalist and separatist terrorism in the post colonial era, the internationalization of terrorism heralded by acts perpetrated by the Palestine Liberation Organisation (PLO), and after the Cold War, religious motivation becoming prevalent characteristics of terrorist activity. In addition, the book also discussed the evolution of targets, tactics and technologies of terrorists and explored the relationship between terrorism, the media and public opinion. The author concluded, *inter alia*, that religiously motivated terrorism, especially with the use of weapons of [mass] destruction (WMD), would present the most serious threat to global stability.

Dr Hoffman started by explaining the difficulties in defining terrorism, and was able to provide readers with the meaning of the word from different viewpoints and contexts. For instance, while contemporary terrorism, defined as general violence or threat of violence used in service of political aims, has decidedly a negative conno-

tation, Dr Hoffman highlighted that the word "during the French Revolution in fact had a positive connotation, where system of terror was an instrument of governance wielded by the revolutionary state to remind citizens of the necessity of virtue and democracy."[1] Dr Hoffman discussed the growth of ethno-nationalist terrorist groups in the period leading to WWI, which resulted from the unrest and irredentist ferment in the decaying Ottoman and Habsburg Empires. By the 1930s, the meaning of terrorism could be used to describe the practices of mass repression employed by totalitarian states against their citizens. In addition, Dr Hoffman surfaced the difficulty of defining some of the contemporary terrorist groups who consciously proclaimed themselves as "freedom or liberation fighters". This ambiguity of "terrorism is in the eye of the beholder" has complicated the international community's effort to respond to acts of terror. To use a widely quoted example, the use of violence by the Palestinians has been justified, by some, as a war of liberation against Israel's oppression and the expression of the right to form an independent Palestinian state. In this manner, Dr Hoffman has devoted a chapter to explain why one could not be defined in a consistent manner, as its usage and meaning have been altered over time to accommodate the political context of each era.

Another important takeaway from this book was Dr Hoffman's distinctions between the motivations that drive political (or ethno-nationalist) terrorism and religious terrorism. He pointed out that terrorism during the Cold War was motivated by Marxist, Leninist or Maoist ideologies. From the 1960s to '80s, politico-ideological, the ethno-nationalist and the separatist organizations dominated terrorism. These terrorist groups espoused the political and social aim of gaining independence from colonial rule, or fighting to establish a new social order. Radical leftist organizations such as the Japanese Red Army, Red Army Faction and the Red Brigade (Italy), as well as ethno-nationalist/separatist terrorist movements like the Irish Republican Army and the *Euskadi ta Askatasuna* (Freedom for the Basque Homeland) conformed to the notion of the "traditional" terrorist group.[2] One of the main characteristics of these organizations is that they avoid the deliberate causing of mass casualties, mainly because of fears that such attacks would undermine political support for their aims, or raise the risk of government retaliation.

Dr Hoffman explained that with the end of Cold War and the collapse of communism, left-wing terrorist groups were no longer appealing to the general populace, thus gradually leading to their demise. In their place, groups with less comprehensible nationalist, ideological and religious motivations have emerged. Some harbour apocalyptic visions, while others are inspired by hate agendas against targets ranging from the state and authority to ethnic groups. These groups have little regard of public image or any qualms in inflicting mass civilian casualties. Dr Hoffman cited examples of such acts of terror, which included the release of sarin nerve gas in a Tokyo subway station on March 1995 by the Japanese religious cult, *Aum Shinrikyo* (Aum 'Supreme Truth' sect) led by Shoko Asahara, who claimed to be entrusted with a messianic mission; and the bombing of the Alfred P. Murrah Federal Office Building in Oklahoma City in April 1995 by Timothy McVeigh and his co-conspirators of the Christian Patriots, an American anti-government Christian White Supremacist movement, which sought to foment a nation-wide revolution. Keeping in mind that *Inside Terrorism* was published in 1998, Dr Hoffman's views about the dangers of religious fanaticism seem prophetic. However he also cautioned acts of terrorism had not been confined exclusively to Islamic militants, but involved deviant elements of the world's other major religions, as well as smaller cults and sects. Thus, this might be a word of warning that it might be a strategic error to focus solely on terrorist acts perpetrated by Islamic extremists.

Dr Hoffman wrote in his preface that he was always dumbstruck by "how disturbingly 'normal' most terrorists seem, who are highly articulate but have nonetheless deliberately chosen a path of bloodshed and destruction."[3] His comments have been vindicated by the grim reality that terrorists who piloted the airliners that crashed into the World Trade Centre and the Pentagon belonged to a new breed of terrorists: intelligent, middle-class men committing mass murder and suicide, united only by Islamic extremism and hatred for the West.[4] They were not disillusioned young Palestinian suicide bombers, brought up in refugee camps with little education, disillusioned with the future, filled with hatred of the West and saw their salvation as winning eternal paradise by killing infidels. Instead the hijackers of September 11 were, for the most part, professionals in their 20s and 30s, well-educated, often living seemingly normal, middle class lives.[5]

However Dr Hoffman also presented some controversial issues. For instance, he commented that religious terrorism, coupled with increased access to critical information and key component, notably with WMD, leading to enhanced terrorist capabilities could spell an even bloodier and more destructive era of violence.[6] Notwithstanding, this reviewer notes that despite the range of sophisticated weaponry and their availability on the market, tried and true methods are still valid. For instance, kidnappings by the Abu Sayyaf group in the Philippines and hijackings by Chechen nationals protesting Russian policies, rely not on advanced technology but on intent and belief.[7]

Dr Hoffman's focus on religion as the major driving force of terrorism was vindicated by the horror of the September 11 attacks. On the other hand, Dr Hoffman's conviction about the propensity of terrorists using WMD to wreak havoc need to be seen in a more circumspect manner; as the September 11 attacks were committed by the creative use of a humble "conventional" weapon in the form of a pocket knife.[8]

Notwithstanding this, Dr Hoffman's focus on religious terrorism could also lead to the provocative thought of whether such terrorism could be seen as a defining conflict in the early years of the 21st century. After all, another authority on this issue, Prof Walter Lacquer, has called the rise of religious terrorism a radical transformation, if not a revolution of terrorism as "postmodern terrorism".[9] According to him, the new terrorism is different in character, aimed not at achieving clearly defined political demands but at the destruction of society and the elimination of large proportions of the population.[10] While debatable, this reviewer is of the view that the defining characteristic of terrorism is how terrorists have transcended territorial borders in such a pervasive manner that they do not merely threaten one state—the prime example being Al-Qaeda with its global reach. As such, never before in the history of terrorism has the international community been expected to co-operate on such a broad range of measures and co-operation, ranging from legislation to operational measures to deal with the threat.

In short, Dr Hoffman's book is a must read to all academics or practitioners who are dealing with the issue of terrorism.

Endnotes

1. Bruce Hoffman, *Inside Terrorism* (New York: Columbia University Press, 1998), p.15.
2. Bruce Hoffman, p.197.
3. Bruce Hoffman, p.1.
4. Louise Branson, quoted by the Straits Times, *The New Breed of Terrorism*, Tuesday, September 25, 2001, p.10.
5. Ibid.
6. Hoffman, p.205.
7. Ibid.
8. Ibid.
9. Walter Laqueur, *The New Terrorism: Fanaticism and the Arms of Mass Destruction* (London: Phoenix Press, 2001), p.4.
10. Ibid., p.81

Mr Tan Puay Seng is a Preventive Security Executive at the Ministry of Home Affairs. He graduated with a BSc in Mathematics from NUS in 1997 and an MA in War Studies from King's College London in 1998. He is currently pursuing a Masters in Social Science (International Studies) at NUS.

From *Pointer*, Vol. 28, No. 4, October-December 2002. © 2002 by Pointer. Reprinted by permission.

Terror as a Strategy of Psychological Warfare

Boaz Ganor
ICT Executive Director

The modern terrorist differs from the common criminal in that he is motivated by a political agenda. The actions of the terrorist—murder, sabotage, blackmail—may be identical to those of the common criminal. However, for the terrorist, these are all means to achieve wider goals, whether ideological, religious, social or economic. The way to the terrorist's ultimate political goal runs through a vital interim objective—the creation of an unremitting paralyzing sensation of fear in the target community. Thus, modern terrorism is a means of instilling in every individual the feeling that the next terror attack may have his name on it. Terrorism works to undermine the sense of security and to disrupt everyday life so as to harm the target country's ability to function. The goal of this strategy is, in turn, to drive public opinion to pressure decision-makers to surrender to the terrorists' demands. Thus the target population becomes a tool in the hands of the terrorist in advancing the political agenda in the name of which the terrorism is perpetrated.

Terrorists are not necessarily interested in the deaths of three, or thirty—or even of three thousand—people. Rather, they allow the imagination of the target population to do their work

for them. In fact, it is conceivable that the terrorists could attain their aims without carrying out a single attack; the desired panic could be produced by the continuous broadcast of threats and declarations—by radio and TV interviews, videos and all the familiar methods of psychological warfare.

Modern terrorism, in defiance of the norms and laws of combat, focuses its attacks on civilians, thus turning the home front into the frontline. The civilian population is not only an easy target for the terrorist, but also an effective one; the randomness of the attack contributes to the general anxiety. The message is: anyone, anywhere, at any time, may be the target of the next attack. This threat undermines the ability of the civilian population to live a normal life. When every action must involve planning for how to survive a potential terror attack at a random time and place, the daily routine becomes fraught with anxiety.

A "conventional" terror attack usually has a fairly limited physical effect. Its effectiveness lies in its ability to get the terrorists' message across. These messages are intended for three different audiences. To the terrorist organization's supporters, and the population which it purports to serve, the message is:

"We have succeeded. We have neutralized the power of the enemy and hit them at their most sensitive point." The attack thus serves to strengthen this public's support of the terror organization, to encourage enlistment to their ranks and, in general, to raise the morale of this community.

To the community targeted by the terror attack, the opposite message is sent: Despite all your defenses—your army, your police force, your military hardware—you are never safe from us. Once civilians feel unsafe in their own homes and work-places, daily life is disrupted, causing considerable harm to personal and national morale. The message is: until you accede to our demands, you will not be safe.

At the same time, the terror attacks sends still a third message to international public opinion. To the rest of the world, the terrorists present the attack as an example of their determination to achieve their political aims by any means and at any cost. The terror attack is intended to draw the attention of international public opinion to the conflict and the terrorists' demands. A more sinister message is concealed in this show of determination: "You, the countries uninvolved in the conflict, must put pressure on our enemies to give us what we want. Otherwise you might be next."

Classifying fear

The terrorists' primary aim is to create fear within the target population, with the intention that this fear is translated into pressure on the government to accede to the terrorists' demands in order to stave off further terror attacks. The success of this strategy is dependent on the degree to which the fear of attack can be magnified out of all proportion to the actual danger. The fear engendered in a population living in the shadow of terrorism has two components—a rational component and an irrational component. The rational fear is simply a product of the possibility of meeting a violent death as a result of a terror attack, with the degree of anxiety being proportional to the actual likelihood of the event occurring. In a society experiencing a large number of attacks, such anxiety is natural. However, there is also a more insidious element—an "irrational" anxiety—a fear that bears no relation to the actual statistical probability of ones being killed or injured in a terror attack, or even of a terror attack taking place at all.

It is this irrational anxiety that is the interim goal of the terrorist organization, and the means by which it exerts pressure on the target population. By magnifying the threat—making it seem that violent death lies around every corner—the terrorists hope to amplify the victim's anxiety to the point where he looses a sense of proportion. Terrorism is psychological warfare pure and simple. It aims to isolate the individual from the group, to break up a society into so many frightened individuals, hiding in their homes and unable to go about their daily lives as citizens, employees, and family members. Further the terrorist aims to undermine the individual's belief in the collective values of his society, by amplifying the potential threat to the extent that security appears to outweigh all other political concerns. Terrorism uses the victim's own imagination against him.

Terrorist use of psychological manipulation

Modern terror organizations invest much time and effort, as well as extensive resources into methods of psychological warfare. They carefully observer their target population to find weaknesses and cracks in the society which can be widened or exploited. The terrorists study the target country's media to learn how best to get their threats across and how to magnify the fears of the population and stimulate or amplify criticism of the government and its policies. Dissenting views in the society are carefully collected and used to undermine the population's beliefs in the rightness of its own ways. The terror organization knows from the outset that it will not achieve its goals purely by means of terror attacks. It must enlist the help of its victims themselves in gaining its objectives. A victory that would be impossible by military means is thus brought within reach through a protracted, gnawing campaign of psychological warfare—a war of attrition that gradually erodes the target population's will to fight and turns the tables against the stronger power.

Personalizing the attack

One of the most telling examples of such a policy in action is the effect that a terror attack has on members of the target population not directly hit by the attack. This influence—the "personalization of the attack"—can be seen immediately after a terror attack on a busy street or crowded shopping center. The immediate reaction of most people upon hearing of the attack is: "I was there only last week!" or "my wife works on the next block," or "my aunt lives just down the street." People have a natural tendency to seek a personal connection to events—a tendency of which the terrorist organization is well aware. By such "personalizing" of terror attacks, the effect on the target population is made to extend beyond the immediate victims to include people who weren't even in the area at the time of the attack. The message conveyed—even though totally unfounded—is nevertheless highly dangerous. Members of the target population come to believe that only by a coincidence were they or someone dear to them, saved from harm, and that such a coincidence cannot be counted upon next time.

Of course, statistically these fears have no connection to reality. The likelihood of being harmed in a terror attack is less than the likelihood of being harmed in a traffic accident or even an accident in the home or workplace. In fact, the chances of dying of serious illness are much greater than the chances of being even slightly injured in a terror attack. Nonetheless, by using psychological manipulation, the terrorists succeed in creating disproportionate anxiety in relation to the actual threat—a kind of irrational panic. While the physical damage caused by terrorism may be statistically less than that of traffic accidents or other mishaps, the atmosphere created by a terrorist act casts a greatly magnified shadow over society, far in excess of its statistical risk to the individual.

Terrorists' use of the media

Governments and policies have foundered under the influence of terrorism. The ability of a small group of individuals to manipulate public opinion, and thus the highest policies of the land, is what makes terrorism a strategic threat to Israel and other democratic societies.

An example of terrorist organizations' understanding of the psychological ramifications of its deeds can be seen in the way in which the Hamas organization uses the media in Israel. After any Israeli military operation against the organization, Hamas spokesman can be counted on to declare via the news media that, because of this operation, Hamas will now carry out a series of attacks in retaliation. "Our organization has ten suicide bombers standing by to retaliate," the spokesman declares in ominous tones. But what is the real significance of such threats? Does he mean that had the military not acted against the organization, all Hamas terrorism would cease? And when he speaks of ten suicide bombings, does this mean ten attacks in the next few hours, or the next week, or the next three years? And after these ten attacks, will the organization suddenly cease attacks, or will it merely use a different excuse for the eleventh attack.

Despite the threat's lack of significance, it serves to arouse anxiety during the calm periods between attacks. What's more, it plays on the fears of the target population, which, after the first attack will be inclined to think to itself, "Oh no! There are still nine more attacks like this to come!"

Sometimes the terror organizations will exploit fears raised by a successful attack, upon learning that the attack had some special, and unintended, significance to the target population. Most of the victims of the June 2001 bombing at Tel-Aviv's Dolphinarium discotheque were teenaged new immigrants from Russia. Upon learning of this, Hamas attempted to exploit the fears of new immigrants by claiming that the attack was intended from the start to target this particular group and that henceforth, they would focus their attacks on new immigrants. Their aim was clear: to create panic within the new immigrant population, and thereby harm immigration to Israel and to encourage emigration out of Israel.

Toward a comprehensive counter-terrorism policy

Decision-makers and security personnel in countries affected by terrorism, not to mention as members of the media, often appear to be woefully ignorant of the psychological manipulations used by terrorist organizations. These people all too often play into the hands of the terrorists, helping to increase the effectiveness of the terrorists' psychological campaign. The media often grants the terrorists a platform to publicize their views and psychological manipulations, not only by the coverage of the attack itself, but also in airing interviews with terrorists themselves and videotapes made by them. Decision-makers publicly make reference to baseless threats made by the terrorists, thus granting them a credibility that they would not otherwise have. All of this naturally increases the public's anxiety. In addition,

security personnel sometimes choose to publish vague intelligence warnings of impending attacks, even where such publicity does not add to public security. This increases the level of anxiety and contributes to a feeling of insecurity and confusion amongst the public, who have no idea how to act in the light of these warnings.

Those tasked with dealing with terrorism must examine their methods of coping from the point of view of terrorism's psychological effect, and not just with a view to countering the physical threat. Otherwise they risk winning the battle—succeeding in detecting and foiling a specific attack—while losing the war. When terrorism succeeds in creating such anxiety within a society that daily life becomes impossible, then that society has lost the war against terrorism.

The population that must live under the threat of terrorism can, and is entitled to, receive aid and instruction to enable it to reduce the "irrational" anxiety caused by terrorism. It is the responsibility of the State to provide its citizens with the tools and information necessary to counter the terrorist's manipulation. And this can only be done through education, arming the population with knowledge in order to prevent the strategic damage of modern terrorism. This must be based on comprehensive research on the goals of the terrorists and the psychological manipulations used by them to achieve these goals. On the basis of this information, tools can be developed to neutralize these manipulations.

The target community must be taught to view media coverage of terrorist attacks with a critical eye, to avoid falling for terrorist manipulation. Individuals must be taught to recognize the moment when the manner in which they relate to terrorism changed—the instant when "rational" fear became "irrational" anxiety. At this stage, the instruction should give the individual psychological tools to enable him to lower the level of his personal "irrational" anxiety on his own. As a rule, members of a targeted population must constantly ask themselves: how do the terrorists expect me to behave in the light of their attacks? Am I willing to play the part that they have assigned to me in their terrorism strategy?

The role of the media

The media need not be a tool in the hands of the terrorist organization. On the contrary, it can play a crucial role in neutralizing the psychological damage of terrorism. In a democratic society, the media's role is to provide reliable information in real time. However, they must be wary of their natural tendency to amplify the horror of a terror attack, and thus serve as a platform for the terrorists. The media should avoid taking close-ups whilst a terror attack is taking place and they should downplay expressions of extreme fear and panic in the heat of the moment. Above all, they should avoid broadcasting tapes made by terror organizations and interviews with individual terrorists.

In a democratic society there is no place for censorship, even on such a problematic and sensitive issue. However, even though the journalist must remain professional, he must also be aware of his responsibility as a member of his society, and avoid being used as a tool by the terrorists to attain their political aims.

The role of the government

Psychological victory and the ensuing changes in public policy are the primary strategic goals of terrorist groups. This manipulation of governments through public opinion is especially dangerous to democracies. Thus, the decision-makers and politicians have a responsibility to their constituencies to help neutralize the effects of terrorist manipulation. Among other things, decision-makers can help by allocating the necessary funds for educational and instructional activities within the target community. In addition, they must be careful not to inten-sify the fear of terror attacks, by using the attacks as a tool in inter-party political struggles.

Above all, decision-makers must recognize the strategic psychological damage which could be caused by a policy of counter terrorism that does not take into account the physio-logical influence of terror attacks—on the morale of the nation's citizens, as well as on the terrorist groups supporters and activists.

A terror attack is not an end in itself, but only a means to an end. Those faced with countering terrorism must have at least as thorough an understanding of the terrorists and their methods as the terrorist has of his target society. Often, the knowledge that one is being manipulated—and how this is being done—is itself a powerful weapon for countering such manipulation.

From *The International Policy Institute for Counter-Terrorism*, July 15, 2002. © 2002 by ICT-At the Interdisciplinary Center.

CURRENT AND FUTURE TRENDS IN DOMESTIC AND INTERNATIONAL TERRORISM: IMPLICATIONS FOR DEMOCRATIC GOVERNMENT AND THE INTERNATIONAL COMMUNITY

Prof Paul Wilkinson
Director: Centre for the Study of Terrorism
and Political Violence
University of St Andrews, United Kingdom*

ABSTRACT

This article distinguishes terrorism from other forms of violence and identifies the main types of terrorism in the contemporary international system. The major current trends in International and domestic terrorism are then briefly outlined. The article emphasises the key role of government response and argues that although democracies are inherently vulnerable to terrorist activity their popular legitimacy gives them an inner resilience to prevent terrorists from attaining their strategic goals. The value of prophylactic political, diplomatic and other socio-economic measures in helping to prevent the escalation of conflicts, which spawn terrorism is also emphasised. In conclusion, some of the key components of an effective counter-terrorism strategy are identified, drawing from the recent history of democratic responses. These include enhanced law-enforcement and criminal justice measures to combat organised crime, enhanced counter-terrorism intelligence and international intelligence co-operation, enhanced aviation security, and measures to combat terrorist fund raising.

1. CONCEPT AND TYPOLOGY

Terrorism is a special form of political violence. It is not a philosophy or a political movement. Terrorism is a weapon or a method, which has been used throughout history by both state and sub-state organisations for a whole variety of political causes or purposes. This special form of political violence has five major characteristics.

- It is premeditated and aims to create a climate of extreme fear or terror;
- it is directed at a wider audience or target than the immediate victims of the violence;
- it inherently involves attacks on random and symbolic targets, including civilians;
- the acts of violence committed are seen by the society in which they occur as extra-normal, in the literal sense that they breach the social norms, thus causing a sense of outrage; and
- terrorism is generally used to try to influence political behaviour in some way: for example to force opponents into conceding some or all of the perpetrators' demands, to provoke an over reaction, to serve as a catalyst for more general conflict or to publicise a political or religious cause, to inspire followers to emulate violent attacks, to give vent to deep hatred and the thirst for revenge, and to help undermine governments and institutions designated as enemies by the terrorists.

Terrorism is a very broad concept.[1] The role of typology is to sub-divide the field into categories, which are more manageable for research and analysis. One basic distinction is between state and factional terror. There is of course a very considerable historical and social science literature on aspects of state terror.[2] In view of the sheer scale of crimes against humanity, war crimes, and mass terror that have been and are being committed by regimes, this is a more severe and intractable problem for humanity than the containment and reduction of factional terror by often very tiny groups. It is also important to observe that historically state terror has often been an antecedent to, and, to varying degrees, a contributory cause of, campaigns of sub-state terrorism. Once regimes come to assume that their ends justify the means they tend to get locked into a spiral of terror and counter-terror against their adversaries.

Another important distinction is between international terrorism, involving the citizens of two or more states, and domestic or internal terrorism, which confines its activities within the borders of a specific state or province. Terrorism analysis based entirely on international incident statistics cannot provide an accurate picture of world trends in terrorism because it excludes well over 90 per cent of terrorist activity around the globe.[3] A further complication is that almost all prolonged domestic terrorist campaigns have an international dimension. In most cases their leaders expend considerable effort seeking external sources of political support, cash, weapons, safe haven, and other useful assets, from friendly governments and political movements as well as from their own diasporas.

A particularly useful way of mapping different types of sub-state terrorist groups active in the contemporary international system is to classify them according to their underlying political motivation or ideological orientation.[4] No broad categorisation can do full justice to the variety and complexity of the modern phenomena of terrorism but a comprehensive review of the social science literature on terrorism reveals abundant evidence of currently active groups involved in terrorist activity motivated by one or more of the following: nationalism, separatism, racism, vigilantism, ultra-left ideology, religious fundamentalism, millennialism, and single-issue campaigns (for example animal rights, antiabortion). To obtain a preliminary map of the main types of terrorism in the world today, sub-state terrorism, the phenomena of state terror and state sponsored terrorism need to be added to this list. Although the ending of the Cold War and the collapse of the former Soviet Union and Warsaw Pact communist regimes dramatically reduced the number of states involved in the routine use of regime terror and state sponsorship of terrorism for both domestic and foreign policy purposes, it by no means eradicated these forms of terrorism.

2. MAJOR CURRENT TRENDS IN TERRORISM

A major trend during the 1980s and 1990s has been an upsurge in the number and severity of ethnic and ethno-religious conflicts in which the use of mass terror against the designated "enemy" civilian population has become a standard weapon for forcing them to flee from their land and homes. Over 90 per cent of the significant armed conflicts in the world today are intra-state conflicts, the majority with an underlying ethnic or religious conflict at their root. The causes of this upsurge are to be found not only in the historical ethnic rivalries and hatreds but also in the structure of post-Cold War international system. The spread of a new world disorder is becoming more evident, in which bitter ethnic and ethno-religious conflicts have become the characteristic mode of warfare from the Balkans and the Caucasus to South Asia and Central Africa. Typically these wars are interwoven with mass terror, ethnic cleansing and a total disregard for the international humanitarian laws of war.

A second significant trend common to both internal and international terrorism is the emergence and the consolidation of terrorist groups wholly or in part motivated by religious fanaticism.[5] In the late 1970s all active international terrorist groups had secular goals and beliefs, a majority professing some variant of Marxism. By the end of the 1990s no less than a third of all currently active international terrorist groups were religiously motivated, the majority professing Islamic beliefs. It has been argued that religious fanaticism causes a greater propensity for mass-lethality indiscriminate attacks, because a bomber who believes he is carrying out the will of God or Allah and waging a Holy War is unlikely to be inhibited by the prospect of causing large-scale carnage. However, it is worth recalling that members of secular nationalist terrorist groups such as the Tamil Tigers and the Kurdistan Workers' Party (PKK) have also carried out suicide bombings.

It would be wise to avoid exaggerating the religious aspects of many of these groups. For example, although the fundamentalist Islamic groups constantly use religious language and justifications, as for example Osama Bin Laden's notorious Fatwa[6] there is a very strong political agenda underlying their campaigns: the Armed Islamic Group (GIA) demands an Islamic Republic be established in Algeria, Hezbollah wants an Islamic Republic in Lebanon. Hamas wants an Islamic Republic in Palestine, and so on. Moreover, the intensive activity of these groups in attempting to build political parties, where this is permitted by the state, and to create a social base of health, welfare and educational facilities, belies the idea that these movements should be solely perceived in religious terms.

There are five other major recent general trends at work among domestic terrorist groups in many countries which have been widely observed in the specialist literature, namely the trend towards huge bomb attacks on city centres; the trend towards mass-lethality attacks; the trend towards attacks designed to inflict mass damage on national economies, either by bombing key financial and commercial districts or by attacking vulnerable key sectors (for example, terrorist attacks on tourist industries in Egypt and Turkey); the trend in many countries towards a major escalation in hostage-taking for the purpose of extortion against families, companies and governments; and much more extensive and closer collaboration between political terrorist groups and international organised crime (for example the alliance between the degenerate guerrilla" organisations of Colombia and the drug barons).

3. THE KEY ROLE OF GOVERNMENT RESPONSE TO TERRORISM

The overwhelming majority of conflicts involving the use of terrorism are waged within the borders of nation-states. In theory, if not always in practise, each nation-state has sovereignty over its own territory and is responsible for maintaining national security and for upholding law and order. When domestic or intra-state conflicts do spill over into the territory of other states it is of course the national authorities of the affected states, which exercise jurisdiction and have the right to respond as they see fit. In this age of increasing globalisation it is hard to find any example of a terrorist movement involved in a protracted campaign of domestic terrorism which fails to take the opportunity of establishing overseas support networks to provide fundraising, access to weapons, supplies, political and propaganda support, safe haven, and other valuable assets. In all such cases, it is, once again, the national governments in the host states, which have the power and authority to control these support activities, provided they have the will to do so. Similarly, international conventions on co-operation against terrorism depend entirely for their implementation on the will, capabilities and efficiency of the national governments that ratified them.

3.1 Terrorism and liberal democracy

The history of political violence in the 20th century shows that while liberal democracies are, by definition, free of the massive sufferings caused by regimes of state terror within their own borders, they are inherently more vulnerable to the activities of sub-state terrorist groups. Terrorist groups can exploit the very freedoms, which are the hallmark of an open, pluralistic democracy—freedom of movement within and across borders, freedom of association and freedom of expression to attack others in the name of some cause they believe to be just. Groups using bombings, shooting attacks and hostage taking in liberal democracies have proved time and again that they have the ability to cause death and injury and to inflict severe damage and disruption. They are no doubt encouraged by the ample evidence that terrorism can win them useful tactical gains such as huge publicity for their cause and opportunities to raise funds and obtain weapons, explosives, and additional recruits.

However, the good news for governments of well-established and effective liberal democracies is that their popular legitimacy in the eyes of the vast majority of their citizens means that they have enormous resilience in resisting the strategic agendas of the terrorists. Citizens will rally in support of their democratic institutions against those who seek to impose on democracy by the gun and the bomb what they are unable to win at the ballot box. A dramatic display of this inner resilience was the vast popular demonstrations in Spain against Basque Fatherland and Liberty (ETA) following the kidnap and murder of a young Popular Party Councillor and other recent ETA atrocities.

Liberal democratic leaders and theorists extol the virtues of their pluralistic, open form of government as a vehicle for achieving individual liberties and the benefits of a free market economy. There is also much evidence to back up the claim that liberal democracies do not go to war with each other. A valuable additional argument for supporting the spread of the liberal democratic form of government is that it has a strong "immune system" to protect against take over by extremists using the weapon of terrorism.

It would be very foolish to pretend that the old-established liberal democracies provide perfect models for other governments in fashioning their responses to terrorism. All have skeletons to hide, including major scandals, such as the Iran-Contra

affair, illegal actions by individual members of the security forces, cover-ups and egregious cases of over-reaction. However, it is possible to draw some general lessons from the experience of democratic responses to terrorism over the past 30 years, which have a wider applicability.

3.2 Prophylactic measures

In view of the tragic effects of terrorism when it becomes deeply entrenched in any society it should be obvious that "prevention is better than cure". As indicated earlier, the majority of terrorist violence today is spawned by ethnic or ethno-religious conflicts. Generally it is used in combination with other methods of struggle, including guerrilla and full-scale conventional warfare. Therefore it is of crucial importance for governments and non-governmental and international organisations to work together to address the underlying grievances, alleged injustices, and mutual fears and suspicions which may become the cause of violent conflict. If national governments put much greater effort into promoting dialogue, mediation and conciliation in internal conflicts many insurgencies and terrorist campaigns could be avoided. Time and effort expended in ensuring greater democratic participation for ethnic and religious minorities and determined protection of the basic human rights of all members of society including members of minority communities, could save many lives and help ensure the conditions of greater social peace and stability that will allow a civil society and greater economic prosperity to develop in tandem.

Governments should at all times seek to ensure that peaceful political channels exist for communication and for resolving legitimate ethnic, religious and socio-economic concerns. The experience of many liberal democracies shows that multi-ethnic states can succeed in the peaceful management of ethnic diversity while at the same time achieving political stability and economic growth. Above all, governments should try to avoid over-reaction and repression by their security forces. There are numerous examples, which show that acts of brutality and repression of the civilian population by the security forces tend to generate and sustain campaigns of insurgency, guerrilla warfare and terrorism more rapidly than any other factor.

An efficient democratic government will attempt to remain sensitive to the needs of all sectors of society and take effective action to remedy widely perceived injustices before they fester into full-blown rebellion. It is a common mistake to assume that such injustices are always perceived in purely materialistic terms, such as access to jobs, housing and so forth. Social scientific research suggests that perceived deprivation of civil and political rights, such as downgrading the status of a language, is far more of a danger to stability than purely material deprivation.[7] Timely and effective political, social and economic measures should be introduced because of their inherent worth and the degree of popular support they enjoy. At the same time, such measures can have the inestimable advantage of serving as prophylactics against violence, insurrection and terrorism.

In the case of long-standing and potentially bitter and violent ethnic conflicts within liberal democratic states, imaginative policies designed to give fuller recognition and rights to a minority population can be the most effective way of preventing or greatly diminishing polarisation and armed conflict. An outstanding example of this method of heading off a potentially bitter and prolonged civil war was the Italian government's 1972 statute granting a considerable degree of autonomy to the German-speaking province of South Tyrol, where terrorist violence was an increasing danger at that time. There is wide agreement that Italy's policy on the South Tyrol issue was pretty effective.

Similarly, the *Statute of Autonomy, 1978* granted to the Basque region by the Madrid government, appears to have been very successful, and has led to the increased isolation of ETA-M, which has so far refused to abandon its demand for a totally independent Marxist Basque State. The *Statute of Autonomy* has not been sufficient to eradicate ETA violence, but it has helped it to marginalise it and it has captured the allegiance of the overwhelming majority of Basques. The French have tried similar approaches in their attempts to resolve the Corsican conflict, but so far with little success.

However, attempts to resolve bitter international conflicts, which have spawned international terrorism, are fraught with even more difficulties and dangers. The current efforts by the Israeli government and the moderates in the Palestinian movement to counteract rejectionist terrorism deserve the widest possible support from liberal democratic countries throughout the world. There is no doubt that the recent barbaric terrorist attacks by Hamas and Islamic Jihad were aimed at derailing the peace process. All states supporting the peace process must constantly reaffirm their determination not to allow the terrorists to get their own way and to press on with patient and determined efforts so vital to the long-term security of Israel and its Arab neighbours.

4. SOME KEY COMPONENTS OF AN EFFECTIVE COUNTER-TERRORISM STRATEGY

High-quality intelligence is the heart of the pro-active counter-terrorism strategy. It has been used with notable success against many terrorist groups. By gaining advanced warning of terrorist-planned operations, their weaponry, personnel, financial assets and fund-raising tactics, communications systems and so on, it becomes feasible to pre-empt terrorist attacks, and ultimately crack open the terrorist cell structure and bring its members to trial. Impressive examples of this pro-active intelligence-led counter-terrorism are frequently ignored by the public, but this should not result in underestimating their value.

However, it is of course not sufficient to have a highly-trained and effective counter-terrorism intelligence capability. It is also essential to have professionally trained and dedicated police and military personnel available for counter-terrorism duties who are capable of putting the counter-terrorism intelligence to fullest possible use, and who themselves provide additional arms for intelligence gathering and analysis.

A key requisite for an effective and well-calibrated response by the security forces is to ensure not only highest standards of

training, leadership and morale, but also to develop a culture of democratic control and accountability under the firm authority of the civilian government. Security force units that begin to function outside this framework of accountability are a potential source of danger. They may, by simply ignoring all considerations of constitutionality and legality, become a law unto themselves. In the worst case they begin to commit gross human rights abuses in the name of defending "national security". By resorting to the tactics of terror and brutal and indiscriminate repression, they become a root cause of further insurgency and internal conflict.

The experience of democratic states confronting protracted terrorism shows that the creation and maintenance of a democratic ethos for all the units involved in combating terrorism is vital to creating a response to terrorism fully compatible with the rule of law.

4.1 Organised crime and terrorism

The overall enhancement of police professionalism, expertise and resources makes the task of combating terrorism far more manageable. One of the key issues to be faced in many national law enforcement systems is that police corruption and collusion with organised crime undermines the viability and integrity of the entire criminal justice system. Therefore, major reforms aimed at eliminating police corruption will have a direct bearing on the ability of emerging democracies to combat terrorism. An additional benefit is that, owing to the ever increasing interdependency of transnational organised crime and terrorism improved police capabilities enable national governments to make substantial progress in combating both these serious threats to national security and law and order. Indeed many terrorist organisations themselves are heavily involved in organised crime, particularly drug trafficking, human smuggling, credit card fraud, and racketeering.

It may be of value to identify certain national measures for combating terrorism which have been found to be effective in combating terrorism in the old-established democracies, and which can be recommended for more general adoption. However, it should be remembered that every terrorist campaign is different. Responses to terrorism must be custom-built to meet the particular nature of the threat(s) confronted. If the measures are to have any chance of preventing, deterring or reducing violence they must also take full account of the political, socio-economic, strategic and cultural context of the conflict involved.

Above all, the following specific recommendations should be placed firmly in the context of the general principles of the approach outlined earlier. If the measures proposed here are taken without regard to these general principles they are, at best, unlikely to be effective and, at worst, could be counterproductive.

4.2 Intelligence measures

All law-abiding governments need to utilise the best possible available intelligence to assess the changing domestic and international terrorist threats to national security, to the lives and well being of their citizens, to neighbouring states, and to the wider security and stability of the region. Governments should also be prepared to share counter-terrorism intelligence with other states in order to enhance the capability to prevent and deter attacks, to strengthen mutual legal assistance and to help prevent terrorists from acquiring weapons and funding.

National authorities should only withhold this intelligence sharing if they have good reason to believe that one or more of the following is the case: the state requesting intelligence is itself engaged in sponsorship or support or collaboration with terrorists; the requesting state is so incompetent that valuable sources of intelligence and data that should be kept secret are compromised, thus endangering counter-terrorism operations; or the requesting state is using the excuse of combating terrorism to cover up its use of terror and general repression against its own population or other gross human rights violations.

National authorities should encourage the exchange of counter-terrorism intelligence both at the highest levels of decision-making and crisis management and in direct bilateral inter-agency co-operation. The latter is the most effective of all forms of international co-operation against terrorism. The following types of intelligence data have been found to be particularly useful in the experience of law-abiding states co-operating to combat terrorism:

- data on the activities of groups and individuals suspected of involvement in terrorism;
- information concerning the forgery or falsification of travel documents;
- intelligence on trafficking in explosives, weapons, or nuclear, biological or chemical material which could be used by terrorists, and on activities by individuals or groups pointing to the possibility of terrorists using chemical, biological, radiological and nuclear (CBRN) attacks or threats;
- information on the use of sophisticated communications technologies by terrorist groups, for example the use of encryption; and
- intelligence on links between terrorists and international organised crime, especially using drug trafficking.

4.3 Border controls

All law-abiding states can help enhance co-operation against terrorism by taking effective national measures to prevent terrorist groups and individuals from moving across borders to plan or mount attacks, to evade justice, or to obtain weapons, funds, training facilities or other assets.

It should be stressed that by applying thorough border controls and strict rules on the issuing of passports and other travel documents, and by taking firm steps to prevent and deter the forgery or falsification of travel documents, national authorities will also be enhancing their capacity to combat international organised crime.

4.4 Aviation security

Closely intertwined with the improvement of border controls is the important issue of aviation security.[8] Civil aviation is such

a predominant and fast growing method of international travel that national authorities can make a major contribution not only to the security of domestic and international civil aviation but also to security against terrorism and international organised crime in general by ensuring that they are implementing a well-designed, well-managed and adequately resourced national aviation security system. Sadly, there are still many countries, by no means always the poorest, with airports, which are weak links in the international aviation security chain. Determined and resourceful terrorist groups are quite capable of finding where these weak links are and exploiting them to the full.

National authorities throughout the international aviation system are enjoined to abide by the security standards laid down by the International Civil Aviation Organisation (ICAO).[9] These are contained in Annex 17 of the ICAO convention. It is a grave weakness that there is, to date, no adequate system of international inspection and enforcement of aviation security and safety standards.

Of particular importance in strengthening prevention of the continuing threat of airliner hijacking, and the far more lethal threat of sabotage bombing which caused so many deaths in the 1980s, are the following measures:

- enhanced X-ray and other advanced explosive detection systems;
- effective and comprehensive Positive Passenger Baggage Match Systems to ensure that no unauthorised unaccompanied bag is loaded on to an airliner; and
- high standards of management, training and morale of airport security staff.

The last part is often neglected, but is of crucial importance. Recent major serious aviation security lapses revealed by security inspectors in the United States (US) and the United Kingdom (UK), in which bombs and guns have been successfully smuggled through airport security checks, underline the fact that good technology for detecting explosives and metallic objects is not a magic formula for obtaining high standards of security. Sadly, there are still many airports around the world where security staff lack the management skills, training and basic morale to perform effectively.

4.5 Combating the hostage-taking plague

Hostage-taking for political objectives and for large cash ransoms is the fastest growing form of terrorist activity worldwide. In some areas, such as Colombia and the Philippines it has become a major growth industry, netting millions of dollars for the hostage-takers. A particularly worrying trend is the mass-hostage taking of United Nations (UN) peacekeepers, officials and aid workers, as witnessed in Bosnia, East Timor, and Sierra Leone for example. If the UN is to be able to continue with its tasks of peacekeeping and intervention for humanitarian purposes it must be provided with the means of protecting its peacekeepers and civilian officials and aid workers when they are deployed in volatile areas. The national authorities of law-abiding states should also be concentrating their efforts on enhancing their capability of handling hostage crises once they occur. For example, they need highly trained hostage negotiators with the skills to help bring a peaceful end to the hostage situation.[10] They also need highly trained hostage rescue commandos. As shown in the Lima hostage crisis (Peru), and recently in Sierra Leone, elite rescue commandos are a critical asset for saving hostages' lives when negotiations break down and the hostage-takers start killing their captives.

It is folly to pretend that there is any magic solution to hostage crises. The best strategy is to prevent terrorists and organised crime gangs from being able to establish, and operate with impunity in, ungovernable areas, so-called "gray" areas of so many countries. The reestablishment of sovereign control and the general strengthening of law and order using truly professional police and judicial systems, free of corruption, and adopting a multi-pronged strategy of combating terrorism, including terrorist infrastructures of financial and logistic support, offers the best hope of bringing the hostage-taking problem under control.[11]

4.6 National judicial measures

In *Terrorism and the Liberal State* (1986), and *Terrorism Versus Democracy: The Liberal State Response* (2000), this author emphasises the importance of national criminal justice systems in combating terrorism. In any rule of law state, acts of terrorism are regarded as serious crimes under the penal code. Therefore it is entirely appropriate that the normal response to such actions should be by the law enforcement agencies and the courts. But it is a snare and a delusion to believe that the existence of laws alone is a solution to the problem of terrorism. The floors of national parliaments and the UN General Assembly could be carpeted with laws, declarations, conventions and agreements, on terrorism. The key problem is that most of them are more honoured in the breach. It takes will, courage and determination to ensure that the law is properly implemented, and to ensure that the legal system is kept updated to contend with new developments in terrorism, with sufficient powers to deal with it effectively.

All law-abiding governments should pursue any individuals or groups suspected of involvement in the planning, preparation and perpetrating of acts of terrorism, including assisting in such activities. They should seek to ensure that all terrorist acts are made serious criminal offences with appropriately severe sentences. National laws against terrorism should be accompanied by strong laws controlling the manufacture, trading, transport and export of explosives and firearms.[12]

4.7 Measures to combat terrorist fundraising

All law-abiding governments should also enact and implement laws to prevent terrorist groups financing their activities either directly through their terrorist organisations or indirectly *via* charitable or cultural organisations or through legal "front" organisations and businesses, which are also involved in drugs, arms trafficking and racketeering.

Experience shows that to be effective these laws need to include controls on cash transfers and procedures for bank disclo-

sures. National authorities should develop regulatory laws and measures to prevent the movement of funds suspected of being destined for terrorist organisations. They should also take bilateral measures to ensure seizures and forfeiture of terrorist assets—for example, by bilateral financial agreements with other law-abiding states willing to co-operate.

5. CONCLUSION

There is no universally applicable counter-terrorism policy. Every conflict involving terrorism has its unique characteristics. In order to design an appropriate and effective response, each national government will need to take into account the nature and severity of the threat and the political, social, economic and strategic context, and the preparedness of their intelligence, police, and judicial systems, their anti-terrorism legislation (if any) and, where necessary, the availability and potential value of their military forces in aid to the civil power in combating terrorism. In other words what is needed is a custom-built, multi-pronged approach geared to the type of terrorist threat confronted.

REFERENCES

1. On the conceptual and typological aspects see the discussion in: Schmid, A and A Jongman, *et al, Political Terrorism: A New Guide to Actors, Authors, Concepts, Data Bases, Theories and Literatures*, North Holland Publishing Go, Amsterdam, 1988; Kegley Jr, C (ed), *International Terrorism: Characteristics, Causes, Controls*, St Martin's Press, New York, 1990; Walter, E V, *Terror and Resistance*, Oxford University Press, London, 1969; Wilkinson P, *Political Terrorism*, Macmillan, London, 1974, Chapter One; Wilkinson, P, *Terrorism and the Liberal State*, second edition, Macmillan, Basingstoke, 1986, Part 1; and Wilkinson, P, "Terrorism" in Foley, M G (ed), *Ideas that Shape Politics*, Manchester University Press, Manchester, 1994, pp 189–198.

2. See: Arendt, H, *The Origins of Totalitarianism*, Allen & Unwin, London, 1967; Conquest, R, *The Great Terror*, Macmillan, London, 1968; Dallin, A and G W Breslauer, *Political Terror in Communist Systems*, Stanford University Press, Stanford, 1970; Fainsod, M, *How Russia is Ruled*, Harvard University Press, Cambridge MA, 1964; Friedrich, C J (ed), *Totalitarianism*, Harvard University Press, New York, 1954; Friedrich, C J and S K Brzezinski, second edition, *Totalitarian Dictatorship and Autocracy*, Harvard University Press, Cambridge, 1956; Levytsky, B, *The Uses of Terror: The Soviet Secret Service, 1917–1970*, Coward, McCann & Geoghegan, New York, 1972; Loomis, S, *Paris in the Terror, June 1793–July 1794*, J Cape, London, 1965; Lopez, G A and M Stohl (eds), *Government Violence and Repression*, Greenwood Press, New York, 1986; Medvedev, R A, *Let History Judge: The origins and consequences of Stalinism*, Macmillan, London, 1972; Moore Jr, B, *Terror and Progress, USSR: Some sources of change and stability in the Soviet dictatorship*, Harvard University Press, Cambridge, MA, 1954; Rubin, B, *Paved with Good Intentions: The American experience in Iran*, Penguin, Harmondsworth, 1981; Schapiro, L B, *Totalitarianism*, Macmillan, Basingstoke, 1972; Solzhenitsyn, A, *Gulag Archipelago 1918–1956*, Harper & Row, New York, 1973; Stohl, M and G Lopez (eds), *The State as Terrorist*, Greenwood Press, Westport, Conn, 1984; and Walter, E V, *Terror and Resistance*, Oxford University Press, London, 1969.

3. See, for example, US Department of State, *Patterns of Global Terrorism* (annual publication), Washington, DC; Mickolus, E F, *et al,*

International Terrorism in the 1980s: A Chronology of Events, Iowa State University Press, Ames, 1989; and Hoffman, B and D Hoffman, "A Chronology of International Terrorism 1995", *Terrorism and Political Violence*, Vol 8, No 3, Autumn 1996, pp 87–127.

4. The author developed a typology based on political motivation and political ideology in *Terrorism and the Liberal State*, Macmillan, Basingstoke, 1986; and in "Fighting the Hydra: International terrorism and the rule of law", in O'Sullivan, N (ed), *Terrorism, Ideology and Revolution*, Harvester/Wheatsheaf, Brighton, 1986, pp 205–224.

5. For a seminal article on terrorism motivated by religious fanaticism, see Rapoport, D, "Fear and Trembling: Terrorism in Three Religious Traditions", *American Political Science Review*, September 1984, pp 658–667.

6. On Bin Laden's Fatwa, see valuable commentary by Ranstrop, M, in *Studies in Conflict and Terrorism*, Volume 21, No 4, 1998.

7. See discussion by Gross, F, "Political Violence and Terror in the 19th and 20th Century Russia and Eastern Europe", in Vol 8 of *A Report to the National Commission on the Causes and Prevention of Violence*, edited by Kirkham, J F, Levy, S G and W J Crotty, Washington DC, 1969; and Wilkinson, P, "Social Scientific Theory and Civil Violence", in Alexander, Y, Carlton, D and P Wilkinson, *Terrorism: Theory and Practice*, Westview Press, Boulder, 1979.

8. See Wilkinson, P and B Jenkins (eds), *Aviation Terrorism and Security*, Frank Cass, London, 1998.

9. See Wallis, R, "The Role of the International Aviation Organisations in Enhancing Security", in Wilkinson, P and B Jenkins (eds), *op cit*, pp 83–100.

10. On the prerequisites for effective hostage negotiation, see Clutterbuck, R, *Kidnap and Ransom: The Response*, Faber & Faber, London, 1978, pp 115–127.

11. It is often suggested that the best way to fight hostage-taking would be to prohibit families and business organisations from negotiating the release of hostages by payment of ransom. Experience shows that attempts to prohibit ransom payment are virtually unenforceable. Moreover, allowing families and companies to pay ransom for the release of a family member/employee provides the police with the best possibility of capturing and convicting the kidnappers, because a highly trained professional police force can monitor the contacts between the captors and the negotiators. The success of the police in the US in following this policy helps explain the remarkably low incidence of kidnap for ransom in the US.

12. Although this was one of the recommendations of the Ministerial Summit on Terrorism held in Paris on 30 July 1996, few countries have taken any serious progress towards implementation.

*Edited version of a paper delivered at a conference entitled *Urban Terror in the New Millennium: Implications for South Africa*, presented by the Institute for Strategic Studies, University of Pretoria, on 4 April 2001. Professor of International Relations, Paul Wilkinson, was a research associate at the Institute for Strategic Studies during April 2001.

UNIT 2
Causes of Terrorism

Unit Selections

4. **Ghosts of Our Past**, Karen Armstrong
5. **The Terrorist Mentality**, Paul B. Davis
6. **The Pentagon's New Map**, Thomas P. M. Barnett

Key Points to Consider

- Why do Islamic fundamentalists feel threatened by modern, secular society? What can America and the West do to address growing fear and resentment in the Islamic world?

- What characteristics have been generally observed in terrorists around the world? How does the terrorist mindset contribute to the continuation of violence?

- What does Thomas Barnett mean by a Non-Integrating Gap? What are the potential implications for our future security?

 **Links: www.dushkin.com/online/**
These sites are annotated in the World Wide Web pages.

Al Queda vs. the US—Winning the Hearts and Minds of the Islamic World
http://www.nsuc.org/sermons/al_queda.htm

FrontPage Magazine—Ecoterrorism and Us
http://www.frontpagemag.com/Articles/Printable.asp?ID=1277

The Irish Republican Army
http://users.westnet.gr/~cgian/irahist.htm

Muhammad, Islam, and Terrorism
http://answering-islam.org.uk/Silas/terrorism.htm

This section focuses on the hypothesized causes of political violence. The political, economic, social, religious, and psychological causes of terrorism have long been the subject of academic discourse.

Terrorists often portray themselves as victims of political, economic, social, religious, or psychological oppression. By virtue of their courage, their convictions, or their condition, terrorists see themselves as the chosen few, representing a larger population, in the struggle against the perceived oppressors. The actions of the oppressor, real or imagined, against the population terrorists claim to represent, serve as motivation and moral justification for their use of violence. Existing institutional mechanisms for change are deemed either illegitimate or in the hands of the oppressors. Hence, political violence becomes the primary means of asserting their interests and the interests of the people they claim to represent.

Governments and policymakers also see themselves as victims of violence. They too see themselves as chosen, by whatever mechanism, to protect the interests of the people they represent. Fearful of appearing to legitimize or justify terrorist violence, policymakers often portray terrorists as irrational and illogical. Discussions of potential causes of terrorist violence are deemed irrelevant and dismissed, because the crazed actions of small groups of fanatics surely cannot be representative of the legitimate interests of larger populations. The declaration of moral outrage and the demonization of perpetrators, in the wake of particularly gruesome acts of violence, often undermine the legitimate search for answers and the causes of such violence.

Both terrorists and governments contribute to distortions of facts. By claiming the moral high ground and demonizing the opposition, they leave little room for a debate about the causes of violence. Understanding these causes of contemporary terrorism, however, provides important insights into the behaviors and actions of terrorists.

In unit 2, Karen Armstrong, Paul Davis, and Thomas Barnett search for potential causes of violence and come to vastly different conclusions.

GHOSTS
OF OUR PAST

To win the war on terrorism, we first need to understand its roots

BY KAREN ARMSTRONG

ABOUT A HUNDRED YEARS AGO, almost every leading Muslim intellectual was in love with the West, which at that time meant Europe. America was still an unknown quantity. Politicians and journalists in India, Egypt, and Iran wanted their countries to be just like Britain or France; philosophers, poets, and even some of the *ulama* (religious scholars) tried to find ways of reforming Islam according to the democratic model of the West. They called for a nation state, for representational government, for the disestablishment of religion, and for constitutional rights. Some even claimed that the Europeans were better Muslims than their own fellow countrymen since the Koran teaches that the resources of a society must be shared as fairly as possible, and in the European nations there was beginning to be a more equitable sharing of wealth.

So what happened in the intervening years to transform all of that admiration and respect into the hatred that incited the acts of terror that we witnessed on September 11? It is not only terrorists who feel this anger and resentment, although they do so to an extreme degree. Throughout the Muslim world there is widespread bitterness against America, even among pragmatic and well-educated businessmen and professionals, who may sincerely deplore the recent atrocities, condemn them as evil, and feel sympathy with the victims, but who still resent the way the Western powers have behaved in their countries. This atmosphere is highly conducive to extremism, especially now that potential terrorists have seen the catastrophe that it is possible to inflict using only the simplest of weapons.

Even if President Bush and our allies succeed in eliminating Osama bin Laden and his network, hundreds more terrorists will rise up to take their place unless we in the West address the root cause of this hatred. This task must be an essential part of the war against terrorism.

We cannot understand the present crisis without taking into account the painful process of modernization. In the 16th century, the countries of Western Europe and, later, the American colonies embarked on what historians have called "the Great Western Transformation." Until then, all the great societies were based upon a surplus of agriculture and so were economically vulnerable; they soon found that they had grown beyond their limited resources. The new Western societies, though, were based upon technology and the constant reinvestment of capital. They found that they could reproduce their resources indefinitely, and so could afford to experiment with new ideas and products. In Western cultures today, when a new kind of computer is invented, all the old office equipment is thrown out. In the old agrarian societies, any project that required such frequent change of the basic infrastructure was likely to be shelved. Originality was not encouraged; instead people had to concentrate on preserving what had been achieved.

So while the Great Western Transformation was exciting and gave the people of the West more freedom, it demanded fundamental change at every level: social, political, intellectual, and religious. Not surprisingly, the period of transition was traumatic and violent. As the early modern states became more centralized and efficient, draconian measures were often required to weld hitherto disparate kingdoms together. Some minority groups, such as the Catholics in England and the Jews in Spain, were persecuted or deported. There were acts of genocide, terrible wars of religion, the exploitation of workers in factories, the despoliation of the countryside, and anomie and spiritual malaise in the newly industrialized mega-cities.

Successful modern societies found, by trial and error, that they had to be democratic. The reasons were many. In order to preserve the momentum of the continually expanding economy, more people had to be involved—even in a humble capacity as printers, clerks, or factory workers. To do these jobs, they needed to be educated, and once they became educated, they began to demand political rights. In order to draw upon all of a society's resources, modern countries also found they had to bring outgroups, such as the Jews and women, into the mainstream. Countries like those in Eastern Europe that did not become secular, tolerant, and democratic fell behind. But those that did fulfill these norms, including Britain and France, became so powerful that no agrarian, traditional society, such as those of the Islamic countries, could stand against them.

In the West, we have completed the modernizing process and have forgotten what we had to go through. We view the Islamic countries as inherently backward and do not realize we're seeing imperfectly modernized societies.

Today we are witnessing similar upheaval in developing countries, including those in the Islamic world, that are making their own painful journey to modernity. In the Middle East, we see constant political turmoil. There have been revolutions, such as the 1952 coup of the Free Officers in Egypt and the Islamic Revolution in Iran in 1979. Autocratic rulers predominate in this region because the modernizing process is not yet sufficiently advanced to provide the conditions for a fully developed democracy.

In the West, we have completed the modernizing process and have forgotten what we had to go through, so we do not always understand the difficulty of this transition. We tend to imagine that we have always been in the van of progress, and we see the Islamic countries as inherently backward. We have imagined that they are held back by their religion, and do not realize that what we are actually seeing is an imperfectly modernized society.

The Muslim world has had an especially problematic experience with modernity because its people have had to modernize so rapidly, in 50 years instead of the 300 years that it took the Western world. Nevertheless, this in itself would not have been an insuperable obstacle. Japan, for example, has created its own highly successful version of modernity. But Japan had one huge advantage over most of the Islamic countries: It had never been colonized. In the Muslim world, modernity did not bring freedom and independence; it came in a context of political subjection.

Modern society is of its very nature progressive, and by the 19th century the new economies of Western Europe needed a constantly expanding market for the goods that funded their cultural enterprises. Once the home countries were saturated, new markets were sought abroad. In 1798, Napoleon defeated the Mamelukes, Egypt's military rulers, in the Battle of the Pyramids near Cairo. Between 1830 and 1915, the European powers also occupied Algeria, Aden, Tunisia, the Sudan, Libya, and Morocco—all Muslim countries. These new colonies provided raw materials for export, which were fed into European industry. In return, they received cheap manufactured goods, which naturally destroyed local industry.

This new impotence was extremely disturbing for the Muslim countries. Until this point, Islam had been a religion of success. Within a hundred years of the death of the Prophet Muhammad in 632, the Muslims ruled an empire that stretched from the Himalayas to the Pyrenees. By the 15th century, Islam was the greatest world power—not dissimilar to the United States today. When Europeans began to explore the rest of the globe at the beginning of the Great Western Transformation, they found an Islamic presence almost everywhere they went: in the Middle East, India, Persia, Southeast Asia, China, and Japan. In the 16th century, when Europe was in the early stages of its rise to power, the Ottoman Empire [which ruled Turkey, the Middle East, and North Africa] was probably the most powerful state in the world. But once the great powers of Europe had reformed their military, economic, and political structures according to the modern norm, the Islamic countries could put up no effective resistance.

Muslims would not be human if they did not resent being subjugated this way. The colonial powers treated the natives with contempt, and it was not long before Muslims discovered that their new rulers despised their religious traditions. True, the Europeans brought many improvements to their colonies, such as modern medicine, education, and technology, but these were sometimes a mixed blessing.

Thus, the Suez Canal, initiated by the French consul Ferdinand de Lesseps, was a disaster for Egypt, which had to provide all the money, labor, and materials as well as donate 200 square miles of Egyptian territory gratis, and yet the shares of the Canal Company were all held by Europeans. The immense outlay helped to bankrupt Egypt, and this gave Britain a pretext to set up a military occupation there in 1882.

Railways were installed in the colonies, but they rarely benefited the local people. Instead they were designed to further the colonialists' own projects. And the missionary schools often taught the children to despise their own culture, with the result that many felt they belonged neither to the West nor to the Islamic world. One of the most scarring effects of colonialism is the rift that still exists between those who have had a Western education and those who have not and remain perforce stuck in the premodern ethos. To this day, the Westernized elites of these countries and the more traditional classes simply cannot understand one another.

After World War II, Britain and France became secondary powers and the United States became the leader of the Western world. Even though the Islamic countries were no longer colonies but were nominally independent, America still controlled their destinies. During the Cold War, the United States sought allies in the region by supporting unsavory governments and unpopular leaders, largely to protect its oil interests. For example, in 1953, after Shah Muhammad Reza Pahlavi had been deposed and forced to leave Iran, he was put back on the throne in a coup engineered by British Intelligence and the CIA. The United States continued to support the Shah, even though he denied Iranians human rights that most Americans take for granted.

Fundamentalists are convinced that modern, secular society is trying to wipe out the true faith and religious values. When people feel that they are fighting for their very survival, they often lash out violently.

Saddam Hussein, who became the president of Iraq in 1979, was also a protégé of the United States, which literally allowed him to get away with murder, most notably the chemical attack against the Kurdish population. It was only after the invasion in 1990 of Kuwait, a critical oil-producing state, that Hussein incurred the enmity of America and its allies. Many Muslims resent the way America has continued to support unpopular rulers, such as President Hosni Mubarak of Egypt and the Saudi royal family. Indeed, Osama bin Laden was himself a protégé of the West, which was happy to support and fund his fighters in the struggle for Afghanistan against Soviet Russia. Too often, the Western powers have not considered the long-term consequences of their actions. After the Soviets had pulled out of Afghanistan, for example, no help was forthcoming for the devastated country, whose ensuing chaos made it possible for the Taliban to come to power.

When the United States supports autocratic rulers, its proud assertion of democratic values has at best a hollow ring. What America seemed to be saying to Muslims was: "Yes, we have freedom and democracy, but you have to live under tyrannical governments." The creation of the state of Israel, the chief ally of the United States in the Middle East, has become a symbol of Muslim impotence before the Western powers, which seemed to feel no qualm about the hundreds of thousands of Palestinians who lost their homeland and either went into exile or lived under Israeli occupation. Rightly or wrongly, America's strong support for Israel is seen as proof that as far as the United States is concerned, Muslims are of no importance.

In their frustration, many have turned to Islam. The secularist and nationalist ideologies, which many Muslims had imported from the West, seemed to have failed them, and by the late 1960s Muslims throughout the Islamic world had begun to develop what we call fundamentalist movements.

Fundamentalism is a complex phenomenon and is by no means confined to the Islamic world. During the 20th century, most major religions developed this type of militant piety. Fundamentalism represents a rebellion against the secularist ethos of modernity. Wherever a Western-style society has established itself, a fundamentalist movement has developed alongside it. Fundamentalism is, therefore, a part of the modern scene. Although fundamentalists often claim that they are returning to a golden age of the past, these movements could have taken root in no time other than our own.

Fundamentalists believe that they are under threat. Every fundamentalist movement—in Judaism, Christianity, and Islam—is convinced that modern, secular society is trying to wipe out the true faith and religious values. Fundamentalists believe that they are fighting for survival, and when people feel their backs are to the wall, they often lash out violently. This is especially the case when there is conflict in the region.

The vast majority of fundamentalists do not take part in acts of violence, of course. But those who do utterly distort the faith that they purport to defend. In their fear and anxiety about the encroachments of the secular world, fundamentalists—be they Jewish, Christian, or Muslim—tend to downplay the compassionate teachings of their scripture and overemphasize the more belligerent passages. In so doing, they often fall into moral nihilism, as is the case of the suicide bomber or hijacker. To kill even one person in the name of God is blasphemy; to massacre thousands of innocent men, women, and children is an obscene perversion of religion itself.

Osama bin Laden subscribes roughly to the fundamentalist vision of the Egyptian ideologue Sayyid Qutb, who was executed by President Nasser in 1966. Qutb developed his militant ideology in the concentration camps in which he, and thousands of other members of the Muslim Brotherhood, were imprisoned by Nasser. After 15 years of torture in these prisons, Qutb became convinced that secularism was a great evil and that it was a Muslim's first duty to overthrow rulers such as Nasser, who paid only lip service to Islam.

Bin Laden's first target was the government of Saudi Arabia; he has also vowed to overthrow the secularist governments of Egypt and Jordan and the Shiite Republic of Iran. Fundamentalism, in every faith, always begins as an intra-religious movement; it is directed at first against one's own countrymen or co-religionists. Only at a later stage do fundamentalists take on a foreign enemy, whom they feel to lie behind the ills of their own people. Thus in 1998 bin Laden issued his fatwa against the United States. But bin Laden holds no official position in the Islamic world; he simply is not entitled to issue such a fatwa, and has, like other fundamentalists, completely distorted the essential teachings of his faith.

The Koran insists that the only just war is one of self-defense, but the terrorists would claim that it is America which is the aggressor. They would point out that during the past year, hundreds of Palestinians have died in the conflict with Israel, America's ally; that Britain and America are still bombing Iraq; and that thousands of Iraqi civilians, many of them children, have died as a result of the American-led sanctions.

None of this, of course, excuses the September atrocities. These were evil actions, and it is essential that all those implicated in any way be brought to justice. But what can we do to prevent a repetition of this tragedy? As the towers of the World Trade Center crumbled, our world changed forever, and that means that we can never see things in the same way again. These events were an "apocalypse," a "revelation"—words that literally mean an "unveiling." They laid bare a reality that we had not seen clearly before. Part of that reality was Muslim rage, but the catastrophe showed us something else as well.

In Britain, until September 11, the main news story was the problem of asylum seekers. Every night, more than 90 refugees from the developing world make desperate attempts to get into Britain. There is now a strong armed presence in England's ports. The United States and other Western countries also have a problem with illegal immigrants. It is almost as though we in the First World have been trying to keep the "other" world at bay. But as the September Apocalypse showed, if we try to ignore the plight of that other world, it will come to us in devastating ways.

So we in the First World must develop a "one world" mentality in the coming years. Americans have often assumed that they were protected by the great oceans surrounding the United States. As a result, they have not always been very well-informed about other parts of the globe. But the September Apocalypse and the events that followed have shown that this isolation has come to an end, and revealed America's terrifying vulnerability. This is deeply frightening, and it will have a profound effect upon the American psyche. But this tragedy could be turned to good, if we in the First World cultivate a new sympathy with other peoples who have experienced a similar helplessness: in Rwanda, in Lebanon, or in Srebrenica.

We cannot leave the fight against terrorism solely to our politicians or to our armies. In Europe and America, ordinary citizens must find out more about the rest of the world. We must make ourselves understand, at a deep level, that it is not only Muslims who resent America and the West; that many people in non-Muslim countries, while not condoning these atrocities, may be dry-eyed about the collapse of those giant towers, which represented a power, wealth, and security to which they could never hope to aspire.

We must find out about foreign ideologies and other religions like Islam. And we must also acquire a full knowledge of our own governments' foreign policies, using our democratic rights to oppose them, should we deem this to be necessary. We have been warned that the war against terror may take years, and so will the development of this "one world" mentality, which could do as much, if not more, than our fighter planes to create a safer and more just world.

Karen Armstrong is the author of The Battle for God: A History of Fundamentalism *and* Islam: A Brief History.

From *AARP Modern Maturity*, January/February 2002, pp. 44-47, 66. © 2001 by Karen Armstrong.

The Terrorist Mentality

By Paul B. Davis, Ph.D

Terrorism has left its mark of fear on America as never before. The upsurge in worldwide terrorism had been unfolding, in lurid detail, on network television, showing ordinary Americans how vulnerable they were. With the September 11 hijacking of four civilian jets, the deliberate destruction of the World Trade Center, and the attack on the Pentagon, terrorism in the United States reached critical and unprecedented proportions. The loss of life and the financial repercussions of these attacks shocked the nation and world. Some previous events, however—an attack on the World Trade Center (February 1993), the Tokyo subway nerve-agent attack (March 1995), and the Oklahoma City Federal Building bombing (April 1995)—had already shown that if an enemy were determined enough he could create a truly frightening atmosphere in the United States. The enemy has succeeded.

When we analyze the terrorist mentality, we should strive to be clear what we are discussing. Because the word "terrorist" evokes such strong emotions and is so politically charged, it has become difficult to get a definition that is universally accepted. It is difficult, for example, to avoid value judgments. Yasir Arafat told the United Nations that nobody is a terrorist who stands for a just cause. How does one determine a just cause? Some have even concluded that terrorism is a concept with no real essence, making it pointless to seek to define it.[1] Despite these difficulties, there are common elements in many definitions of terrorism that will be used in this discussion. Terrorism is an act of violence that has a political goal or motive. It is usually perpetrated against innocent victims, and it is staged to be played before an audience whose reaction of fear—and terror— is the desired result.[2]

RESENTMENT AND SELF-RIGHTEOUSNESS

Why do people become terrorists? Are they thrill seekers? Religious fanatics? Ideologues? Can we tell who is likely to become a terrorist?

Much contemporary terrorism seems to be predicated on excessive resentment and extreme self-righteousness. Terrorists tend to believe that their causes—whether they stem from ethnic, religious, or ideological convictions—have been undermined, exploited, or betrayed by powerful forces internal or external to their nation. The perception of themselves as being morally charged, as victims, is a core component of their belief system that is often passed on from generation to generation. Because of this, they feel justified in victimizing others and believe that they have been left no choice in that matter by a cruel and insensitive world. It has been argued that people predisposed to recruitment by modern terrorist organizations have learned to see the world in very simple terms. For many, things are either black or white, all good or all bad.

In the end, however, the threat we face is not from a weapon but from a cluster of beliefs, motivations, and cultural forces that have molded the human mind.

Terrorists are collectors of injustice. They are extremely sensitive to slights and humiliations inflicted on themselves or on members of social groups to which they belong or with which they identify themselves.[3] As one observer remarks: "The terrorist seems to be hypersensitive to the sufferings and injustices of the world at large, but totally insensitive to immediate, palpable suffering directly around him, especially if he has produced it himself."[4] This may be due to the terrorist's propensity to dehumanize his victims by regarding them as objects or impersonal concepts. Indeed, the dehumanization of the enemy is a critical component within the belief system of terrorists in general.[5]

The terrorist perceives himself part of an elite engaged in a heroic struggle to right the injustices of a cruel world. "The struggle in which they are engaged is an obligation, a duty, not a voluntary choice, because they are the enlightened in a mass of unenlightened," says Cindy Combs in *Terrorism in the Twenty-First Century*. Going beyond these characteristics, some observers have speculated that many terrorists may be stress seekers with a need to interrupt the monotony of this daily lives by the pursuit of adventure and excitement.

Rushworth M. Kidder, a prominent researcher on terrorism, has identified seven characteristics observed in interviewing well-known terrorists around the world:

- oversimplification of issues
- frustration about an inability to change society
- a sense of self-righteousness
- a utopian belief in the world
- a feeling of social isolation
- a need to assert his own existence
- a cold-blooded willingness to kill.

WHAT OF THE FUTURE?

Terrorism, then, represents an absolutist approach to resolving political problems. This approach has increasingly become infected, as well, with an anti-Western bias. The membership of terrorist groups has become more ruthless and violent as the more moderate and compassionate members have been eliminated or cast aside.[6]

Much contemporary terrorism is inspired, motivated, and justified by fundamentalist religious doctrine. Muslims have no monopoly on martyrdom or mass murder. Throughout history we see religions presuming the approval of God for the killing of pagans, heathens, or infidels. For example, Muslim extremists who strap on explosives and blow themselves up often see themselves fighting injustice inflicted against their people. Islamic tradition professes to assert that those who sacrifice themselves and become martyrs for the benefit of God will be justly and richly rewarded: "They are alive in the presence of their Lord," says the Koran, "and are granted gifts from him."[7]

Based on this mindset, what can we expect of terrorism in the future? The trend will probably be toward more violent attacks on mass civilian targets using more powerful bombs and other weapons. Since terrorists need publicity to inspire fear and paranoia, it is logical to believe that they will seek more sensational and horrific events to hold the public's attention and maintain the momentum they achieved on September 11. Will this mean the use of biological or chemical weapons of mass destruction and more catastrophic disasters? Is the unthinkable now thinkable: the use of nuclear explosions? Many people believe that nuclear terrorism may, in fact, be inevitable.[8]

In the end, however, the threat we face is not from a weapon but from a cluster of beliefs, motivations, and cultural forces that have molded a human mind. The individual terrorist can be captured, killed, or rendered less dangerous by attacking his support system or increasing our own security—as we are doing now. But how can we combat the terrorist mindset? It has been said that bad ideas can be fought only by better ideas, but exactly how to fight that battle on the most complex terrain we know—the human brain and mind—is still far beyond our knowledge. To understand more is now our urgent task.

Notes

1. Jonathan R. White, *Terrorism: An Introduction* (California: Brooks/Cole, 1997) 7.
2. Cindy C. Combs, *Terrorism in the Twenty-First Century* (New Jersey: Prentice-Hall, 1997) 17.
3. Frederick Hacker, "Dialectical Interrelationships of Personal and Political Factors in Terrorism," in Lawrence Freedom and Yonah Alexander (eds.), *Perspective on Terrorism* (Wilmington, Del.: Scholarly Resources, 1983) 24–25.
4. Konrad Kellen, *Terrorists—What Are They Like?* (Santa Monica, Ca: The Rand Corporation, 1979) 39.
5. Martha Crenshaw, "The Psychology of Political Terrorism," in Margaret Hermann (ed.), *Political Psychology* (San Francisco: Josey-Bass, 1968) 384–390.
6. Brian Jenkins, *The Future Course of International Terrorism* (Santa Monica, Ca.: The Rand Corporation, 1985) 14.
7. Jeffery L. Sheler, "Alive in the Presence of Their Lord," *U.S. News & World Report* (October 1, 2001) 38.
8. Jenkins, op. cit., 24.

PAUL DAVIS, PH.D., an international expert on terrorism, is professor of political science at the University of Nevada at Reno. He is the co-author of *Introduction to Political Terrorism* (McGraw-Hill, 1989) and participated in the United States State Department Scholar-Diplomat Program on National Security.

This article originally appeared in *Cerebrum: The Dana Forum on Brain Science,* Summer 2001, Vol. 3, No. 3. © 2001 by The Dana Press (www.dana.org). Reprinted by permission.

THE PENTAGON'S NEW MAP

IT EXPLAINS WHY WE'RE GOING TO WAR. AND WHY WE'LL KEEP GOING TO WAR.

BY THOMAS P.M. BARNETT, U.S. NAVAL WAR COLLEGE [MAPS BY WILLIAM MCNULTY]

Since the end of the cold war, the United States has been trying to come up with an operating theory of the world—and a military strategy to accompany it. Now there's a leading contender. It involves identifying the problem parts of the world and aggressively shrinking them. Since September 11, 2001, the author, a professor of warfare analysis, has been advising the Office of the Secretary of Defense and giving this briefing continually at the Pentagon and in the intelligence community. Now he gives it to you.

LET ME TELL YOU why military engagement with Saddam Hussein's regime in Baghdad is not only necessary and inevitable, but good.

When the United States finally goes to war again in the Persian Gulf, it will not constitute a settling of old scores, or just an enforced disarmament of illegal weapons, or a distraction in the war on terror. Our next war in the Gulf will mark a historical tipping point—the moment when Washington takes real ownership of strategic security in the age of globalization.

That is why the public debate about this war has been so important: It forces Americans to come to terms with what I believe is the new security paradigm that shapes this age, namely, *Disconnectedness defines danger.* Saddam Hussein's outlaw regime is dangerously disconnected from the globalizing world, from its rule sets, its norms, and all the ties that bind countries together in mutually assured dependence.

The problem with most discussion of globalization is that too many experts treat it as a binary outcome: Either it is great and sweeping the planet, or it is horrid and failing humanity everywhere. Neither view really works, because globalization as a historical process is simply too big and too complex for such summary judgments. Instead, this new world must be defined by where globalization has truly taken root and where it has not.

Show me where globalization is thick with network connectivity, financial transactions, liberal media flows, and collective security, and I will show you regions featuring stable governments, rising standards of living, and more deaths by suicide than murder. These parts of the world I call the Functioning Core, or Core. But show me where globalization is thinning or just plain absent, and I will show you regions plagued by politically repressive regimes, widespread poverty and disease, routine mass murder, and—most important—the chronic conflicts that incubate the next generation of global terrorists. These parts of the world I call the Non-Integrating Gap, or Gap.

Globalization's "ozone hole" may have been out of sight and out of mind prior to September 11, 2001, but it has been hard to miss ever since. And measuring the reach of globalization is not an academic exercise to an eighteen-year-old marine sinking tent poles on its far side. So where do we schedule the U.S. military's next round of away games? The pattern that has emerged since the end of the cold war suggests a simple answer: in the Gap.

The reason I support going to war in Iraq is not simply that Saddam is a cutthroat Stalinist willing to kill anyone to stay in power, nor because that regime has clearly supported terrorist networks over the years. The real reason I support a war like this is that the resulting long-term military commitment will finally force America to deal with the entire Gap as a strategic threat environment.

FOR MOST COUNTRIES, accommodating the emerging global rule set of democracy, transparency, and free trade is no mean feat, which is something most Americans find hard to understand. We tend to forget just how hard it has been to keep the United States together all these years, harmonizing our own, competing internal rule sets along the way—through a Civil War, a Great Depression, and the long struggles for racial and sexual equality that continue to this day. As far as most states are concerned, we are quite unrealistic in our expectation that they should adapt themselves quickly to globalization's very American-looking rule set.

But you have to be careful with that Darwinian pessimism, because it is a short jump from apologizing for globalization-as-forced-Americanization to insinuating—along racial or civilization lines—that "*those* people will simply never be like us." Just ten years ago, most experts were willing to write off poor Russia, declaring Slavs, in effect, genetically unfit for democracy and capitalism. Similar arguments resonated in most China-bashing during the 1990's, and you hear them today in the debates about the feasibility of imposing democracy on a post-Saddam Iraq—a sort of Muslims-are-from-Mars argument.

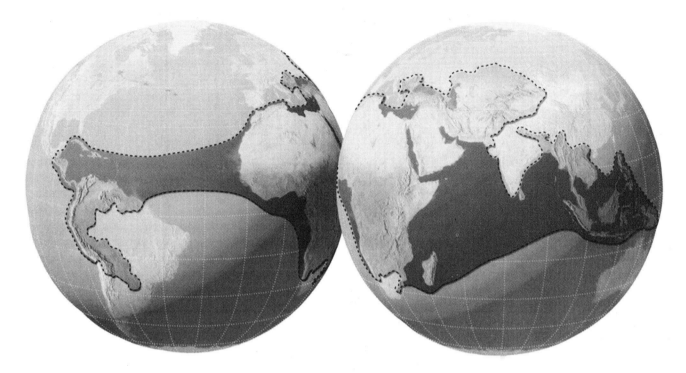

DISCONNECTEDNESS DEFINES DANGER Problem areas requiring American attention (outlined) are, in the author's analysis, called the Gap. Shrinking the Gap is possible only by stopping the ability of terrorist networks to access the Core via the "seam states" that lie along the Gap's bloody boundaries. In this war on terrorism, the U.S. will place a special emphasis on cooperation with these states. What are the classic seam states? Mexico, Brazil, South Africa, Morocco, Algeria, Greece, Turkey, Pakistan, Thailand, Malaysia, the Phillipines, Indonesia.

So how do we distinguish between who is really making it in globalization's Core and who remains trapped in the Gap? And how permanent is this dividing line?

Understanding that the line between the Core and Gap is constantly shifting, let me suggest that the direction of change is more critical than the degree. So, yes, Beijing is still ruled by a "Communist party" whose ideological formula is 30 percent Marxist-Leninist and 70 percent *Sopranos*, but China just signed on to the World Trade Organization, and over the long run, that is far more important in securing the country's permanent Core status. Why? Because it forces China to harmonize its internal rule set with that of globalization—banking, tariffs, copyright protection, environmental standards. Of course, working to adjust your internal rule sets to globalization's evolving rule set offers no guarantee of success. As Argentina and Brazil have recently found out, following the rules (in Argentina's case, *sort of* following) does not mean you are panicproof, or bubbleproof, or even recessionproof. Trying to adapt to globalization does not mean bad things will never happen to you. Nor does it mean all your poor will immediately morph into stable middle class. It just means your standard of living gets better over time.

In sum, it is always possible to fall off this bandwagon called globalization. And when you do, bloodshed will follow. If you are lucky, so will American troops.

SO WHAT PARTS OF THE WORLD can be considered functioning right now? North America, much of South America, the European Union, Putin's Russia, Japan and Asia's emerging economies (most notably China and India), Australia and New Zealand, and South Africa, which accounts for roughly four billion out of a global population of six billion.

Whom does that leave in the Gap? It would be easy to say "everyone else," but I want to offer you more proof than that and, by doing so, argue why I think the Gap is a long-term threat to more than just your pocketbook or conscience.

If we map out U.S. military responses since the end of the cold war, (see following maps), we find an overwhelming concentration of activity in the regions of the world that are excluded from globalization's growing Core—namely the Caribbean Rim, virtually all of Africa, the Balkans, the Caucasus, Central Asia, the Middle East and Southwest Asia, and much of Southeast Asia. That is roughly the remaining two billion of the world's population. Most have demographics skewed very young, and most are labeled, "low income" or "low middle income" by the World Bank (i.e., less than $3,000 annual per capita).

If we draw a line around the majority of those military interventions, we have basically mapped the Non-Integrating Gap. Obviously, there are outliers excluded geographically by this simple approach, such as an Israel isolated in the Gap, a North Korea adrift within the Core, or a Philippines straddling the line. But looking at the data, it is hard to deny the essential logic of the picture: If a country is either losing out to globalization or rejecting much of the content flows associated with its advance, there is a far greater chance that the U.S. will end up sending forces at some point. Conversely, if a country is largely

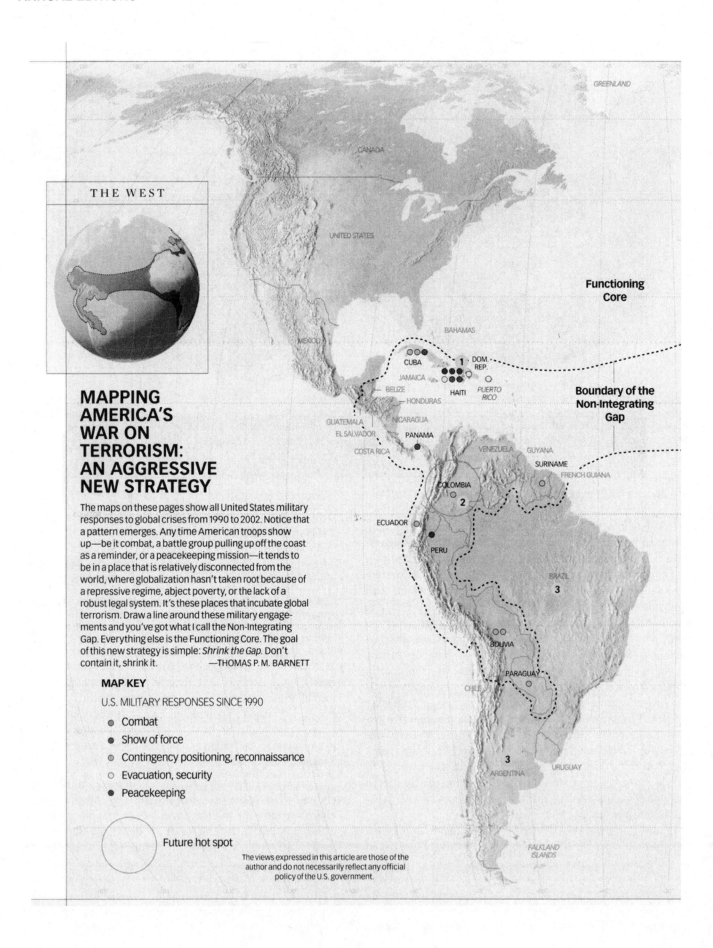

THE WEST

MAPPING AMERICA'S WAR ON TERRORISM: AN AGGRESSIVE NEW STRATEGY

The maps on these pages show all United States military responses to global crises from 1990 to 2002. Notice that a pattern emerges. Any time American troops show up—be it combat, a battle group pulling up off the coast as a reminder, or a peacekeeping mission—it tends to be in a place that is relatively disconnected from the world, where globalization hasn't taken root because of a repressive regime, abject poverty, or the lack of a robust legal system. It's these places that incubate global terrorism. Draw a line around these military engagements and you've got what I call the Non-Integrating Gap. Everything else is the Functioning Core. The goal of this new strategy is simple: *Shrink the Gap.* Don't contain it, shrink it.
—THOMAS P. M. BARNETT

MAP KEY

U.S. MILITARY RESPONSES SINCE 1990

- Combat
- Show of force
- Contingency positioning, reconnaissance
- Evacuation, security
- Peacekeeping

Future hot spot

The views expressed in this article are those of the author and do not necessarily reflect any official policy of the U.S. government.

Functioning Core

Boundary of the Non-Integrating Gap

HANDICAPPING THE GAP

My list of real trouble for the world in the 1990s, today, and tomorrow, starting in our own backyard:

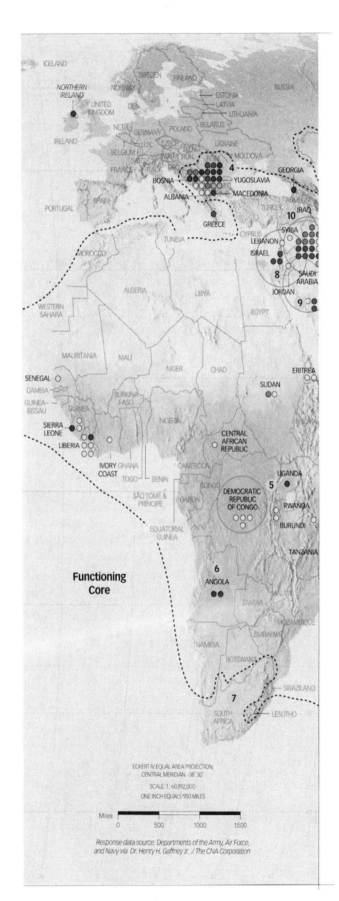

Functioning Core

ECKERT IV EQUAL AREA PROJECTION,
CENTRAL MERIDIAN -38°30'

SCALE 1:60,192,000
ONE INCH EQUALS 950 MILES

Miles
0   500   1000   1500

Response data source: Departments of the Army, Air Force, and Navy via Dr. Henry H. Gaffney Jr. / The CNA Corporation

1) HAITI Efforts to build a nation in 1990s were disappointing. • We have been going into Haiti for about a century, and we will go back when boat people start flowing in during the next crisis—without fail.

2) COLOMBIA Country is broken into several lawless chunks, with private armies, rebels, narcos, and legit government all working the place over. • Drugs still flow. • Ties between drug cartels and rebels grew over decade, and now we know of links to international terror, too. • We get involved, keep promising more, and keep getting nowhere. Piecemeal, incremental approach is clearly not working.

3) BRAZIL AND ARGENTINA Both on the bubble between the Gap and the Functioning Core. Both played the globalization game to hilt in nineties and both feel abused now. The danger of falling off the wagon and going self-destructively leftist or rightist is very real. • No military threats to speak of, except against their own democracies (the return of the generals). • South American alliance MERCOSUR tries to carve out its own reality while Washington pushes Free Trade of Americas, but we may have to settle for agreements with Chile or for pulling only Chile into bigger NAFTA. Will Brazil and Argentina force themselves to be left out and then resent it? • Amazon a large ungovernable area for Brazil, plus all that environmental damage continues to pile up. Will the world eventually care enough to step in?

4) FORMER YUGOSLAVIA For most of the past decade, served as shorthand for Europe's inability to get its act together even in its own backyard. • Will be long-term baby-sitting job for the West.

5) CONGO AND RWANDA/BURUNDI Two to three million dead in central Africa from all the fighting across the decade. How much worse can it get before we try to do something, anything? Three million more dead? • Congo is a carrion state—not quite dead or alive, and everyone is feeding off it. • And then there's AIDS.

6) ANGOLA Never really has solved its ongoing civil war (1.5 million dead in past quarter century). • Basically at conflict with self since mid-seventies, when Portuguese "empire" fell. • Life expectancy right now is under forty!

7) SOUTH AFRICA The only functioning Core country in Africa, but it's on the bubble. Lots of concerns that South Africa is a gateway country for terror networks trying to access Core through back door. • Endemic crime is biggest security threat. • And then there's AIDS.

8) ISRAEL-PALESTINE Terror will not abate—there is no next generation in the West Bank that wants anything but more violence. • Wall going up right now will be the Berlin Wall of twenty-first century. Eventually, outside powers will end up providing security to keep the two sides apart (this divorce is going to be very painful). • There is always the chance of somebody (Saddam in desperation?) trying to light up Israel with weapons of mass destruction (WMD) and triggering the counterpunch we all fear Israel is capable of.

9) SAUDI ARABIA The let-them-eat-cake mentality of royal mafia will eventually trigger violent instability from within. • Paying terrorists protection money to stay away will likewise eventually fail, so danger will come from outside, too. • Huge young population with little prospects for future, and a ruling elite whose main source of income is a declining long-term asset. And yet the oil will matter to enough of the world far enough into the future that the United States will never let this place really tank, no matter what it takes.

10) IRAQ Question of when and how, not if. • Then there's the huge rehab job. We will have to build a security regime for the whole region.

11) SOMALIA Chronic lack of governance. • Chronic food problems. • Chronic problem of terrorist-network infiltration. • We went in with Marines and Special Forces and left disillusioned—a poor man's Vietnam for the 1990s. Will be hard-pressed not to return.

12) IRAN Counterrevolution has already begun: This time the students want to throw the mullahs out. • Iran wants to be friends with U.S., but resurgence of fundamentalists may be the price we pay to invade Iraq. • The mullahs support terror, and their push for WMD is real: Does this make them inevitable target once Iraq and North Korea are settled?

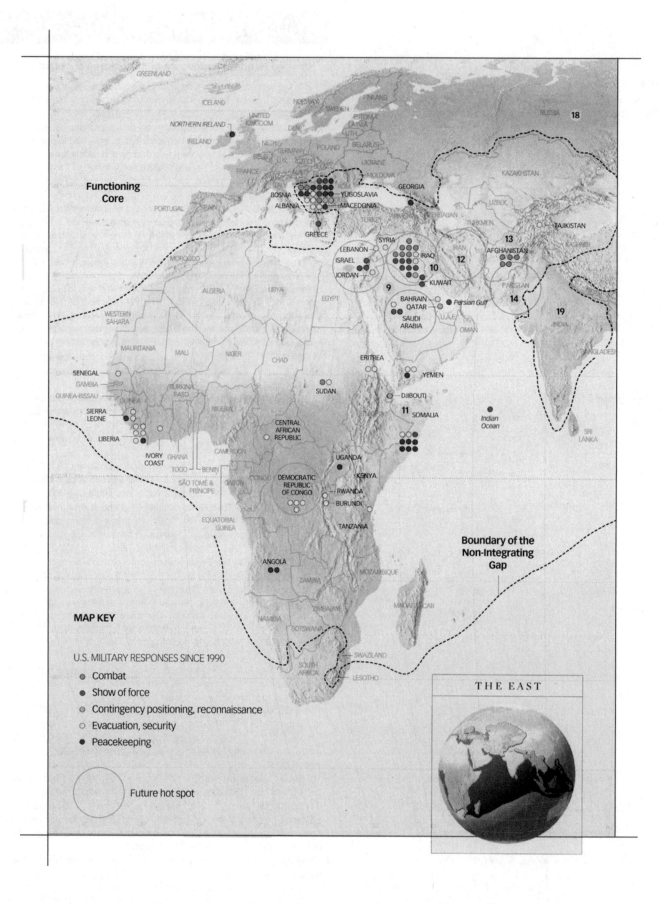

Functioning
Core

Boundary of the
Non-Integrating
Gap

MAP KEY

U.S. MILITARY RESPONSES SINCE 1990

- Combat
- Show of force
- Contingency positioning, reconnaissance
- Evacuation, security
- Peacekeeping

Future hot spot

THE EAST

HANDICAPPING THE GAP

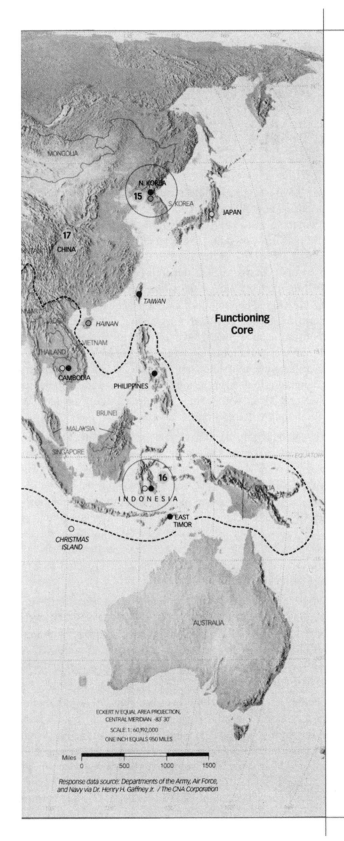

Functioning
Core

ECKERT IV EQUAL AREA PROJECTION,
CENTRAL MERIDIAN -83°30'
SCALE 1: 60,192,000
ONE INCH EQUALS 950 MILES

Miles
0   500   1000   1500

*Response data source: Departments of the Army, Air Force,
and Navy via Dr. Henry H. Gaffney Jr. / The CNA Corporation*

13) AFGHANISTAN Lawless, violent place even before the Taliban stepped onstage and started pulling it back toward seventh century (short trip). • Government sold to Al Qaeda for pennies on the dollar. • Big source of narcotics (heroin). • Now U.S. stuck there for long haul, rooting out hardcore terrorists/rebels who've chosen to stay.

14) PAKISTAN There is always the real danger of their having the bomb and using it out of weakness in conflict with India (very close call with December 13, 2001, New Delhi bombing). • Out of fear that Pakistan may fall to radical Muslims, we end up backing hard-line military types we don't really trust. • Clearly infested with Al Qaeda. • Was on its way to being declared a rogue state by U.S. until September 11 forced us to cooperate again. Simply put, Pakistan doesn't seem to control much of its own territory.

15) NORTH KOREA Marching toward WMD. • Bizarre recent behavior of Pyongyang (admitting kidnappings, breaking promises on nukes, shipping weapons to places we disapprove of and getting caught, signing agreements with Japan that seem to signal new era, talking up new economic zone next to China) suggests it is intent (like some mental patient) on provoking crises. • We live in fear of Kim's Götterdämmerung scenario (he is nuts). • Population deteriorating—how much more can they stand? • After Iraq, may be next.

16) INDONESIA Usual fears about breakup and "world's largest Muslim population." • Casualty of Asian economic crisis (really got wiped out). • Hot spot for terror networks, as we have discovered.

New/integrating members of Core
I worry may be lost in coming years:

17) CHINA Running lots of races against itself in terms of reducing the unprofitable state-run enterprises while not triggering too much unemployment, plus dealing with all that growth in energy demand and accompanying pollution, plus coming pension crisis as population ages. • New generation of leaders looks suspiciously like unimaginative technocrats—big question if they are up to task. • If none of those macro pressures trigger internal instability, there is always the fear that the Communist party won't go quietly into the night in terms of allowing more political freedoms and that at some point, economic freedom won't be enough for the masses. Right now the CCP is very corrupt and mostly a parasite on the country, but it still calls the big shots in Beijing. • Army seems to be getting more disassociated from society and reality, focusing ever more myopically on countering U.S. threat to their ability to threaten Taiwan, which remains the one flash point that could matter. • And then there's AIDS.

18) RUSSIA Putin has long way to go in his dictatorship of the law; the mafia and robber barons still have too much power. • Chechnya and the near-abroad in general will drag Moscow into violence, but it will be kept within the federation by and large. • U.S. moving into Central Asia is a testy thing—a relationship that can sour if not handled just right. • Russia has so many internal problems (financial weakness, environmental damage, et cetera) and depends too much on energy exports to feel safe (does bringing Iraq back online after invasion kill their golden goose?). • And then there's AIDS.

19) INDIA First, there's always the danger of nuking it out with Pakistan. • Short of that, Kashmir pulls them into conflict with Pak, and that involves U.S. now in way it never did before due to war on terror. • India is microcosm of globalization: the high tech, the massive poverty, the islands of development, the tensions between cultures/civilizations/religions/et cetera. It is too big to succeed, and too big to let fail. • Wants to be big responsible military player in region, wants to be strong friend of U.S., and also wants desperately to catch up with China in development (the self-imposed pressure to succeed is enormous). • And then there's AIDS.

functioning within globalization, we tend not to have to send our forces there to restore order or eradicate threats.

Now, that may seem like a tautology—in effect defining any place that has not attracted U.S. military intervention in the last decade or so as "functioning within globalization" (and vice versa). But think about this larger point: Ever since the end of World War II, this country has assumed that the real threats to its security resided in countries of roughly similar size, development, and wealth—in other words, other great powers like ourselves. During the cold war, that other great power was the Soviet Union. When the big Red machine evaporated in the early 1990's, we flirted with concerns about a united Europe, a powerhouse Japan, and—most recently—a rising China.

What was interesting about all those scenarios is the assumption that only an advanced state can truly threaten us. The rest of the world? Those less-developed parts of the world have long been referred to in military plans as the "Lesser Includeds," meaning that if we built a military capable of handling a great power's military threat, it would always be sufficient for any minor scenarios we might have to engage in the less advanced world.

That assumption was shattered by September 11. After all, we were not attacked by a nation or even an army but by a group of—in Thomas Friedman's vernacular—Super-Empowered Individuals willing to die for their cause. September 11 triggered a system perturbation that continues to reshape our government (the new Department of Homeland Security), our economy (the de facto security tax we all pay), and even our society (*Wave to the camera!*). Moreover, it launched the global war on terrorism, the prism through which our government now views every bilateral security relationship we have across the world.

In many ways, the September 11 attacks did the U.S. national-security establishment a huge favor by pulling us back from the abstract planning of future high-tech wars against "near peers" into the here-and-now threats to global order. By doing so, the dividing lines between Core and Gap were highlighted, and more important, the nature of the threat environment was thrown into stark relief.

Think about it: Bin Laden and Al Qaeda are pure products of the Gap—in effect, its most violent feedback to the Core. They tell us how we are doing in exporting security to these lawless areas (not very well) and which states they would like to take "off line" from globalization and return to some seventh-century definition of the good life (any Gap state with a sizable Muslim population, especially Saudi Arabia).

If you take this message from Osama and combine it with our military-intervention record of the last decade, a simple security rule set emerges: *A country's potential to warrant a U.S. military response is inversely related to its globalization connectivity.* There is a good reason why Al Qaeda was based first in Sudan and then later in Afghanistan: These are two of the most disconnected countries in the world. Look at the other places U.S. Special Operations Forces have recently zeroed in on: northwestern Pakistan, Somalia, Yemen. We are talking about the ends of the earth as far as globalization is concerned.

But just as important as "getting them where they live" is stopping the ability of these terrorist networks to access the Core via the "seam states" that lie along the Gap's bloody boundaries. It is along this seam that the Core will seek to suppress bad things coming out of the Gap. Which are some of these classic seam states? Mexico, Brazil, South Africa, Morocco, Algeria, Greece, Turkey, Pakistan, Thailand, Malaysia, the Philippines, and Indonesia come readily to mind. But the U.S. will not be the only Core state working this issue. For example, Russia has its own war on terrorism in the Caucasus, China is working its western border with more vigor, and Australia was recently energized (or was it cowed?) by the Bali bombing.

IF WE STEP BACK for a minute and consider the broader implications of this new global map, then U.S. national-security strategy would seem to be: 1) Increase the Core's immune system capabilities for responding to September 11–like system perturbations; 2) Work the seam states to firewall the Core from the Gap's worst exports, such as terror, drugs, and pandemics; and, most important, 3) *Shrink the Gap*. Notice I did not just say *Mind the Gap*. The knee-jerk reaction of many Americans to September 11 is to say, "Let's get off our dependency on foreign oil, and then we won't have to deal with *those* people." The most naïve assumption underlying that dream is that reducing what little connectivity the Gap has with the Core will render it less dangerous to us over the long haul. Turning the Middle East into Central Africa will not build a better world for my kids. We cannot simply will *those* people away.

The Middle East is the perfect place to start. Diplomacy cannot work in a region where the biggest sources of insecurity lie not between states but within them. What is most wrong about the Middle East is the lack of personal freedom and how that translates into dead-end lives for most of the population—especially for the young. Some states like Qatar and Jordan are ripe for perestroika-like leaps into better political futures, thanks to younger leaders who see the inevitability of such change. Iran is likewise waiting for the right Gorbachev to come along—if he has not already.

What stands in the path of this change? Fear. Fear of tradition unraveling. Fear of the mullah's disapproval. Fear of being labeled a "bad" or "traitorous" Muslim state. Fear of becoming a target of radical groups and terrorist networks. But most of all, fear of being attacked from all sides for being different—the fear of becoming Israel.

The Middle East has long been a neighborhood of bullies eager to pick on the weak. Israel is still around because it has become—sadly—one of the toughest bullies on the block. The only thing that will change that nasty environment and open the floodgates for change is if some external power steps in and plays Leviathan full-time. Taking down Saddam, the region's bully-in-chief, will force the U.S. into playing that role far more fully than it has over the past several decades, primarily because Iraq is the Yugoslavia of the Middle East—a crossroads of civilizations that has historically required a dictatorship to keep the peace. As baby-sitting jobs go, this one will be a doozy, making our lengthy efforts in postwar Germany and Japan look simple in retrospect.

But it is the right thing to do, and now is the right time to do it, and we are the only country that can. Freedom cannot blossom in the Middle East without security, and security is this country's most influential public-sector export. By that I do not mean arms exports, but basically the attention paid by our military forces to any region's potential for mass violence. We are the only nation on earth capable of exporting security in a sustained fashion, and we have a very good track record of doing it.

Show me a part of the world that is secure in its peace and I will show you strong or growing ties between local militaries and the U.S. military. Show me regions where major war is inconceivable and I will show you permanent U.S. military bases and long-term security alliances. Show me the strongest investment relationships in the global economy and I will show you two postwar military occupations that remade Europe and Japan following World War II.

This country has successfully exported security to globalization's Old Core (Western Europe, Northeast Asia) for half a century and to its emerging New Core (Developing Asia) for a solid quarter century following our mishandling of Vietnam. But our efforts in the Middle Ease have been inconsistent—in Africa, almost nonexistent. Until we begin the systematic, long-term export of security to the Gap, it will increasingly export its pain to the Core in the form of terrorism and other instabilities.

Naturally, it will take a whole lot more than the U.S. exporting security to shrink the Gap. Africa, for example, will need far more aid than the Core has offered in the past, and the integration of the Gap will ultimately depend more on private investment than anything the Core's public sector can offer. But it all has to begin with security, because free markets and democracy cannot flourish amid chronic conflict.

Making this effort means reshaping our military establishment to mirror-image the challenge that we face. Think about it. Global war is not in the offing, primarily because our huge nuclear stockpile renders such war unthinkable—for anyone. Meanwhile, classic state-on-state wars are becoming fairly rare. So if the United States is in the process of "transforming" its military to meet the threats of tomorrow, what should it end up looking like? In my mind, we fight fire with fire. If we live in a world increasingly populated by Super-Empowered Individuals, we field a military of Super-Empowered-Individuals.

This may sound like additional responsibility for an already overburdened military, but that is the wrong way of looking at it, for what we are dealing with here are problems of success—not failure. It is America's continued success in deterring global war and obsolescing state-on-state war that allows us to stick our noses into the far more difficult subnational conflicts and the dangerous transnational actors they spawn. I know most Americans do not want to hear this, but the real battlegrounds in the global war on terrorism are still *over there*. If gated communities and rent-a-cops were enough, September 11 never would have happened.

History is full of turning points like that terrible day, *but no turning-back points*. We ignore the Gap's existence at our own peril, because it will not go away until we as a nation respond to the challenge of making globalization truly global.

UNIT 3

Strategies and Tactics of Terrorism

Unit Selections

7. **The Terrorist Notebooks**, Martha Brill Olcott and Bakhtiyar Babajanov
8. **Hostage, Inc.**, Rachel Briggs
9. **Inside Suicide, Inc.**, Christopher Dickey

Key Points to Consider

- What do the methods and tactics taught in terrorist training camps in the 1990s tell us about the future of terrorism?

- What are the benefits and drawbacks of kidnapping as a terrorist tactic? Why do kidnappings by terrorists often receive less media attention than other types of terrorist violence?

- What factors have led to the emergence of a culture where martyrdom is considered heroism? How can the threat posed by suicide bombers be addressed?

 **Links: www.dushkin.com/online/**
These sites are annotated in the World Wide Web pages.

JCSS Military Resources
http://www.tau.ac.il/jcss/lmas.html
Security Resource Net's Counter Terrorism
http://nsi.org/terrorism.html
Terrorist Groups Profiles
http://web.nps.navy.mil/~library/tgp/tgpndx.htm

The strategies and tactics of terrorism appear to be universal. While ideologies and motivations vary, terrorist organizations in different parts of the world use similar methods. Whether this is the consequence of increased communications among terrorist organizations or the result of greater access to information in an age of global media remains unclear. Some argue that terrorists simply tend to be conservative in their selection of tactics, relying on methods that have proven successful rather than risking failure. Regardless of the underlying reasons, the tactics used by terrorists have remained remarkably consistent. While they have increased in size and sophistication, bombs are still the primary tool employed by terrorist organizations around the world. According to the latest U.S. State Department report, despite a significant drop in bombings against U.S. oil pipelines in Colombia, bombings accounted for more than 85 percent of attacks against U.S. interests in 2002. In addition to bombings, kidnapping, armed attacks, arson, hostage-taking, and hijacking are the tactics most commonly used by terrorists.

The three articles in this unit reflect some of the challenges posed by contemporary terrorist tactics. Martha Brill Olcott and Bakhtiyar Babajanov's article "The Terrorist Notebooks" provides an introduction to the ABCs of terrorist training. It examines 10 notebooks maintained by students attending terrorist training camps in Uzbekistan in the 1990s and provides an insider perspective of the methods and tactics that were taught in these camps. In "Hostage, Inc." Rachel Briggs provides the latest statistics and a comparative analysis of kidnapping and hostage-taking around the world. Finally, Christopher Dickey examines suicide terrorism in the West Bank and Gaza and provides a glimpse into a culture where suicide bombing has become part of everyday life "from which no child is spared."

THE TERRORIST NOTEBOOKS

During the mid-1990s, a group of young Uzbeks went to school to learn how to kill you. Here is what they were taught.

By Martha Brill Olcott and Bakhtiyar Babajanov

"Jews, Russians, and Americans are always against Muslims and kill Muslims. And the Muslims are sound asleep."

—Notebook #3 page 16

The world of a young man recruited for jihad or holy war is a frightening one. His training teaches hatred in the name of religious purification. He learns to divide people into those who embrace the true faith and properly follow its precepts and those who do not. His former colleagues and neighbors become enemies he must destroy with deadly weapons he learns to fashion out of everyday objects.

That reality describes the world of a group of Central Asians, mostly Uzbek by nationality, who went through local terrorist schools in the mid-1990s. Their course of study is laid out in 10 remarkable notebooks we acquired in 2001–2002. Covering topics such as the use of weapons, the making of poison, and the ideology of jihad, the notebooks offer a unique window into a frightening mind-set that predates the expansion of Osama bin Laden's network in the region and still holds sway in much of Central Asia.

References in the notebooks suggest that much of this training took place in Uzbekistan's Fergana Valley. Long a center of Islamic revival in the region, the Fergana Valley is a mix of scrub desert, low hills, and lush oases. It is the most densely populated area of Central Asia and one of the most densely populated regions in the world. Throughout Soviet rule, the valley was home to a host of underground mosques and religious "schools" that thrived even as Islamic teachings were banned or re-

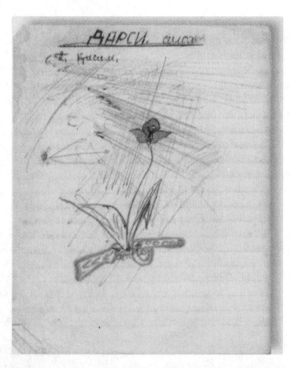

This page is from the notebook belonging to "Ayub," probably a Tajik from the city of Namangan, whom we nicknamed "the gunner" because of his single-minded focus on weapons and targeting. Ayub notes in his text that the AKM-59, a version of the AK-47, is "pretty and well put together and is comfortable to handle."

stricted. When the Soviet Union began to collapse, graduates of these schools played an important role in the revival of Islam in Central Asia, as thousands of new mosques and religious schools opened. Clerics who preached radical Islam gained new contacts and sources of financing when the mujahideen started fighting the Soviets in the Afghan war and when Saudi groups began what became a global crusade.

Covering the period from 1993 to 1994, this notebook belonged to "Abdumalik," also from Namangan, whose name is written on the cover in Russian, Uzbek, and Arabic. Among other subjects, his notes cover the characteristics of various pistols and detailed diagrams for making bombs and fuses.

The late 1980s and early 1990s were difficult and confusing years for young people living in Central Asia. A seemingly invincible state had virtually disintegrated and was replaced by fragile new ones. Conditions were almost apocalyptic: The economy was in disarray, an expansive social safety net had shredded, and the powerful Red Army was in tatters, with those who served it selling off their weaponry to survive. Muslim activists who claimed that moral turpitude brought down the Soviet regime found it easy to muster arguments to bolster their cause, and they organized the Islamic Renaissance Party (IRP). Although the Uzbek government refused to register the IRP, a number of charismatic clerics who preached rejection of the secular state continued to gain supporters, especially in the Fergana Valley. And these men in turn developed armed supporters, who in the first months of Uzbekistan's independence briefly took control of key government buildings in the city of Namangan. Fearing the outbreak of civil war, Uzbek President Islam Karimov authorized a purge of the official Islamic establishment and the arrest or disappearance of prominent unlicensed clerics and leaders of "extremist" Islamic groups.

Several prominent figures escaped the official dragnet, fleeing with followers into neighboring Tajikistan and the Tajik- and Uzbek-dominated parts of northern Afghanistan, long a host site for jihadi training camps. Thus was born the Islamic Movement of Uzbekistan (IMU), led by Soviet Army veteran Juma Namangani.

ABDUMALIK'S WORLD

During the mid- to late 1990s, hundreds, and, some claim, even thousands, of young Uzbeks belonging to the IMU passed through terrorist camps in Afghanistan, Pakistan, and elsewhere in the region. Some of the Uzbek mujahideen went home to train their countrymen, and they created clandestine terrorist schools for this purpose. The notebooks we acquired belonged to students who attended such courses during the period of 1994 to 1996. [For more information on the origins of the notebooks, consult the section Want to Know More at the end of this article.] We purchased or otherwise acquired these books through various intermediaries, each unaware that we were collecting material from others as part of an effort to document the Islamic revival in Uzbekistan.

Taken collectively, the notebooks allow us to reconstruct the training of the young mujahideen. Students seem to have spent the bulk of their time on military subjects. Once they mastered these subjects, the students focused on when and how to make jihad—and some of the students may have heard lectures on jihad by Namangani himself, or one of his close associates.

We don't know much for certain about the students themselves. Some of the notebooks have the names (or pseudonyms) of the fighters in training who wrote them—for example, Abdumalik or Ayub. We have reason to think some of them studied in Namangan, possibly in the basement of the Juma mosque; reopened during the 1990s under pressure from the community, the mosque had been used as a storehouse for alcoholic beverages during the Soviet era. Our sources told us that all of the students were eventually arrested—in one case, for smuggling consumer goods (and "trade" was, in fact, their livelihood). Uzbek security forces picked up most of the others as suspected terrorists. Their parents, who gave us or our intermediaries the notebooks, were reluctant to talk about them, save to disassociate themselves from their children's "mistakes."

We do not know whether the young men who studied in these schools were devout Muslims, but their notes suggest they were not very knowledgeable about Islam. The same may also be said about their teachers: In the lessons on jihad, for example, references to the Koran, offered by chapter and verse, sometimes cite passages unrelated to the subjects under discussion. These errors are clearly those of the teachers; most students at this early stage of religious education would not have possessed their own copies of the Koran, and they also lacked

Dangerous neighborhood: The Fergana Valley where most of the notebooks were acquired cuts across Tajikistan, Uzbekistan, and Kirgizstan and is near Afghanistan.

the necessary Arabic-language skills to read the Holy Book in the original.

We can also say with certainty that the students were not very educated. They made many grammatical mistakes when writing in Arabic, Russian, and even their native Uzbek. Some of the students seem to have had poor attention spans, and they were careless in taking notes and studying.

THE ABCs OF TERROR: HOW TO KILL

One thing is clear, though: These students learned how to make deadly weapons. As their notes show, these pupils "learned by doing" in every field of terrorism from instructors proficient in their respective subject matter. The teachers who used Russian terminology clearly had experience with the Red Army and Soviet system of military instruction, and those who used Arabic likely passed through terrorist camps in Afghanistan and maybe even those of the Middle East. In many cases, several different instructors taught the various military subjects.

Cartography Students first learned to orient themselves to their surroundings. When we showed some of the notebooks to a professor of cartography in Tashkent—without revealing the source of the material—he was able to identify them as terrorist manuals and was certain the instructor was a cartographer. All high-school students in the Soviet Union were required to receive paramilitary

The basic language of instruction in the notebooks was Uzbek; those who taught the technical subjects knew Russian or Arabic, and in some cases both languages.

training, so there was no shortage of people capable of teaching cartography or most other military subjects, even in the remotest areas of Uzbekistan. Moreover, with some modification, textbooks from the Soviet courses would have been a good starting point of instruction.

Small Arms Students then went on to study how to handle small firearms—a fixture of life in a region where military service was compulsory and where anyone familiar with the black market could buy an AK-47. During the years of the Soviet occupation of Afghanistan (1979–1989), more local youth acquired combat experience than at any time since the end of World War II. Much of our knowledge about this field of study comes from the notebook of Ayub, a Tajik from Namangan (writing in Uzbek), who spent so much time mastering this material that we dubbed him "the gunner."

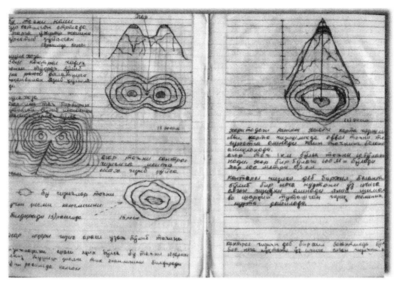

Detail from the eight lessons on maps contained in the notebook acquired in Tashkent oblast, in which students learned to use compasses and natural measurements.

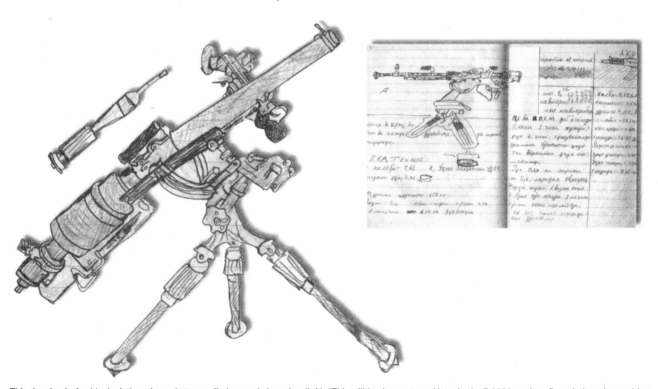

This drawing is Ayub's depiction of a rocket-propelled grenade launcher (left). "This will be demonstrated later in the field," he writes. Description of a machine gun, including discussion of speed, caliber, and other technical specifications (right).

Many of the weapons the students learned to use were common Soviet-era ones, including various forms of the Kalashnikov rifle (AK-47, AK-56, and AKM). Ayub, though, also learned to handle several weapons of choice from Afghanistan, including the Egyptian rocket-propelled grenade launcher. This 82-millimeter weapon is based on a Russian or Chinese modification of an earlier U.S. weapon, writes Ayub in broken Arabic. All of these weapons appear in detailed illustrations, with accompanying notes on their functions and maintenance.

Targeting Ayub was also diligent in learning how to target the enemy, on the ground and in the air. His notebook includes tables with elaborate calculations on how to target planes and helicopters in varying wind and weather conditions. His teacher used both Arabic and Russian military terminology. In the course of his lessons, Ayub handled various forms of sighting instruments, writing in one case that "the front glass reflects many colors" and "the plus sign that regulates distance is easily obscured by finger marks."

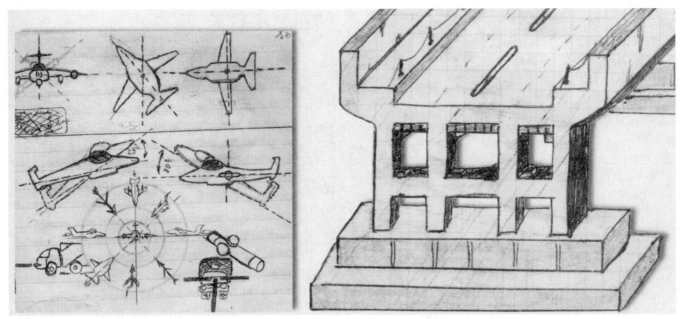

Left: Part of Ayub's notes on calculating target data and using sighting mechanisms. Right: One of several drawings by Abdumalik on the correct placement of explosive charges for blowing up a bridge.

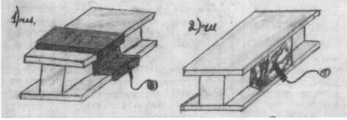

Left: Part of a series of diagrams on how to set mines, from a notebook shared by two students. Right: details from another notebook on the best explosive placement in wells, bridges, and support structures.

Mines and Demolitions The notebooks suggest this subject was a standard part of the instruction that all young mujahideen in Uzbekistan received. Many of the mines the mujahideen learned to make had been commonly used in Afghanistan and other guerrilla war settings, including the MI8AI antipersonnel mine—a plastic-bodied directed fragmentation mine that has ball bearings embedded in the facing of the target. Variations of this mine were produced in the Soviet Union, Pakistan, South Africa, South Korea, and Chile. The students also received instruction in the POMZ-2 antipersonnel mine, activated through the use of a trip wire, with a lethal radius of 4 meters. Variations of this mine were manufactured in the Soviet Union, China, North Korea, and throughout Europe's Eastern bloc.

One notebook includes information on making 16 different explosive devices. The two students who prepared this notebook learned reaction times and temperatures for blowing up buildings, bridges, railroad ties, and electricity relay stations. They were taught everything necessary to become competent arsonists, including how to escape unharmed, a subject emphasized in some of the lessons. These young men were not trained to be suicide bombers but guerrilla fighters who would endure long periods of battle.

Poisons Students also learned how to make poisons with readily accessible substances, such as tobacco or toxic mushrooms. Precise information on the amounts of each ingredient, how to mix them properly, and reaction times are carefully documented. The students penned lengthy instructions on safety techniques, when to wear gloves and masks, and how to conceal noxious odors so potential targets would not be alerted. Alongside instructions for making and using cyanide, one student writes, "And the power of Allah is mightier"—a phrase commonly used at deathbeds—as if to see off his future victims.

WHO DESERVES TO DIE?

The section on jihad—the final course of study—is also the most terrifying. At one level, the lectures on jihad were designed to mobilize students for battle with the enemy. But stripped of their pedagogical intent, these lectures make clear that the explicit goal of the students' military studies was to kill people, preferably as many as possible.

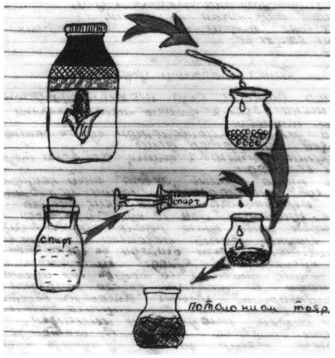

Entries in the notebook from Tashkent on how to make poison using corn flour, beef, yak dung, alcohol, and water.

Since Islam was spread by the sword, holy war is an important theme in the Koran. But since the time of Mohammed, theologians have fought over when jihad is required and when it is forbidden. The view of jihad presented in the notebooks is both simplistic and uniform—so much so that the same person may have taught students studying in different cities. The teacher likely lacked even a middling religious education (8–10 years of study) and was instead a fighter with a religious background, perhaps someone like Namangani or Tohir Yuldashev, the leaders of the IMU.

Jihad is depicted as a cleansing act, as "Jafar" (owner of one of the notebooks) writes, "so the old ideology makes way for the new"—by which he supposedly meant that Uzbekistan's dominant Hannafi school of religious law would make way for Salafi (or fundamentalist) Islam. Central Asian theologians from the Hannafi school preached accommodation with secular rulers; most, in

fact, argued that Islamic law demanded such accommodation, for to do otherwise was to put the community of believers at risk.

By contrast, these students learned that Uzbekistan's secular rulers were betrayers of the faith, and, as Jafar writes, holy war is imperative: "for our faith of Islam, to make Allah pleased with us, to eradicate oppression against Muslims, to establish Islamic rule in perpetuity."

Jafar and his fellow mujahideen were taught that jihad has multiple goals—that economic, political, ideological, and military goals have to be mutually reinforcing. The propaganda that precedes military action, they learned, is critical.

As another student writes, the goal of this propaganda is to raise popular awareness of the enemies among them:

> To make a declaration of the fact that unbelievers and the government are oppressors; that they are connected with Russians, Americans, and Jews, to whose music they are dancing; and that they don't think about their people. We spread true knowledge about Islam in our country [Uzbekistan]. We speak of the fate of faith betrayers, according to Islamic law, and about how people should distance themselves from those who breach the faith and should side with the mujahideen. At the same time, it has to be announced that jihad is a necessary religious requirement, for all social groups of people. And in life, everyone must either be a Muslim or a non-Muslim, that is, no one can remain in the middle. After this, the declaration will be done, the mujahideen will inform the people of the beginning of jihad.

Targeted enemies are depicted in political cartoons, which the students appear to have been asked to draw outside of class. In a perverse manifestation of continuity with the Communist years, many of these cartoons are variants of the anti-imperialist and anti-Zionist pictures that Soviet students sometimes drew during their studies. The drawings in these notebooks, however, include caricatures of Russians alongside those of Americans and Jews.

The anti-Semitism taught to these Uzbek students in their classes was primitive, based on perverse distortions of history, but effective:

> All the countries of the world are today ruled by Jews. This people who is cursed by God began to rule everyone 120 years ago, at the time of Napoleon. It was so. At the time of the fighting between the armies of Napoleon and the British, the Jews spread rumors among the people of England that Napoleon won the battle. Upon hearing these rumors, the British fell into panic and began to sell their stores, factories, plants, and

"Now the first task is to kill Jews, and then the rest," reads the caption above this drawing of a three-headed dragon. The knife of jihad has already cut off the head of the Jews, but the heads of the United States and Russia remain.

Left: "This is how America destroys Muslims. Muslims, rise up in holy war." The drawing on the right is of an insignia to be worn by "the most faithful troops, those especially prepared for purging enemies." Note the faint swastika at the bottom.

other kinds of enterprises. They thought as following: "After the victory of Napoleon, he will arrive in England, and we will lose everything." And so lots of enterprises were sold, and very cheaply. The Jews took advantage of this opportunity and started buying everything very cheaply. A week later, it became known that the British won the battle against Napoleon. Upon hearing this news, all the people began to buy back their things. The Jews sold all this, but for 5 to 10 times more than they paid, and received enormous profit. That the Jews are cursed by God is demonstrated in Ayat 14 of sura al-Khashr. (59:14)

The first Jews came to the region long before the Arab conquests in the mid-seventh century. Traditionally, anti-

Semitism was much worse in the Slavic parts of the Russian Empire than in Central Asia. And historically, Uzbeks have had more resentment for the Russians, who conquered Uzbek lands in the late 19th century and restricted the practice of their faith. Russians remain a target in the notebooks, despite their withdrawal from Uzbekistan after the country gained independence in 1991.

Now, the mujahideen are determined to rout out these enemies and kill them, as part of larger economic, political, and ideological goals. Such economic goals mentioned in one notebook include:

1. To attack the joint ventures that have been organized by the officials of our city [perhaps Namangan—M.B.O. and B.B.]. That is, in the first instance, those enterprises with Russians, Jews, and American [partners] at the head.

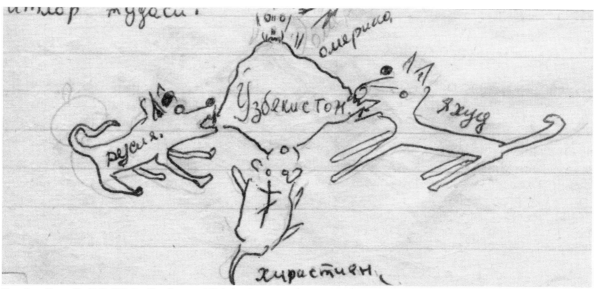

Four dogs (Jews, the United States, Russians, and Christians) attack a map of Uzbekistan.

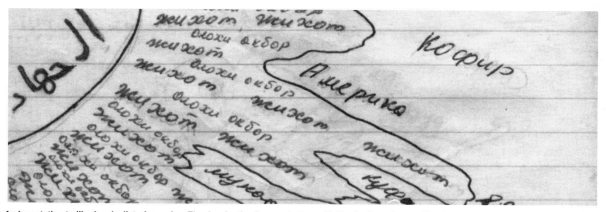

An incantation to jihad and a list of enemies: The drawing is of an explosion, with jihad at its epicenter. The fire of the explosion is an incantation of Allah Akbar (God is great) and jihad. Those who have been blown up include unbelievers, Americans, Jews, two-faced people who put themselves forward as Muslims, Russians, and Christians.

2. To destroy all that is imported from the countries of the enemy, whatever it may be, food, clothes, etc. This, too, is an economic and political blow.

3. To destroy all raw materials exported from the country by unbelievers. This includes fruit… one or two cases of fruit should be poisoned, and when this is discovered, it should be announced that all the fruit that was sent (for example) to Russia, is poisoned…. [This threat is very serious, since Uzbekistan is such an important source of fruit and vegetables for Russia—M.B.O. and B.B.] Those who transport things for personal use will be warned once or twice, and then everything will be confiscated from them.

4. Specialists from Russia, Jews, and Americans working in the economy will be destroyed.

The same groups were targeted under political goals: "At the time of the political strike against the state, we should also kill Russians, Americans, and Israeli citizens.

That is, ambassadors, or others of them, who live here, they all must be beaten."

Clerics and missionaries of other faiths are slated for extermination as part of the ideological program:

From among religious people we will kill:

1. Those who try to gain converts to Christianity on Muslim soil

2. Spies who work as Christian clerics [During Soviet times, there were many KGB employees among Christian clerics—M.B.O. and B.B.]

3. We will kill those Christians and Jews who speak against the mujahideen and those who propagate against Islam

4. Those Christians who collect money for the struggle against Muslims, and those who speak against Muslims. They will be stabbed or shot or hung or beaten to death.

The Christian missionaries targeted here were fairly recent arrivals in Central Asia. Many belonged to U.S. evangelical groups that saw the fall of communism as a signal to expand proselytizing efforts throughout the former Soviet Union.

But it's important to remember that the mujahideen who were trained in Uzbekistan at this time were mobilized to fight a local war, for local causes. Their goal was to prevent enemies of Islam from using new economic structures, like joint ventures, to keep down true believers. Such arguments echo those of radical Muslim thinkers such as Egypt's Sayyid Qutb, who died in 1966. Qutb's works had circulated clandestinely among Islamic activists in Central Asia for decades. Only occasionally do the notebooks make a connection between the efforts in Uzbekistan and a larger, global cause. Those teaching and studying in these schools were keenly aware of the situation in Tajikistan and the ongoing struggle in Afghanistan. But the notebooks make no mention of or link between their efforts and the ongoing Chechen war nor to conflicts in more distant places such as Bosnia or Somalia.

THE FIRE NEXT TIME

The good news is that the owners of these notebooks were never able to execute the number or kind of operations planned with the deadly knowledge they acquired. True, in February 1999, the IMU was credited with masterminding the simultaneous bombings of key government offices in Uzbekistan's capital, Tashkent, killing 13 people. But these attacks did not set off the panic or chain reaction of other violent acts predicted in the notebooks. After the bombings, the Uzbek government successfully pressured the United States to list the IMU as an international terrorist group. And faced with heightened Uzbek security, the IMU made do with taking hostages and raiding parts of nearby Kirgizstan. The group did become part of the al Qaeda network, with camps in Afghanistan and safe havens over the border in Tajikistan. But its founder, Namangani, and many of his fighters were reportedly killed during the U.S. bombings in Afghanistan; the whereabouts of another prominent leader, Yuldashev, are still unknown.

The bad news is that the threat posed by such terrorist groups is infinitely renewable in states such as those in Central Asia, where large numbers of young people with limited education and diminishing economic prospects live in densely populated communities. Moreover, popular resentment toward these countries secular leaders remains high: Many of these leaders were local masters of the openly atheistic Soviet regime, and most of them have profited mightily from the unprecedented increase in corruption since independence.

Each of the budding Central Asian states has attempted to carve out an identity in the past decade. But conditions have not favored the development of authentic moderate Islamic clerics. State authorities view leaders who are credible to religious believers as too threatening, and religious believers are suspicious of those championed by state authorities.

These conditions are made-to-order for those preaching more radical forms of Islam. The best known of these groups is Hizb-ut-Tahrir (Party of Liberation), which attracts young people despite the extraordinary efforts of the Uzbek government to harshly punish those associated with the group. Its numbers are increasing in Kirgizstan, Kazakhstan, and Tajikistan. This movement is committed to the reestablishment of the Caliphate—the rule of Islam as it was practiced by the Prophet Mohammed. For now, the group maintains, this goal can be advanced only through persuasion, not force.

Whatever the fate of Hizb-ut-Tahrir, other radical groups seem certain to emerge from the turmoil of the transitions that Central Asian states are still undergoing. Notwithstanding the presence of new U.S. military bases in Uzbekistan and Kirgizstan and expanded assistance in the war on terrorism, no amount of force alone will defeat such groups. Any security agency capable of routing out all potential terrorists would inevitably become a source of terrorism. Not only would such an organization tread on the basic civil rights of peaceful citizens, but, by targeting "radical" Islam, it would invariably cause those who consider themselves devout Muslims to see the government as an enemy of Islam.

In every part of the world, there are heroes who have died fighting for their faith and who make ready role models. In Central Asia, it is Namangani or Ahmed Shah Massoud, the Lion of Panjshir in Afghanistan. As the disturbing contents of these notebooks attest, purveyors of jihad supply their own credentials and design their own curricula. They require no licenses for their undertakings. The proof of their success is whether they can gain recruits and successfully teach them how to kill.

Want to Know More?

The authors acquired the 10 notebooks between 2001 and 2002. Six were obtained in the Fergana Valley, three in the Tashkent region, and one from an Uzbek village just over the Uzbek border in Kazakhstan. Those interested in more information about the notebooks should contact Martha Brill Olcott at the Carnegie Endowment for International Peace.

For more guidance on Islam, readers can refer to Cyril Glassé's *The Concise Encyclopedia of Islam* (San Francisco: Harper & Row, Publishers, Inc., 1989) and *The Oxford History of Islam* (New York: Oxford University Press, 1999), edited by John L. Esposito. Ira Lapidus's *A History of Islamic Societies* (New York: Cambridge University Press, 2002) is also recommended as an all-purpose guiding tool. The authors used J.M. Rodwell's translation of the *Koran* (London: J.M. Dent, 1994).

Readers interested in learning more about political Islam should consider Graham Fuller's **"The Future of Political Islam"** (*Foreign Affairs*, March/April 2002), Gilles Kepel's *Jihad: The Trial of Political Islam* (Cambridge: Harvard University Press, 2002), Ahmed Rashid's *Jihad: The Rise of Militant Islam in Central Asia* (New Haven: Yale University Press, 2002), and Olivier Roy's *The Failure of Political Islam* (Cambridge: Harvard University Press, 1994). The Carnegie Endownment's Husain Haqqani provides a unique firsthand view of life in a *madrasa* in **"Islam's Medieval Outposts"** (FOREIGN POLICY, November/December 2002). In addition, astute accounts of fundamentalism are provided by Daniel Pipes in *Militant Islam Reaches America* (New York: W.W. Norton, 2002) and Daniel Benjamin and Steven Simon's *The Age of Sacred Terror* (New York: Random House, 2002).

Insightful books on Central Asia include Roy's *The New Central Asia: The Creation of Nations* (New York: New York University Press, 2000) and Rashid's *The Resurgence of Central Asia: Islam or Nationalism?* (Karachi: Oxford University Press, 1994). Another comprehensive source is a recent collection of essays edited by Boris Rumer, *Central Asia: A Gathering Storm?* (New York: M.E. Sharpe, 2002).

The **Institute for War & Peace Reporting** and **EurasiaNet** provide information and analysis about political, economic, environmental, and social developments in the countries of Central Asia and the Caucasus in both Russian and English. Some of the regional sources of reliable information are the Web sites of the information agency **"AkiPress,"** the **Central Asia Information Center**, and the **Central Asian Information Agency**.

Martha Brill Olcott is a senior associate at the Carnegie Endowment for International Peace (CEIP) and author of Kazakhstan: Unfulfilled Promise *(Washington: CEIP, 2002). Bakhtiyar Babajanov is a senior research fellow at the Institute of Oriental Studies of the Academy of Sciences of Uzbekistan in Tashkent.*

PRIME NUMBERS

Hostage, Inc.

By Rachel Briggs

Kidnapping in the 1980s, when the Beirut hostage cases were making headlines, became both a tabloid staple and the stuff of high diplomacy. Groups motivated by political goals demanded everything from the release of a few prisoners to the dissolution of Israel. Although still widely regarded as political crimes perpetrated by fanatics, today's kidnappings, which affect 10,000 people annually, neither make much news nor much of a political point. Instead, kidnapping has become a big business in many countries—one in which kidnappers adapt their business models in response to market conditions and carefully balance the risks of operating against the rewards on offer.

tries and regions reveals a common, profit-driven profile. First, kidnappers need networks to sustain their activities over the long term. Second, they operate where there is relatively low risk of being caught. And third, significant financial reward, from either local middle classes or multinational companies with local presence, must be probable. Most important, kidnappers must balance the risks against the rewards. Therefore, kidnapping doesn't happen where risk is low, as is the case in failed states, where the rewards are unlikely to make the effort worthwhile. Conversely, in rich countries, where the returns are highest, tough standards of law enforcement carry the highest risk and thus ward off kidnappers.

Balancing Risk and Reward

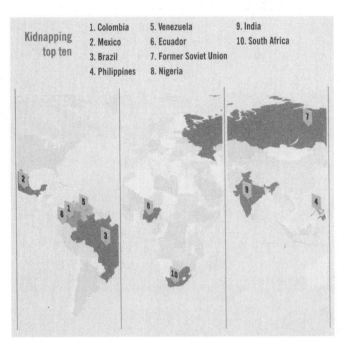

CHARTS (4) BY MANUEL BEVIA PEREZ

In 1999, Latin America was the site of nearly 80 percent of the world's kidnappings. Because the crime is often seen as uniquely Latin American, its root causes remain unexplored. Yet countries elsewhere—the Philippines, India, and Pakistan, for instance—have long-standing kidnapping problems as well. And a comparison across coun-

Nabbing Their Own

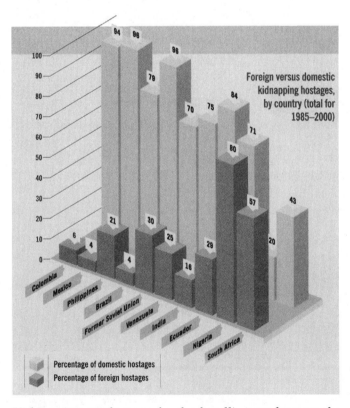

Kidnapping tends to make the headlines at home only when a compatriot has been taken, and this publicity exaggerates Western publics' sense of their own risk abroad. In reality, the vast majority of hostages are locals. In Mexico and Brazil, only 4 percent of hostages are foreigners because both countries have significant local wealth. Nigeria is an exception: Foreigners account for 80 percent of hostages, largely due to local poverty, which makes kidnappers dependent on the rich pickings of foreign oil workers on the Niger Delta.

Price List

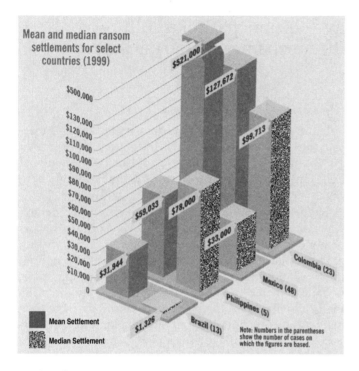

Mean and median ransom settlements for select countries (1999)

$521,000
$127,672
$99,713
$59,033
$78,000
$33,000
$31,944
$1,326

Colombia (23)
Mexico (48)
Philippines (5)
Brazil (13)

Mean Settlement
Median Settlement

Note: Numbers in the parentheses show the number of cases on which the figures are based.

In this fast-growing criminal industry, kidnappers globally take home well over $500 million each year, and the figure is rising. The market value of hostages depends on their ability to pay—ranging from as little as $200 for a local farmer to $2,000 for a local professional to tens of thousands of dollars for a foreign aid worker to several million for the CEO of a large multinational. Ransom levels also differ between countries. Ransoms tend to be lower in Brazil, where the majority of cases are "quick-naps" in which hostages are held for just a few hours or days and are forced to withdraw their credit limit from ATMs. In Colombia, kidnappers operate in rural areas, where they can hold hostages longer and bargain harder.

King of Kidnapping

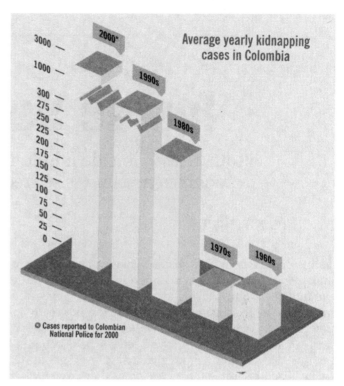

Average yearly kidnapping cases in Colombia

3000
2000*
1000
1990s
1980s
300
275
250
225
200
175
150
125
100
75
50
25
0
1970s
1960s

© Cases reported to Colombian National Police for 2000

Colombia has earned its title as the "kidnap capital of the world." Kidnappers face few risks: Detection is rare, and impunity stands at approximately 95 percent. *El Tiempo*, the national daily newspaper, estimates that 80 percent of kidnappings are carried out by the country's main guerrilla groups, the Marxist-Leninist Revolutionary Armed Forces of Colombia (FARC) and the National Liberation Army (ELN). Estimates about how much the groups earn from kidnapping vary from $150 million to $500 million per year. The U.S. Senate Foreign Relations Committee guesses that 40 percent of the FARC's budget comes from kidnapping, with the rest coming from the drug trade and extortion.

Rachel Briggs is manager of the Risk and Security Programme at The Foreign Policy Centre, a London think tank, and author of The Kidnapping Business *(London: The Foreign Policy Centre, 2001).*

Source: Data are from the Control Risks Group (CRG) and represent only cases that CRG can confirm.

Inside Suicide, Inc.

Death wishes: Suicide missions have become part of a culture from which no child is spared. The mechanics of martyrdom

BY CHRISTOPHER DICKEY

Little boys love to play soldier. They want so badly to look like men, standing at attention in their crinkly little camouflage fatigues, trying to harden their soft eyes and their baby-toothed grins and show they're not really as powerless as they almost always feel. In other generations, in other places, they have been cowboys conquering the Wild West or Jedi knights up against the Empire. In the Israeli-occupied territories today, they're would-be suicide bombers killing Israelis. And unlike most little boys and girls, for whom the games of war are passing fantasies, the children of Palestine are taught by everything and everyone around them that they'll have their chance. When they grow up they'll trade their cardboard bombs for real ones, and kill the real Israelis who man the omnipresent checkpoints, who intimidate and humiliate their parents, or fight their brothers in the streets.

"They want to be martyrs even if they don't know the meaning of the word," says Muhammad Abu Rukbah, principal of an elementary school in Gaza's Jabaliya refugee camp. "They see the images on TV, the posters in the streets, the honor of the martyrs' families, and they want that kind of honor for themselves, for their families." Out on the dusty street of the camp, 10-year-old Aya, a pretty, bright-eyed girl in a school smock, is asked how she feels about kids just like her who are blown up by murderer-martyrs in Israel. "I don't feel sorry for them," she says. "Their families and their mothers are pushing them to fight us and kill us." She adds that she'd like to be a doctor someday, "or maybe a martyr myself."

What kind of madness is this? Since September 11, the answer to that question has become vital to Americans as well as Israelis. When the World Trade Center was destroyed, Flight 93 hijacked and the Pentagon blasted by 19 terrorists (all of them Arabs, none of them Palestinians), the security of the most massively armed country on earth seemed in peril at the hands of men with box cutters and a passionate will to die. The suicidal killers came on the scene as the ultimate weapon of asymmetric warfare,

one that could penetrate to the democratic core of American society. "A human bomb is like a very sophisticated guided missile," says Ely Karmon of Israel's International Policy Institute for Counter-Terrorism. But no multibillion-dollar antimissile system can stop it.

Now that Israel has come under an unprecedented wave of suicide attacks, Prime Minister Ariel Sharon has responded with a relentless, if temporary, reoccupation of Palestinian cities. Protests spread last week throughout the Muslim world and Europe. But for at least four days, no suicide bomb thundered through the daily life of Israeli civilians. Were the bombers broken? Or were they just biding their time, and possibly looking for new targets? If we are to believe a recent Israeli propaganda film, "irrevocable seeds of hatred have been planted into an entire generation," and Palestinian children—by the hundreds of thousands—will grow, irrevocably, to be killers. And if death-cult terrorists can do what they've done to mighty little Israel, making life a daily dance with carnage, what can they do to the U.S.A.? As one Palestinian academic suggests, without meaning it as a threat, "if the present situation continues, you are going to see the kind of terrorism all over the world that we had in the 1970s, but this time with suicide attacks." Are there really thousands of would-be martyrs "out there," whole populations—whole cultures ready to clash with Western civilization? And if so, what possible defense can there be?

In fact, there are defenses, and some of them are diplomatic. The anger of the Palestinians is not immune to negotiation, and there's no reason to think it's irrevocable. Nor is the anger of other Arabs and Muslims throughout the world, for whom the suffering of the Palestinians has become a satellite-broadcast passion play, inspiring their own most violent currents. But diplomacy works slowly, and suicide bombers don't.

How do you address the immediate threat? There, too, answers exist. The despair that afflicts—and motivates—so much of Palestinian society is not enough to launch a concerted campaign of suicide bombings. For that, cynical technicians are required who build an infrastructure to encourage, discipline and arm the would-be shahid, or martyr. Those same technicians have worked to create a mystique around the dead, which attracts still more recruits. And all this takes money, so contributions have had to be collected from sympathizers around the world.

Bottom line: In an invoice Israel says it found in Arafat's compound, the 'largest expense' is a bomb—roughly $150

In Gaza and the West Bank, Islamic fundamentalists from Hamas and other groups have nurtured a cult of death for years, having learned from the example of Lebanon's Hizbullah. At least since 1992, when several Hamas leaders were exiled to Lebanon by the Israeli government, the two organizations have had extensive contacts. Teachers in Hamas day camps and preachers in mosques have kept up a constant chorus of praise for 'martyrs' defending Palestinian lands. Like Hizbullah, they called for an end to the Jewish state. "It's a religious war," says Hani, a bearded 23-year-old Hamas disciple in Gaza who neighbors say is destined for martyrdom. "This is not about land."

In the past, Hamas and Islamic Jihad fundamentalists operated highly secretive cells that recruited young men deemed to be suitable candidates for suicide missions. For the most part, these men, like Hani, were unmarried and unemployed. Most were educated (at least to the high-school level), but faced bleak futures. Many were enticed, in part, by the promise of a wondrous "marriage" in heaven, where they would be greeted by 72 dark-eyed virgins.

Over the past year, secular militants connected to Palestinian Authority Chairman Yasir Arafat have stolen the banner of martyrdom that was growing so popular in the territories. Not to be outdone by Islamic fundamentalist rivals, terrorists from Arafat's Al Aqsa Martyrs Brigades have taken up suicide attacks. "When the Al Aqsa Brigades saw that Hamas was taking a lead in the *intifada* and threatening their status in the street, they adopted this suicide strategy," says Ely Karmon of the counterterrorism institute. Neither Freud nor Allah is the primary motivator here; the dream of "Palestine" is. And the demographics and culture of the Palestinians are such that there is potentially an endless supply of cannon fodder to this cause: in 1995 and 1996, when Hamas mounted its first major suicide-bombing campaigns, only 20 percent of Palestinians approved; in the most recent poll, it's 80 percent.

A document that Israeli military intelligence says it captured in Yasir Arafat's headquarters last week gives a weirdly banal picture of the infrastructure of terror that took shape. The paper, denounced as a fabrication by the Palestinians, appears to be an invoice from the 'Al-Aqsa

Martyrs Troops.' By Israel's count, the Aqsa Brigades have mounted at least 22 attacks since last August, killing 26 Israelis and wounding 613. Among the itemized expenses from its early operations are "various electrical components and chemical supplies (for the production of charges and bombs)." The author of the memo goes on to point out that "this has been our largest expense"—the cost of a prepared bomb being at least 700 shekels, or roughly $150. "We need about five to nine bombs a week for our cells in various areas." There are also expense items for printing posters of some 'martyrs', mounting the portraits of others on wooden boards and the cost of memorial ceremonies for the dead. Other captured documents purport to show a request from Marwan Barghouti, the most popular of Arafat's militia leaders in the West Bank, requesting funds for a dozen men, of whom several were on Israel's wanted list of fugitives. Barghouti asked $1,000 for each. Arafat signed off on $350.

Compared with the impact of the operations, the amounts are truly insignificant. But the money trail is not. Cash is needed not only to fund the operations but to maintain morale and propagate the hero worship that is at the heart of the suicide movement. Some funds from Palestinian factions go to creating special martyrs' videos that serve as recruitment tapes. "There's a special unit in the military wing that's in charge of it," Hamas official Ismail Abu Shanab told NEWSWEEK. "It's done on the last day of training, before the operation. Making the video is a way of getting media exposure. It gets the message out that these people are martyrs of their own free will. And it encourages others to become martyrs."

At wakes for Hamas bombers, it has become routine for an activist to approach the father with an envelope containing $10,000. Abu Shanab says the money is a form of reparation to help the family rebound from their loss, but Israelis say it provides the bomber some incentive. "If a guy knows that the money will serve as a dowry for his sister, for instance, that it will allow her to marry a good husband, this is a factor," says one Israeli security official.

Sorrow is often masked—or overwhelmed—by the cheers and praise of the community, but it is not erased. Shuhail Masri was never proud of what his son did. Last August, 22-year-old Izzedine Masri walked into the Sbarro pizza restaurant in downtown Jerusalem and blew himself up for Hamas, killing 15 people. But the hundreds of well-wishers who went to the Masri home in the West Bank town of Aqqaba after the attack helped comfort Shuhail and his wife, Fatima. In nearby Jenin, Palestinians handed out candy on the streets to celebrate the bombing. "It took our minds off the loss of our son," Masri says. Now the crowds are gone and the misery remains: "I lost my health. I wish I still had my son around. If I knew, I would have stopped him."

Iyad Sarraj, a Palestinian psychologist who studies the phenomenon of suicide attacks, says families of the bombers are initially comforted by the status accorded to

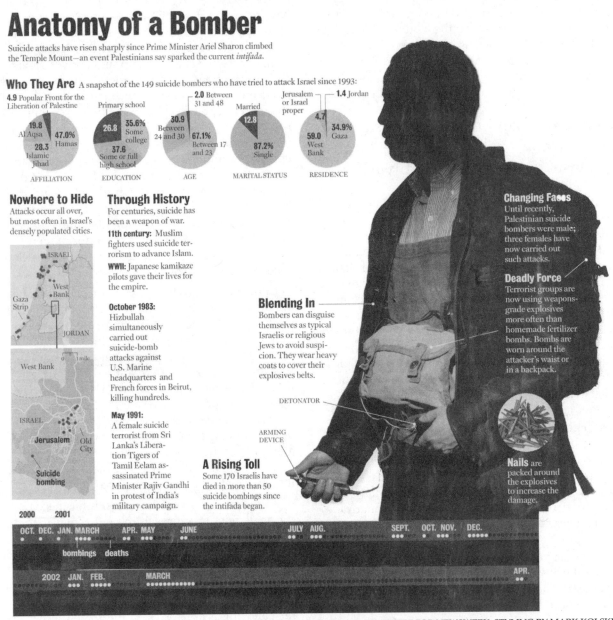

Anatomy of a Bomber

Suicide attacks have risen sharply since Prime Minister Ariel Sharon climbed the Temple Mount—an event Palestinians say sparked the current *intifada*.

Who They Are A snapshot of the 149 suicide bombers who have tried to attack Israel since 1993:

4.9 Popular Front for the Liberation of Palestine
19.8 Al Aqsa
28.3 Islamic Jihad
47.0% Hamas
AFFILIATION

Primary school
26.8
35.6% Some college
37.6 Some or full high school
EDUCATION

2.0 Between 31 and 48
30.9 Between 24 and 30
67.1% Between 17 and 23
AGE

Married
12.8
87.2% Single
MARITAL STATUS

Jerusalem or Israel proper
4.7
1.4 Jordan
34.9% Gaza
59.0 West Bank
RESIDENCE

Nowhere to Hide

Attacks occur all over, but most often in Israel's densely populated cities.

ISRAEL
Gaza Strip
West Bank
JORDAN

West Bank
0   1 mile

ISRAEL
Jerusalem   Old City
Suicide bombing

Through History

For centuries, suicide has been a weapon of war.

11th century: Muslim fighters used suicide terrorism to advance Islam.

WWII: Japanese kamikaze pilots gave their lives for the empire.

October 1983: Hizbullah simultaneously carried out suicide-bomb attacks against U.S. Marine headquarters and French forces in Beirut, killing hundreds.

May 1991: A female suicide terrorist from Sri Lanka's Liberation Tigers of Tamil Eelam assassinated Prime Minister Rajiv Gandhi in protest of India's military campaign.

Blending In

Bombers can disguise themselves as typical Israelis or religious Jews to avoid suspicion. They wear heavy coats to cover their explosives belts.

DETONATOR

ARMING DEVICE

A Rising Toll

Some 170 Israelis have died in more than 50 suicide bombings since the intifada began.

Changing Faces

Until recently, Palestinian suicide bombers were male; three females have now carried out such attacks.

Deadly Force

Terrorist groups are now using weapons-grade explosives more often than homemade fertilizer bombs. Bombs are worn around the attacker's waist or in a backpack.

Nails are packed around the explosives to increase the damage.

2000   2001
OCT. DEC. JAN. MARCH   APR. MAY   JUNE   JULY AUG.   SEPT. OCT. NOV. DEC.
bombings   deaths
2002 JAN. FEB.   MARCH   APR.

PHOTO ILLUSTRATION BY DAVID N. BERKWITZ FOR NEWSWEEK, STYLING BY MARK KOLSKI,
ALAIN KELER-CORBIS SYGMA, JAKUB MOSUR-AP.

their sons. "But if you go back to these families six months later, you see nothing but grief."

The money to support organizations like Hamas, as well as Arafat's Fatah, largely comes from outside the Palestinian territories. Iraq said last week it would now up its contribution to $ 25,000 (from $ 10,000) for the family of each suicide bomber. But U.S. intelligence and law-enforcement officials say Iraq probably plays a minor role in financing suicide networks. The bulk of the money comes from the same sources that provide funds to a wide assortment of radical Islamic groups and causes, including Al Qaeda: wealthy Arab businessmen, particularly from Saudi Arabia and other oil states, and well-off Islamic families in the Western world. Saudi Arabia's foreign minister, Saud al-Faisal, told NEWSWEEK last week that private Saudi do-

nations to Hamas had been cut since the group was put on a special terrorist list by the U.S. Treasury Department in November. Now "support goes only to the Palestinian Authority of Yasir Arafat," said al-Faisal.

Earthly reward: At Hamas wakes, the father of a suicide bomber is usually handed an envelope with $10,000

Money has also come from the United States. Treasury Department officials say they are convinced that some U.S.-based groups whose assets have been frozen by the president since September 11 were raising money for Palestinian bombing missions. A 49-page report sent by the FBI to the Treasury Department last November explicitly accuses one of the largest U.S. Islamic charities, the Holy Land Foundation for Relief and Development, of providing "crucial" financial support to the families of Hamas suicide bombers. Established in 1989, the Texas-based Holy Land Foundation has openly raised money to help Palestinians in the West Bank and Gaza. But the FBI report says "evidence strongly suggests" that by providing "annuities" to the families of Hamas members, the Holy Land Foundation had helped Hamas over the years by "providing a constant flow of suicide volunteers."

According to the FBI document, Holy Land Foundation officials have talked at meetings inside the United States about how their organization was supporting the families of Palestinian "martyrs". An FBI informant reported that, at a 1994 Muslim youth association conference in Los Angeles attended by the foundation's chief, a spokesman for the Hamas military wing said, "I hope no one is recording me or taking any pictures… because I'm going to speak the truth to you. It's simple. Finish off the Israelis. Kill them all! Exterminate them! No peace ever! Do not bother to talk politics." According to the FBI report, $207,000 was raised after this speech for "the cause." The Holy Land Foundation has denied government allegations that it supports terrorism and has sued the Justice and Treasury Departments, seeking to have the courts order the government to unfreeze its assets. In a written statement, the foundation said that it is "dedicated to alleviating the suffering of people… around the world… particularly in Palestine." The organization said it "rejects terrorism by anyone," and denied that it has ever acted on behalf of Hamas.

Another U.S.-based group that apparently has ties to Hamas is the Islamic Association for Palestine. An INS report obtained by NEWSWEEK alleges that a top Hamas official, Mousa Abu Marzook, had contributed $490,000 to the IAP's budget. The report notes that the IAP distributed Hamas recruitment videos and published two pro-Hamas newspapers. But the precise links between groups like IAP and operations against civilians in Israel are hard, if not impossible, to find. IAP president Rafeeq Jabar told NEWSWEEK that he was unaware who had made the $490,000 contribution, and that his organization's funds are used to produce position papers, videos and other materials dedicated to "educating our fellow Americans about what's going on in Palestine. We don't send money to martyrs." Asked about his appearance at a conference two years ago, when he read the will of a Palestinian "martyr" who had driven his car into Israeli soldiers and died in a hail of gunfire, Jabar said: "I read his will so that people will feel the despair that Palestinians feel. These people feel they have nothing to live for."

So, is the world—or more to the point, are Americans—due for a new wave of attacks by suicidal mass murderers? The possibility is there, but on balance, the likelihood is not. There is nothing natural about killing yourself in any culture. In those who have waged suicide-war, the strongest motivation is protection of home and hearth. Japan's kamikaze pilots saw themselves as the last line of defense for their families in World War II. Sri Lanka's Tamil Tigers, who have carried out more than 170 suicide attacks in the last 25 years, are fighting at the behest of a charismatic leader to secure their homeland. Lebanon's Hizbullah has a radical Islamic ideology, but it was created and grew as a response to Israel's 1982 invasion of their country. Although martyrdom is revered in Islam, the Qur'an recognizes the martyrdom only of those who fight to defend their faith and their land. Suicide, as a means of escape from this life, is regarded as a sin.

ALL OF WHICH MAY EXPLAIN why Osama bin Laden, after processing tens of thousands of foreign recruits through his Afghan camps, appears to have produced only a relatively small number of suicide attackers. His ideas might have inspired most recruits to fight ferociously, but not to embrace certain death. With the destruction of bin Laden's infrastructure for indoctrinating, training and equipping his international terrorist brigades of America-haters, the threat that he can organize future large-scale attacks really is reduced.

Palestinian suicide bombers pose a more difficult problem. Precisely because the terrorism is a reaction to occupation, the use of more intense and brutal occupation to try to wipe them out is not likely to have the desired effect. And the issue of Palestine's liberation is of such passionate interest to Muslims throughout the world that it could provide the impetus for new waves of terror that have nothing whatsoever to do with Al Qaeda, or could be exploited by the group's remnants.

And meanwhile, the youngest generation of Palestinians wakes up every morning with more reason to die. After Israeli troops stormed into the Jabaliya refugee camp last month, schoolteacher Samira Abu Shamak was shocked to hear her 6-year-old daughter begging for a gun or a bomb. "She said, I want to be a martyr," remembers Abu Shamak. "What could I say? I didn't know. I told her, "Wait until you're grown up, dear. Maybe—maybe things will change. At least wait until then."

With DAN EPHRON *in Jerusalem and* JOHN BARRY, MARK HOSENBAL *and* MICHAEL ISIKOFF *in Washington*

UNIT 4
State-Sponsored Terrorism

Unit Selections

Key Points to Consider

- What is the purpose of the designation "state sponsor of international terrorism"? Which states are currently listed by the U.S. government as state sponsors? Which states are not?

- What was the relationship between Saddam Hussein and al Qaida? Does a link between Iraq and al Qaida justify the U.S. government's intervention in Iraq?

- What was the link between Osama bin Laden and the Sudanese government? To what extent does the Sudanese government bear responsibility for subsequent events?

- How can the U.S. government more effectively deal with state sponsors of international terrorism?

 **Links: www.dushkin.com/online/**
These sites are annotated in the World Wide Web pages.

Arab.Net Contents
http://www.arab.net/sections/contents.html

International Association for Counterterrorism and Security Professionals
http://www.iacsp.com/index.html

President Bush's Axis of Evil
http://wire.ap.org/APpackages/axis_flash/

The role of states in international terrorism has long been the subject of controversy. It is clear that states often support foreign groups with similar interests. This support can take a number of forms. States may provide political support, financial assistance, safe havens, logistic support, training, or in some cases, even weapons and equipment to groups that advocate the use of political violence. State support for terrorist organizations, however, does not necessarily translate into state control over terrorism. As Martha Crenshaw has noted, "while terrorists exclude no donors on principle the acceptance of support does not, however, bind clients to the wishes of their patrons."

Despite this apparent contradiction, since the passage of the Export Administration Act of 1979, the U.S. government has sought to make certain states responsible for the actions of these groups by requiring economic sanctions. The resulting list of state sponsors of terrorism provides the basis for contemporary U.S. antiterrorism and sanctions policy. Included on this list of state sponsors of international terrorism are Cuba, Iran, Iraq, Libya, North Korea, Sudan, and Syria. Not surprisingly, the list

includes only so-called rogue states perceived to be, for a wide variety of reasons, a threat to U.S. interests. States in which the United States has significant political or economic interests are generally excluded.

The first article in this unit, published in the State Department's annual report *Patterns of Global Terrorism,* provides an overview of the states currently on the list of state sponsors and justifies their inclusion.

Next, U.S. secretary of state Colin Powell, in his remarks to the United Nations Security Council on February 5, 2003, makes his case, outlining what the administration sees as the link between the Iraqi government and terrorist organizations. Secretary Powell urges the members of the UN Security Council to act and confront a regime that "provides haven and active support for terrorists." Finally, Ann Lesch examines the complex relationship between Osama bin Laden and the Sudanese government. She argues that without the support of Sudan, bin Laden could not have "incubated the networks that have caused such devastation."

Overview of State-Sponsored Terrorism

"Every nation in every region now has a decision to make. Either you are with us, or you are with the terrorists."

President George W. Bush
20 September 2001

President Bush put state supporters of terrorism on notice in his 20 September address to the joint session of Congress: "Every nation, in every region, now has a decision to make. Either you are with us, or you are with the terrorists." The seven designated state sponsors—Cuba, Iran, Iraq, Libya, North Korea, Syria, and Sudan—clearly heard the President's message. While some of these countries appear to be reconsidering their present course, none has yet taken all necessary actions to divest itself fully of ties to terrorism.

Sudan and Libya seem closest to understanding what they must do to get out of the terrorism business, and each has taken measures pointing it in the right direction. Iran, North Korea, and Syria have, in some narrow areas, made limited moves to cooperate with the international community's campaign against terrorism. Iran and Syria, however, seek to have it both ways. On the one hand, they clamped down on certain terrorist groups, such as al-Qaida. On the other hand, they maintained their support for other terrorist groups, such as HAMAS and Hizballah, insisting they were national liberation movements. North Korea's initial positive moves halted abruptly.

Until all states that support or tolerate terrorism cease their sponsorship, whether by choice or coercion, they remain a critical foundation for terrorist groups and their operations. Even though the year 2001 saw a continuation of a slow trend away from state sponsorship as the guiding force behind the overall global terrorist threat, state sponsors still represent a key impediment to the international campaign against terrorism.

In certain areas, including Israel, the West Bank, and Gaza Strip, state sponsors remain an important driving force behind terrorism. Iran continues its firm support for Hizballah, HAMAS, and the Palestine Islamic Jihad. Iraq employs terrorism against dissident Iraqi groups opposed to Saddam Hussein's regime. Syria continued its support for Hizballah and allowed HAMAS, the Palestine Islamic Jihad, and other Palestinian rejectionist groups to maintain offices in Damascus.

Cuba

Since September 11, Fidel Castro has vacillated over the war on terrorism. In October, he labeled the US-led war on terrorism "worse than the original attacks, militaristic, and fascist."

When this tactic earned ostracism rather than praise, he undertook an effort to demonstrate Cuban support for the international campaign against terrorism and signed all 12 UN counterterrorism conventions as well as the Ibero-American declaration on terrorism at the 2001 summit. Although Cuba decided not to protest the detention of suspected terrorists at the US Naval Base at Guantanamo Bay, it continued to denounce the global effort against terrorism—even by asserting that the United States was intentionally targeting Afghan children and Red Cross hospitals.

Cuba's signature of UN counterterrorism conventions notwithstanding, Castro continued to view terror as a legitimate revolutionary tactic. The Cuban Government continued to allow at least 20 Basque ETA members to reside in Cuba as privileged guests and provided some degree of

State Sponsor: Implications

Designating countries that repeatedly support international terrorism (i.e., placing a country on the "terrorism list") imposes four main sets of US Government sanctions:

1. A ban on arms-related exports and sales,

2. Controls over exports of dual use items, requiring 30-day Congressional notification for goods or services that could significantly enhance the terrorist list country's military capability or ability to support terrorism,

3. Prohibitions on economic assistance; and

4. Imposition of miscellaneous financial and other restrictions, including

- Requiring the United States to oppose loans by the World Bank and other international financial institutions;
- Lifting the diplomatic immunity to allow families of terrorist victims to file civil lawsuits in US courts;
- Denying companies and individuals tax credits for income earned in terrorist list countries;
- Denial of duty-free treatment for goods exported to the United States;
- Authority to prohibit any US person from engaging in a financial transaction with terrorism list government without a Treasury Department license;
- Prohibition of Defense Department contracts above $100,000 with companies controlled by terrorist list states.

---

safehaven and support to members of the Colombian FARC and ELN groups. In August, a Cuban spokesman revealed that Sinn Fein's official representative for Cuba and Latin America, Niall Connolly, who was one of three Irish Republican Army members arrested in Colombia on suspicion of providing explosives training to the FARC, had been based in Cuba for five years. In addition, the recent arrest in Brazil of the leader of a Chilean terrorist group, the Frente Patriotico Manuel Rodriguez (FPMR), has raised the strong possibility that in the mid-1990s, the Cuban Government harbored FPMR terrorists wanted for murder in Chile. The arrested terrorist told Brazilian authorities he had traveled through Cuba on his way to Brazil. Chilean investigators had traced calls from FPMR relatives in Chile to Cuba following an FPMR prison break in 1996, but the Cuban Government twice denied extradition requests, claiming that the wanted persons were not in Cuba and the phone numbers were incorrect.

Numerous US fugitives continued to live on the island, including Joanne Chesimard, wanted in the United States for the murder in 1973 of a New Jersey police officer and living as a guest of the Castro regime since 1979.

Iran

Iran remained the most active state sponsor of terrorism in 2001. Iran's Islamic Revolutionary Guard Corps (IRGC) and Ministry of Intelligence and Security (MOIS) continued to be involved in the planning and support of terrorist acts and supported a variety of groups that use terrorism to pursue their goals. Although some within Iran would like to end this support, hardliners who hold the reins of power continue to thwart any efforts to moderate these policies. Since the outbreak of the *intifadah,* support has intensified for Pal-

estinian groups that use violence against Israel. During the past year, however, Iran appears to have reduced its involvement in other forms of terrorist activity. There is no evidence of Iranian sponsorship or foreknowledge of the September 11 attacks in the United States. President Khatami condemned the attacks and offered condolences to the American people.

During 2001, Iran sought a high-profile role in encouraging anti-Israeli activity by way of increasing its support for anti-Israeli terrorist groups. Supreme Leader Khamenei continued to refer to Israel as a "cancerous tumor" that must be removed. Matching this rhetoric with action, Iran continued to provide Lebanese Hizballah and the Palestinian rejectionist groups—notably HAMAS, the Palestine Islamic Jihad, and the PFLP-GC—with varying amounts of funding, safehaven, training, and weapons. It also encouraged Hizballah and the rejectionist Palestinian groups to coordinate their planning and to escalate their activities.

In addition, Iran provided limited support to terrorist groups in the Gulf, Africa, Turkey, and Central Asia. This support is at a considerably lower level than that provided to the groups opposed to Israel and has been decreasing in recent years. The Iranian Government took no direct action in 2001 to implement Ayatollah Khomeini's *fatwa* against Salman Rushdie, but the decree has not been revoked nor has the $2.8 million bounty for his death been withdrawn. Moreover, on the anniversary of the *fatwa* in February, some hardline Iranians stressed again that the decree is irrevocable and should be carried out.

During Operation Enduring Freedom, Tehran informed the United States that, in the event US warplanes went down inside Iran, Iranian forces would assist downed air crews in accordance with international convention. Iran also worked with the United States and its allies at the Bonn

Chemical, Biological, Radiological, Nuclear (CBRN) Terrorism

The September 11, 2001 attacks on the World Trade Center and the Pentagon confirmed the resolution and capability of terrorists to plan, organize, and execute attacks to produce mass casualties. In the wake of these unprecedented attacks, terrorists increasingly may look to use chemical, biological, radiological, or nuclear (CBRN) materials—many of which can cause significant casualties—to rival the events of September 11. Such materials, information about the technology required to create them, and information about how to deliver the materials continue to be available through a variety of means.

Usama Bin Ladin has professed the acquisition of "weapons of mass destruction" (WMD) to be a "religious duty" and he has threatened to use such weapons. Reports that documents retrieved from al-Qaida facilities in Afghanistan contain information on CBRN materials underscore Bin Ladin's rhetoric. The threat is not limited to Bin Ladin and al-Qaida. Other information indicates interest in acquiring and using CBRN materials by a small but growing number of other terrorist groups. The use by HAMAS of poisons and pesticides to coat shrapnel in improvised explosive devices is one example. The recent arrest in Italy of a group which had in its possession a compound that could produce hydrogen cyanide (HCN) gas under certain circumstances, along with maps of the underground utility systems near the US Embassy, is also demonstrative of terrorist intentions to employ CBRN materials in their activities.

CBRN terrorism events to date have generally involved crude and improvised delivery means that have been effective but only marginally so. The lethal materials employed in some events (with the exception of the anthrax used in the incidents in the United States) also have been crudely manufactured. Other events have featured materials (toxic industrial chemicals and materials, poisons and pesticides, radiological source materials embedded in legitimate measuring instruments, etc.) that have been acquired legitimately or illegitimately and used for purposes other than those for which they were intended. While terrorist events involving these materials and improvised delivery systems can be lethal and can cause significant damage and disruption, they pale in comparison to the number of casualties and damage levels that could occur should terrorists ever acquire militarized Weapons of Mass Destruction (WMD) and the systems to deliver them.

Preventing the proliferation of WMD, relevant materials, and related technologies, while long a pillar of national security, has become an even more urgent global priority since September 11. President George Bush made clear in his 29 January 2002 State of the Union address that the United States has as one of two great objectives to "…prevent the terrorists and regimes who seek chemical, biological, or nuclear weapons from threatening the United States and the world." Nations around the world have joined the United States in calling for greater efforts to prevent terrorist acquisition of WMD, relevant materials, and related technologies.

The United States is working within appropriate multilateral nonproliferation and other international forums and is encouraging countries worldwide to adopt more stringent nonproliferation policies and programs to help ensure that terrorists or the states who sponsor and support them cannot acquire WMD, materials, or related technologies.

Active involvement by the nonproliferation communities in the United States and other nations is a welcome addition to the capabilities of the international Coalition engaged in the war on terrorism. Such cooperative activities should help buttress existing international counterterrorism strategies and programs for combating CBRN terrorism in the areas of diplomacy, intelligence sharing, cooperative law enforcement arrangements, technology exchange, security and force protection, and training that have been traditionally undertaken.

Conference in late 2001 to help in the formation of the Afghan Interim Authority. Tehran pledged to close its borders with Afghanistan and Pakistan to prevent the infiltration of Taliban and al-Qaida escapees. There are, however, reports that Arab Afghans, including al-Qaida members, used Iran as a transit route to enter and leave from Afghanistan.

Iraq

Iraq was the only Arab-Muslim country that did not condemn the September 11 attacks against the United States. A commentary of the official Iraqi station on September 11 stated that America was "…reaping the fruits of [its] crimes against humanity." Subsequent commentary in a newspaper run by one of Saddam's sons expressed sympathy for Usama Bin Ladin following initial US retaliatory strikes in Afghanistan. In addition, the regime continued to provide training and political encouragement to numerous terrorist groups, although its main focus was on dissident Iraqi activity overseas.

Iraq provided bases to several terrorist groups including the Mujahedin-e-Khalq (MEK), the Kurdistan Workers' Party (PKK), the Palestine Liberation Front (PLF), and the Abu Nidal organization (ANO). In 2001, the Popular Front for the Liberation of Palestine (PFLP) raised its profile in the West Bank and Gaza Strip by carrying out successful terrorist attacks against Israeli targets. In recognition of the PFLP's growing role, an Iraqi Vice President met with former PFLP Secretary General Habbash in Baghdad in January 2001 and expressed continued Iraqi support for the *intifadah*. Also, in mid-September, a senior delegation from the PFLP met with an Iraqi Deputy Prime Minister. Baghdad also continued to host other Palestinian rejectionist groups, including the Arab Liberation Front, and the 15 May Organization.

Meanwhile, Czech police continued to provide protection to the Prague office of the US Government-funded Radio Free Europe/Radio Liberty (RFE/RL), which produces Radio Free Iraq programs and employs expatriate journalists. The police presence was augmented in 1999 and 2000, following reports that the Iraqi Intelligence Service might retaliate against RFE/RL for broadcasts critical of the Iraqi regime. As concerns over the facility's security mounted through 2000, the Czechs expelled an Iraqi intelligence officer in April 2001.

The Iraqi regime has not met a request from Riyadh for the extradition of two Saudis who had hijacked a Saudi Arabian Airlines flight to Baghdad in 2000. Disregarding its obligations under international law, the regime granted political asylum to the hijackers and gave them ample opportunity to voice their criticisms of alleged abuses by the Saudi Government in the Iraqi Government-controlled and international media.

Libya

Following the September 11 terrorist attacks, Libyan leader Muammar Qadhafi issued a statement condemning the attacks as horrific and gruesome and urging Libyans to donate blood for the US victims. On 16 September he declared that the United States had justification to retaliate for the attacks. Since September 11, Qadhafi has repeatedly denounced terrorism.

Libya appears to have curtailed its support for international terrorism, although it may maintain residual contacts with a few groups. Tripoli has, in recent years, sought to recast itself as a peacemaker, offering to mediate a number of conflicts such as the military standoff between India and Pakistan that began in December 2001. In October, Libya ransomed a hostage held by the Abu Sayyaf Group, although it claimed that the money was not a ransom and would be used for "humanitarian assistance."

Libya's past record of terrorist activity continued to hinder Qadhafi's efforts to shed Libya's pariah status. In January, a Scottish court found Libyan intelligence agent Abdel Basset Ali al-Megrahi guilty of murder, concluding that in 1988 he planted an explosive device on Pan Am Flight 103 whose detonation resulted in the murder of all 259 passengers and crew on board as well as 11 persons on the ground in Lockerbie, Scotland. The judges found that Megrahi had acted "in furtherance of the purposes of...Libyan Intelligence Services." His codefendant, Libyan Arab Airlines employee Al-Amin Khalifa Fhima, was acquitted on the grounds that the prosecution failed to prove his role in the bombing "beyond a reasonable doubt." At year's end, Libya had yet to comply fully with the remaining UN Security Council requirements related to Pan Am 103, including accepting responsibility for the actions of its officials, fully disclosing all that it knows about the bombing, and paying appropriate compensation to the victims' families. Libya's hesitation to do so may have reflected a hope that Meghahi's appeal would overturn his conviction. (On 14 March 2002, a Scottish appellate court upheld Megrahi's conviction.)

In November, a German court convicted four defendants in the bombing in 1986 of La Belle Discotheque in West Berlin. In rendering his decision, the judge stated that Libyan Government officials had clearly orchestrated the attack. In response to the court's findings, the German Government called on Libya to accept responsibility for the attack and provide compensation to the victims. Two US servicemen and one Turkish civilian died in the bombing, and more than 200 persons were wounded.

North Korea

The Democratic People's Republic of Korea's (DPRK) response to international efforts to combat terrorism has been disappointing. In a statement released after the September 11 attacks, the DPRK reiterated its public policy of opposing terrorism and any support for terrorism. It also signed the UN Convention for the Suppression of the Financing of Terrorism, acceded to the Convention Against the Taking of Hostages, and indicated its willingness to sign five others. Despite the urging of the international community, however, North Korea did not take substantial steps to cooperate in efforts to combat terrorism, including responding to requests for information on how it is implementing the UN Security Council resolutions, and it did not respond to US proposals for discussions on terrorism. It did not report any efforts to search for and block financial assets as required by UN Security Council Resolution 1373. Similarly, the DPRK did not respond positively to the Republic of Korea's call to resume dialogue, where counterterrorism is an agenda item, nor to the United States in its call to undertake dialogue on improved implementation of the agreed framework. In light of President Bush's call to recognize the dangerous nexus between Weapons of Mass Destruction and terrorism, this latter failure, with its implications for nuclear development and proliferation, was especially troublesome.

In addition, Pyongyang's provision of safehaven to four remaining Japanese Communist League-Red Army Faction members who participated in the hijacking of a Japanese Airlines flight to North Korea in 1970 remained problematic in terms of support for terrorists. Moreover, some evidence suggested the DPRK may have sold limited quantities of small arms to terrorist groups during the year.

Sudan

The counterterrorism dialogue begun in mid-2000 between the US and Sudan continued and intensified during 2001. Sudan condemned the September 11 attacks and pledged its commitment to combating terrorism and fully cooperating with the United States in the campaign against terrorism. The Sudanese Government has stepped up its counterterrorism cooperation with various US agencies, and Sudanese authorities have investigated and apprehended extremists suspected of involvement in terrorist activities. In late September, the United Nations recognized Sudan's positive steps against terrorism by removing UN sanctions.

Sudan, however, remained a designated state sponsor of terrorism. A number of international terrorist groups including al-Qaida, the Egyptian Islamic Jihad, Egyptian al-Gama'a al-Islamiyya, the Palestine Islamic Jihad, and HAMAS continued to use Sudan as a safehaven, primarily for conducting logistics and other support activities. Press speculation about the extent of Sudan's cooperation with the United States probably has led some terrorist elements to depart the country. Unilateral US sanctions remained in force.

Syria

Syria's president, Bashar al-Asad, as well as senior Syrian officials, publicly condemned the September 11 attacks. The Syrian Government also cooperated with the United States and with other foreign governments in investigating al-Qaida and some other terrorist groups and individuals.

The Government of Syria has not been implicated directly in an act of terrorism since 1986, but it continued in 2001 to provide safehaven and logistics support to a number of terrorist groups. Ahmad Jibril's Popular Front for the Liberation of Palestine—General Command (PFLP-GC), the Palestine Islamic Jihad (PIJ), Abu Musa's Fatah-the-Intifadah, George Habash's Popular Front for the Liberation of Palestine, and HAMAS continued to maintain offices in Damascus. Syria provided Hizballah, HAMAS, PFLP-GC, the PIJ, and other terrorist organizations refuge and basing privileges in Lebanon's Beka'a Valley, under Syrian control. Damascus, however, generally upheld its September 2000 antiterrorism agreement with Ankara, honoring its 1998 pledge not to support the Kurdistan Workers' Party (PKK).

Damascus served as the primary transit point for the transfer of Iranian-supplied weapons to Hizballah. Syria continued to adhere to its longstanding policy of preventing any attacks against Israel or Western targets from Syrian territory or attacks against Western interests in Syria.

From *Patterns of Global Terrorism—2001*, May 2002. Published by the U.S. State Department.

Article 11

Excerpt from

Remarks to the United Nations Security Council

Secretary Colin L. Powell

New York City
February 5, 2003

Iraq and terrorism go back decades. Baghdad trains Palestine Liberation Front members in small arms and explosives. Saddam uses the Arab Liberation Front to funnel money to the families of Palestinian suicide bombers in order to prolong the Intifadah. And it's no secret that Saddam's own intelligence service was involved in dozens of attacks or attempted assassinations in the 1990s.

But what I want to bring to your attention today is the potentially much more sinister nexus between Iraq and the al-Qaida terrorist network, a nexus that combines classic terrorist organizations and modern methods of murder. Iraq today harbors a deadly terrorist network headed by Abu Musab al-Zarqawi, an associate and collaborator of Usama bin Laden and his al-Qaida lieutenants.

Zarqawi, Palestinian born in Jordan, fought in the Afghan war more than a decade ago. Returning to Afghanistan in 2000, he oversaw a terrorist training camp. One of his specialties, and one of the specialties of this camp, is poisons.

When our coalition ousted the Taliban, the Zarqawi network helped establish another poison and explosive training center camp, and this camp is located in northeastern Iraq.

The network is teaching its operatives how to produce ricin and other poisons. Let me remind you how ricin works. Less than a pinch—imagine a pinch of salt—less than a pinch of ricin, eating just this amount in your food, would cause shock, followed by circulatory failure. Death comes within 72 hours and there is no antidote. There is no cure. It is fatal.

Those helping to run this camp are Zarqawi lieutenants operating in northern Kurdish areas outside Saddam Hussein's controlled Iraq. But Baghdad has an agent in the most senior levels of the radical organization Ansar al-Islam that controls this corner of Iraq. In 2000, this agent offered al-Qaida safe haven in the region.

After we swept al-Qaida from Afghanistan, some of those members accepted this safe haven. They remain there today. Zarqawi's activities are not confined to this small corner of northeast Iraq. He traveled to Baghdad in May of 2002 for medical treatment, staying in the capital of Iraq for two months while he recuperated to fight another day.

During his stay, nearly two dozen extremists converged on Baghdad and established a base of operations there. These al-Qaida affiliates based in Baghdad now coordinate the movement of people, money and supplies into and throughout Iraq for his network, and they have now been operating freely in the capital for more than eight months.

Iraqi officials deny accusations of ties with al-Qaida. These denials are simply not credible. Last year, an al-Qaida associate bragged that the situation in Iraq was "good," that Baghdad could be transited quickly.

We know these affiliates are connected to Zarqawi because they remain, even today, in regular contact with his direct subordinates, including the poison cell plotters. And they are involved in moving more than money and materiel. Last year, two suspected al-Qaida operatives were arrested crossing from Iraq into Saudi Arabia. They were linked to associates of the Baghdad cell and one of them received training in Afghanistan on how to use cyanide.

From his terrorist network in Iraq, Zarqawi can direct his network in the Middle East and beyond. We in the United States, all of us, the State Department and the Agency for International Development, we all lost a dear friend with the cold-blooded murder of Mr. Laurence Foley in Amman, Jordan, last October. A despicable act was committed that day, the assassination of an individual whose sole mission was to assist the people of Jordan. The captured assassin says his cell received money and weapons from Zarqawi for that murder. After the attack, an associate of the assassin left Jordan to go to Iraq to obtain weapons and explosives for further operations. Iraqi officials protest that they are not aware of the whereabouts of Zarqawi or of any of his associates. Again, these protests are not credible. We know of Zarqawi's activities in Baghdad. I described them earlier.

Now let me add one other fact. We asked a friendly security service to approach Baghdad about extraditing Zarqawi and providing information about him and his close associates. This service contacted Iraqi officials twice and we passed details that should have made it easy to find Zarqawi. The network remains in Baghdad. Zarqawi still remains at large, to come and go.

As my colleagues around this table and as the citizens they represent in Europe know, Zarqawi's terrorism is not confined to the Middle East. Zarqawi and his network have plotted terrorist actions against countries including France, Britain, Spain, Italy, Germany and Russia. According to detainees Abu Atiya, who graduated from Zarqawi's terrorist camp in Afghanistan, tasked at least nine North African extremists in 2001 to travel to Europe to conduct poison and explosive attacks.

Since last year, members of this network have been apprehended in France, Britain, Spain and Italy. By our last count, 116 operatives connected to this global web have been arrested.

We know about this European network and we know about its links to Zarqawi because the detainees who provided the information about the targets also provided the names of members of the network. Three of those he identified by name were arrested in France last December. In the apartments of the terrorists, authorities found circuits for explosive devices and a list of ingredients to make toxins.

The detainee who helped piece this together says the plot also targeted Britain. Later evidence again proved him right. When the British unearthed the cell there just last month, one British police officer was murdered during the destruction of the cell.

We also know that Zarqawi's colleagues have been active in the Pankisi Gorge, Georgia, and in Chechnya, Russia. The plotting to which they are linked is not mere chatter. Members of Zarqawi's network say their goal was to kill Russians with toxins.

We are not surprised that Iraq is harboring Zarqawi and his subordinates. This understanding builds on decades-long experience with respect to ties between Iraq and al-Qaida. Going back to the early and mid-1990s when bin Laden was based in Sudan, an al-Qaida source tells us that Saddam and bin Laden reached an understanding that al-Qaida would no longer support activities against Baghdad. Early al-Qaida ties were forged by secret high-level intelligence service contacts with al-Qaida, secret Iraqi intelligence high-level contacts with al-Qaida.

We know members of both organizations met repeatedly and have met at least eight times at very senior levels since the early 1990s. In 1996, a foreign security service tells us that bin Laden met with a senior Iraqi intelligence official in Khartoum and later met the director of the Iraqi intelligence service.

Saddam became more interested as he saw al-Qaida's appalling attacks. A detained al-Qaida member tells us that Saddam was more willing to assist al-Qaida after the 1998 bombings of our embassies in Kenya and Tanzania. Saddam was also impressed by al-Qaida's attacks on the *USS Cole* in Yemen in October 2000.

Iraqis continue to visit bin Laden in his new home in Afghanistan. A senior defector, one of Saddam's former intelligence chiefs in Europe, says Saddam sent his agents to Afghanistan sometime in the mid-1990s to provide training to al-Qaida members on document forgery. From the late 1990s until 2001, the Iraqi Embassy in Pakistan played the role of liaison to the al-Qaida organization.

Some believe, some claim, these contacts do not amount to much. They say Saddam Hussein's secular tyranny and al-Qaida's religious tyranny do not mix. I am not comforted by this thought. Ambition and hatred are enough to bring Iraq and al-Qaida together, enough so al-Qaida could learn how to build more sophisticated bombs and learn how to forge documents, and enough so that al-Qaida could turn to Iraq for help in acquiring expertise on weapons of mass destruction.

And the record of Saddam Hussein's cooperation with other Islamist terrorist organizations is clear. Hamas, for example, opened an office in Baghdad in 1999 and Iraq has hosted conferences attended by Palestine Islamic Jihad. These groups are at the forefront of sponsoring suicide attacks against Israel.

Al-Qaida continues to have a deep interest in acquiring weapons of mass destruction. As with the story of Zarqawi and his network, I can trace the story of a senior terrorist operative telling how Iraq provided training in these weapons to al-Qaida. Fortunately, this operative is now detained and he has told his story. I will relate it to you now as he, himself, described it.

This senior al-Qaida terrorist was responsible for one of al-Qaida's training camps in Afghanistan. His information comes firsthand from his personal involvement at senior levels of al-Qaida. He says bin Laden and his top deputy in Afghanistan, deceased al-Qaida leader Muhammad Atif, did not believe that al-Qaida labs in Afghanistan were capable enough to manufacture these chemical or biological agents. They needed to go somewhere else. They had to look outside of Afghanistan for help.

Where did they go? Where did they look? They went to Iraq. The support that this detainee describes included Iraq offering chemical or biological weapons training for two al-Qaida associates beginning in December 2000. He says that a militant known as Abdallah al-Iraqi had been sent to Iraq several times between 1997 and 2000 for help in acquiring poisons and gasses. Abdallah al-Iraqi characterized the relationship he forged with Iraqi officials as successful.

As I said at the outset, none of this should come as a surprise to any of us. Terrorism has been a tool used by Saddam for decades. Saddam was a supporter of terrorism long before these terrorist networks had a name, and this support continues. The nexus of poisons and terror is new. The nexus of Iraq and terror is old. The combination is lethal.

With this track record, Iraqi denials of supporting terrorism take their place alongside the other Iraqi denials of weapons of mass destruction. It is all a web of lies.

When we confront a regime that harbors ambitions for regional domination, hides weapons of mass destruction, and provides haven and active support for terrorists, we are not confronting the past; we are confronting the present. And unless we act, we are confronting an even more frightening future.

And, friends, this has been a long and a detailed presentation and I thank you for your patience, but there is one more subject that I would like to touch on briefly, and it should be a subject of deep and continuing concern to this Council: Saddam Hussein's violations of human rights.

Underlying all that I have said, underlying all the facts and the patterns of behavior that I have identified, is Saddam Hussein's contempt for the will of this Council, his contempt for the truth, and, most damning of all, his utter contempt for human life. Saddam Hussein's use of mustard and nerve gas against the Kurds in 1988 was one of the 20th century's most horrible atrocities. Five thousand men, women and children died. His campaign against the Kurds from 1987 to '89 included mass summary executions, disappearances, arbitrary jailing and ethnic cleansing, and the destruction of some 2,000 villages.

He has also conducted ethnic cleansing against the Shia Iraqis and the Marsh Arabs, whose culture has flourished for more than a millennium. Saddam Hussein's police state ruthlessly eliminates anyone who dares to dissent. Iraq has more forced disappearance cases than any other country—tens of thousands of people reported missing in the past decade.

Nothing points more clearly to Saddam Hussein's dangerous intentions and the threat he poses to all of us than his calculated cruelty to his own citizens and to his neighbors. Clearly, Saddam Hussein and his regime will stop at nothing until something stops him.

For more than 20 years, by word and by deed, Saddam Hussein has pursued his ambition to dominate Iraq and the broader Middle East using the only means he knows: intimidation, coercion and annihilation of all those who might stand in his way. For Saddam Hussein, possession of the world's most deadly weapons is the ultimate trump card, the one he must hold to fulfill his ambition.

We know that Saddam Hussein is determined to keep his weapons of mass destruction, is determined to make more. Given Saddam Hussein's history of aggression, given what we know of his grandiose plans, given what we know of his terrorist associations, and given his determination to exact revenge on those who oppose him, should we take the risk that he will not someday use these weapons at a time and a place and in a manner of his choosing, at a time when the world is in a much weaker position to respond?

The United States will not and cannot run that risk for the American people. Leaving Saddam Hussein in possession of weapons of mass destruction for a few more months or years is not an option, not in a post-September 11th world.

My colleagues, over three months ago, this Council recognized that Iraq continued to pose a threat to international peace and security, and that Iraq had been and remained in material breach of its disarmament obligations.

Today, Iraq still poses a threat and Iraq still remains in material breach. Indeed, by its failure to seize on its one last opportunity to come clean and disarm, Iraq has put itself in deeper material breach and closer to the day when it will face serious consequences for its continue defiance of this Council.

My colleagues, we have an obligation to our citizens. We have an obligation to this body to see that our resolutions are complied with. We wrote 1441 not in order to go to war. We wrote 1441 to try to preserve the peace. We wrote 1441 to give Iraq one last chance. Iraq is not, so far, taking that one last chance.

We must not shrink from whatever is ahead of us. We must not fail in our duty and our responsibility to the citizens of the countries that are represented by this body.

Thank you, Mr. President.

Published by the U.S Department of State, February 5, 2003.

Osama bin Laden's "Business" in Sudan

"What was the importance of the Sudanese sojourn for Osama bin Laden? One can argue that, without the sanctuary in Sudan, the Arabs who had fought in Afghanistan would have dispersed. Some would have gone home; others would have scattered in exile. Over time, their strength would have waned and they would have had difficulty communicating and coordinating their efforts.... Without Sudan, bin Laden could not have incubated the networks that have caused such devastation in subsequent years."

Ann M. Lesch

During a newspaper interview a few months ago, Hasan al-Turabi—the former éminence grise behind Sudan's Islamist regime—shook his head, seemingly bewildered at the claim that he worked closely with Osama bin Laden during the Saudi militant's four and a half years in Khartoum: "I knew bin Laden in Sudan briefly, through his work in roads and agriculture.... I met him once...."[1] Those few words conveniently rewrote the story—a rewriting that was essential for Turabi in the wake of September 11. The actual history of their relationship was quite different.

TURABI'S PAN-ISLAMIST ZEAL...

Well before bin Laden arrived in Khartoum in December 1991, Turabi eagerly spread his version of Islamic politics throughout the Middle East, North Africa, and East Africa. Bringing his National Islamic Front to power through a military coup in June 1989, he took advantage of the Persian Gulf crisis in 1990–1991 to launch a pan-Islamic, anti-imperialist front to resist America's "recolonization of the Islamic world." Turabi's Popular Arab Islamic Conference (PAIC) brought together leaders of militant Islamist groups, inaugurated by conferences in Khartoum in April and August 1991.

Sudan provided a sanctuary for many of these militants. Battle-hardened by their jihad (holy struggle) against the Soviet Union in Afghanistan (a struggle that ended in February 1989) and disillusioned by the subsequent warlordism in Afghanistan, many Arab mujahideen (holy warriors) were perceived as threats to security in their own countries and therefore could not re-turn home without risking arrest. In 1990 Sudan dropped its visa requirement for Arabs and opened its doors to them. (It even began to grant Arabs immediate permanent residency and passports in 1993). Turabi disbursed Sudanese diplomatic passports to favored Islamist politicians, such as leaders of the Nahda (Islamic Revival) Party in Tunisia and the Islamic Salvation Front (FIS) in Algeria. His movement also funneled money to the FIS during the 1991 parliamentary election campaign. (The final stage of these elections was canceled when the government feared the FIS might win.) And in November 1991, the first armed operation against the Algerian government—in what has become a bloody 11 years of war—occurred when a group of Algerian veterans of the Afghan war, who had trained in Sudan, attacked a police post on the Algerian-Tunisian border.

Turabi also welcomed Egyptian militants, arguing that the Egyptian government was hostile to Islam and that Sudan must support that government's enemies until it was overthrown. Egypt's Islamic Jihad leader, Sheikh Umar Abd al-Rahman, on trail in absentia for political incitement, lived in a government villa in Khartoum in April 1990 and again in July of that year before he flew to the United States. (Abd al-Rahman obtained a "green card" but was jailed for complicity in attempts to bomb buildings and tunnels in New York City in 1993.) By the end of 1991, Sudan hosted about a thousand Egyptians, who were affiliated with both Islamic Jihad and Ayman al-Zawahiri's wing of the Islamic Group. These comprised nearly half the Egyptian fighters who had remained in Pakistan after the Afghan war ended.

Sudan set up training camps for African militants on the Ethiopian border and helped overthrow the Marxist regime in Addis Ababa in May 1991. Camps to train Arabs were located outside Port Sudan and Khartoum. As early as May 1990, some 60 Arabs from North Africa, France, and Belgium began to train in the Shambat district of Khartoum for sabotage operations in Europe. And in December 1991 the first 19 fighters from Kashmir completed a six-month training program; Turabi joined government officials to address their graduation ceremony.

These actions angered Arab and African rulers well before bin Laden arrived in Khartoum. In October 1990 the Egyptian government closed its airspace to flights from Sudan, seized nearly 200 machine guns that had been smuggled across the desert into upper Egypt, and asserted that the men who had killed the speaker of parliament in September had trained in Sudan. Libyan leader Muammar Qaddafi complained that Turabi sent saboteurs trained in Sudan to destabilize Libya and abruptly raised the price of oil deliveries to pressure Khartoum. Tunisia recalled its ambassador in the fall of 1991 after receiving credible reports that Turabi and Sudanese government officials had plotted with Nahda leaders during the August PAIC meeting to assassinate the Tunisian president and to smuggle weapons into the country. (The head of Nahda then relinquished his Sudanese diplomatic passport and left Khartoum for Europe.) The Algerian military government, which seized power in January 1992, cold-shouldered Khartoum because of its support for Algerian Islamic groups. Governments in East Africa also protested Sudan's support for violent underground opposition movements.

...AND BIN LADEN'S MUTUAL INTEREST

A strong coincidence of interest united Turabi, the senior Islamist political operative, and bin Laden, the wealthy young Saudi businessman. Bin Laden had fought in Afghanistan alongside Arab mujahideen he had recruited and funded. He had gloried in the victory against Soviet troops, but had returned to Jeddah discouraged by the postwar Afghan infighting. When Iraq invaded Kuwait in August 1990, bin Laden offered to mobilize 10,000 mujahideen to defend the kingdom. He was shocked when the rulers instead brought in thousands of American soldiers.

Bin Laden's deeply felt beliefs crystallized during his stay in Sudan.

Although placed under severe restrictions by the Saudi regime, bin Laden managed to leave for Pakistan in April 1991 on the pretext of a business trip. But the political situation was too unstable for him to remain there. He was already in contact with Sudanese Islamists and had vis-

ited the country in October 1990. Therefore, he eagerly accepted Turabi's invitation to relocate to Khartoum.

It is not clear what their exact relationship was at that time. One report claims that Turabi appealed to bin Laden to use his contacts in the Persian Gulf to set up an international banking network to launder and transfer money to support PAIC and the armed movements. Bin Laden himself said that he had been considering investing in Sudan since 1990 and that, while dining with Turabi soon after his arrival, Turabi promised to give him all the help he needed. In any event, Turabi quickly provided him with an office and security guards and arranged to exempt his newly established construction company from customs duties on the import of trucks and tractors. Bin Laden moved into a villa in the upscale Riyadh district in Khartoum, next door to Turabi's spacious home.

Bin Laden launched a wide variety of businesses, starting with a construction company that built a new highway from Khartoum to Port Sudan, constructed a new airport outside Port Sudan, repaved the 500-kilometer road from Khartoum north to Shendi and Atbara, and raised the height of the Rusayris hydroelectric dam. He said that when he contributed a million dollars toward the capitalization of the new Shamali Bank, he was awarded a million acres in western Sudan for agriculture and cattle raising. Bin Laden also claimed that, when the government was desperately short of wheat in 1993, he underwrote an $8-million loan with lenient terms to finance the necessary imports. Then, when the government failed in 1994 to pay him for his multimillion-dollar construction projects, it handed over ownership of its money-losing tannery and reportedly even awarded him a 10-year monopoly on the export of gum arabic, maize, sunflowers, and sesame.

Bin Laden provided substantial sums to help Turabi realize his pan-Islamic ambitions. By bin Laden's own account, he paid $5,000 on arrival to become a member of Turabi's National Islamic Front, contributed $1 million to support PAIC, and spent $2 million to fly Arab mujahideen to Sudan from Pakistan when Iran reneged on paying that sum. He also affirmed that he built and equipped 23 training camps for mujahideen at his own expense. By the summer of 1994 at least 5,000 mujahideen trained in Sudan, often while working on bin Laden's agricultural and construction projects. The largest camp was said to be based on a 5,000-acre farm in the mountains near Shendi, north of Khartoum.

Bin Laden's Egyptian partner, Ayman al-Zawahiri, apparently managed the international financial networks for bin Laden and Turabi, using Islamic banks, couriers, and charities to accumulate and move funds from Zawahiri's safe haven in Geneva. Bin Laden also spent three months in London in 1994 setting up the Advice and Reform Committee, which complemented Zawahiri's efforts by fund raising, propagandizing against the Saudi regime, and supporting cells in Europe and the United

States. Bin Laden is said to have left Jeddah with a million dollars in cash. However, although he accessed additional funds before the Saudi government blocked his bank accounts, he was not the multimillionaire that is often alleged. His business ventures in the Sudan and the global fund-raising network were essential for the support of military and political operations.

Bin Laden's deeply felt beliefs crystallized during his stay in Sudan. From his viewpoint, he had fought a legitimate defensive jihad against the foreign presence in Afghanistan and had helped build an international movement of mujahideen, ready to fight against the infidels wherever they attacked. Jihad became the "acme of religion"—a drastic shift in the way Islamic principles are prioritized. He shared the foot soldiers' postwar disillusionment and sympathized with their eagerness to confront their own authoritarian, seemingly antireligious governments. And he was dismayed when United States troops defiled Saudi Arabia's holy soil. He accused the royal family of lying when they promised that those troops would leave as soon as they liberated Kuwait. Instead, the United States armed forces established permanent bases to enforce the crippling sanctions against Iraq that were imposed during the Persian Gulf conflict.

Bin Laden's interests therefore overlapped with Turabi's ambitions and with the goals of exiled Egyptian Islamists such as Zawahiri, with whom he had worked closely in Afghanistan. The camps that bin Laden set up expanded the training of militants to include attacks on neighboring countries. Libyans who had trained in Sudan attempted to assassinate Qaddafi in 1993, launched attacks inside Libya in 1995, and killed several Libyan security officers in 1996. Some of the Palestinian Hamas operatives who had trained in Sudan organized suicide bombings on Israeli civilian buses after they returned to Gaza in 1995. Bin Laden and Turabi worked closely with the radical wing of Yemen's Islah (Reform) Party to achieve an Islamic military government similar to that in Sudan. The Sudanese government accelerated its training to Eritrean Jihad and Oromo fighters, and Egyptian Islamists continued to cross the border to attack targets in upper Egypt. The movement's reach extended to Lebanon: assassins of a prominent Lebanese politician escaped to Khartoum in November 1995, and two Sudanese arrested in January 1996 for casing the Egyptian embassy and other targets admitted to receiving funds from the Sudanese consul in Beirut.

Bin Laden shared the Sudanese government's concern about the situation in Somalia, which descended into chaos after the overthrow of United States ally General Siad Barre in January 1991. When the United Nations sent in peacekeepers in December 1992, Khartoum feared that this would establish a bridgehead for the United States (which spearheaded the peacekeeping force) to invade southern Sudan. Soon after, bin Laden's allies in Yemen tried to kill United States soldiers stationed in the city of Aden. Following a coordinating meeting in Khartoum in February 1993, the Sudanese government began to send arms to General Muhammad Aidid, a Somali warlord opposed to the UN–United States presence. The arms were shipped overland through Oromo-controlled areas of Ethiopia or by bin Laden's ships, which sailed from Port Sudan to offload along the Somali coast. Bin Laden flew at least 3,000 Arab fighters from Yemen to support Aidid's militia (at the cost of $3 million) and bought land for training camps inside Somalia. Zawahiri helped raise funds and coordinate these efforts from his base in Europe. Aidid's confrontation with the United States forces culminated in the latter's disastrous attack on his headquarters in September 1993. Bin Laden celebrated the United States withdrawal in March 1994 as a victory for the expanding Islamist movement.

The bin Laden network also assisted the beleaguered government in Bosnia, under attack by Serbia and Croatia after it declared independence in 1991 but faced with an arms embargo from the West. Islamists argued that the Christian West refused to aid the Bosnian Muslims against the Christian Serbs and Croats. The mufti of Bosnia appealed for support at a PAIC conference in December 1993, and Islamists responded by sending funds, arms, and some 5,000 fighters to defend the only Muslim political entity in Europe. They denounced the United States–brokered Dayton accords of November 1995 that ended fighting in Bosnia, saying that Dayton ratified territorial gains made by Serbs and Croats at the expense of Muslims. Although Zawahiri hastened to Bosnia, threatening to attack the UN peacekeepers that had been deployed there, most of the fighters were deported to their home countries before and after the accords were implemented.

Further afield, militants apparently linked to Sheikh Abd al-Rahman attacked the World Trade Center in February 1993 and plotted to blow up the UN headquarters, the Holland Tunnel, and other important structures in New York City. The Algerian Armed Islamic Group (GIA) conspired to crash an Air France airliner into the Eiffel Tower on Christmas Day in 1994, the same year that a plot was discovered to fly a plane into the CIA's headquarters near Washington, D.C. And bin Laden visited Manila in 1993, seemingly to lay the groundwork to support the Abu Sayyaf rebel group, assassinate foreign leaders, and blow up United States airliners over the Pacific Ocean. (The Manila plots were discovered accidentally in early 1995.)

Bin Laden was personally preoccupied with the need to expel United States forces from the sacred soil of Arabia. He sought to expose the royal family as liars and hypocrites who would be punished on the day of judgment. They responded by stripping him of his citizenship in April 1994 and freezing his assets. In April 1995 a leaflet appeared that threatened strikes on United States and British troops and on the Saudi government if the "crusader" foreign forces did not evacuate Saudi Arabia by June 28, 1995. This threat was followed by attacks on the

Saudi national guard headquarters in Riyadh in November 1995, which killed 5 American soldiers, and on the United States military barracks in Khobar in June 1996, which killed 19 American soldiers.[2] Bin Laden praised the bombings for targeting United States troops while sparing Saudi citizens. He probably viewed the attacks as a success when the United States reacted by recalling many dependents and moving its bases to isolated locations in the desert.

CLASH OF IDEOLOGIES

Although Turabi and bin Laden had common interests in opposing Untied States domination and undermining regional governments, ideological differences began to mar their relationship. The mercurial Turabi espoused a modernist Islamist that (among other things) sought to reconcile the various currents of Islam, promote women's participation in public life, and avoid violence against civilians. In contrast, bin Laden and many of the Arab militants who settled in Sudan adopted the *salafi* approach preached by Wahhabis in Saudi Arabia.[3] These militants denounced all other Islamic currents as apostate, restricted the activities of women, and endorsed attacks on civilians as well as security forces to overthrow un-Islamic regimes.

By 1995 Turabi openly criticized the Algerian GIA and Zawahiri's Egyptian Islamic Group for killing civilians and foreign tourists. He also criticized the militants for repressing women and denounced Iran's clerical rule. Similarly, President Omar al-Bashir argued that the Sudan upheld the "return to our roots [and to] the principles of justice…under the aegis of a modern state.… We are against extremism and against bigotry."

The militants responded in kind. At the PAIC conference in April 1995, a Lebanese Hezbollah leader accused Turabi of delusions of grandeur and pointedly asserted that he lacked the charisma and stature of the late Ayatollah Ruhollah Khomeini. Later, Egyptian operative Mustafa Hamza accused the Sudanese government of distorting Islam by deviating from the precepts and practices of the early Muslim forefathers.

By mid-1995 Turabi and the government had banned Arab militants from preaching in mosques after the five daily prayers. They had preached and circulated leaflets and cassettes that accused Turabi of blasphemy and atheism. Members of the militant Takfir wal-Hijra even killed 28 worshippers in the conservative and nonviolent Ansar al-Sunna al-Muhammadiya mosque in February 1994. The Libyan-born leader of the cell declared that all contemporary Muslim societies were infidel and must be fought; bin Laden and Turabi were both on his hit list. Banned from the mosques, the young militants then preached on street corners against corruption, blasphemy, and the evils of modern society. In December 1995 police killed eight Takfir zealots who tried to force residents of a shantytown near Wad Medani to convert to their creed of Islam.

These ideological differences alone would not have caused the government to expel bin Laden and the Arab militants. The security forces could contain their excesses, and most of them could be kept isolated from the Sudanese public in bin Laden's training camps. Some could also be sent to fight in the jihad in southern Sudan, a move that bin Laden strongly opposed. (The civil war in Sudan, renewed in 1983, pitted the Arab-Islamic northern government against the African, non-Muslim peoples in the south.) So long as they served Turabi and the regime's regional political goals, they would be allowed to reside and train in Sudan.

THE TURNING POINT

On June 26, 1995, several Egyptians tried to assassinate Egyptian President Hosni Mubarak shortly after his convoy left the Addis Ababa airport en route for the Ethiopian capital itself. Cells coordinated by Zawahiri, Mustafa Hamza, and others had tried to kill Mubarak many times, first in Cairo and later in New York, Sarajevo, Rome, and Manila. This plan was allegedly initiated at the PAIC meeting in Khartoum in March 1995, where Turabi met with Zawahiri (based in Geneva), Rifat Ahmad Taha (a terrorist trainer based in Peshawar, Pakistan), and Hamza (who was based in Sudan). Turabi tasked Hamza with preparing the plan; Zawahiri would put the final touches on it. Hamza rented a villa in Addis Ababa, flying in operatives and weapons from Sudan in May on Sudanair as well as on bin Laden's private plane. Turabi met with Zawahiri in Geneva, followed by meetings between Hamza and the senior European commander to finalize the plans.

Zawahiri made an inspection trip to Sudan and Ethiopia in mid-June, culminating in a final meeting in Geneva on June 23 to coordinate three separate teams. One entered Ethiopia from Sudan, a second flew in from Pakistan (transiting at the Khartoum airport), and the third infiltrated Egypt to launch simultaneous attacks there. Hamza had trained the first and third teams separately on a farm north of Khartoum. When the attack failed, Ethiopian and Egyptian security arrested most of the participants, but three escaped to Sudan.

Turabi and his agents in the security forces seem to have been fully involved in the plot. Those agents included the head of security, Nafi Ali Nafi, and Brigadier General al-Fatih Urwah, who headed training camps in eastern Sudan and now serves as the Sudanese ambassador to the United Nations. Indeed, Nafi was in Addis Ababa on the day of the attack. While denying prior knowledge, Turabi quickly hailed the "mujahideen who pursued the pharaoh of Egypt."

President Bashir apparently had no prior knowledge of the plot. He immediately fired Nafi and began to overhaul the security services to reduce Turabi's control. The government reimposed entry visas for Arabs in September. When Egypt and Ethiopia formally accused the government of organizing the attack, Sudanese diplomats scrambled to deflect the accusation and repeatedly denied that they were hiding the three Egyptians. They were already concerned about ongoing censure from Libya and other North African regimes for hosting Arab militants; they also feared that the November bombing in Riyadh would be blamed on Khartoum. Although relations had been cold since Sudan had embraced Iraq during the Gulf War, Khartoum could ill afford complete isolation from Riyadh.

On January 31, 1996, the UN Security Council unanimously accused the Sudanese government of supporting terror, imposed limited sanctions, and demanded that the government extradite the three wanted Egyptians to Ethiopia. The United States simultaneously closed its embassy in Khartoum, on the grounds that the Sudanese government could not guarantee the diplomats' security so long as extremist groups operated freely in the capital city. The United States antiterrorism act of April 1996, which blocked the assets of terrorist organizations, was swiftly invoked against bin Laden's organization.

THE EXPULSION

Bin Laden was already anxious about his status when he flew to London in December 1995 (and soon after traveled to Mogadishu). He tried to obtain a visa to the United States and gain political asylum in England; instead, the British issued an exclusion order. He also prepared to send some of his followers from Sudan to Somalia.

In the wake of bin Laden's expulsion, Sudanese government officials vigorously denied responsibility for his actions.

The ever-pragmatic Turabi realized that, to save the Khartoum regime, bin Laden had to leave. In January 1996 he contacted mujahideen leaders in Afghanistan to see if they would host their former ally. Turabi may have wanted to protect bin Laden from the outcome that Bashir was considering: turning bin Laden over to the United States or Saudi government.

Turabi later noted that, when no other country would accept bin Laden, "we worked out a plan under which the government apologetically permitted bin Laden to leave and proceed to Afghanistan." Turabi reportedly went to bin Laden's office in March [to] tell him this, expressing his hope that bin Laden would retain his business interests in the country. But Turabi said bin Laden "left Sudan angry at being banished to Afghanistan."

In February 1996 the Sudanese interior ministry required all Egyptians to register with the police. During April the government ordered the nearly 200 Egyptian militants in the country to leave within three weeks or face the threat of extradition to Egypt. Mustafa Hamza

appears to have been one of those who abruptly left for Afghanistan that month.[4] In fact, the Egyptian government gave Khartoum a detailed list of wanted persons, of whom 64 were detained in May. The government closed the Hamas office and expelled several Palestinians; militants from North Africa also quickly departed.

When Bashir performed the pilgrimage in early May, he piously told King Fahd that bin Laden entered Sudan as a businessman: "When the Saudis complained…we stopped him from performing these hostile activities." Bin Laden departed that same month, flying into Jalalabad on May 10 to be welcomed by his former Afghan mujahideen ally, Gulhuddin Hekmetyar. Over the next few weeks, he was joined by his family, the families of Zawahiri and other key colleagues, and hundreds of fighters.

THE RETURN TO AFGHANISTAN

The globalization of the Islamist network peaked after bin Laden returned to Afghanistan. He quickly switched allegiance from Hekmetyar to the Pakistani-supported Taliban, which he later called the only pure "Muslim state that enforces God's laws, that destroys falsehoods, and that does not succumb to the American infidels." Afghanistan also provided an ideal sanctuary for training new militants from the Middle East, Asia, and Europe. Indeed, the old training camps in Afghanistan had never entirely closed; in the early 1990s they were used to train Chechen and Central Asian militants.

In February 1998 bin Laden and Zawahiri formalized their long-standing ties by announcing the World Front for Jihad Against Jews and Crusaders, which endorsed attacks against American civilians and military personnel for occupying and, in bin Laden's words, "desecrating my land and holy shrines, and plundering the Muslims' oil." That August its operatives bombed the United States embassies in Kenya and Tanzania; the "sleeper" cells that carried out the attacks had been planted in East Africa in 1994 while bin Laden was still *persona grata* in Khartoum. The September 11, 2001 terrorist attacks on the symbols and center of American military and financial power were the logical outcome of the front's ideology. Zawahiri boasted afterward that, for the first time, Americans felt danger coming directly at them.

SUDAN'S DENIALS

In the wake of bin Laden's expulsion, Sudanese government officials vigorously denied responsibility for his actions. They argued that they expelled any Arab residents who were wanted in their own country or who undertook illegal actions. Bin Laden may have retained some of his businesses, however, and may have revisited Sudan at least once, in part because the government still owed him substantial amounts of his construction projects. Moreover, Qaddafi was compelled to issue an ultimatum to President Bashir in January 1997 to force Sudan to hand over two dozen Libyans, some of whom he accused of killing Libyan security officers. And not until the summer of 2001 did the Sudanese government deport the Egyptian Rifat Ahmad Taha, who had been sentenced to death in absentia for his role in the bloody attack on Luxor in November 1997.[5] By then Bashir had sidelined and arrested Turabi, closed the PAIC, reestablished cooperative relations with Egypt and Ethiopia, and held lengthy security talks with the CIA in an effort to prove that the country no longer hosted wanted terrorists.

This clean-up effort became frantic after September 11 as the government sought to ensure that it would not be a target of a United States military attack that would be presumably much more severe than the cruise missile strike the United States carried out in August 1998 in retaliation for the attacks on the United States embassies in Kenya and Tanzania. The government gave United States security agents access to hundreds of files on Islamists who had lived in Sudan. It was rewarded when the UN lifted the five-and-a-half-year-old sanctions and the United States made its first serious effort to resolve the nearly 20-year-old war in the south.

What was the importance of the Sudanese sojourn for Osama bin Laden? One can argue that, without the sanctuary in Sudan, the Arabs who had fought in Afghanistan would have dispersed. Some would have gone home; others would have scattered in exile. Over time, their strength would have waned and they would have had difficulty communicating and coordinating their efforts.

Sudan provided a welcoming environment. The government worked closely with bin Laden and the Egyptian Islamists to reinvigorate the transnational mujahideen movement and to train a new generation of militants. The Islamists could undertake weapons training and travel freely in and out of the country. While Turabi initiated this support before bin Laden's arrival and provided cover through PAIC for the leaders to plan terrorist attacks, bin Laden's presence expanded the range of activities. His and Zawahiri's organizations opened up new arenas for operations in East Africa, the Balkans, and Central Asia. Without Sudan, bin Laden could not have incubated the networks that have caused such devastation in subsequent years.

NOTES

1. *Al-Sharq al-Awsat* (London), January 23, 2002.
2. Allegedly targets began to be cased in 1993 and the Riyadh attack was planned in 1995 at meetings in Turabi's office in Khartoum and in Mecca during the pilgrimage. The 27-year-old Saudi executed as the leader of the cell had fought in Afghanistan and lived in Peshawar in one of bin Laden's hostels for Arab fighters. The bombers also demanded the release of Abd al-Rahman and others jailed in the United States for the 1993 New York terrorist plots. See Mary Anne Weaver, *A Portrait of Egypt* (New York: Farrar, Straus and Giroux, 2000), pp. 188–189; Yossef Bodansky, *Bin Laden* (Roseville, Calif.: Prima Publishing, 2001), p. 104.
3. The *salafi* approach is based on the return to what are viewed as the principles followed by the pious ancestors in Mecca at the time of the prophet and the first four caliphs.
4. Interviewed by *al-Hayat* (London), April 22, 1996, he claimed that the last time that he had been to Sudan was in 1994, a year before the attempt to kill Mubarak, and that his Egyptian Islamic Group undertook the operation alone, without Sudanese assistance. Two persons, he claimed, merely passed through Khartoum on the way from Pakistan to Ethiopia, and others went from Pakistan across Sudanese territory to infiltrate into Egypt. These statements must have been part of a deal to let him leave if he would distance himself from the regime.
5. Taha was put on a plane to Syria. The Syrian government realized that he was a political hot potato and deported him to Egypt in November 2001, where he was immediately jailed.

ANN M. LESCH *is a professor of political science at Villanova University and the author of* The Sudan: Contested National Identities *(Bloomington: Indiana University Press, 1998).*

From *Current History*, May 2002, pp. 203-209. © 2002 by Current History, Inc. Reprinted by permission.

UNIT 5
International Terrorism

Unit Selections

13. **Extremist Groups in Egypt**, Jeffrey A. Nedoroscik
14. **Colombia and the United States: From Counternarcotics to Counterterrorism**, Arlene B. Tickner
15. **"Déjà Vu All Over Again?" Why Dialogue Won't Solve the Kashmir Dispute**, Arun R. Swamy

Key Points to Consider

- What are the conditions that have contributed to the emergence of extremist groups in Egypt? What lesson can be learned from the Egyptian example?

- What are the root causes of the current crisis in Colombia? What impact has U.S. policy had on the problems in Colombia?

- What factors led to the formation of terrorist groups in Kashmir? What role can diplomacy play in the potential resolution of this conflict? How has the U.S. campaign in Afghanistan affected the conflict in Kashmir?

 **Links: www.dushkin.com/online/**
These sites are annotated in the World Wide Web pages.

The International Policy Institute for Counter-Terrorism
http://www.ict.org.il

International Rescue Committee
http://www.intrescom.org

ISN International Relations and Security Network
http://www.isn.ethz.ch

International terrorism has changed significantly in the past decade. Simply said, it has become more complex. While some of the actors remain the same, increased organizational complexity, improved communications, and an increased willingness to cause mass casualties pose new challenges for the international community.

Individuals and small groups dominated international terrorism in the 1970s. Larger groups and organizations played a critical role in international terrorism in the 1980s. More complex multinational terrorist networks emerged in the 1990s. As we enter the twenty-first century, all three generations and levels of organizational structure appear to exist. Sometimes terrorists act, locally or regionally, to pursue independent agendas. At other times they take advantage of cross-national links to obtain greater access to weapons, training, or financial resources. On occasion, they may even temporarily set aside local interests and objectives to cooperate within loosely connected international networks to pursue broader ideological agendas. At any given point in time, international terrorists may appear to be engaged in activities at all three levels, posing unique challenges to those engaged in the study of international terrorism.

Modern communications technologies have changed the way international terrorists operate. The cell phone and the laptop computer have become as important as the bomb and the AK-47 in the terrorist's arsenal. The Internet has provided terrorists access to instant global communications. It enhances their ability to exchange information and provides them with an effective vehicle to rally their supporters. Almost all major international terrorist organizations operate their own Web sites and communicate via the Internet.

A particularly disturbing trend in contemporary international terrorism is the increased willingness of some terrorists to cause mass casualties. While the potential causes of this trend are subject to debate, the trend itself has again elevated terrorism to the top of the international agenda. While the number of interna-

tional terrorist incidents has significantly declined, the casualties caused by international terrorism have steadily increased. More important, this trend has focused international attention on terrorist methods deemed unlikely only a few years ago. Potential threats posed by biological, chemical, or radiological weapons are again at the forefront of international concern.

The three selections in this unit reflect some of the diversity in international terrorism. The first article traces the development of Islamic extremism in Egypt from the Muslim Brotherhood to al Qaida. It argues that there are important lessons to be learned from the Egyptian experience. The second article focuses on the second shift in U.S. policy in Colombia "from counternarcotics to counterterrorism." The article argues that U.S. policy may have made "an already grave situation" even worse. The final article in this section focuses on the complexity of the Kashmir dispute, examining myriad actors and motives at various levels of analysis, arguing that engaging in dialogue at one level may not resolve the conflict at other levels.

Extremist Groups in Egypt

On 11 September, terrorism became a much greater reality for Americans and much of the rest of the world. Indeed, that date marks the beginning of a new era for the global community, an era that may be called the Violent New World Order, or the Age of Fear. Since the events of 11 September, the United States has been working to build a coalition against terrorism consisting of countries throughout the world. More recently, the United States launched attacks on positions inside Afghanistan in order to wipe out Osama bin Laden's al-Qaeda organization and assisted the Northern Alliance in the overthrow of the Taliban government that had protected al-Qaeda. Given the military prowess of the United States and its allies, these acts have largely achieved their short-term goals. Over the long term, however, the United States, its allies, those countries that have been breeding grounds for terrorist organizations and those whose citizens sympathize with terrorist organizations need to look deeper at the causes of terrorism. On the surface, the religious zeal associated with the most prolific terrorist organizations appears to be something with which the United States and its allies cannot negotiate. The frustrations that drive people to acts of terror, however, are often rooted in adverse socio-economic conditions as well as cultural and political tensions that need to be addressed by underdeveloped nations and the larger international community. Since the deserts of Egypt gave birth to the rise of the first Islamic militant organizations, the Egyptian experience provides a perspective.

JEFFREY A. NEDOROSCIK

In the early 1990s, Egypt was gripped by years of terrorist acts by radical Islamic groups. This violence helped cause the demise of the country's economy, which relies on tourism for hard currency, and sent the government scrambling for control. The Western press largely dismissed these acts as those of religious fanatics with whom it is impossible to reason or negotiate. Rather, according to traditional thought, they needed to be eliminated. In a project that spanned two continents, however, I joined some of my colleagues in investigating the roots of the violent internal conflict that was growing stronger in Egypt.

The foundation for our project rested on the theory that there could be lessons learned about the roots of violent internal conflict in underdeveloped nations by comparing conflicts such as those in Mexico and Egypt.[1] A workshop in Cairo in 1996 took a deeper look into these two conflicts to understand what they had in common. Three hypotheses emerged from our investigation. The first and primary hypothesis was that violent internal conflict results from socio-economic, cultural and political tensions. These tensions are exacerbated by the mobilizing efforts of anti-status quo activists, as well as by the impact and perceived impact of economic liberalization and structural adjustment policies. There are various sub-hypotheses:

a. The actors in the conflict stretch across four intricately linked levels: the locus of the conflict, the institutional system, civil society and the international environment. The locus of the conflict is the geographic area from which the conflict has erupted or a group of people who, for various reasons, are somehow separated from mainstream society and are in a less advantageous position socially and economically than their countrymen.

b. The locus is in a situation where it is being marginalized by the institutional system.

c. Civil society demonstrates sympathetic tendencies towards the anti-status quo group.

d. The international environment strongly influences the response of the government towards the conflict.

This workshop led to further investigation of violent internal conflict. Again, the efforts focused on the conflict situations in Egypt and Mexico. In Egypt, it soon became clear that the movement that had caused acts of terror throughout the country was not simply one based on religious extremism. Rather, this movement grew out of the socio-economic conditions as well as the cultural and political tensions existing for the poorest of Egypt's poor.

The militant groups carrying out these acts of terror were from Upper Egypt, and the movement was very region-biased as they viewed other Islamist groups, largely from the north, as having failed to address what they saw as the immediate issues at hand—the dire socio-economic conditions faced by their people each day. While other groups tended to look beyond Egypt's borders at issues such as Pan-Arabism and the liberation of Palestine as priorities, Upper Egyptian Islamists looked homeward at the dismal socio-economic conditions of the region and the policies of the government in power that perpetuated the status quo. This was evident in the assassination of President Anwar Sadat at the hands of Upper Egyptian Islamists as he attempted to roll back reforms that President Nasser had set in place that had benefited Upper Egyptians.

Upper Egypt has historically been isolated, geographically, politically and economically, from the rest of Egypt. Until recently, there was little effort at development in Upper Egypt, by either the Government of Egypt or the international donor community, as efforts focused on Cairo and the Nile Delta region. As a result, Upper Egypt has soaring rates of unemployment, illiteracy, malnutrition, morbidity and mortality. Upper Egypt ranks at the bottom of virtually every social and economic indicator for Egypt and has the highest percentage of ultra-poor—those who survive on a day-to-day basis. As such, it served as a perfect breeding ground for militant activity.

The rise of low-intensity conflict in Egypt culminated in November 1997, when 58 tourists were brutally killed in Luxor, Upper Egypt. This attack was attributed to the southern militant movement al-Gama'a al-Islamiyya, one of the organizations included on the US Government's list of 'terrorist organizations' later released following the 11 September attacks. In recent years, al-Gama'a al-Islamiyya is said to have increasingly close ties to Osama bin Laden as he sought to create a worldwide terrorist network.

The attack in Luxor succeeded in devastating Egypt's economy by scaring away tourists and their much-needed hard currency. This attack was the pinnacle of the movement that began its terrorist operations with vigor in 1992, when anti-status quo groups such as al-Gama'a al-Islamiyya began targeting Egypt's secular government. During the height of fundamentalist activity in Egypt (between April 1992 and October 1993), some 222 people were killed in anti-status quo violence, including 66 members of government security forces, 76 'terrorists' and 6 foreign tourists.

The Egyptian government has mostly fought violence with violence. Whereas they have succeeded in keeping the movement under control in recent years, the root causes of the Upper Egyptian movement continue to exist: the bleak socio-economic conditions characterizing the lives of most Upper Egyptians. As a result, Upper Egypt has become the breeding ground for the fundamentalist movement and is the area where the movement receives its most widespread support. Still, the media, the Egyptian government and the international community focused on the violence itself and largely ignored its root causes.

The fundamentalist groups that have grown up in Egypt trace their roots to an ideology that dates to the immediate post-independence period and in the creation of the Muslim Brotherhood in the 1920s. Although the Brotherhood has historically been a more mainstream organization that operated within the established institutional system, they have had a profound influence on the groups that are active today.

The Muslim Brotherhood in Egypt

The Muslim Brotherhood was founded in 1928 by Hasan al-Banna. Al-Banna was born in the Nile Delta in 1906, the son of an Islamic scholar. He grew up in the Delta province of al-Buhayra before attending the teacher's college in Cairo. There, al-Banna learned the concept of Islam as a self-sufficient ideology and became aware of the 'dangers' of Westernization.

A rural-to-urban migrant, al-Banna was initially shocked by life in Cairo. In his memoirs he wrote,

> Young men were lost, and the educated were in a state of doubt and confusion… I saw that the social life of the beloved Egyptian nation was oscillating between her dear and precious Islamism which she had inherited, defended, lived with and become accustomed to, and made powerful during thirteen centuries, and this severe western invasion which is armed and equipped with all destructive and degenerative influences of money, wealth, prestige, ostentation, material enjoyment, power and means of propaganda.[2]

Al-Banna began to think of all of the problems that Egypt faced as a result of the influence of the West and the straying of Egyptians from the straight path of Islam.

In 1927, al-Banna began teaching at a government primary school in Ismaliya. There, he came into daily contact with British soldiers and he found their presence to be offensive. He began to form the goal of ridding Egypt of this foreign occupation.

The following year, al-Banna established the Muslim Brotherhood, predicated on radical nationalist ideas and religious practices. At first, the group was simply an Islamic revivalist movement. Quickly, however, the group developed a political orientation that was very anti-Western and opposed to secular politics. An underground paramilitary wing was also established, primarily to fight against the British occupation of Egypt. It was also active, however, in attacking Jewish interests in Egypt as well as government figures.

The Muslim Brotherhood has often been called the first wide-ranging, organized and international Islamic movement of modern times. The group's message: struggle to rid Egypt of foreign occupation and defend and obey Islam. Its slogan: 'God is our purpose, the Prophet our leader, the Qur'an our constitution, Jihad our way and dying for God's cause our supreme objective.' Its banner: two crossing swords, a copy of the Holy Qur'an and the word 'prepare'.

The Brotherhood recognized early on the power of education in spreading its message and engaged in many educational activities. The group established primary and secondary schools for boys and girls as well as technical schools for workers.

There were also Qur'anic classes and basic skill classes for the illiterate. Many of the Brotherhood's members were recruited from among the students of these institutions. In her book, *Egypt from Independence to Revolution*, historian Selma Botman commented that,

> From the beginning of its organization, the Muslim Brotherhood took the recruitment of students seriously and considered them the organization's 'striking force'. Student members were organized in 'families' which met regularly every week in the house of one of them to study an Islamic educative syllabus specially designed to suit their age group and educational level.[3]

The Brotherhood has also been active in encouraging 'appropriate' social and economic reform in Egypt. As part of their programme, they set up urban projects that provided jobs for the unemployed and poor and set up industrial and commercial enterprises that could compete with Egypt's non-Islamic entrepreneurs.

The Brotherhood drew much of its support from recent rural-to-urban migrants who had found little satisfaction in Cairo. To them, the Brotherhood offered associations that embraced each member as a family. Soon, however, support for the Brothers grew beyond students and the urban poor to the middle classes, who were equally disenchanted with the government, the economy and the continued presence of foreigners on Egypt's soil.

The Depression of 1929 and the economic distress experienced by Egyptians contributed to the growing popularity of the Brotherhood and its message. By the time of the Second World War, Brotherhood membership was estimated to be anywhere from hundreds of thousands to greater than one million members. These included government employees, students, policemen, lawyers and soldiers, as well as the urban and rural poor. John Esposito wrote that, 'The Muslim Brotherhood grew at a time when the Egyptian community was in crisis. They blamed European imperialism and Westernized Muslim leadership for many of the problems Egypt faced.'[4] He later continued, 'In the 1930s and 1940s, the Muslim Brotherhood reasserted the relevance of Islam to all areas of life, diagnosed the ills of Muslim society, and offered an Islamic activism aimed at redressing issues of religious identity and social justice.'[5]

The Brotherhood was strongest in the mid to late 1940s, when its influence on lower- and middle-class Egyptians was considerable. The Brotherhood organized numerous demonstrations, marches and protests during this period and acted as a counterweight to the Communists and Wafdists. These organizations were secular and envisioned a more democratic, constitutional and cosmopolitan society. In contrast, the Brotherhood spread a message of Islam as a self-sufficient, all-encompassing way of life, an alternative to Marxism and Western capitalism. John Esposito argued that, 'the message of the Brotherhood... was the conviction that Islam provided a divinely revealed and prescribed third alternative to Western capitalism and Soviet Marxism'.[6] The Brotherhood told people to turn to religion, as opposed to political parties, for answers.

The Brotherhood was frequently accused of sabotaging meetings of the Communists and Wafdists, precipitating clashes in public, damaging property and carrying out political assassinations. According to Botman, 'the Brotherhood advocated a militancy that went far beyond the imaginations of Egypt's established political leaders'.[7]

It is clear that the Brotherhood was hostile to the West. They saw Egypt as dependent on the West, politically ineffectual and socially and culturally weak. They viewed Westernization as threatening not only independence, but the identity and way of life of Muslims. Still, the Brothers made a distinction between Westernization and modernization. Esposito explains, 'They engaged in modern organization and institution building, provided educational and social welfare services, and used modern technology and mass communications to spread their message and mobilize popular support.'[8]

At the same time that the Brotherhood condemned the West, they realized that the predicament that Egypt was in was foremost a Muslim problem, that is, the result of Muslims failing adequately to observe their religion. Indeed, 'Rebuilding the community and redressing the balance of power between Islam and the West must begin with a call or invitation (*dawa*) to all Muslims to return to and appropriate their faith in its fullness— to be born again in the straight path of God.'[9]

After the Second World War, the Brotherhood continued to be active in education and enjoyed enormous popularity on university campuses. The group continued to recruit heavily among students, who joined their ranks in large numbers.

At the same time that students were being recruited, the Brotherhood was also recruiting workers. Al-Banna's interest here was twofold: to save all Muslims and to protect Egyptians from the dangers of having foreigners controlling Egypt's economy. To help carry out its interest in this area, the Brotherhood formed labour unions among workers in many different trades. In its union activities, the Brotherhood spread its fundamentalist ideas among workers. The Brotherhood also hoped that these activities would weaken the force of the Communists and Wafdists in labour affairs and would demonstrate their commitment to the average wage-labourer.

The Brothers also looked beyond Egypt's borders and became deeply concerned with and involved in the struggle in Palestine. The group collected money and arms, trained volunteers and sent troops to Palestine in 1948 to fight alongside the Palestinians and other Arab soldiers. By most accounts, the participation of many Brothers in the effort to liberate Palestine was an event that led to the strengthening of a growing paramilitary wing of the Brotherhood. In this respect, Palestine served as a training ground for Brotherhood militants.

The Palestine conflict made the growing power and popularity of the Brotherhood all too obvious. The Egyptian government began to fear the growing strength of the Brotherhood and recognized the danger the group posed to state security. During the political tension of the Palestine conflict, Egyptian Prime Minister Mahmoud al-Nuqrashi imposed military law and outlawed the Muslim Brotherhood in December 1948. He claimed that the group had plotted revolution against the government and had repeatedly carried out terrorist attacks on individuals.

In retaliation to the government's actions, an angry member of the Brotherhood assassinated al-Nuqrashi. The government did not sit by idly, however. Revenge was sought after: as the 'Supreme Guide' of the Brotherhood, al-Banna was also murdered in 1949, presumably by a member of the government's police forces.

The Brotherhood movement was forced underground as it tried to regroup after the loss of its founder and leader. After the Wafd regained power in 1951, the Brotherhood was temporarily allowed to resume activities. They were restricted, however, to cultural, social and spiritual services. The group soon resumed banned activities, however, and was an active presence in the guerrilla war being fought against British occupation in the Suez Canal area.

Sharing many of the same goals, the Muslim Brotherhood gave their support to the Free Officers' movement in the early 1950s in its attempt to overthrow the government. The Officers succeeded with the Brothers' help and set up a government under the leadership of Gamal Abdul Nasser. In doing so, however, the revolutionaries cut the Brotherhood out of any leadership role. Afaf Lutfi Marsot wrote that,

> They [the Muslim Brothers] had helped the Free Officers come to power and had expected a share in the government of the country. But once in power, the Officers saw no need to associate the Brethren with their government, especially since the Brethren possessed a massive, popular power base, and the officers had no power base yet.[10]

In October 1954, an assassination attempt was carried out against Nasser. Popular thought was that the Brotherhood was responsible. As a result, the Brotherhood was banned by the government, and many of the Brothers were arrested, imprisoned and tortured. The remaining members of the organization were forced underground again.

The late 1950s and the 1960s saw an increased militancy among the Brotherhood as a consequence of the group's hostility toward the Egyptian government. This new trend of radical Islam was led by Muslim Brotherhood member Sayyid Qutb (1906–66). Qutb took the ideological writings and beliefs of al-Banna and built them into a revolutionary call to *jihad*. Esposito attested that, during the 1950s,

> Qutb emerged as a major voice of the Muslim Brotherhood and its most influential ideologue. His commitment, intelligence, militancy, and literary style made him especially effective within the context of the growing confrontation between a repressive regime and the Brotherhood. Government harassment of the Brotherhood and Qutb's imprisonment and torture in 1954 for alleged involvement in an attempt to assassinate Nasser only increased his radicalization and confrontational worldview.[11]

Qutb's major work, *Signposts on the Road,* is said to mark the beginnings of Islamic fundamentalism. Qutb, an Upper Egyptian, wrote about the concept of *jahiliyya.* He wrote that there exist two kinds of societies: Muslim and *jahiliyya.* In Muslim societies, Islam is fully applied across the board. In *jahiliyya* societies, it is not applied. He went on to say that even if its members proclaim themselves as Muslim, they are not if their legislation does not have divine law as a basis. This statement was made in order to point out that the government of Nasser was *jahiliyya.* Qutb then went on to describe how the *jahiliyya* government must be destroyed so that an Islamic state could be established in its place. Qutb called for a revolution under the vanguard of the *umma* (the community of believers). Qutb called for a *jihad* and said that this holy war could not be waged by words alone. Thus, it was under Qutb that the Muslim Brotherhood began to splinter into moderate and radical factions. Both factions retained the same objective (that is, the creation of an Islamic system of government in Egypt) but disagreed on the means of attaining this objective. More moderate and traditional members of the Brotherhood felt that change could be brought about by working within the existing political system. Radical members, however, felt that attempts at change within the system were futile (given the authoritarian nature of the existing government). These Brothers, inspired by the writings and leadership of Qutb, felt that the only option was armed struggle.

The two different paths taken by the moderate and radical factions—evolutionary and revolutionary—are described as thus,

> Qutb's formulation became the starting point for many radical groups. The two options—evolution, a process which emphasizes revolutionary change from below, and revolution, the violent overthrow of established (un-Islamic) systems of government—have remained the twin paths of contemporary Islamic movement.[12]

In 1965, the government clamped down on the Muslim Brotherhood once again. Many Brotherhood leaders, including Qutb, were arrested and executed. Thousands of other Brotherhood members were arrested and tortured. Those who escaped the grasp of the government went underground or left the country. Those who went underground were again faced with the task of rebuilding the organization while consciously avoiding confrontation with the government.

The Brotherhood was seen by many as a broken and harmless organization in the early years of the Sadat presidency. In fact, Sadat released the Brotherhood's Supreme Guide, Omar Tilmassani, from prison and formed a somewhat co-operative relationship with the group. Taking advantage of this relative freedom, the Brotherhood was soon preaching and publishing its message once again, as well as setting up institutions for its social welfare and financial activities.

At the same time, more radical factions had gone underground and were planning violent activities aimed at overthrowing the government. They criticized the Brotherhood as a 'has been' organization that had allowed itself to be co-opted by the Egyptian government. These factions received great inspiration in the 1970s from the Islamic Revolution in Iran. Sociologist Saad Eddin Ibrahim (recently jailed for criticizing the

Egyptian government on human rights practices) interviewed a number of jailed militants during this period. Although they demonstrated a respect for al-Banna and other Brotherhood leaders, they criticized the state of the post-1965 Brothers. He wrote,

> But these militants took some exception to the current practices of surviving members of the Brotherhood. They consider some of the surviving members as weak and 'burned out' or bought off. Some of the early members of the Military Academy group reported having gone to visit older members of the Brotherhood, to seek advice and offer support. They were advised to mind their individual businesses, to stay out of trouble, and to worship God. Quite disillusioned, the youngsters then decided to form their own organization.[13]

Still, the Brotherhood continued to attract members from the lower and middle classes and began to rebuild its power base. They quietly criticized the government but strongly and consistently denounced violence and criticized the armed struggle of the radical Islamic groups.

> It [the Brotherhood] clearly opted for socio-political change through a policy of moderation and gradualism which accepted political pluralism and parliamentary democracy, entering into political alliances with secular political parties and organizations as well as acknowledging the rights of Coptic Christians… Though sympathetic to many of the concerns of extremist groups, it remained steadfast in its rejection of violence and terrorism and stayed scrupulously within the limits of Egyptian law.[14]

Following this trend, the 1980s and 1990s have witnessed the Muslim Brotherhood's return as a major force in Egyptian society and politics, having rebuilt its wealth and power. The group gathered such institutions among its assets as banks, schools, factories and mass communication organizations. In addition, the Brotherhood became a major force in professional organizations. In the 1990s, they gained control of the powerful doctors', lawyers' and engineers' syndicates. They also returned as a force in university politics.

At the national level, although the Brotherhood could not compete in elections as a political party, it joined forces in 1984 with the Wafd party. In 1987, it formed an 'Islamic Alliance' with the Labour Party and won 17 per cent of the general vote, making the coalition the major opposition to President Hosni Mubarak's National Democratic Party.

Since 1993, Mubarak's government has become increasingly aware of the Brotherhood's growing power base and has sought to break its hold over professional syndicates and university politics. Law 100 of 1993 made syndicate elections valid only if winners received greater than a 50 per cent quorum of syndicate member voters, a plateau that is rarely achieved. In the event of receiving less than 50 per cent, the government reserves for itself the right to appoint people to the most powerful

positions in the syndicate's legislative bodies. The government has also undertaken audits of Brotherhood-controlled syndicates, accusing the Brotherhood leadership of financial irregularities. Likewise, in university elections, the names of Islamist candidates have been removed from election lists in an effort to break their hold over student unions.

General elections were held in November 1995. Unlike previous elections, candidates were allowed to run for office as independents. In the months leading up to the election, the Brotherhood announced that it would field some 150 candidates. Many of these candidates and their supporters, however, ended up watching election results from behind bars, as the government once again clamped down on the Brotherhood in three sets of arrests carried out over six weeks in September and October. Seventy-nine members of the Brotherhood were ordered to stand trial in military court for 'increasing their activity in the Muslim Brotherhood organization and provoking citizens against the government, inciting hatred for it and claiming that it strives to strike at the Islamist movement in the country on the advice of foreign powers'.[15] Human rights activist Hesham Kassem denounced the government's actions, saying, 'it is a direct reaction to the declaration by the Muslim Brotherhood to field 150 candidates in the elections'.[16]

Even with many of its leaders and its most efficient organizers in prison, the Brotherhood still succeeded in fielding 150 candidates in the elections, competing in 17 governorates. This marked the first time in the organization's history that they had such a large number of candidates and covered such a large geographical area. Hisham Mubarak, of the Centre for Human Rights Legal Aid, commented on the Brotherhood's presence in the election. He said, 'It proves that it [the Brotherhood] is a big political force, that it can stand the blows from security, and that it has not lost its political viability.'[17]

1996 brought other changes and challenges for the Muslim Brotherhood as well. In January, the group's Supreme Guide, Mohamed Hamed Aboul Nasser, died after a long battle with illness. In a swift transfer of power, Mustafa Mashour was named as Aboul Nasser's successor on the same day of his death. Mashour has effectively exercised leadership of the organization for the previous two years while Aboul Nasser's health was fading. Therefore, radical changes in the organization's leadership and activities did not occur. The new leader reiterated the Brotherhood's commitment to 'moderate, non-violent, non-extremist' activities. He stated in an interview, 'We will not turn to violence and we hope that God will allow an opening between us and the government to put an end to injustice of which we have been victims.'[18]

Another challenge for the Brotherhood came with the announcement that a group of younger Brotherhood members had officially requested to establish a new political party called al-Wasat (Centre Party). The group, which also includes women and Christians on its slate, was led by the deputy secretary-general of the engineers' syndicate, Abul Ella Madi. Although the request received limited attention in the mass media, one journalist claimed that it 'represents the first open move by the young generation of syndicate activists in the Muslim Brotherhood to break with the aging leadership of the organization who have opted to lie low while the state rages against them'.[19]

Islamic Militant Groups in Egypt

As demonstrated above, armed Islamic militant groups in Egypt grew out of the Muslim Brotherhood and were a response to the Brotherhood's increasing moderation in the face of confrontation with the state. Former Egyptian minister of the interior General Hasan al-Alfi (fired after the 1997 massacre in Luxor) has stated that,

> If we go back to the 1940s we realize that the Muslim Brothers are the root group to all these [militant] organizations. If we look at the leaders of the radical terrorists groups—they are all defected Muslim Brotherhood members, there is a link—not a direct one but an indirect one.[20]

Both the Muslim Brotherhood and militant groups share a common vision for Egypt: the establishment of an Islamic state based on the principles of *shari'a*. They disagree, however, on the means of achieving this goal. Still, their common vision and historical ties leave them intricately connected and sympathetic to each other's causes.

The Muslim Brotherhood had an underground paramilitary group as early on as the late 1930s. It was particularly active in the 1940s, carrying out major violent activities aimed at British forces, Jewish businesses and government officials. Amira Howeidy wrote that,

> In just one week in 1946, four attacks, in which guns and explosives were used, were directed at British occupation forces, wounding 128 people. A group of Brotherhood figures were put on trial and found guilty by judge Ahmed El-Khazindar. Eight months later, the judge was assassinated by two Brotherhood members.[21]

The paramilitary group also bombed several Jewish-owned businesses in Cairo in 1947 and 1948.

After the Brotherhood was outlawed in 1948 by Prime Minister Mahmoud El-Naqrashi, the paramilitary wing responded by assassinating the prime minister inside the interior ministry building. At this point, Hassan al-Banna appeared to realize that the paramilitary wing was raging out of control. He denounced the assassination and declared that the members who had carried it out were 'neither Brothers nor Muslims'.[22]

Al-Banna was assassinated in 1949. Without his voice of moderation, militancy increased among the Brotherhood's ranks as it began its split into competing factions. Esposito explained that,

> Though ostensibly one organization, the Muslim Brothers had in fact split into several factors. After al-Banna's death, no single leader enjoyed his authority. While radical rhetoric appealed to a more militant

wing, especially disaffected youth, many other Brothers, including their leader or Supreme Guide, were wary of direct confrontation with the regime. The political strategy of the Brotherhood remained unresolved, with two competing models, evolution and revolution. While some Brothers conspired to overthrow the government, many of the older guard, fully aware of the power of the state, preferred to pursue change through preaching and social activism.[23]

After government crackdowns on the Brotherhood in the 1950s and 1960s, it became evident that the two Brotherhood factions could no longer live together in the same group. Whereas the older and more traditional members continued to moderate their stand, younger members chose a more militant route. Among them were Shukri Mustafa, founder of Takfir wal-Hijra, and Salih Siriya, founder of the Military Academy group. These leaders drew heavily on the ideology of Hassan al-Banna and Sayyid Qutb, taking their call for Islamic revolution and pushing it to its logical conclusion.

When Egyptian sociologist Saad Ibrahim interviewed jailed militants in the late 1970s, he was quick to recognize that the militants were intricately connected with the ideological view of the Brotherhood and that they were building on the foundation that the Brotherhood had established in Egypt. He wrote, 'In terms of religious dimensions of ideology, their reading of history and their overall vision for the future, the militants expressed no differences with the Muslim Brotherhood. In fact, they consider themselves a natural continuation of the Brotherhood.'[24]

Militant Islamic groups have continued to orchestrate campaigns of terror in Egypt in their violent attempt to overthrow the government. At the same time, the Muslim Brotherhood has been consolidating its power base in professional organizations, universities and on the national political scene. They represent two groups that share a common ideological basis, a common history and a common vision for the future. The difference between the two lies in the lengths they feel their religion allows them to go to in order to achieve that vision. El-Sayid Yassan, former director for the al-Ahram Centre for Political and Strategic Studies, argued that these commonalities create an underlying bond between the militant groups and the Brotherhood: 'They both have the same project, the establishment of an Islamic state. It is true that one of them believes in violence while the other denounces it, but the unity of goals definitely creates sympathy.'[25]

There are many well-known northern Islamic militancy groups that have been active in Egypt for years. These include the Islamic Liberation Organization (also known as 'Shabab Mohamed' or Mohamed's youth as well as Salvation from Hell). Most of the recent violence, however, has been carried out by militants from Upper Egypt. Indeed, most of the acts of terrorism that have occurred since 1992 have been attributed to al-Gama'a al-Islamiyya, the main violent anti-status quo group from Egypt's south. In the last decade, al-Gama'a has stepped up its activities and has been blamed for attacks on the Egyptian minister of information, Safwat Sharif, as well as an attack against General Hasan al-Alfi, the former Egyptian minister of the interior. The group has also been blamed for the murder of secular commentator Farag Foda, the 1994 assassination attempt on nobel laureate Naguib Mahfouz, the fatal shooting of 18 Greek tourists in Cairo in 1996, the bombing of the Egyptian Embassy in Islamabad, Pakistan in 1995, the failed attack on the American Embassy in Albania in 1998, as well as numerous other bombings, assassination attempts and attacks on foreign tourists, including the massacre in Luxor in 1997. Since 1992, more than 1,200 people have been killed in violence attributed to Islamic fundamentalists in Egypt. More recently, al-Gama'a appears to have become closely associated with Osama bin Laden's terrorist network. Whereas some of al-Gama'a's leadership formally renounced acts of terrorism, others joined the ranks of al-Qaeda.

Another Egyptian fundamentalist group was the Jamaat al-Muslimin, or Society of Muslims (also known as Takfir wal-Hijra, or Excommunication and Emigration—this was the popular name given to the organization by the Egyptian media). This group was founded by Shukri Mustafa, an Upper Egyptian from Asyut. Shukri's group earned its name because it chose to withdraw (hijra) from the jahiliyya society governing Egypt by hiding in caves in the desert outside of Asyut. In 1977, this group succeeded in kidnapping Muhammad al-Dhahabi, the former Egyptian minister of waqfs (property whose funds are used to support religious foundations). The group killed al-Dhahabi when their demands were not met, causing the government to hunt down the members of the organization, including Shukri Mustafa, imprison and execute them.

Jamaat al-Jihad, another Egyptian militant group, gained notoriety when it orchestrated the assassination of Egyptian President Anwar Sadat in 1981. Al-Jihad was formed by survivors of another group, Muhammad's Youth, which had staged an abortive coup in 1974. The ideology of al-Jihad was put forward in The Neglected Obligation, by Muhammad al-Farag. Building upon al-Banna's writings as well as those of Sayyid Qutb, al-Farag called true believers to rise up and fight a holy war against Egypt's un-Islamic government. Al-Farag saw jihad as the only effective way to fight for the establishment of an Islamic state, because all other means had been tried before and failed. Only through jihad could the glory of Islam be restored. Khalid al-Islambuli was the al-Jihad member who killed President Sadat in 1981. Upon firing the bullets that killed Sadat, he reportedly exclaimed, 'I have killed Pharoah'. Al-Islambuli was incited into action when his brother Mohammad, leader of the al-Gama'a organization at the university in Asyut, was taken out of bed in the middle of the night and arrested by Egyptian police forces during Sadat's crackdown on Islamists. Al-Jihad was led by the infamous Sheikh Omar Abdel Rahman. The group drew further worldwide attention after claiming responsibility for the February 1993 bombing of the World Trade Center in New York (for which Abdel Rahman is serving a life sentence in the United States).

Another prolific militant group that became active in Egypt in the 1990s and a sibling of al-Jihad is Jihad al-Gadid, or New Holy War. This group has been claiming responsibility for acts of violence since 1993. Still, many observers do not feel that this group is new at all. Rather, it is believed that the group is made up of veterans of the Afghanistan war splintered off from al-Gama'a. Indeed, the level of success of its acts of terrorism (27 people were killed in 3 attacks in 1993 and 1994) indicates that the group is familiar with sophisticated weaponry and explosives, most likely a result of training in al-Qaeda camps in Afghanistan.

Militant groups are said to receive support from abroad. This is becoming evident as the United States and its allies try to break the flow of finances to terrorist groups as part of their current campaign. In the past, the Sudan, Iran and Saudi Arabia were often listed as the chief external financiers of the movement in Egypt (as argued by the Egyptian government). Egyptian government officials have also accused Western governments such as Britain of harboring so-called 'terrorists' who influence the activities of militants in Egypt.[26] Today, we know that terrorist cells existed throughout Europe and the United States. In the month following the 11 September attacks, some 225 people in a dozen countries outside of the United States were rounded up after intelligence indicated that they were involved in plotting or assisting terrorism.

The Afghanistan Connection

Al-Gama'a al-Islamiyya has historically been made up of two types of members, one of which has a strong connection to Afghanistan and the al-Qaeda network. The first type consists of Egyptians recruited locally from Upper Egypt, including those who rose and who continue to rise through the ranks of the universities. A second and important type of member includes those Upper Egyptians who fought in the war of independence in Afghanistan and then returned home to their native country. Indeed, as the Islamic Revolution in Iran fuelled Islamic extremism in Egypt in the 1970s, the Soviet withdrawal from Afghanistan in 1989 and the subsequent formation of an Islamic state boosted the fundamentalist movement in Egypt in the 1990s. Alongside the Afghan mujahideen who were fighting against the Soviets were between 5,000 and 10,000 zealous youths from around the Muslim world, including many from Egypt. These youths were trained in military camps set up along the Pakistan–Afghanistan border and sent to the front lines. These camps continued to operate after the rise to power of the Taliban, and continued to be a training ground for youths from around the Muslim world who prescribed to a more militant form of Islam.[27]

After the Soviets withdrew from Afghanistan, these young fighters, fresh from the battle, looked throughout the Muslim world for places where they could try to replicate their victory. Many sided with al-Gama'a al-Islamiyya in its fight against the Egyptian government. The subsequent rise in terrorist attacks in the 1990s in Egypt is largely a result of the return home of fighters from Afghanistan's war of independence. The presence of these members in al-Gama'a has made the continuation of ties with Afghanistan and Osama bin Laden's al-Qaeda organization a natural consequence. Al-Qaeda continued to nurture these ties, recruit from al-Gama'a, and provide training and other support to Egypt's militants. After the mujahideen succeeded in ridding Afghanistan of Soviet occupation, al-Qaeda, originally set up to provide logistical, financial and military support for the fight for independence, decided to stay intact. The group, led by bin Laden, chose to use the skills, resources and experience that it had acquired to fight for Islam on a more global scale. Originally, the targets for this fight were the governments of Egypt and Saudi Arabia. As a result, al-Qaeda provided significant support to al-Gama'a al-Islamiyya. Indeed, al-Gama'a had its foreign headquarters in Peshawar, Pakistan (the origin of many of the faxes that have been sent out by the group), allowing the group to be in close contact and co-ordination with al-Qaeda operatives. During the crackdown of the Egyptian government on fundamentalist groups, some al-Gama'a members fled Egypt and took up posts within al-Qaeda in Afghanistan and Pakistan. As the focus of al-Qaeda began to shift to the United States, al-Gama'a soon began to join al-Qaeda in its attacks on the US and its allies around the world. The connection between Egyptian militants and al-Qaeda has remained strong. Today, bin Laden's lieutenant is Ayman al-Zawahiri, an Egyptian physician who headed the Egyptian group al-Jihad until its effective merger with al-Qaeda in 1998. Al-Qaeda's military commander, Mohamed Atef, is a former Egyptian policeman and member of al-Jihad. He recently married off his daughter to bin Laden's son Mohamed. Suspected bin Laden finance operative, Mustafa Ahmed, has typically worked out of Egypt and the United Arab Emirates.

Why Upper Egypt?

It is clear that the militant activity that grew up in Upper Egypt is rooted in the experience and ideology of the Muslim Brotherhood. Militants in Upper Egypt, however, more than in any other part of the country, have come to view the Muslim Brotherhood and other fundamentalist groups as having failed to address the immediate issues at hand. This sense of failure has caused a new Upper Egyptian militant movement to grow that is very regional in outlook. Whereas the Brotherhood and other groups have tended to look beyond Egypt's borders as international issues, such as the promotion of pan-Arabism and the liberation of Palestine as major priorities, Upper Egyptian Islamists, until their recent union with al-Qaeda, have looked homeward, focusing on the dismal socio-economic conditions in Upper Egypt created by policies of the Sadat and Mubarak regimes. Islam as the solution to poverty and injustice in Egypt, and in particular in Upper Egypt, has been their overriding conviction. As the Muslim Brotherhood grew in force during the distress of the Depression and as a reaction to the influence of Western powers in Egypt, the Upper Egyptian militant movement similarly grew as a result of a regime in power that has been perceived as corrupt, and as a reaction to the implementation of Western policies of economic liberalization.

The Upper Egyptian movement, as an entity separate from other Islamic organizations, originated in the 1970s at Asyut University and its various regional campuses across southern Egypt. The movement's leadership consisted of university students. This was in sharp contrast to the fundamentalist movements in northern Egypt that were made up of doctors, engineers and other

professionals for the bourgeoisie. Unlike their northern brothers, these southern students who sought solace in Islam were mainly from lower middle- and working-class families. Many were the sons and daughters of *fallaheen,* Egypt's peasant farmers, who were able to get an education thanks to the reforms of President Nasser. Even though their education was free, the conditions in which these students had to study were often destitute, especially in Asyut. Gilles Kepel described the scene,

> In Asyut in particular there has grown up around the university what can only be called a 'belt', al-Hamra. An entire universe of poverty-stricken students is packed into it, cut off from their family milieu and highly receptive to any voices that manage to make themselves heard and promise an improvement in their conditions.[28]

The students were united in the southern universities, as the education code in Egypt prevents a student from studying outside of the region from which they originate, unless the subject that they wish to study is not offered in the given region. The fact that the students were all from the south helped to solidify the growing Islamist movement's southern focus.

The difference in the backgrounds of the southern and northern Islamists contributed to them having significantly different agendas. Whereas both groups agreed that Islam is the solution, they differed in answering the question: *a solution to what?* Upper Egyptians agree with northern Islamic revolutionaries that the system must be changed and that it cannot be changed from within the current legal system. The Upper Egyptian militants, however, have a much more regional focus given their particular situation. This became starkly clear when President Sadat began to roll back many of Nasser's reforms. Nasser's form of socialism had attempted to be an equalizer among Egyptians. His many programmes included providing free university education, giving government jobs to graduates and instituting a program of land reform. Whereas many of Nasser's programmes can be seen as having failed, they were a source of hope and promise for Egypt's poor. Through his de-Nasserization program, Sadat was destroying the hopes of millions of Egypt's less fortunate and restoring the bond between the government and Egypt's wealthy, land-owning elite. The Muslim Brotherhood and its Islamist colleagues in the north (largely from the bourgeoisie) supported the de-Nasserization programme. The southern Islamist movement, formed by university students—the sons and daughters of peasant farmers who had been given hope and opportunity by the very programmes that Sadat sought to recall—stood firmly against the de-Nasserization programme; a programme that they viewed as an attack against the lower classes. They began to view the northern government as greedy, corrupt and un-Islamic.

On 6 October 1981, President Anwar Sadat was shot and killed by Lieutenant Khalid al-Islambuli, an Upper Egyptian from the town of Minia. Out of the 280 people implicated in the conspiracy surrounding the death of President Sadat, 183 were Upper Egyptians. Another 73 were from neighbourhoods in Cairo where a significant portion of the population consists of rural-to-urban migrants from Upper Egypt.[29] Hence, the Upper Egyptian Islamic militant movement had risen from secluded university classrooms in Asyut and Minia to having forced a major change in Egyptian politics, shocking all of Egypt and the world in the process.

The assassination of Sadat was followed by massive sweeps and arrests of suspected Islamists. Those who were not taken into custody were forced underground. President Hosni Mubarak, Sadat's successor, has largely continued the political and economic policies that Sadat had set in motion. Given the crackdown, the Islamists' resources and strength were largely depleted. Still, their grievances against a government that they continued to see as un-Islamic and as oppressive to Upper Egypt's disenfranchised remained. Given time to rebuild and regroup, the southern Islamists would begin a new attack aimed at destabilizing Egypt's government in the 1990s, as Egypt's accelerated programme of structural adjustment, as recommended by Western institutions such as the International Monetary Fund (IMF) and the World Bank, began to squeeze the majority of poor Egyptians, in particular Upper Egyptians, who felt even further ostracized from Egypt's developmental goals. This attack against the Government of Egypt culminated in the massacre in Luxor in November 1997.[30]

As stated earlier, it is very easy to look at the conflict between Upper Egyptian Islamic fundamentalists and the Egyptian government and security forces as a confrontation based simply in religion. It has been demonstrated, however, that the roots of the conflict in Upper Egypt lie much deeper, and the Upper Egyptian movement, although it has a basis in the ideological thought of the Muslim Brotherhood, stands in stark contrast to northern Islamist movements. This unique movement has grown out of the experience of poverty, discrimination and a history of neglect that the majority of Upper Egyptians have felt throughout Egypt's modern period. This argument was put forward by political scientist Mamoun Fandy. Mamoun stated that the targets of these militants offer proof that this co-called holy war is not merely based in religion. If this were true, he argued, the militants would be targeting Sufi mystics and Muslims who combine pagan and Christian rituals into their religion. For instance, many Muslim Upper Egyptian peasants still practice annual celebrations that date to pharaonic times and have strong pagan characteristics. However, Fandy wrote,

there is no single report of the Islamists objecting to these 'un-Islamic' practices of the common folk. The difference is that these are the indigenous customs of the poor and powerless, whereas the practices of the government are part of the corrupt, pseudo-Westernized upper classes' monopoly of political and economic power.[31]

Upper Egypt has been left behind in many aspects of Egypt's development so that today, not only does it have the worst socio-economic indicators of any area in Egypt, its inhabitants also have a culture and a legal system that sets itself apart from the rest of the country.

In Egypt, the Arabic word used for Cairo is *Misr*—the same name in Arabic for Egypt. In many ways, Cairo is Egypt, that is, Cairo is where the government is centred and where the government spends the vast majority of its resources. Cairo is the unchallenged economic, political and cultural centre of Egypt and dominates all other areas of the country, the south in particular. The south does not even have its own media. Dr Abdel-Mo'ati Shaarawi, a professor of sociology at Cairo University, summed up the feelings of Upper Egyptians:

They do not feel they belong to the country because in the south, justice is denied, poverty is enforced, ignorance prevails, and people feel that society is conspiring to oppress, rob, and degrade them, so neither person nor property will be safe.[32]

Upper Egypt has historically been isolated geographically, politically and economically from the rest of the country. Up until the last two decades, travel between Middle and Upper Egypt was difficult. Even the British never truly colonized Upper Egypt, failing to maintain an outpost there. In the post-revolutionary period, Egypt's central government has also left Upper Egypt largely to itself, relying on local notables to enforce order. These notables have allowed the traditional customs and traditional structure of society to govern, and Upper Egypt has largely remained divided along tribal lines. Egyptian civil law has been widely ignored in Upper Egypt. Political thought and economic growth has been concentrated in the north. Until recently, there was little effort at development in Upper Egypt, with the notable exception of the Aswan Dam and a few other agricultural and manufacturing projects. Still, these projects were controlled by the north and the north has reaped their benefits. The donor community in Egypt, including the United States Agency for International Development (USAID), was also late in realizing the great developmental needs of Upper Egypt and how this area was falling behind the rest of the country. Therefore, traveling between the north and south of Egypt often seems like travelling between two different worlds: one desperately trying to modernize and the other left far behind and losing ground.

Upper Egyptians are typically classified as three different groups of people. These groupings have structured the hierarchy of Upper Egyptian society in the following way: the *ashraf* claim descent from the Prophet Muhammed and see themselves as superior to all other Upper Egyptians. The Arabs claim lineage from central Arabia. They are inferior to the *ashraf* but superior to the majority of Upper Egyptians who are the *falaheen,* or the non-Arab Egyptians. The *falaheen* consider themselves the direct descendants of the pharaohs. But the *ashraf* and the Arabs see the *falaheen* as those who converted to Islam under threat of the sword and therefore as inferior. The *ashraf* and the Arabs have typically filled any positions of power and influence and tend to own land, be wealthier, and to have better access to social services such as health care and education than the *falaheen,* who are typically peasant farmers.

The above structure dates back to the Arab conquest of Egypt (AD 622) and has remained the norm throughout Upper Egypt's modern history as well. The *ashraf* and the Arabs have typically used interpretations of Islam that appear to accept inequality in society to solidify their hold on society and their dominance over the *falaheen.*

The post-revolutionary reforms of President Nasser posed the first serious challenge to the social structure of Upper Egypt. Under Nasser, for the first time ever, there was talk of equality among Egyptians, and the sons and daughters of *falaheen* were allowed to receive a free government education and to qualify for government jobs. Educated, many of these children of farmers began to challenge the local hierarchy and to prescribe to other interpretations of the Qur'an that preached that there is no difference between the Arab and non-Arab Muslims. Still, very little else changed. The economic situation for the majority of the *falaheen* remained dismal and the status of the *falaheen* as third-class citizens was upheld by the *ashraf* and Arabs, who continued to be favoured by Cairo. In addition, the local administrators were largely able to avoid Nasser's attempts at land reform as well.

President Sadat offered hope for the *falaheen* at the start of his presidency through his use of Islamic rhetoric. His de-Nasserization programme, however, left these poor Upper Egyptians disillusioned, as they became afraid of losing even the small gains that they had received during Nasser's legacy. Sadat's economic programme clearly favoured the southern families that had historically held wealth and power. The *falaheen* began to feel that Egypt was going back in time, given that some of the few plots of land that had been redistributed under Nasser were even taken back by the government. This was a source of enormous frustration for the *falaheen.* As stated earlier, it is from the ranks of these newly educated sons and daughters of the *falaheen* that Upper Egypt's unique Islamic movement rose. Mamoun Fandy noted, 'the *falaheen* took refuge in Islam and Sai'di [Upper Egyptian] regionalism… The Islamists' reform and revolt in the south is informed by the *falaheen's* desire to rearrange the rules of southern social structure and centre-periphery relations'.[33]

As Fandy also noted, another major force in the growth of the Islamist movement in Upper Egypt was the influx of oil money from the Gulf Arab states. At the same time that Sadat was introducing his economic liberalization programme, the Gulf states were experiencing an oil boom and needed migrant workers from surrounding poorer countries. Many of the sons of Upper Egyptian *falaheen,* eager to do hard labour for cash, travelled to the Gulf. Many later returned with significant savings that were used to buy land and start businesses. Many of these returning migrant labourers also used their newly found wealth to influence society and challenge the traditional hierarchy by building mosques and setting up social services for poor Upper Egyptian communities. These mosques preached a message that was non-traditional to Upper Egypt: that all Muslims, Arab and non-Arab, are equal. Differences should be recognized in terms of one's piety, not one's ancestral background. As the number of mosques grew, this message was spread across Upper Egypt and the new Islamist force grew.[34] Fandy claimed that, 'The power of the Islamic network in Upper Egypt rivals that of the government and other social organizations and has emerged as

an alternative to the old *'umdas* [governors] in mediating local disputes.'

Dr Mohamed Abul-Issad, a Professor of History at Minia University in Upper Egypt, once stated that,

> The deadliest disease is despair. Poverty is only a symptom. The lack of any governmental attention to development has created a vast underclass which has no stake in the society or government.

Development Indicators in Upper Egypt

A visitor to rural areas in Upper Egypt quickly becomes aware of the desperate situation that many of the Upper Egyptian *falaheen* live in on a daily basis. According to World Bank senior economist Marcelo Giugale, Upper Egypt has the highest percentage of Egypt's so-called 'ultra poor', those surviving on a day-to-day basis.[35] With an annual per capita income of just over $300, and soaring rates of unemployment, illiteracy, malnutrition, morbidity and mortality, Upper Egypt ranks at the bottom of virtually every social and economic indicator for Egypt. In 1995, during the height of Islamist activity, the Institute of National Planning published a human development report that looked at various social and economic indicators in the numerous governorates of Egypt. Each governorate was then ranked as low, medium or high in terms of human development. Only Giza and Aswan in Upper Egypt achieved the rank of medium. The remaining six governorates were all ranked at the bottom of the human development survey.[36] A project paper by USAID's Cairo Mission, completed during the same period, reiterated these facts by stating that, 'according to every indicator, [developmental] progress has been slowest in Upper Egypt, especially rural Upper Egypt'.[37] Given that the 1999 United Nations development index ranked Egypt as a whole as 105th out of 162 countries, Upper Egyptians face conditions of dire poverty.

A look at a few of the key development indicators paints a very bleak picture:

a. *Health.* Upper Egypt suffers from important health problems and lags behind the progress made in other parts of the country. There is a general lack of health facilities. Clinics are rare, and physicians can often not be found for miles. This is a considerable journey when your only means of transportation may be on the back of a donkey. Even if healthcare is available, it is mostly unaffordable for rural Upper Egyptians, who will attempt to cure illnesses with traditional homemade remedies in order to avoid doctors' fees. Most babies are born in the home without the assistance of a medical professional. Almost every mother has a story of a stillborn birth or a child who died before the age of five. Many of these deaths were from diarrhoea or respiratory infections that could have been cured given the proper care. The rate of immunization coverage is much lower in Upper Egypt than in other parts of the country, and many *fallaheen* have never heard of vaccinations that are standard practice in other parts of the country. Knowledge of proper hygiene practices is also minimal in many areas. It is important to point out that not only does Upper Egypt lag far behind Cairo and other urban areas in Egypt, but it lags far behind Lower Egypt as well. A USAID Cairo report pointed out that, 'The gaping discrepancies between Lower and Upper Egypt and between rural and urban areas according to all human development indicators cannot be ignored.'[38]

b. *Population.* In the area of population, Upper Egyptians are less educated in family planning methods and less likely to use family planning. As a result, families in Upper Egypt tend to be much larger than in Egypt's urban governorates and in Lower Egypt. Women in Upper Egypt get married at the average age of 17.2 years. The median age for the first time to give birth is 19.3 years and the average number of births is six. This figure is some 2 births higher than in rural Lower Egypt. This is due in part to the fact that the rate of usage of modern family planning methods in Lower Egypt is some 20 per center higher than in Upper Egypt, where 19 per cent of households expressed disapproval of family planning and 24 per cent claimed that it is against their religious practices.[39]

c. *Education.* As noted earlier, Nasser's education reforms gave many of the sons and daughters of Upper Egyptian peasants the opportunity to receive an education. Still, Upper Egypt trails the rest of the country in terms of educational facilities and educational attainment. Many villages have no educational facilities at all. As a result, children have to walk for miles to get to the nearest school. Many of the educational facilities that do exist are overcrowded and poor. After a few years of schooling, a child may know little more than how to write his or her name. Given this, parents often feel that it is more practical for a child to be assisting in harvesting or other household and manual tasks. In addition, there still exists a strong unwillingness among a large part of the rural Upper Egyptian population to educate girls. For Upper Egyptian males, the average number of years spent in school is 4.2. Approximately 44 per cent of men have no education at all. Only 30 per cent of women have had any formal schooling. The adult literacy rate in Upper Egypt is 46.7 per cent.

d. *Infrastructure.* Many of the villages of Upper Egypt have no electricity or piped-in water. Few have sanitation facilities beyond primitive drainage tanks attached to a homemade latrine. Access to villages is oftentimes difficult. Some villages can only be accessed by boat or on foot. Homes are typically simple mud huts with dirt floors that are poorly constructed. Huts that collapse during rainstorms or for various other reasons are commonplace. Villages are often centred along a canal from the Nile, with stagnant and unclean water that is used to launder clothes, wash dishes, as well as for bathing and drinking. Water buffalo, donkeys, geese, ducks and other creatures are scattered about making use of the same water source. Only around 38 per cent of households in Upper Egypt have piped-in water. Around 32 per cent of households do not have any toilet facilities. Nearly three-quarters of households in Upper Egypt have sand or dirt floors and the number of people sleeping per room averages 3.6.

The above statistics and description of life demonstrate that rural Upper Egyptians are more likely than their fellow countrymen to live in ill-constructed dwellings that are overcrowded and that lack clean, piped-in water, sanitation facilities, electricity and durable goods. In addition, their access to health care and education is limited and, due to a lack of knowledge about family planning as well as a lack of modern family planning products, large families are the norm in Upper Egypt.

The militant groups that have formed in Upper Egypt, with their unique characteristics that have set them apart from other Egyptian Islamist groups, have risen from the experience described above; an experience that is seen as being perpetuated by the current regime in power and by the spread of globalization. In this sense, it becomes clearer that the rise of militant activity in Upper Egypt is not only a call for a more Islamic government, but a call for a more just government as well as a protest against the dismal status quo. The Islamists view the government as a puppet of the West that has bought into a globalization and an Americanization that is leaving most of Egypt's people behind and given them little voice in the future. Desperate for change, they have resorted to acts of violence to bring attention to the plight of Upper Egyptians and to the disparity that exists in the country.

Responses to the Development Challenge and Terrorism

As stated earlier, the Egyptian government has responded to the militant's threats and activities in Upper Egypt with force. Police and security battles with militants have been frequent. The government has used massive sweeps through the countryside to gather up suspected militants, who may be detained without trial, tortured into confessing crimes that they may or may not have committed, and tried at a military court. They have also offered incentives for people who have information on suspected militants or militant activities and have burned thousands of square kilometers of sugarcane fields—traditional hideouts for the militants.

After the violence in Luxor in November 1997, President Mubarak fired many of the security personnel in that district and forced the resignation of General Hassan al-Alfi, the then minister of the interior. These moves, however, were largely symbolic gestures meant to assure the international community that he was acting to improve security.

The government's anti-terrorism policies have been met with mixed reactions. Cairenes and other northerners have generally supported the government's heavy-handed actions and have seen them as justified to stop the growing militancy movement. Still, there is evidence of much support for the militants in Upper Egypt. In addition, there are countless others who, although they may not support the militants' activities, are sympathetic to the militants' cause. Many Upper Egyptians who claimed not to be supporters of the militancy movement declared that, nonetheless, they fear and do not trust the police and the security forces as much as they fear and do not trust the militants. One Western diplomat living in Cairo in the mid-1990s commented that, 'The populace [of Upper Egypt], for the most part, stands aside or sympathizes with the militants. The Government is losing the war down there.'[40]

Egypt's central government has also acknowledged that the development of Upper Egypt will play a role in the fight to cease the violence of the region's Islamic militants (although it has not been widely publicized). In 1996, the government announced the formulation of an Upper Egyptian development campaign. The campaign, to be financed 25 per cent by the Egyptian government and 75 per cent from private sources, aims at establishing sustainable development programmes in the region over 22 years. Still, the government appears to have realized the fact that development is a major component needed in the fight against militants only years after the violence actually began.

The government's plan for Upper Egypt is to be undertaken in four stages and will cost between $60bn and $100bn. The plan is expected to produce some 2.8 million new jobs in the agricultural and industrial sectors. Still, this plan is seen by many as constituting too little too late. In autumn 1996, after the plan was announced, journalist Ahmed Ragab wrote,

> We have to stretch our hands, like good neighbours do, to the state of Upper Egypt which is south of Cairo and belongs to the Fourth World. We have to change the concept that Upper Egypt is the exile of bad employees. If the government is taking care of the slums in the city, why doesn't it take care of the slum south of Cairo which suffers from poverty, unemployment and terrorism.[41]

The rise of terrorism in Egypt did not occur in a vacuum and is not a problem specific to Egypt. Rather, the story of Upper Egypt and the rise of militant factions has been duplicated in other countries around the world as the people react to the adverse socio-economic conditions and neglect that they face in their everyday lives, with little hope for the future. For some, religious extremism and desperate militant acts become a favourable alternative.

Osama bin Laden has succeeded in creating a worldwide network among various loosely knit terrorist cells and organizations, including some of Egypt's militant groups, around the world. Most likely, there is no single master plan that exists that dictates the actions of terrorists worldwide. Rather, terrorist organizations are united in their vision as well as their admiration for bin Laden and his cause. They have received necessary training, financial and logistical support from bin Laden and al-Qaeda. It is largely believed that within al-Qaeda exists a *shura* council that acts as a board of directors and includes representatives from various terrorist groups and cells from across the globe. This group meets in Afghanistan and reviews and approves terrorist operations proposed by members of the network. As a result of this networking and of his efforts to build an umbrella structure that unites so many groups, bin Laden has succeeded in streamlining the activities of these groups into actions that serve the purpose of a single, larger Islamic crusade

against the West and those governments viewed as puppets of the West. At their heart, however, these individual militant/terrorist movements have homegrown objectives that have arisen out of their individual experiences—experiences often rooted in poverty, lack of opportunity, neglect and discrimination. Osama bin Laden has succeeded in moving these groups beyond their regional causes and in convincing them that American-driven globalization is the larger force that keeps the governments that they are fighting against in power and that perpetuates the dismal living conditions of the people they claim to represent. Indeed, bin Laden has been very good at calling on sympathizers of causes such as the Palestinian and Iraqi causes, as well as militants from Algeria, Egypt and numerous other nations, and focusing their energies and directing their anger towards the United States and its allies. For the network that he has created, globalization is a continuation of the imperialism, colonialism and neo-colonialism that has kept the Muslim world from advancing since the seventeenth century.

Today, the world is in a battle against the forces of terror. In this fight, President Bush has stated that the nation states of the world are either against the US or with it. It is countries such as Egypt, however, for which this choice is very difficult to make. Certainly, the Egyptian government would like to pledge their fully-fledged support to the US-led war. At the same time, this could provoke another rise of militant activity in the country as a significant portion of the population sympathizes with the fundamentalist cause. Whereas many may not support the specific actions that took place on 11 September, they feel that the United States is guilty of worsening and perpetuating a situation of social and economic injustice around the world, particularly against Muslims.

What Can the United States and the Coalition Learn from the Egyptian Experience?

The Egyptian experience demonstrates that the argument that religious fundamentalism cannot be dealt with logically and cannot be negotiated with is largely untrue. Many of these groups have been able to rise in force and in numbers because they offer an 'Islamic' alternative to governments that are seen as corrupt and not representing the common person. They represent hope to people living in dire socio-economic conditions with no political voice. In countries such as Egypt, there is a large, dissatisfied, underemployed or unemployed segment of the population that is easily susceptible to ideas put forth by Islamic fundamentalist groups. These groups, in addition to establishing charities, businesses, schools and hospitals for those people whom the official governments have ignored, have conducted acts of terror in an attempt to make their cause known and to destabilize the governments that they are fighting against. Osama bin Laden was able to take some of these groups 'global' by convincing them that the system that has created and perpetuated the conditions that they are fighting to escape is driven by American-led globalization. The ties that have brought these groups together were forged in the military training camps in Afghanistan. As a result of these alliances, terrorist attacks have escalated beyond the countries that gave birth to these groups and to a global level that culminated in the 11 September attacks. Today, it is believed that bin Laden's group controls 3–5,000 terrorists worldwide in a loose organization.

In the war against terrorism, the United States and its allies cannot just focus on the fight at the global level to which Osama bin Laden and his al-Qaeda organization has elevated terrorism. Certainly, the military strikes in Afghanistan aimed at wiping out al-Qaeda's base may succeed in destroying the network of communication, logistical and financial support among terrorist organizations that bin Laden has achieved. As demonstrated by the Egyptian experience, however, this is a short-term solution to a much larger and widespread problem. Indeed, Egyptian authorities may have been overly successful in their violent crackdown on terrorists. As a result of the crackdown, many of Egypt's militants fled the country only to set up terrorist cells elsewhere, including the United States. If al-Qaeda is destroyed, individual terrorist and militant organizations will continue to exist. If governments are able to use this environment to crack down on these groups, others will surely rise in their place. This will continue to happen until the root causes of their existence— so often the adverse socio-economic and political conditions existing in the loci of their countries—are cured. Egyptian sheikh Yusef al-Qaradawi has stated on Egyptian television that fighting terrorism by merely waging a huge war would be using the same logic as the terrorists. He argued instead that true Muslims need to advocate for the middle path of Islam, and that the United States and its allies need to make efforts to understand the psychology of the terrorists.[42] Similarly, Algerian President Abdelaziz Bouteflika recently stated that the international coalition against terrorism would gain more support if it included efforts to 'settle problems and injustices which fanaticism exploits to feed despair that nurtures terrorism'. He continued, 'We should all work together to correct the flagrant injustices of the world today, which globalization only exacerbates.'[43] The Egyptian government realized this quite late in the game in its fight against terrorism. It is hoped that the coalition that the United States has built will not. Secretary of State Colin L. Powell recently stated that international development programmes are 'at the core of our engagement with the world… over the long-term, our foreign assistance programs are among the most powerful national security tools'.[44] Military and police measures alone will not eradicate the forces of terrorism. Americans must learn that globalization does not just facilitate the movement of products or capital around the world, it also brings with it the risk of facilitating the movement of terrorism grown in another country into its own backyard. A long-term battle aimed at ridding the world of large-scale terrorism must be comprehensive in scope. The battle must include an intensified fight against the poverty existing in the world that drives individuals with no hope to such extreme acts of violence and terrorism as well as facilitating greater political participation for those people who are under represented. Such an approach will also benefit non-Islamic countries, such as Mexico, that have witnessed the rise of militant anti-status quo groups. If the military campaign does not go hand-in-hand with a campaign for international development and social justice, the United States

and its allies risk creating more enemies than the ones that they will eliminate. Only by working to create a world where social justice is distributed more equitably can the ideological roots of terrorism, as demonstrated in the rise of the Muslim Brotherhood and subsequent militant organizations in Egypt, be eradicated.

The views expressed in this article are those of the author and not necessarily those of USAID or the US Government.

NOTES

1. This concept originated with Dr Dan Tschirgi of the Political Science Department of the American University in Cairo.
2. See Selma Botman, *Egypt from Independence to Revolution* (Syracuse: Syracuse University Press 1991) p. 120.
3. Ibid. p. 94.
4. John Esposito, *Islam: The Straight Path* (Oxford: Oxford University Press 1998) p. 120.
5. Ibid.
6. John Esposito, *The Islamic Threat* (Oxford: Oxford University Press 1992) p. 123.
7. Botman (note 2) p. 122.
8. Esposito (note 6) p. 122.
9. Ibid. p. 124.
10. Afaf Lutfi al-Sayyid Marsot, *A Short History of Modern Egypt* (Cambridge: Cambridge University Press 1992) p. 109.
11. Esposito (note 6) p. 128.
12. Ibid. p. 129.
13. Saad Eddin Ibrahim, 'Egypt's Islamic Militants', in Nicholas Hopkins and Saad Eddin Ibrahim (ed.), *Arab Society* (Cairo: American University in Cairo Press 1998) p. 501.
14. Esposito (note 6) p. 132.
15. See Andrew Hammond, 'State Defies Support for Brothers', *Middle East Times,* 22–28 Oct. 1995, p. 1.
16. Ibid. p. 20.
17. See Fatemeh Farag and Steve Negus, 'Brothers Form Electoral Pact with Liberals and Labour', *Middle East Times,* 15–21 Oct. 1995, p. 1.
18. See Fatemeh Farag, 'New Guide for the Brotherhood', *Middle East Times,* 21 Jan–3 Feb. 1996, p. 1.
19. See Andrew Hammond, 'New Centre Party Takes State by Surprise', *Middle East Times,* 21–27 Jan. 1996, p. 1.
20. See Miriam Shahin, 'Egypt Cracks Down on Terrorism', *Middle East,* May 1996, p. 15.
21. Amira Howeidy, 'Politics in God's Name', *al-Ahram Weekly,* 16–22 Nov. 1995, p. 3.
22. Ibid. p. 3.
23. Esposito (note 6) p. 130.
24. Ibrahim (note 13) p. 500.
25. Amira Howeidy, 'Debating Democratic Credentials', *al-Ahram Weekly,* 2–8 Feb. 1995, p. 2.
26. For example, London is home to Yasir al-Siri, who has claimed asylum in Britain from Egypt, where he was sentenced to death for the attempted murder of the prime minister in 1993.

27. Note that, in 1992, the Egyptian government passed a law stating that anyone having received military training in a foreign country could face the death penalty. This law was aimed at Egyptians who had received training in camps in Afghanistan, Pakistan and the Sudan.

28. Gilles Kepel, *Muslim Extremism in Egypt* (Berkeley, CA: University of California Press 1993) p. 137.

29. See Mamoun Fandy, 'Egypt's Islamic Group: Regional Revenge', *Middle East Journal* 48/4 (Autumn 1994) p. 607.

30. Note that only one of the six attackers in the Luxor incident was identified. The identified attacker, Medhat Abdel Rahman, had been trained in military camps in Afghanistan.

31. See Mamoun Fandy, 'The Tensions Behind the Violence in Egypt', *Middle East Policy* 2/1 (1993) pp. 25–34.

32. These comments were made in an interview with Omayma Abdel-Latif, *al-Ahram Weekly,* 29 Aug.–4 Sept. 1996, p. 15.

33. See Fandy (note 29) p. 614.

34. In 1992, the Egyptian government passed a law stating that all mosques, including those that were built privately, would come under the control of the government. As a result, all sermons being delivered at mosques had to be approved by government officials.

35. See Omayma Abdel-Latif, 'Making the Future into a Site of Hope', *al-Ahram Weekly,* 29 Aug.–4 Sept. 1996, p. 14.

36. See Egypt Human Development Survey, the Institute of National Planning, Nasr City, Cairo, Egypt, 1995.

37. See USAID/Cairo, 'Healthy Mother/Healthy Child', project paper, 8 June 1995, p. 1.

38. Ibid.

39. The statistics are taken from the Egypt Demographic and Health Survey, The Population Council, Cairo 1993.

40. See Chris Hedges, 'Egypt Loses Ground, to Muslim Militants and Fear', *New York Times,* 5 Feb. 1994.

41. Quoted in Abdel-Latif (note 35) p. 14.

42. Al-Qaradawi's comments were cited in the special report on fighting terrorism, *Economist,* 20 Oct. 2001.

43. Comments reported in 'Algeria says U.S. Should Address Arab Discontent', CNN.com, 5 Nov. 2001.

44. Secretary of State Colin Powell, speech given at USAID's 40th anniversary celebration.

Colombia and the United States: From Counternarcotics to Counterterrorism

"The worldview that has molded Washington's twin wars on drugs and terrorism constitutes an extremely narrow framework through which to address the complex problems Colombia faces. National security, defined exclusively in military terms, has taken precedence over equally significant political, economic, and social considerations."

ARLENE B. TICKNER

During the past several years, United States foreign policy toward Colombia has undergone significant transformations. Long considered a faithful ally in the fight against drugs, as well as showcasing Washington's achievements in this camp, Colombia became widely identified as an international pariah in the mid-1990s during the administration of Ernesto Samper because of the scandal surrounding the president's electoral campaign, which was said to have been funded by drug money. Although the inauguration in 1998 of President Andrés Pastrana—a man untainted by drugs—marked the official return to friendly relations with the United States, Colombia came to be viewed as a problem nation in which the spillover effects of the country's guerrilla war threatened regional stability. The events of September 11, combined with the definitive rupture of the Colombian government's peace process with the rebels in February 2002, have converted this country into the primary theater of United States counterterrorist operations in the Western Hemisphere today.

THE PERVERSE EFFECTS OF THE "WAR ON DRUGS"

Any discussion of United States policy in Colombia must begin with drugs. Since the mid-1980s, when illicit narcotics were declared a lethal threat to America's national security, the drug issue has been central to relations with Colombia. Washington's counternarcotics policies have been based on repressive, prohibitionist, and hardline language and on strategies that have changed little in the last few decades. The manner in which Colombia itself has addressed the drug problem derives substantially from the United States approach, with most of Bogotá's measures to fight drug trade the result of bilateral agreements or the unilateral imposition of specific strategies designed in Washington.[1] These American-guided efforts to combat illegal drugs "at the source" have produced countless negative consequences for Colombia, aggravating the armed conflict that continues to consume the country and forcing urgent national problems such as the strengthening of democracy, the defense of human rights, the reduction of poverty, and the preservation of the environment to become secondary to countering the drug trade.

Perhaps the most perverse result of the United States–led "war on drugs" is that it has failed to reduce the production, trafficking, and consumption of illicit substances. Between 1996 and 2001, United States military aid to Colombia increased fifteenfold, from $67 million to $1 billion.[2] During this same period, data from the United States State Department's annual *International Narcotics*

THE "REALIST" APPROACH TO DRUGS AND TERRORISM

WITH THE END of the cold war the United States lost its most significant "other," the Soviet Union; it also lost a clear sense of the national security interests of the United States. Drugs, long considered a threat to United States values and society, became an obvious target. Viewed in this light, the "threat" represented by illegal drugs in the United States is not an objective condition; rather, narcotics constitute one of the "cognitive enemies" against which United States national identity attempted to rebuild, albeit only partially, until September 11. In this sense, drugs are seen as "endangering" the American way of life and social fabric, much like the challenge posed by the communist threat to America's values during the bipolar conflict.

Given the sense of moral superiority that has traditionally characterized United States relations with the rest of the world, drug consumption is understood as being prompted by the availability of illegal drugs, which are concentrated, unsurprisingly, in the countries of the periphery; it is not seen as a problem originating in the demand for drugs in the United States or in the prohibitionist strategies that have traditionally characterized America's handling of this issue. While this rationale clearly runs contrary to commonsense economic rules of supply and demand, it tends to reinforce the underlying assumption of moral purity on which America's sense of self is partly based.

The terrorist attacks of September 11, 2001 and the United States–led retaliation mirror this perspective on drugs. Just as the drug issue fails to conform to typical notions of security and threat from a realist perspective, so September 11 challenges traditional views of international relations. The attacks came from within America's borders, not without, and were perpetrated by nonstate actors with little or no military power. But terrorism, rather than being seen as a diffuse, nonterritorial problem, has been associated by the Bush administration with state-based territories—Afghanistan and the entire "axis of evil"—and personified in figures such as Osama bin Laden and Saddam Hussein. The exercise of military power in countries threatening "freedom" and "justice" in the world constitutes the cornerstone of the United States strategy. And the zealous language accompanying the fight against terrorism—"those who are not with us are against us"—eerily recalls the cold war period.

The similarities between the wars on drugs and terrorism and the war on communism notwithstanding, a crucial difference exists: the enemies of these new wars are not readily identifiable, making victory nearly impossible. Hence, any explanation of the role of drugs and terrorism in United States domestic and international politics must necessarily return to the concepts of danger and threat. Although the policies implemented by the United States have failed in reducing the availability of illegal substances—and will most likely be unsuccessful in erasing terrorism from the globe—drugs and, more important, terrorism occupy a crucial discursive function in support of American identities and values. Both are considered lethal threats to United States security—and the political costs associated with directly challenging existing policies in Washington are extremely high. At the same time, the need to persevere in the war on drugs has received an additional push from the war on terrorism; the financing of terrorist activities with drug money has received much greater attention in United States policymaking circles in the aftermath of September 11.

A.B.T.

Drug Control Strategy report show that coca cultivations in Colombia grew 150 percent, from 67,200 to 169,800 hectares (1 hectare = 2.471 acres). Clearly, the high levels of military assistance received by Colombia have had little effect on illicit crop cultivation in the country.

Efforts to eradicate coca cultivation, primarily through aerial spraying, have also increased progressively in Colombia. In 1998, for example, 50 percent more hectares were fumigated than in 1997; in 2001 the Colombian National Police fumigated nearly two times more coca than in 2000. In both instances, fumigation had no effect or even an inverse effect on the total number of hectares cultivated.

Intensive aerial fumigation—particularly in southern Colombia, where Plan Colombia efforts are concentrated—has created public health problems and led to the destruction of licit crops. According to exhaustive studies conducted by Colombia's national human rights ombudsman in 2001 and 2002, aerial spraying with glyphosate has not only killed the legal crops of many communities in southern Colombia but has also caused health problems associated with the inhalation of the pesticide and contact with human skin.[3] On two separate occasions, the ombudsman called for a halt to aerial fumigation until its harmful effects could be mitigated. Echoing similar concerns, in late 2001 the United States Congress, as a precondition for disbursing the aerial-fumigation portion of the 2002 aid bill to the Andean region, requested the State Department to certify that drug-eradication strategies currently employed in Colombia do not pose significant public health risks. On September 4, 2002 the State Department issued its report, arguing that no adverse effects had been found. Members of the scientific community and environmental nongovernmental organizations in the United States and Europe criticized the report, primarily on methodological grounds.

Eradication efforts also have not affected the costs to users: in November 2001 the United States Office of National

Drug Control Policy acknowledged that the price of cocaine in principal American cities has remained stable during the past several years. Yet Washington and Bogotá continue to insist that the war on drugs can be won simply by intensifying and expanding current strategies.

The United States war on drugs is nearly inseparable from counterinsurgency efforts in Colombia.

THE "WAR ON DRUGS" AND COUNTERINSURGENCY

The cold war's end saw drugs replace communism as the primary threat to United States national security in the Western Hemisphere. Military assistance to Latin America became concentrated in the "source" countries, particularly Colombia. At the same time, the definition of "low-intensity conflict"—the term used to describe the political situation in Central America during the 1980s—was expanded to include those countries in which drug-trafficking organizations threatened the stability of the state. And the strategies applied in the 1980s to confront low-intensity conflict in the region were subsequently adjusted in the 1990s to address the new regional threat: drugs.

In Colombia this view of the drug problem, and of the strategies needed to combat it, is especially troublesome, given that illegal armed actors, especially the leftist Revolutionary Armed Forces of Colombia (FARC) and the paramilitary United Self-Defense Force of Colombia (AUC), maintain complex linkages with the drug trade. At conceptual and practical levels, the United States war on drugs is nearly inseparable from counterinsurgency efforts in Colombia.[4]

The conflation of low-intensity counterinsurgency tactics with counter-narcotics strategies was facilitated initially through the "narcoguerrilla theory" (a term first made popular in the 1980s by former United States Ambassador to Colombia Lewis Tambs, who accused the FARC of sustaining direct links with drug traffickers). However, the fact that paramilitary organizations, most notably MAS (Muerte a Secuestradores, or Death to Kidnappers), were created in the early 1980s and financed by drug traffickers in retaliation for guerrilla kidnappings, seemed to belie the theory's validity. Yet by the mid-1990s, references to the "narcoguerrilla" slowly began to find their way into the official jargon of certain sectors of the United States and Colombian political and military establishment. Robert Gelbard, United States assistant secretary of state for international narcotics and law enforcement, referred to the FARC as Colombia's third-largest drug cartel in 1996. During his administration, President Ernesto Samper himself began to use the narcoguerrilla label domestically in an attempt to discredit the FARC, given the group's unwillingness to negotiate with a political figure that the guerrilla organization considered illegitimate.

Ironically, when the Colombian military during the Samper administration tried to convince Washington that the symbiosis between guerrillas and drug-trafficking organizations was real, and that counternarcotics strategies needed to take this relationship into consideration, the United States argued against the idea that the guerrillas were involved in the drug traffic. Indeed, although Tambs and others had made the accusation, the United States had never categorically associated Colombian guerrilla organizations with the latter stages of the drug-trafficking process. Only in November 2000 did the State Department accuse the FARC of maintaining relations with Mexico's Arellano-Félix Organization, one of the most powerful drug cartels in that country; it also argued that "since late 1999 the FARC has sought to establish a monopoly position over the commercialization of cocaine base across much of southern Colombia." One week later, United States Ambassador to Colombia Anne Patterson affirmed that both the FARC and the paramilitaries had "control of the entire export process and the routes for sending drugs abroad" and were operating as drug cartels in the country.

In principle, the "narcoguerrilla theory," as employed in Colombia, argues that: 1) the FARC controls most aspects of the drug trade, given the demise of the major drug cartels in the mid-1990s; 2) the Colombian state is too weak to confront this threat, primarily due to the inefficacy of the country's armed forces; and 3) United States military support is warranted in wresting drug-producing regions from guerrilla control.

The events of September 11 and America's war on terrorism have introduced an additional ingredient to United States policy in Colombia: counterterrorism.

Although bearing a certain degree of truth, this description grossly oversimplifies the Colombian situation. For example, while a general consensus exists that the FARC derives a considerable portion of its income from the taxation of coca crops and coca paste and that members of this organization have participated in drugs for arms transactions, the involvement of the FARC in the transportation and distribution of narcotics internationally is still uncertain. (Contrary to the claims made by the United States State Department and its representative in Colombia, for example, the Drug Enforcement Agency has never directly accused the FARC of operating as an international drug cartel.)

The involvement of paramilitaries in drug-related activities clouds this picture even further. According to some sources, paramilitary expansion in southern Colombia during late 2000, in particular in the Putumayo region, was largely financed by drug-trafficking organizations in response to the FARC-imposed increases in the price and taxation of coca paste. This is not surprising, since the leader of the AUC, Carlos Castaño, has personally acknowledged since March 2000 that a large percentage of this organization's revenues, especially in the departments of Antioquia and Córdoba, are derived from participation in the drug trade.

Yet even with evidence that the "narcoguerrilla theory" is simpleminded, it seems to have informed many United States and Colombian political and military actors in the search for policy options in the country, while also lending credence to those who argue that counterinsurgency techniques used in other low-intensity conflicts can be applied successfully in Colombia.

SEPTEMBER 11 AND COUNTERTERRORISM

The events of September 11 and America's war on terrorism have introduced an additional ingredient to United States policy in Colombia: counterterrorism. On the day of the attacks, United States Secretary of State Colin Powell was to have visited Bogotá on official business. Although Washington's concern about the FARC's abuse of a swath of Colombia designated as a demilitarized zone created to facilitate peace talks was clear (the FARC was accused of using the zone to cultivate coca, hold kidnapping victims, and meet with members of the Irish Republican Army, allegedly to receive training in urban military tactics), some members of the American government were beginning to express reservations about the depth and nature of United States involvement in Colombia and the effectiveness of counternarcotics strategies in the country. To a large degree, the incidents of the day facilitated shifts in United States policy that had begun taking shape much earlier.

Colombia's insertion into the global antiterrorist dynamic leaves scant room for autonomous decision-making by the new president.

In a congressional hearing held on October 10, 2001, Francis Taylor, the State Department's coordinator for counterterrorism, stated that the "most dangerous international terrorist group based in this hemisphere is the Revolutionary Armed Forces of Colombia." Both Secretary of State Colin Powell and United States Ambassador to Colombia Patterson also began to refer to Colombian armed actors, in particular the FARC, as terrorist organizations that threaten regional stability.[5] Given that the global war on terrorism has targeted the links that exist among terrorism, arms, and drugs, a new term was coined, "narcoterrorism," to describe actors such as the

FARC and the AUC that fund terrorist-related activities with drug money.

The Colombian government's termination of the peace process with the FARC on February 20, 2002 placed Colombia squarely within Washington's new counterterrorist efforts. Until that day, the government of President Andrés Pastrana had never publicly referred to the guerrillas as terrorists. In a televised speech announcing his decision to call off the peace talks, however, Pastrana made this association explicit. Echoing this change, the presidential electoral battle of 2002 centered on the issues of counterterrorism and war, and led to the election of hard-liner Álvaro Uribe on May 26.

Colombia's insertion into the global war on terrorism has been reflected in concrete policy measures in the United States. In simple terms, Colombia is now viewed through the lens of counterterrorism. Public officials from both countries must frame Colombia's problems along antiterrorist lines to assure continued United States support. This shift in terminology has led to the complete erasure of differences between counternarcotics, counterinsurgency, and counterterrorist activities that formerly constituted the rhetorical backbone of United States policy in Colombia. For many years, Washington stressed the idea that its "war" in Colombia was against drug trafficking and not against the armed insurgents. As was noted, some began to openly advocate reconsideration of this policy as early as November 2000. Tellingly, United States Representative Benjamin Gilman (R., N.Y.), in a letter written that month to drug czar Barry McCaffrey that criticized the militarization of counternarcotics activities in Colombia, suggested the need for public debate concerning counterinsurgency aid to the country. A RAND report published in March 2001 also affirmed that Washington should reorient its strategy in Colombia toward counterinsurgency to help the local government regain control of the national territory.[6]

On March 21, 2002 President George W. Bush presented a supplemental budgetary request to the United States Congress totaling $27 billion for the war on terrorism and the defense of national security. The request solicited additional funding for Colombia as well as authorization to use counternarcotics assistance already disbursed to the country. The antiterrorist package finally approved by Congress in July contains an additional $35 million for counterinsurgency activities in Colombia as well as authority to use United States military assistance for purposes other than counternarcotics—namely, counterinsurgency and counterterrorism.

In its 2003 budget proposal submitted to Congress on February 4, 2002, the Bush administration also requested, for the first time, funding for activities unrelated to the drug war in Colombia. The aid package, which totals over $500 million, includes a request for approximately $100 million to train and equip two new Colombian army brigades to protect the Caño Limón-Coveñas oil pipeline, in which the American firm Occidental Petroleum is a large shareholder.

MILITARIZATION AND HUMAN RIGHTS

One of the most severe challenges to United States policy derives from the human rights situation in Colombia. According to the United States State Department *Report on Human Rights* for 2001, political and extrajudicial actions involving government security forces, paramilitary groups, and members of the guerrilla forces resulted in the deaths of 3,700 civilians; paramilitary forces were responsible for approximately 70 percent of these. During the first 10 months of 2001, 161 massacres occurred in which an estimated 1,021 people were killed. Between 275,000 and 347,000 people were forced to leave their homes, while the total number of Colombians displaced by rural violence in the country during only the last five years grew to approximately 1 million. More than 25,000 homicides were committed, one of the highest global figures per capita, and approximately 3,041 civilians were kidnapped (a slight decline from the 3,700 abducted in 2000).

Although Colombian security forces were responsible for only 3 percent of human rights violations in 2001 (a notable improvement over the 54 percent share in 1993), the report notes that government security forces continued to commit abuses, including extrajudicial killings, and collaborated directly and indirectly with paramilitary forces. And although the government has worked to strengthen its human rights policy, the measures adopted to punish officials accused of committing violations and to prevent paramilitary attacks nationwide are considered insufficient. In the meantime, paramilitary forces have increased their social and political support among the civilian population in many parts of the country. Increasingly, Colombians sense that the paramilitaries constitute the only force capable of controlling the guerrillas' expansion. The AUC have also adopted parastate functions in those regions in which the government's presence is scarce or nonexistent.

Because of the questionable human rights record of the Colombian armed forces as well as Bogotá's unwillingness to denounce this publicly, United States military assistance to the country was severely limited during much of the 1990s. Nevertheless, the United States continued to provide the armed forces with military training, weapons, and materials. In 1994 the United States embassy in Colombia reported that counternarcotics aid had been provided in 1992 and 1993 to several units responsible for human rights violations in areas not considered to be priority drug-producing zones. As a result, beginning in 1994 the United States Congress anchored military aid in Colombia directly to antidrug activities. The Leahy Amendment of September 1996—introduced by Senator Patrick Leahy (D., Vt.)—sought to suspend military assis-

tance to those units implicated in human rights violations that were receiving counternarcotics funding, unless the United States secretary of state certified that the government was taking measures to bring responsible military officers to trial.

The Colombian government itself began in 1994 to adopt a stronger stance on human rights and in January 1995 publicly claimed responsibility in what became known as the Trujillo massacres (committed between 1988 and 1991): more than 100 assassinations carried out by government security forces in collaboration with drug-trafficking organizations. Other measures directly sponsored by the Samper government in this area included the creation of a permanent regional office of the UN High Commissioner for Human Rights; the ratification of Protocol II of the Geneva Conventions; and the formalization of an agreement with the International Red Cross that enabled this organization to establish a presence in the country's conflict zones. Unfortunately, as the Colombian newsweekly *Semana* noted, "Little by little, the novel proposals made at the beginning of the Samper administration became relegated to a secondary status, given the government's need to maintain the support of the military in order to stay in power."

The moderate changes implemented by the Colombian government in its handling of human rights issues—combined with the intensification of the armed conflict and the military's need for greater firepower and better technology—facilitated the signing of an agreement in August 1997 in which the Colombian armed forces accepted the conditionality imposed by the Leahy Amendment. In the past, the Colombian military had repeatedly refused United States military assistance on the grounds that such unilateral impositions "violated the dignity of the army." But the marked asymmetries between United States aid earmarked for the Colombian National Police (CNP), which immediately accepted human rights conditionalities, and assistance specifically designated for the Colombian army constituted a strong incentive for the military to finally accept the conditions attached by the United States. Until the late 1990s the CNP was Washington's principal ally in the war on drugs, receiving nearly 90 percent of United States military aid given to Colombia. The 2000–2001 Plan Colombia aid package, however, reversed this trend completely: while the Colombian army received $416.9 million, primarily for the training of several counternarcotics battalions, police assistance only totaled $115.6 million.[7] In the 2002 and 2003 aid packages, the Colombian army continues to be the primary recipient of United States military assistance.

With the approval of the first Plan Colombia aid package in June 2000, the United States Congress specified that the president must certify that the Colombian armed forces are acting to suspend and prosecute those officers involved in human rights violations and to enforce civilian court jurisdiction over human rights crimes, and that concrete measures are being taken to break the links between the military and paramilitary groups. This legislation, however, gives the president the prerogative to waive this condition if it is deemed that vital United States national interests are at stake. On August 22, 2000 President Bill Clinton invoked the waiver. And although human rights organizations, the UN High Commissioner for Human Rights, and the State Department affirm that little or no improvements have been made in satisfying the human rights requirements set forth in the original legislation, President George W. Bush certified Colombia in 2002.

With the end of the peace process, human rights in Colombia have been further marginalized. (President Pastrana called off the process with the FARC on February 20, 2002, after continuous setbacks and halts in the peace talks, as well as late 2001 attempts on the part of the United Nations and several countries to serve as intermediaries and revive the process.) Several components of President Álvaro Uribe's national security strategy have caused alarm in human rights circles. Shortly after taking office on August 7, 2002, Uribe declared a state of interior commotion (*Estado de Conmoción Interio*), a constitutional mechanism that allows the executive to rule by decree. In addition to expanding the judicial powers of the police and military, plans to increase the size of the armed forces, create a network of government informants, and build peasant security forces are already under way. In a letter to the Colombian president on August 26, 2002, UN High Commissioner for Human Rights Mary Robinson expressed concern about Colombia's lack of human rights progress and suggested that some of the security measures adopted by the Uribe administration may be incompatible with international humanitarian law. In its November 2002 report on Colombia, Human Rights Watch also criticized the recent reversal of several investigations of military officers suspected of collaborating with paramilitaries.

WEAKENING THE STATE

Inherent to America's growing concern with Colombia is the perception that the state has become "weak" when it comes to confronting the domestic crisis and maintaining it within the country's national boundaries. (The new National Security Strategy of the United States, made public in September 2002, explicitly identifies weak states as a threat to global security because of their propensity to harbor terrorists.) Thus, in addition to combating drugs and terrorism and reducing human rights violations, another stated goal of United States policy is to enable the Colombian military to reestablish territorial control over the country as a necessary step toward state strengthening.

Although state weakness has been a permanent aspect of Colombian political history, during the 1990s the country's deterioration quickened—with the logic of United

States "drug war" imperatives playing a direct role in this process. The expansion and consolidation of drug-trafficking organizations in Colombia during the 1980s were intimately related to increasing United States domestic consumption of illegal substances, as well as the repressive policies traditionally applied to counteract this problem. America's demand for drugs and Washington's prohibitionist strategies created permissive external conditions in which the drug business in Colombia could flourish. The appearance of these organizations coincided with unprecedented levels of corruption in the public sphere, growing violence, and decreasing levels of state monopoly over the use of force.

The dismantling in the mid-1990s of the Medellín and Cali drug cartels—the two main drug-trafficking organizations in the country—gave way to fundamentally different drug-trafficking organizations that combined greater horizontal dispersion, a low profile, and the use of a more sophisticated strategy that made them even more difficult to identify and eradicate. Part of the void created by the disappearance of these two cartels was filled by the FARC and the AUC, which became more directly involved in certain aspects of the drug business between 1994 and 1998. As a result, one might also conclude—correctly—that United States drug consumption and its counternarcotics strategies have also exacerbated the Colombian armed conflict, providing diverse armed actors with substantial sources of income without which their financial autonomy and territorial expansion might not have been as feasible.

The propensity of the United States to interpret the drug problem as a national security issue, in combination with the use of coercive diplomatic measures designed to effectively confront this threat, has forced the Colombian state to "securitize" its own antidrug strategy. One underlying assumption of this "war" is that the use of external pressure is a crucial tool by which to achieve foreign policy objectives in this area, and that United States power is an enabling condition for the success of coercive diplomacy. But realist-inspired counternarcotics efforts ignore that policy orientations in source countries must necessarily answer to domestic as well as international exigencies. If domestic pressures are ignored on a systematic basis, growing state illegitimacy and state weakness can result; in an already weak state, this strategy can accelerate processes of state collapse.

With the Samper administration, the United States drug decertifications of 1996 and 1997 and the continuous threat of economic sanctions combined with domestic pressures that originated in Samper's lack of internal legitimacy to force the government to collaborate vigorously with the United States.[8] As noted, between 1994 and 1998 the Colombian government undertook an unprecedented fumigation campaign that, while returning impressive results in terms of total coca and poppy crop eradication, saw coca cultivation itself mushroom during the same period. More significantly, the fumigation campaign had tremendous repercussions in those parts of southern Colombia where it was applied. In addition to provoking massive social protests in the departments of Putumayo, Caquetá, Cauca, and (especially) Guaviare, guerrilla involvement with drugs heightened during this period, and the FARC strengthened its social base of support among those peasants involved in coca cultivation. The absence of the Colombian state in this part of the country largely facilitated the assumption of parastate functions (administration of justice and security, among others) by the guerrillas. Paramilitary activity also increased with the explicit goal of containing the guerrillas' expansion. The result was the strengthening of armed actors and the intensification of the conflict. Although the United States was clearly not directly responsible for creating this situation, the excessive pressure placed on the Samper government to achieve United States goals did make it worse.

At the same time, Samper, because of the taint of drug money, was ostracized by the United States; increasingly, Colombia became identified as a pariah state within the international community.[9] The political costs of the country's reduced status globally were significant; during his term in office Samper received only two official state visits to Colombia, by neighboring countries Venezuela and Ecuador. On an official tour through Africa and the Middle East in May 1997, the Colombian president was greeted in South Africa by news that President Nelson Mandela had been unable to meet him. Equally considerable were the economic costs. Colombia was precluded from receiving loans from international financial institutions during the time in which the country was decertified by the United States, while United States foreign investment was dramatically reduced.

THE "RENARCOTIZATION" OF RELATIONS

Confronted with growing evidence that it had aggravated Colombia's domestic crisis, Washington became increasingly sensitive to the issue of state weakness and attempted to develop a more comprehensive strategy toward the country when Andrés Pastrana was elected president in 1998. This shift in policy partly explains the initial willingness of the United States to adopt a "wait-and-see" strategy regarding the peace process Pastrana initiated with the FARC in early November 1998. Moreover, because of the marked deterioration in the political sphere, it became difficult to ignore the calls of an increasingly strong civil movement for a negotiated solution to the country's armed conflict. Thus, during the first year of his government, Pastrana was able to effectively navigate between domestic pressures for peace and United States exigencies on the drug front. But less than a year later, the assassination in early March 1999 of three United States citizens at the hands of the FARC, along with growing difficulties in the peace process itself, led to a change in both the United States and the Colombian postures and facilitated the ascendance of the drug-war logic once again.

This "renarcotization" of the bilateral agenda saw the emergence of Plan Colombia in late 1999. At home the Colombian government was able to circumvent domestic pressures by manipulating information about its intentions. This was achieved mainly through the publication of distinct versions for public consumption (in both Colombia and Europe) of arguments in which peace (and not the drug war) were adeptly presented as the centerpiece of Plan Colombia's strategy. Public statements by the government downplaying the strong emphasis the United States version of the plan placed on the drug problem reinforced this idea. When the United States Congress approved the Colombian aid package in mid-2000, sustaining this argument became increasingly difficult, primarily due to the large military component (80 percent of the total) that was designated for the drug war. Instead, the Pastrana government attempted to highlight the approximately $200 million earmarked for initiatives related to alternative development, assistance to displaced persons, human rights, and democracy, while discouraging public debate concerning the significant weight attached to the military and counternarcotics aspects of the package.

Just as war-weary Colombians welcomed Andrés Pastrana's proposal for peace in 1998, a country tired of the failed peace process overwhelmingly elected Álvaro Uribe on a national security and war platform in 2002. Uribe's plans for reestablishing state control over the national territory and for crushing militarily those armed actors unwilling to negotiate on the government's terms—goals widely supported by the Colombian population—rely heavily on United States military assistance. The use of that aid for counterinsurgency and counterterrorism is conditioned on a series of measures with which the Colombian government must comply. In addition to adopting explicit commitments in the "war on drugs," including fumigation efforts that surpass those of previous administrations, the Uribe government must implement budgetary and personnel reforms within the military and apportion additional national funding for its own war on drugs and terrorism. Some of these monies will be accrued through the creation of new taxes and reductions in the size of the state, but social spending is likely to be reduced as well. In early August 2002, Washington also requested a written statement from Bogotá conferring immunity for United States military advisers in Colombia as a precondition for the continuation of military aid.

Although at first glance Colombia and the United States share a common objective—winning the war against armed groups in the country—Colombia's insertion into the global antiterrorist dynamic leaves scant room for autonomous decision-making by the new president. In the future, the hands-on, take-charge attitude that has won Uribe a high public approval rating could be blocked by decisions made in Washington. For example, the September 2002 request for the extradition to the United States of a number of paramilitary leaders and several members of the FARC on charges of drug trafficking may work at cross-purposes with future peace talks. Although it is highly unlikely that negotiations with the FARC will resume anytime soon, on December 1, 2002 a cease-fire was declared by the paramilitaries, who have said they would like to negotiate with the government. The United States has been reluctant to state whether the extradition requests, or its classification of Colombia's armed groups as terrorists, would be revoked in the event of new peace negotiations.

THE WRONG PROFILE

United States policy in Colombia has worked at cross-purposes in terms of reducing the availability of illegal substances, confronting human rights violations, and strengthening the state. In all these areas, United States actions may actually have made an already grave situation worse. The worldview that has molded Washington's twin wars on drugs and terrorism constitutes an extremely narrow framework through which to address the complex problems Colombia faces. National security, defined exclusively in military terms, has taken precedence over equally significant political, economic, and social considerations. Until this perspective undergoes significant change, United States policy will continue to be ill equipped to assist Colombia in addressing the root causes of its current crisis.

NOTES

1. For a discussion of the role of drugs in United States–Colombian relations from 1986 to the present, see Arlene B. Tickner, "Tensiones y contradicciones en los objetivos de la política exterior de Estados Unidos en Colombia," *Colombia Internacional*, nos. 49–50, May–December 2000; and "U.S. Foreign Policy in Colombia: Bizarre Side-Effects of the 'War on Drugs,'" in Gustavo Gallón and Christopher Welna, eds., *Democracy, Human Rights, and Peace in Colombia* (Notre Dame: University of Notre Dame Press, Kellogg Series, forthcoming).

2. The first disbursement of United States aid for Plan Colombia, a multipronged strategy presented by the Pastrana administration to address problems of peace, state building, poverty, drugs, and the rule of law in the country, was made in fiscal year 2000–2001.

3. The United States and the Colombian governments argue that Roundup Ultra, which is a type of glyphosate and is used for aerial fumigation in Colombia, does not have secondary effects in human beings or surrounding plant life. But the manner in which Roundup is used in Colombia is troubling because it is applied in concentrations that exceed the technical specifications established by the manufacturer and sprayed from planes at a great distance as a defensive measure against ground fire; moreover, an additive mixed with the glyphosate to make it better stick to coca leaves also causes it to adhere to human skin and other plants.

4. In the mid-1990s, before United States military assistance to Colombia began to increase, government officials often admitted that, for Colombia, counternarcotics and counterinsurgency were essentially the same. In a 1996 interview conducted by Human Rights Watch with Barry McCaffrey, then head of the United States Southern Command, McCaffrey conceded that these facets constituted "two sides of the same coin."

5. All three of Colombia's largest armed groups, FARC, the leftist National Liberation Army (ELN), and the AUC, are classified by the United States State Department as terrorist organizations.

6. Angel Rabasa and Peter Chalk, *Colombian Labyrinth: The Synergy of Drugs and Insurgency and Its Implications for Regional Stability* (Santa Monica, Calif.: RAND, 2001).

7. An additional $330 million in police and military aid was provided through the counternarcotics budgets of the State and Defense Departments.

8. The decertifications occurred because every March the president of the United States is required to present a report to Congress certifying whether a country involved in the drug trade is in compliance with United States counternarcotics efforts. Colombia was found to be in noncompliance and thus "decertified."

9. On June 20, 1994, one day after Samper won the second round of the presidential elections, Andrés Pastrana, the conservative party candidate, released an audiotape in which Cali cartel leaders Gilberto and Miguel Rodríguez Orejuela were overheard offering several million dollars to the Samper campaign. A series of accusations and denials concerning this allegation, labeled "Proceso 8,000," ensued.

ARLENE B. TICKNER *is the director of the Center for International Studies and professor of international relations at the Universidad de los Andes, Bogotá, Colombia. She is also a professor of international relations at the Universidad Nacional de Colombia.*

"Déjà vu all over again?"

Why Dialogue Won't Solve the Kashmir Dispute

SUMMARY The intensification of a long-standing dispute between India and Pakistan over the state of Kashmir has become the cause of international concern. The stakes for these nuclear-armed rivals are high. Each views Kashmir as the validation of its national ideology; each fears that giving it up will result in serious domestic turmoil. Moreover, each country has plausible legal arguments for its claims along with a long history of grievances. The deep differences over Kashmir that divide the two countries have so far proven intractable, and following September 11 the movement toward confrontation accelerated. There has never been a more urgent need for international attention to Kashmir. While diplomatic engagement seems necessary for a resolution of this dispute, past results indicate that simply pressuring the two sides to talk may be disastrous. In order to avoid such results, any effort to intervene in this dispute must be undertaken with an awareness of how it evolved, why it has been so difficult to resolve, and what kinds of solutions to it might realistically be pursued.

ARUN R. SWAMY

In 2001, a widely anticipated summit meeting between India and Pakistan collapsed over the disputed state of Kashmir. Just months later, the tensions between these nuclear-armed rivals would challenge American efforts to build a coalition against terrorism: India charged Washington with ignoring Pakistan's support for terrorism in the Indian-controlled portion of Kashmir, hinting that it would take military action against Pakistani bases.

The India-Pakistan dispute over Kashmir has already produced two wars, contributed to a nuclear standoff, and stymied U.S. goals during the Cold War. The intensification in the last decade of this long-lived and complex dispute has commanded international attention and concern. Deadlocked for now, the two countries seem to require diplomatic intervention to avoid stepping up the conflict further. But to achieve this purpose, it is vital for policymakers and analysts to have an understanding of the details of the dispute and the reasons why it has proven to be so difficult to resolve. In the case of the Kashmir dispute, dialogue and compromise carry serious risks for both sides.

Sources of Stalemate

The Kashmir dispute grew out of the 1947 division of the British Indian Empire into two independent states, Hindu-majority India and Muslim-majority Pakistan. The division, or Partition as it is referred to in South Asia, came about because many Indian Muslim leaders believed that the cultural identity of Indian Muslims would be threatened in a Hindu-majority India. Their party, the Muslim League, held that Hindus and Indian Muslims constituted two "nations" and deserved separate states. Leaders of India's future ruling party, the Indian National Congress, rejected the "two-nation theory" but accepted the creation of Pakistan as the price of independence, partly in the belief that Pakistan would collapse anyway.

The act of Partition itself left bitter memories. Massacres on both sides of the border left hundreds of thousands dead, and millions from both countries migrated to the state where they would be part of a religious majority. For these refugees—who include Pakistan's president and India's

Historical Origins of the Dispute

Like other Indian princes, the Hindu maharaja of Kashmir had the option of joining either India or Pakistan. However, along with the Muslim ruler of predominantly Hindu Hyderabad, he initially sought independence. The maharaja opted for India when Muslim tribesmen invaded Kashmir from Pakistan. A short war between India and Pakistan in 1948 left India with 64 percent of the state and Pakistan with 36 percent. This division has remained since 1948, with the exception of a region annexed by China in 1962, leaving India with about 47 percent of the original state of Jammu and Kashmir.

minister in charge of internal security—the validity of the two-nation theory carries a personal resonance.

Kashmir as a symbol of ideological differences. Both India and Pakistan thus view Kashmir as the critical test of their founding ideologies. It is India's only Muslim-majority province, it adjoins Pakistan, it is more easily entered from Pakistan, and it was part of the original vision of Pakistan. Despite having a Muslim majority, Kashmir did not go to Pakistan initially because it was part of a larger state, Jammu and Kashmir, which was ruled by a hereditary prince rather than being directly administered by British authorities. For Pakistan, Kashmir is part of the unfinished business of the Partition. For India, possession of Kashmir, with a population in 2001 of 10 million, demonstrates India's secular credentials and guarantees the safety of its 120 million Muslim citizens.

Dialogue and compromise carry serious risks for both India and Pakistan

Separatist movements in both countries increased the importance of Kashmir. In 1971, Pakistan lost its eastern wing when India first supported East Pakistani separatists and then intervened in a Pakistani civil war to create Bangladesh. Two of Pakistan's four remaining provinces experienced separatist violence during the next 15 years. Consequently, Pakistani leaders came increasingly to emphasize Islam as a unifying ideology. India too has faced separatist rebellions in several provinces and, during the 1980s, charged Pakistan with abetting Sikh separatism in India's Punjab State. India fears that giving up Kashmir now would encourage more such movements.

Internationalization of the issue. The Kashmir issue became an international one in 1948 when India appealed to the United Nations Security Council to order Pakistan to withdraw its troops. The Council, however, refused to decide between the rival claims of the two sides and passed a resolution calling for a popular vote to determine the wishes of Kashmiris. India read the resolution to mean that Pakistan should withdraw first, allowing India to hold the vote, but Pakistan insisted on a simultaneous withdrawal. Neither side withdrew.

India eventually maintained that elections held under universal suffrage had met the need to consult Kashmiri sentiment and proceeded to treat Kashmir's accession to India as final. Jammu and Kashmir was incorporated as a state of the Indian Union but, under Article 370 of the Indian constitution, was granted far more autonomy than other Indian states. Pakistan incorporated the Gilgit region of Jammu and Kashmir into Pakistan but declared areas under its control adjoining the Kashmir Valley to be the self-governing republic of Azad (Free) Kashmir.

Over the next decade, both superpowers attempted unsuccessfully to bring about peace in the subcontinent. In the early 1960s the United States attempted to mediate the conflict, but instead a short and inconclusive war over Kashmir followed in 1965. As in 1948, irregular troops entered Indian Kashmir from Pakistan. India responded by attacking Pakistan proper. In a ceasefire agreement brokered by the Soviet Union at Tashkent, both sides forswore the use of force in settling the conflict, but they continue to differ over whether Pakistani support for insurgents in Kashmir violates this agreement. In 1972, after Pakistan lost the Bangladesh war, the two sides agreed at the Indian city of Shimla (formerly Simla), to convert the ceasefire line into a formal Line of Control, but Pakistan rejected an Indian proposal to turn this line into a final border. India interprets Shimla as requiring that the two sides settle future disputes without external intervention or mediation, but Pakistan, which did refrain from raising the issue of Kashmir in international forums until the 1990s, does not.

Legal Claims to Kashmir

India's claim to Kashmir is based on the maharaja of Kashmir's accession to India. However, Pakistan challenges the validity of the accession, claiming that the maharaja had been overthrown by a domestic insurrection before the accession. Pakistan defends this argument by pointing to India's action in another princely state, Hyderabad, which did not adjoin Pakistan, and which India annexed after sponsoring an uprising against the Muslim ruler. India, however, rejects the analogy, arguing that the forces that challenged the maharaja in 1947 were invaders from Pakistan, not domestic rebels.

Formally, India continues to claim Pakistani-held portions of Kashmir, while Pakistan calls for implementing UN resolutions on Kashmir. In practice, neither side is willing to countenance Kahsmiri independence. Although the Indian parliament recently unanimously reiterated its claim to Pakistani-held Kashmir, India would probably be willing to give this up as part of a final settlement. For its part, Pakistan would probably be willing to allow the portion of Indian Kashmir where Muslims are not in a majority to remain with India. However, on the question of whether the Muslim-majority Kashmir Valley should be allowed to join Pakistan if it so chose, neither side is willing to compromise.

The Kashmir Insurgency

The Bangladesh war and India's nuclear test in the 1970s froze the conflict by rendering Pakistan incapable of presenting a political or military challenge. During the 1980s, however, Pakistan's assistance to the U.S. effort to dislodge the Soviet Union from Afghanistan helped to rebuild the Pakistani army and led to the emergence of armed Islamist militias, for whom Kashmir became a salient issue. By the end of the decade, the eruption of an insurgency in Indian Kashmir and Pakistan's acquisition of nuclear weapons created a situation in which these militias could act and provided Pakistan with the opportunity to support them.

The origins of the current insurgency lie in domestic politics within Indian-held Kashmir and in India generally. Before independence, the most popular political force among Kashmiri Muslims was the secular and left-leaning Jammu and Kashmir National Conference, which favored independence or association with India, in that order. In the early 1950s, National Conference leader Sheikh Mohammed Abdullah won elections in Indian Kashmir handily, allowing India to claim popular support among Kashmiris.

Compromised elections in Kashmir. From 1954 to 1975, however, elections in the state were hopelessly compromised, in part because of ethnic divisions in the state. Abdullah alienated the minority regions of Jammu and Ladakh by emphasizing the distinctiveness of Kashmiri identity and undertaking land reforms at the expense of the elites in

these regions. With support from parties on the Hindu Right, Jammu and Ladakh lobbied the central government either to divide Jammu and Kashmir or to rescind its autonomous status. When Abdullah responded to these challenges by promoting independence for the entire state of Jammu and Kashmir, he was imprisoned by the Government of India.

Over the next two decades, India's ruling Congress Party supported pro-India factions of the National Conference, who generally rigged elections to stay in power. Genuine electoral participation was restored to the state in 1975, when Abdullah was released from prison and allowed to govern Kashmir. However, a decade later, Abdullah's son and successor, Farooq Abdullah, was removed from office and then coerced into allying with the ruling Congress Party as a condition for returning to power in 1987.

The 1987 elections, which removed competition from the state's politics and may also have been rigged, are often viewed as having triggered the insurgency. The state was, in any event, ripe for rebellion. Literacy had spread without employment keeping pace, and many of the new literati had been educated in Islamic *madrassas*. In 1989, Kashmir exploded in violence when Indian security forces responded to the kidnapping of a cabinet minister's daughter with brutal repression. Initially led by the pro-independence and nonsectarian Jammu and Kashmir Liberation Front (JKLF), the movement was soon taken over by the Pakistan-supported and Islamist Hizb-ul-Mujahedin. As the Afghanistan war ended, the insurgency drew in pan-Islamist groups based in Pakistan and Afghanistan whose ranks included Arabs, Afghans, and Pakistanis.

Ethnic Diversity

Jammu and Kashmir consisted of four or five regions distinguished by language, culture, and history. Although it contained a Muslim majority overall, two regions, the Hindu-majority, Dogri-speaking region of Jammu and the Tibetan Buddhist region of Ladakh, did not. India controls these two regions and the Muslim-majority Kashmir Valley, home of Kashmiri speakers. Pakistan controls Gilgit, or the Northern Territories, and certain areas adjoining the Valley that contain both Kashmiri and Punjabi speakers. In 1981 the religious breakdown of the various regions in Indian Kashmir was as follows.

Ethnic Region	% of Total Population of Kashmir	Muslims as % of Population
Kashmir Valley	52.37	94.96
Jammu	45.39	29.60
Ladakh	2.24	46.04
All regions	100.00	64.19

Source: Ashutosh Varshney, "Three Compromised Nationalisms" in Raju G.C. Thomas, ed., *Perspectives on Kashmir.* Boulder: Westview Press, 1992, p. 207.

Militant groups operating in Kashmir have been guilty of extensive human rights abuses. While the worst atrocities are believed to have been the work of non-Kashmiri militants, all groups have been guilty of attacks on civilians. Some militant groups have targeted Kashmiri Hindus, who have largely fled the Valley, and all have sought to frustrate the electoral process by threatening retribution against voters and candidates who participate in elections held by India.

Ripe for rebellion, Kashmir exploded in violence in 1989

Kashmiri self-determination. The Islamization of the Kashmir insurgency has made any effort to resolve the Kashmir problem through the principle of self-determination even more problematic. While secular Kashmiri nationalists like Sheikh Abdullah and the JKLF alienated non-Kashmiri ethnic groups, the Hizb and other Islamist groups have attempted to impost orthodox Islam on the historically syncretist Kashmiri culture, making it difficult to know how much support the militants have, even among pro-independence Kashmiris.

The exodus of Kashmiri Hindus form the Valley has strengthened the conviction of the Indian political elite that claims to self-determination on the basis of a region's majority religion violate the rights of minorities in that region. It has also fed the bitterness of Hindu refugees from Pakistan elsewhere in India, adding to the concern among Hindu liberals and Indian Muslims outside Kashmir that if India lost Kashmir, Indian Muslims would suffer from a severe right-wing Hindu backlash. These concerns are especially acute with the rise of the Bharatiya Janata Party (BJP), which leads the current ruling coalition. The BJP won power in 1998, promising to rescind Kashmir's autonomous status and to develop a nuclear arsenal. The BJP government's decision to fulfill the second promise internationalized the conflict again.

Nuclearization and Confrontation

The nuclearization of the India-Pakistan rivalry has brought new international attention to the Kashmir dispute. The 1998 tests by India and Pakistan were followed by economic and military sanctions on both by most industrialized countries. Both countries felt pressured to demonstrate that they were taking measures to reduce tensions between them. However, since no major power was willing to express an opinion on the substantive issues dividing the parties, nothing was necessary to achieve the perception of behaving responsibly other than being willing to engage in talks.

Two facts shape every proposal made. First, India is trying to defend the status quo, while Pakistan seeks to change

it. Therefore India proposes trade and confidence-building measures, while Pakistan insists on settling "core" differences first. Second, India is more powerful militarily, but this is of little use against nuclear weapons or guerrilla activity. Consequently, Pakistan has proposed a no-war pact that would not cover Pakistani support for militants operating in Kashmir, while India has proposed a pact barring the first use of nuclear weapons, which would restore Indian military superiority.

International pressures led to a meeting in February 1999 between Pakistani prime minister Nawaz Sharif and Indian prime minister Atal Behari Vajpayee at Lahore, Pakistan. The meeting produced a joint declaration that focused on measures to reduce the likelihood of accidental nuclear war and emphasized in general the need for both countries to promote development and to pursue peaceful resolution of the Kashmir "issue."

The Kargil conflict. However, several months after Lahore, a major conflict occurred in the Kargil region of Indian Kashmir between Indian troops and infiltrators from the Pakistani side, who probably included soldiers from the Pakistani army. Pakistan's motives in the Kargil incident are unclear, but they probably included the military leadership's desire to undermine the Lahore declaration and pressure India into negotiating on Kashmir.

Pakistan probably also calculated that the fear of nuclear conflict—or of international condemnation for risking nuclear conflict—would keep India from expanding the war as it had in 1965. In this they were correct. While Indian troops suffered heavy casualties for two months and the Indian Air Force undertook bombing missions perilously close to the Line of Control, this boundary was not crossed. The crisis ended when U.S. President Bill Clinton pressured Sharif into withdrawing the infiltrators.

India is trying to defend the status quo, while Pakistan seeks to change it

Kargil and its aftermath disrupted the peace effort for two years. For India, the American role in ending the Kargil conflict was a mixed blessing since it demonstrated Pakistani involvement in the insurgency but also brought in U.S. mediation, which India has consistently rejected. India escaped this dilemma when Nawaz Sharif, discredited by his decision to withdraw the infiltrators, was overthrown in a military coup in October 1999. Shortly after the coup, an Indian Airlines flight was hijacked to Afghanistan; India had to release several militants captured in Kashmir in exchange for the passengers on the flight, and these militants were then allowed to cross into Pakistan. India used the coup and hijacking as reasons to refuse to deal with Pakistan until civilian rule was restored.

For the next year and a half, India sought to allay international concerns regarding Kashmir by attempting to negotiate both with the civilian separatist front, the All-Party Hurriyat Conference (APHC), and with the militant Hizbul-Mujahedin. These efforts failed when India refused either to include Pakistan in the talks or to put secession on the table. In late 2000, India announced a unilateral ceasefire against the militants, hoping to entice them into talks or at least to convince the world that it was trying to negotiate. When this unilateral ceasefire failed to obtain results after six months, India simultaneously lifted its ceasefire and invited Pakistan's military ruler, President Pervez Musharraf, to New Delhi.

A failed 2001 summit. As with Pakistan's motives in Kargil, India's reasons for inviting Musharraf are obscure. India may have wished to balance lifting its unilateral ceasefire with a visibly conciliatory gesture. India probably also believed that a Pakistani military regimen weakened by sanctions and international censure might be more willing to make—and be able to deliver—significant concessions. If so, they were to be disappointed.

Each party was set against discussing the other's main concern

The Vajpayee-Musharraf summit meeting, held at Agra in July 2001, failed to produce even a joint statement defining the countries' differences. A draft declaration negotiated by the two sides was never issued because India refused to concede that the legal status of Kashmir was "in dispute" or that it was the "principal issue" between the two, while Pakistan refused to acknowledge that it was sponsoring "cross-border terrorism" in Indian-held Kashmir. Since Pakistan's principal goal was to negotiate the status of Kashmir, and India's principal goal was to end Pakistani support of militancy, each party was set against discussing the other's main concern. After the summit, India increased military efforts against the insurgency and moved its negotiating position farther away from Pakistan.

The events following September 11 only accelerated the trend toward confrontation. India announced its support for U.S. policy first, hoping to isolate Pakistan. However, Pakistan's strategic location and domestic instability caused the United States to downplay Indian concerns until a suicide bomb attack on the legislative assembly in Indian Kashmir on October 1 led India to warn Washington that it might feel compelled by domestic pressure to retaliate against Pakistan.

Diplomatic exchanges between the United States and India since October 1 have been studiously ambiguous. The United States responded to Indian concerns by calling for restraint on both sides—but without clarifying whether Pakistani support for the insurgency was included in this call—and by emphasizing that it was fighting "terrorism" everywhere—without indicating how it would regard the Kashmir insurgency in this fight. India too responded with general assurances of its support for the U.S. campaign, but it kept the option of military action open while securing Russian support for its position.

The situation could change in dramatic and unpredictable ways with the collapse of the Taliban regime in Afghanistan. This could reduce Indian concerns significantly by weakening the Kashmir insurgency. However, a takeover by the Northern Alliance—which India favors and Pakistan opposes—could lead the Pakistani military to undertake risky actions itself, and Taliban fighters driven from Afghanistan could migrate to Kashmir, raising Indian concerns again. There has never been a more urgent time for international attention to Kashmir.

Policy Recommendations

The analysis so far suggests on the one hand that active diplomatic intervention is necessary to break out of the current impasse and on the other that there are no realistic final solutions acceptable to both parties at present. The two most practical solutions—ratifying the status quo or allowing Kashmir to secede from India—are each unacceptable to one of the parties. Other more creative solutions offered by analysts are hopelessly impractical and would also be rejected by one or the other side. Proposals to turn Kashmir into a joint protectorate of India and Pakistan, for example, are a complete nonstarter for India, which currently possesses most of Kashmir, while proposals to establish a grand confederation between India and Pakistan would be equally unacceptable to most Pakistanis, who would view it as effectively undoing the Partition.

There are few, if any, pure victims in the Kashmir conflict

Any diplomatic intervention will therefore have to be limited to defining a framework for stabilizing the situation in a way both countries can accept as consistent with their long-term goals. A starting point would be to call on India to accept that Kashmir is an issue of international concern and that the insurgency in Kashmir has some domestic causes, while insisting that Pakistan accept responsibility for fueling the insurgency and destabilizing the situation. Since at present most countries accept India's insistence that the conflict be solved bilaterally while remaining silent on Pakistan's support for the insurgency, the position recommended here would maintain the balance between the two positions while promoting dialogue.

Such a dialogue might, with covert encouragement from the outside, focus on ways to channel Kashmiri separatism into political rather than military avenues. A start would be for India to remove the present ban on electoral participation by parties with a separatist agenda, at least in Kashmir, in exchange for some verifiable measures that prevent militants from crossing the ceasefire line. This could be done with or without formal acknowledgment by India of a dispute, or by Pakistan of its responsibility for militant activity in Kashmir.

This solution has the virtue of forcing each side to live up to its own rhetoric. India claims that Kahsmiris have been granted self-determination through the electoral process but has never allowed separatist forces to run for election. Pakistan claims only to demand Kashmiri self-determination but has always insisted on being a party to negotiations and, like India, has refused to allow parties that are not loyal to run for election in its portion of Kashmir. This solution would ensure that Kashmiri separatism receives a fair political hearing, while eliminating military force as a route to a final outcome. Rather than allowing Pakistan and India to promote their own Kashmiri allies as the province's true representatives, this solution would also identify which of the many groups claiming to represent Kashmiris actually do so.

Achieving even this compromise would require active diplomatic engagement, as it carries serious risks for both sides. India might have to decide whether to limit this change in electoral laws to Kashmir or to extend it to the entire country. Either choice contains risks. Pakistan would have to decide whether to crack down on Islamist groups or merely to police the ceasefire line. Any government in Pakistan would face the threat of serious domestic unrest from either decision. To negotiate through these pitfalls, four things need to be remembered.

First, there are few, if any, pure victims in the Kashmir conflict. Neither India nor Pakistan has a clear case in its favor, and Kashmiris have dealt poorly with their own minorities. There are no good solutions to the conflict, and maybe no just ones.

Second, the political leaders of India and Pakistan have held together countries that are, by any criteria, difficult to govern. If they believe that giving up on Kashmir would destabilize their societies, this should be taken seriously. Outside powers, who will not bear the consequences of a mistake, ought to approach the situation with humility.

Third, the United States and other major powers have very little leverage over the two countries, especially India. Both India and Pakistan are large and militarily powerful, and they have both demonstrated their willingness to withstand international censure before. India, in particular, prides itself on having survived three years of economic

sanctions and five decades of American displeasure. Given the states involved in Kashmir, India is more likely to abandon its effort to improve ties with the United States than alter its policy on Kashmir to please Washington. Economic incentives might help stabilize the dispute; they will not obtain permanent substantive concessions.

Finally, simply urging the two sides to talk is the worst of all possible responses. Pressures on the two to discuss their differences were followed by active conflict in 1965 and 1999 and could soon bring the same result. Unless the major powers can convince Pakistan to end its support for the insurgency and India to accept some international role in stabilizing the dispute, another round of talks would simply cause one or both to attempt to coerce the other into making concessions.

For Further Reading

An exhaustive list of sources on Kashmir as well as up-to-date news on the area can be found at http://www.kashmirgroup.freeserve.co.uk, a site maintained by a British scholar working on Kashmiri politics. The following sources were used for the present report.

Cohen, Stephen P. "Kashmir: The Roads Ahead." In *South Asia Approaches the Millenium: Reexamining National Security,* edited by Marvin G. Weinbaum and Chetan Kumar. Boulder: Westview Press, 1995.

Contemporary South Asia, 4, no. 1. Special issue, 1995. (Articles by Indians, Pakistanis, and others.)

Ganguly, Sumit. *The Crisis in Kashmir: Portents of War, Hopes of Peace.* Cambridge: Cambridge University Press and Washington, D.C.: Woodrow Wilson Center Press, 1997.

Thomas, Raju G.C., ed. *Perspectives on Kashmir: The Roots of Conflict in South Asia.* Boulder: Westview Press, 1992. (Articles by Indians, Pakistanis, and others.)

***Arun R. Swamy** is a fellow in the East-West Center Research Program. His work focuses on the consequences of democratic competition for social conflict in developing countries. His Ph.D. dissertation at the University of California, Berkeley, examined the impact of electoral competition, ethnic conflict, and poverty alleviation policies in India, and he has several publications arising out of that research. He is currently developing research projects along similar themes for Southeast Asia.*

He can be reached at:
Telephone: (808) 944-7542
Facsimile: (808) 944-7399
Email: SwamyA@EastWestCenter.org

From *Analysis From the East-West Center,* November 2001. © 2001 by East-West Center.

UNIT 6
Terrorism in America

Unit Selections

16. **From Push to Shove**, Heidi Beirich and Bob Moser
17. **FBI Targets Domestic Terrorists**, Valerie Richardson
18. **Indictment: Smiling Face Hid Hatred**, Richard Willing and Deborah Sharp
19. **Intelligence, Terrorism, and Civil Liberties**, Kate Martin

Key Points to Consider

- Ecoterrorists like the ELF and ALF have caused almost $43 million in damage since 1996. Why do the activities of environmental terrorists in the United States rarely receive national attention and media coverage? Should they?

- How do changes in procedure and legislation, proposed in the wake of the September 11 attacks, affect our civil liberties? At what point do government efforts to prevent future terrorist attacks conflict with or interfere with the individual's right to political dissent?

 **Links: www.dushkin.com/online/**
These sites are annotated in the World Wide Web pages.

America's War Against Terrorism
http://www.lib.umich.edu/govdocs/usterror.html

FBI Homepage
http://www.fbi.gov

The Hate Directory
http://www.bcpl.lib.md.us/~rfrankli/hatedir.htm

The Intelligence Project
http://www.splcenter.org/intelligenceproject/ip-index.html

The Militia Watchdog
http://www.adl.org/mwd/m1.asp

Despite recent experiences, domestic terrorism remains a difficult topic for many in the United States to understand. While Americans are all-too-willing to believe in "evil forces" with origins in other countries, many become uncomfortable at the thought of U.S. citizens, men and women, as perpetrators of political violence. Many refuse to believe that a system as free, open, and democratic as that in the United States can spawn those who hate and wish to destroy the very system that has bestowed on them tremendous individual freedoms, including the right to political dissent.

American reactions to domestic terrorists vary. While many Americans are outraged by domestic terrorism, some terrorists, like Eric Rudolph accused of four bombings, including attacks on the Olympics in Atlanta, two women's clinics, and a bar, have achieved cult-hero status, with bumper stickers and T-shirts popularizing Rudolph's near-legendary flight from law enforcement officials. Groups like the Animal Liberation Front (ALF) and the Earth Liberation Front (ELF) and individuals like Ted Kaczynski or Jane Olson continue to attract apologists, searching for ways to justify or explain the violent behavior of otherwise "good Americans." Even the case of Timothy McVeigh, who was prosecuted and executed for the Oklahoma City bombing, has attracted some who continue to believe in an international conspiracy with origins in the Middle East, despite evidence to the contrary. This apparent schizophrenia is echoed in media reporting, public opinion, and public policy.

While the U.S. media often demonizes foreign terrorists, it tends to humanize American terrorists. Stories of American terrorists often emphasize a human-interest perspective. Stories about the Minnesotan, middle-class soccer mom Jane Olson or the young, idealistic, obviously misguided, "American Taliban" John Walker, or even the psychologically unbalanced, log-cabin-recluse Ted Kaczynski make good copy and are designed to elicit sympathy or empathy in a larger audience. In efforts to explain how or why "good" Americans have gone "so bad," the violent acts committed and the victims are often ignored.

Public opinion and public policy are also subject to this apparent dissonance. While the American public and U.S. policymakers appear to care little about the legal rights or physical detention of foreigners suspected of association with terrorist organizations, the legal rights of domestic terrorists are often the subject of public scrutiny and debate.

The four selections in this unit reflect the apparent contradictions in American perceptions of terrorism at home. In the first two articles, radical environmentalists and animal rights activists are introduced as now employing violent tactics. Heidi Beirich and Bob Moser remind us that when peaceful revolution is impossible, violent revolution becomes inevitable. Valerie Richardson's article expands on this and provides a quick overview of the activities of two groups that the FBI believes to be the "No. 1 domestic terrorist threats": the Animal Liberation Front (ALF) and the Earth Liberation Front (ELF), which link together the activities of a number of ecoterrorist groups in the United States. Despite the fact that there have been over 600 criminal acts linked to these organizations since 1996, there has been little public outcry against their activities.

The third selection in this unit focuses on the arrest of University of South Florida professor Sami Al-Arian. Al-Arian, who has been the subject of FBI investigations since the mid-1990s, was arrested in February of 2003 and charged with a 50-count indictment alleging that he is "the North American leader" of the Palestinian Islamic Jihad. Al-Arian, a resident alien with an application for American citizenship pending, has been a vocal supporter of the Palestinian cause. He claims that his arrest is "political." The final selection in this unit highlights the potential conflict between the collection of domestic intelligence and the protection of civil liberties. Kate Martin suggests that it may be possible to reconcile the two.

From Push to Shove

Radical environmental and animal-rights groups have always drawn the line at targeting humans. Not anymore.

By Heidi Beirich and Bob Moser

A Chicago insurance executive might seem like one of the last people who'd be opening a letter with this succinctly chilling message: "You have been targeted for terrorist attack." But that's what happened last year, when a top official at Marsh USA Inc. was informed that he and his company's employees had landed in the crosshairs of an extremist animal rights group. The reason? Marsh provides insurance for one of the world's biggest animal testing labs. "If you bail out now," the letter advised, "you, your business, and your family will be spared great hassle and humility."

That letter—and the harassment campaign that followed, after Marsh declined to "bail out"—was another shot fired by Stop Huntingdon Animal Cruelty (SHAC). This British-born group, now firmly established in the United States, is waging war on anyone involved with Huntingdon Life Sciences, which tests drugs on approximately 70,000 rats, dogs, monkeys and other animals each year. In the process, SHAC is rewriting the rules by which even the most radical eco-activists have traditionally operated.

In the past, even the edgiest American eco-warriors drew the line at targeting humans. They trumpeted underground activists' attacks on businesses and laboratories perceived as abusing animals or the environment—the FBI reports more than 600 incidents, causing $43 million in damage, since 1996. But spokespeople for the two most active groups in the U.S., the Animal Liberation Front (ALF) and the Earth Liberation Front (ELF), have always been quick to claim that their underground cells have never injured or killed any people.

Since 1999, however, members of both groups have been involved with SHAC's campaign to harass employees of Huntingdon—and even distantly related business associates like Marsh—with frankly terroristic tactics similar to those of anti-abortion extremists. Employees have had their homes vandalized with spray-painted "Puppy killer" and "We'll be back" notices. They have faced a mounting number of death threats, fire bombings and violent assaults. They've had their names, addresses and personal information posted on Web sites and posters, declaring them "wanted for collaboration with animal torture."

Kevin Jonas of SHAC-USA sees no need to mince words about his group's terrorist tactics.

When cowed companies began responding to the harassment by pulling away from Huntingdon, many radical environmentalists cheered—even when SHAC's actions clearly went over the "nonviolent" line. Still, the ELF and ALF insist that they remain dedicated to what their spokespeople describe as nonviolent "economic sabotage," such as tree-spiking and arson. They vigorously deny the label that increasingly sticks to them: "eco-terrorist." Spokespeople continue to chant the public-relations mantra that the ALF's David Barbarash invoked again on National Public Radio this January: "There has never been a single case where any action has resulted in injury or death."

SHAC's escalating violence is not unique. North America's most active and widespread eco-radicals—the ELF and ALF took credit for 137 "direct actions" in 2001 alone—have clearly taken a turn toward the more extreme European model of activism. The rhetoric has begun to change along with the action. Reached by the Intelligence Report, SHAC-USA's Kevin Jonas—a former ALF spokesman—was unusually frank about the lengths to which the new breed of activists will go. "When push comes to shove," Jonas said, "we're ready to push, kick, shove, bite, do whatever to win."

'Igniting the Revolution'

The far left has long been skirting the edge. In the 1980s, the standard-bearer of the movement was EarthFirst!, a radical group inspired by the novels of Edward Abbey, who romanticized a life of "monkey-wrenching," or sabotage, to protect the environment from rapacious corporations and developers. Using the model of "leaderless resistance" long advocated by white supremacist tactician Louis Beam—small, independent underground cells carrying out actions, with no hierarchy for law enforcement to go after—EarthFirst! brought "direct action" to the forefront of the environmental movement.

The most controversial of EarthFirst! techniques was tree-spiking, which involved pounding metal spikes into trees to prevent them from being cut or milled into lumber. Typically, tree-spikings were accompanied by warnings designed to cut down on the possibility of injuring or killing timber workers. But timber companies pointed out that some of the spikes would remain in trees long after the warnings had been forgotten, and said the technique put loggers and sawmill workers at risk of severe injury or even death. Such tactics resulted in the first references to environmentalists as terrorists.

Responding to criticism in the early 1990s, EarthFirst! members began to ponder a more moderate approach. This did not sit well with radicals, who left to found the ELF in Brighton, England, in 1992. In its video, "Igniting the Revolution," the ELF says it realized "that to be successful in the struggle to protect the Earth, more extreme tactics must be utilized. Thus the Earth Liberation Front was born."

Coming to America

It wasn't until 1998, when one of the ELF's underground cells burned down a major part of a brand new ski resort near Vail, Colo., that the group became a household name. The fire caused a whopping $12 million in damage and put eco-radicalism back in the headlines.

But news reports failed to note this was not a home-grown movement. The ELF, in fact, is an outgrowth of the European animal-rights movement more than American environmentalism. Its closely linked predecessor, the ALF, got its starts in Britain in 1976 before crossing the Atlantic Ocean. And while U.S. environmental activists still have a largely positive image, with the Sierra Club's peaceful lobbying efforts setting the tone in most people's eyes, activists of the British ALF and its continental cohorts have given the European movement a very different reputation. Eco-activists there are seen by many as dangerous and reckless criminals—and they often live up to the billing, as the SHAC campaign (along with letter bomb attacks that have maimed one secretary and injured a furrier and his 3-year-old daughter) so vividly demonstrates.

In February 2001, Huntingdon's managing director in Great Britain, Brian Cass, was badly beaten outside his home by three masked assailants swinging baseball bats. Shortly after the attack, British animal rights activist David Blenkinsop, a friend of SHAC-USA's Kevin Jonas,

was arrested and sentenced to three years in prison for the assault. At around the same time, Andrew Gay, Cass' marketing director, was attacked on his doorstep with a spray that left him temporarily blinded, writhing on the ground in front of his wife and young daughter.

Ronnie Lee, one of the British founders of the ALF, applauded the beating of Cass. "He has got off lightly," Lee said. "I have no sympathy for him."

Joining in the jubilation were some American eco-radicals. "If it happens and it works," Last Chance for Animals boss Chris DeRose said of attacks like the Cass beating, "then that's great."

A Growing Radicalism

When longtime ELF spokesperson Craig Rosebraugh was called to testify before Congress about domestic terrorism this February, he invoked the Fifth Amendment with gusto. But Rosebraugh did answer written questions from a congressional subcommittee, and he didn't mince words. Asked whether he feared an ELF action could one day kill someone, Rosebraugh sounded a lot like Ronnie Lee. "No," he wrote, "I am more concerned with massive numbers of people dying at the hands of greedy capitalists if such actions are not taken."

Connections between the ALF and ELF run deep. From the start, they made pledges of solidarity, and they clearly shared a coterie of hard-line activists. They were also structured similarly, with a handful of activists designated as spokespeople who would announce and encourage "direct actions." Essentially, anyone who carried out one of these actions—whether or not they were acquainted with the groups' aboveground spokespeople—became, in effect, a member. The structure is remarkably similar to that of the so-called Army of God, a violent anti-abortion "group" that is "joined" by simply carrying out an attack and claiming credit. Although there is no real "membership," these groups can appear large because every attack undertaken in their name generates significant publicity.

At the Hilton, Violence is Cheered

Rosebraugh signed on to the movement after spending a night in jail with a prominent ALF activist in 1997. Eleven weeks later, he delivered his first message on behalf of the ALF: Activists had broken into a mink farm and released hundreds of animals, costing the business some $300,000. The next year, Rosebraugh switched to the ELF, proudly announcing the Vail arson on the ALF's Web site. (The ELF didn't set up its own site until 2001.)

To this day, the ELF has much more in common—sharing both members and tactics—with the ever-more-radical ALF than with any other environmental group in the U.S. ELF activists like Rosebraugh are regularly invited to speak at the animal rights conference held every year in the Washington, D.C., area on the week of July 4. The event is funded by several animal-rights groups, the most prominent of which are People for the Ethical Treatment of Animals, or PETA, and the more moderate Humane Society of the United States.

The conference setting is surprisingly highbrow, held for the past two years in the marble-clad McLean Hilton, which employs a well-known Vegan chef. But the discussions are down and dirty, dealing forthrightly with the role of violence in the fight for animal rights. At last year's conference, PETA's Bruce Friedrich was candid enough.

"If we really believe that animals have the same right to be free from pain and suffering at our hands," Friedrich told a panel, "then of course we're going to be blowing things up and smashing windows. ... I think it's a great way to bring about animal liberation, considering the level of suffering, the atrocities. I think it would be great if all of the fast-food outlets, slaughterhouses, these laboratories, and the banks that fund them, exploded tomorrow.

"I think it's perfectly appropriate for people to take bricks and toss them through the windows. ... Hallelujah to the people who are willing to do it."

The assembled activists applauded. And as they milled around between speeches and panels, there was still more evidence that the edge of American eco-advocacy is becoming even edgier. Representatives from the ALF, ELF and SHAC—all of whom claim to be independent groups—shared a table, handing out their pamphlets and T-shirts. On the back of one of the shirts was a typical slogan: "Words Mean Nothing ... Action is Everything!"

'Devastate to Liberate'

The terrorist attacks of Sept. 11, 2001, did not dampen the enthusiasm of America's eco-radicals for direct action. But something did change when those attacks brought down the World Trade Center: Americans' tolerance for anything that smacks of terrorism. So when the ALF set a $1 million fire at a primate lab in New Mexico on Sept. 20, and when an ELF cell set a University of Minnesota genetics lab ablaze this Jan. 29, corporate groups, members of Congress, conservative commentators and the FBI joined in a chorus decrying the acts as "eco-terrorism." The targets of these acts couldn't have agreed more. "These are clearly terroristic acts," said Charles Muscoplat, dean of agriculture at the University of Minnesota. "Someone could get hurt or killed in a big fire like we had."

Activists continued to insist that the eco-terror label was "ludicrous," and that law-enforcement officials were engaged in a witch hunt cheered on by corporate interests. "I mean, what was the Boston Tea Party," ALF spokesman Barbarash asked rhetorically on NPR, "if not a massive act of property destruction?" Barbarash went on: "Property damage is a legitimate political tool called economic sabotage, and it's meant to attack businesses and corporations who are profiting from the exploitation, murder and torture of either humans or animals, or the planet. ... [T]o call those acts terrorism is ludicrous."

Their case was bolstered in June, when a San Francisco jury found that law-enforcement officials (including three FBI agents) violated the civil rights of EarthFirst! activists Judi Bari and Darryl Cherney—to the tune of $4.4 million in damages. Bari and Cherney were on their way to an EarthFirst! rally in 1990 when a pipe bomb exploded in Bari's Subaru station wagon. Authorities claimed that the two were planning to use the bomb, but Bari and Cherney consistently denied any knowledge of the explosives, saying they had been falsely pegged as eco-terrorists and in fact were the victims of an assassination attempt.

Though the Bari/Cherney verdict was a setback for those decrying "eco-terrorism," the similarity between eco-radicals' methods and those of more stereotypical "terrorists" has made the comparison seem natural to more and more observers. The increasingly inflammatory rhetoric of the groups hasn't helped.

Last year, the ELF put up two new manuals on its Web site—"Setting Fires With Electrical Timers: An Earth Liberation Guide" and "Arson Around With Auntie ALF." An ELF communiqué went even further, saying the group was now targeting "FBI offices and U.S. federal buildings," "liberal democracy" and even "industrial civilization" itself.

For its part, while it advises non-violence, the ALF's "Beginner's Guide to Direct Action for Animal Liberation" opens with the slogan, "Devastate to Liberate." The booklet goes on to offer handy tips for relatively mild sabotage—gluing locks, spray-painting slogans and threats, smashing windows, "rippin' shit up"—but it also includes easy-to-follow instructions for "a few simple incendiary devices" like Molotov cocktails. A more detailed "ALF Primer" has three single-spaced pages devoted to arson. "As dangerous as arson is," the primer advises, "it is also by far the most potent weapon of direct action."

SHAC Ups the Ante

Meanwhile, SHAC was teaching other potent lessons—and getting results that have only spurred eco-radicals on.

Last year, Barclay's Bank in the United Kingdom pulled its financing of Huntingdon Life Sciences, saying it "couldn't guarantee the safety" of its employees. Charles Schwab, an American financial firm, also pulled out after protesters occupied its offices in Birmingham, England.

When Huntingdon moved to the U.S. last year, hoping to escape the wrath of U.K. activists, the violence didn't let up. SHAC-USA's Web site boasted that a company vice president here "was visited several times, had several car windows broken, tires slashed, house spray painted with slogans. His wife is reportedly on the brink of a nervous breakdown and divorce."

In July 2001, a related group, "Pirates for Animal Liberation," took responsibility for trying to sink the private yacht of a Bank of New York executive to protest the bank's connection with Huntingdon. The Stephens Group, an investment firm in Arkansas, was subjected to a campaign of harassment after announcing a $33 million loan to Huntingdon. After backing out this February, CEO Warren Stephens said the company had been "aware of the activists, but I don't think we understood exactly what lengths they would go to."

SHAC-USA rejoiced along with its allies in the ALF and ELF. "If we can push this domino down," Kevin Jonas told *US News & World Report*, "there is no domino we can't push down."

Targeting Scientists, and Others

Scientists have been increasingly targeted—with similar success. In July, Dr. Michael Podell halted his aids studies and resigned from Ohio State University, giving up a tenured position and a $1.7 million research project. Podell, who was using cats to study why drug users seem to succumb more quickly to aids, received nearly a dozen death threats after PETA (People for the Ethical Treatment of Animals) put the experiment on its "action alert" list. Podell was sent a photograph of a British scientist whose car had been bombed. "You're next" was scrawled across the top of the photo.

The use of animals in research has decreased in the last few decades, according to government estimates—and the use of cats has dropped a whopping 66 percent since 1967. But scientists say that some research, like Podell's, cannot be done with computer modeling or with human subjects. "It's a small number of animals to get information to potentially help millions of people," Podell told The New York Times. But that argument did not hold water with PETA, or with the local protest group that sprung up in Columbus. Eventually, they wore down Podell.

"Scientists tend to be good targets," Frankie Trull, president of the Foundation for Biomedical Research, which promotes "humane and responsible" animal testing, told the Intelligence Report. "Their temperament is such that they don't really fight back. The ALF is like the bully in the schoolyard for them."

Pumped up by their victories, eco-radicals have made it clear that their agenda is broadening in a big—and potentially dangerous—way. If President Bush expands the nuclear-power industry, said a spokesperson for SHAC-USA, that industry will be targeted next. The ultimate target, as the ELF says in a video, is nothing short of "the entire capitalist system."

The Justice Department

While SHAC sets a new standard for eco-terrorism, another British import is making American and Canadian authorities even more nervous. Since it sprang up in 1993, the so-called Justice Department has claimed responsibility for hundreds of violent attacks in the U.K. With an underground cell structure similar to those of the ALF and ELF, the Justice Department has made creative use of let-

ter bombs, which have injured several people, and sent out scores of envelopes rigged with poisoned razor blades. The London *Independent* called the Justice Department's attacks "the most sustained and sophisticated bombing campaign in mainland Britain since the IRA was at its height."

In January 1996, after the group became active in North America, the Justice Department claimed responsibility for sending envelopes with blades dipped in rat poison to 80 researchers, hunting guides and others in British Columbia, Alberta and around the United States. The blades were taped inside the opening edge of the envelopes, poised to cut the fingers of anyone opening the letters. "Dear animal killing scum!" read the note inside. "Hope we sliced your finger wide open and that you now die from the rat poison we smeared on the razor blade." The letter signed off, "Justice Department strikes again."

Authorities in Great Britain have suggested that Keith Mann of the ALF, currently serving an 11-year prison sentence in Britain, founded the Justice Department, although that has not been proven.

A Taste of Fear

Just as EarthFirst! ultimately became too "tame" for the eco-saboteurs who formed the ELF, groups like the Justice Department seem to attract frustrated activists who don't want to hold the line against harming humans. The existence of such violent spin-offs, including the Animal Rights Militia, allows ELF and ALF to continue claiming ethical purity by way of comparison.

How do these groups defend their methods? "If the animals could fight back," says the Justice Department, "there would be a lot of dead animal abusers already."

The group's fact sheet—posted on an ALF Web site— makes it clear that the Justice Department thinks of itself as a more extreme version of the ALF. "The Animal Liberation Front achieved what other methods have not while adhering to nonviolence," the Justice Department manifesto reads. "A separate idea was established that decided animal abusers had been warned long enough. … [T]he time has come for abusers to have but a taste of the fear and anguish their victims suffer on a daily basis."

A similar thought occurred to one of America's legendary terrorists, Ted Kaczynski. And the connection is more than philosophical. During his trial, Kaczynski admitted that he was in contact with EarthFirst! during his Unabomber days. In fact, he found at least one of his targets—Thomas Mosser, a New Jersey advertising executive, who was killed instantly when he opened a package from the Unabomber—by reading about Mosser's firm in the *EarthFirst!* journal.

In his manifesto, Kaczynski sounded for all the world like an eco-extremist as he took credit for Mosser's violent death: "We blew up Thomas Mosser last December because he was a Burston-Marsteller executive. Among other misdeeds, Burston-Marsteller helped Exxon clean up its image after the Exxon Valdez incident." Officials noted that Kaczynski misspelled the company's name—it should be Burson, not Burston—precisely the same way that EarthFirst! did. They also noted that, as reported in the *Washington Post*, the *EarthFirst!* journal got it wrong: Burson-Marsteller "never worked for Exxon on the spill." Thanks to incorrect information from *EarthFirst!*, Mosser was killed for something his company never did.

A Murder in the Netherlands

Frustration with the slow pace of nonviolent change appears to be epidemic in the movement. In September 2001, ALF co-founder Ronnie Lee told *Jane's Intelligence Review*, "So far no one on the other side has ever been seriously harmed or killed. But that may now change."

It didn't take long for Lee to be proved right. This May, as the debate over "eco-terrorism" raged in the United States, an apparent "eco-assassination" in Europe sent shockwaves through the environmental activists and their targets. Less than two weeks before voters in the Netherlands would choose a new government, animal-rights activist Volkert van der Graaf allegedly pumped six bullets into Pim Fortuyn, a right-wing anti-immigration candidate for prime minister. Van der Graaf may have been enraged by Fortuyn's support of pig farmers in a debate with animal rights activists.

Fortuyn's death at the hands of a veteran activist spawned a wave of "I-told-you-so" editorials in European newspapers, which have sharply criticized the escalating violence of radical activists in recent years, warning that murder was the next step. Fortuyn, a dog lover whose environmental views were generally more moderate than his hard-right stance on immigration, had expressed similar exasperation earlier in the campaign, telling the green group Milieudefensie, "I'm sick to death of your environmental movement."

Could eco-activism spawn another van der Graaf—or another Kaczynski—in the United States? If it happens, don't expect the ALF or ELF to take responsibility. The groups' guidelines for cell members always include a crucial escape clause, like this one in "Frequently Asked Questions About the Earth Liberation Front": "If an action similar to one performed by ELF occurred and resulted in an individual becoming physically injured or losing their life, this would not be considered an ELF action."

'Rethinking Nonviolence'

By refusing to take responsibility for any actions that harm humans, the ALF and ELF implicitly acknowledge that violence directed at people is a foreseeable result of the tactics they promote. Their ever-more-fiery rhetoric and increasingly brash methods could inspire future Kaczynskis and van der Graafs. In fact, the 32-year-old van der Graaf was the founder of Zeeland's Animal Liberation Front before he went on to found Milieu Offensief (Environment Offensive). His story reads like a cautionary tale, especially now that the American ELF and ALF seem to take their cues from the Europeans.

While van der Graaf was an avowed enemy of factory farming, most of his attacks on farmers had been peaceful. Environment Offensive filed more than 2,200 lawsuits against big farming interests. "His weapon was the law," a member of Environment Offensive told Dutch television.

But van der Graaf was apparently provoked to more drastic action by his frustration with fighting "the system." When Dutch police searched the suspect's home after Fortuyn's murder, they found documents linking van der Graaf to a recent outbreak of direct-action attacks on a mink factory and a poultry farm. They also found that van der Graaf apparently hadn't intended to stop with Fortuyn: He had floor plans of the homes of three of Fortuyn's fellow List Party candidates for the parliament.

What happens when U.S. companies and politicians keep getting in the way of eco-radicals' goals? Peter Singer, a Princeton University philosopher and long-time darling of many eco-radicals, recently acknowledged the quandary faced by many in the movement—and the direction in which it clearly seems headed. "We who have an affinity with non-human animals and nature," Singer told the Australian *Herald-Sun*, "are finding it increasingly difficult to love our fellow man."

Kevin Jonas of SHAC-USA, which is inspiring a new breed of activist, put it even more bluntly. "There's a very famous quote by John F. Kennedy," he told the *Intelligence Report*. "If you make peaceful revolution impossible, you make violent revolution inevitable."

Indeed, further violence seems almost inevitable. Just ask Craig Rosebraugh, the long-time ELF spokesman who recently left that post to pursue theoretical work for the movement. Attending the Institute for Social Ecology at Goddard College in Vermont, Rosebraugh's master's thesis has a revealing working title: "Rethinking Nonviolence: Arguing for the Legitimacy of Armed Struggle."

Eco-terror: The Record

Extremists within the environmental and animal rights movements have committed literally thousands of violent criminal acts in recent decades — arguably more than those from any other radical sector, left or right. Although these extremists have yet to kill anyone in America, they have carried out ar-

sons, fire-bombings, assaults, and attacks on animal-based businesses and laboratories. This February, an FBI official testified to Congress that what he characterized as the leading eco-terrorist groups —the Animal Liberation Front (ALF) and the Earth Liberation Front (ELF)—had committed more than 600 criminal acts since 1996 that resulted in a minimum of $43 million in damage. What follows is a selection of 1984-2002 incidents, drawn from ALF/ELF communiqués, media reports, law enforcement officials and publications of the movement.

MAY 1984
Philadelphia, Pa.
An ALF raid at the University of Pennsylvania Head Injury Lab caused $60,000 in damage.

DEC. 9, 1984
Duarte, Calif.
The ALF raided the City of Hope National Medical Center, causing $400,000 in damage.

APRIL 1, 1985
Riverside, Calif.
The ALF raided a laboratory at the University of California, Riverside, causing $700,000 in damage. About 500 animals were released.

OCT. 26, 1986
Eugene, Ore.
The ALF claimed an attack on a University of Oregon laboratory that did nearly $120,000 in damage.

APRIL 15, 1987
Davis, Calif.
An ALF arson attack at the University of California, Davis, Animal Diagnostics Laboratory destroyed a building and 20 vehicles, causing $5.1 million in damage.

SEPT. 1, 1987
Santa Clara, Calif.
The Animal Rights Militia, part of the ALF, claimed an arson fire at the San Jose Valley Veal & Beef Company that caused $10,000 in damage.

NOV. 28, 1987
Santa Clara, Calif.
The words "ALF" and "murderers" were sprayed on walls at the V. Melani poultry distribution company, where a fire caused $200,000 in damage.

APRIL 2, 1989
Tucson, Ariz.
The ALF set fires in a laboratory at a Veterans Administration hospital at the University of Arizona that caused $500,000 in damage.

APRIL 15, 1989
Monterey, Calif.
The ALF set timed incendiary devices at a meat company, where an apparently unexpected early morning crew smelled smoke and managed to flee to safety.

JULY 4, 1989
Lubbock, Texas

The ALF destroyed records and smashed computers and other equipment during a laboratory raid at Texas Tech University, causing $700,000 in damage.

JUNE 10, 1991
Corvallis, Ore.
ALF member Rod Coronado and others broke into the Oregon State University's experimental mink farm and set timed incendiary devices that caused $62,000 in damage.

DECEMBER 15, 1991
Yamhill, Ore.
Rod Coronado set fire to a Hynek Malecky facility where mink pelts are dried, causing $96,000 in damage.

FEB. 28, 1992
East Lansing, Mich.
Rod Coronado and other ALF members set a $1.2 million fire at Michigan State University's mink research facility. People for the Ethical Treatment of Animals (PETA) donated $42,000 toward Coronado's defense, but he was imprisoned anyway and not released until 2001.

JANUARY 1995
Henrietta, N.Y.
The ALF set two trucks on fire at the Conti Packing Co.

APRIL 14, 1995
Syracuse, N.Y.
The ALF ignited an incendiary device at Oneata Beef Company, causing $6,000 in damage.

JUNE 15, 1995
Murray, Utah
The ALF torched Tandy Leather, causing $300,000 in damage.

DECEMBER 24, 1995
Eugene, Ore.
The ALF planted incendiary devices under three Dutch Girl Ice Cream trucks, causing $15,600 in damage.

APRIL 2, 1996
Salt Lake City, Utah
The ALF burned an Egg Products store to the ground and damaged two of the firm's trucks, causing over $100,000 in damage.

OCT. 27, 1996
Detroit, Ore.
The ELF and the ALF jointly torched a U.S. Forest Service truck.

OCT. 30, 1996
Eugene, Ore.
The ALF and the ELF burned the U.S. Forest Service Oakridge Ranger Station, causing $5.3 million in damage.

NOV. 12, 1996
Bloomington, Minn.
A firebomb claimed by the ALF was thrown through a window at the Alaskan Fur Company, causing over $2 million in damage.

FEB. 15, 1997
Troy, Mich.
The ALF left butyric acid, a foul-smelling chemical, in a McDonald's and spray-painted "McShit, McMurder, McDeath" on the restaurant's bathroom walls.

MARCH 11, 1997
Sandy, Utah
A series of firebombs claimed jointly by the ALF and the ELF destroyed four trucks and leveled the offices of the Agricultural Fur Breeders Co-Op, causing about $1 million in damage.

MARCH 18, 1997
Davis, Calif.
The "Bay Area Cell of the Earth X ALF" took credit for setting fire to the University of California, Davis, Center for Comparative Medicine facility, which was still under construction.

MARCH 18, 1997
Ogden, Utah
Montgomery Furs, a trapping supply store, was torched by the ALF while a night watchman was inside. The watchman escaped unhurt.

APRIL 19, 1997
Indianapolis, Ind.
The ALF torched an Archer's Meats truck cab.

JULY 21, 1997
Redmond, Ore.
The ALF and ELF used napalm which they referred to as "vegan Jell-O"—to destroy the Cavel West horse slaughtering plant.

AUG. 16, 1997
West Jordan, Utah
Four ALF activists burned a McDonald's restaurant to the ground, causing $400,000 in damage.

AUG. 17, 1997
Morton Grove, Ill.
The ALF threw two Molotov cocktails through a Cosmo's Furs window.

AUG. 19, 1997
Fort Collins, Colo.
The ALF claimed an arson attack on Wildlife Pharmaceuticals.

AUG. 26, 1997
Howell, N.J.
The ALF torched several Jersey Cuts Meat Co. trucks, destroying three that were valued at $60,000 each.

FEB. 28, 1998
Indianapolis, Ind.
The Outdoorsman Sport Shop had its windows broken and was set on fire. ALF slogans were spray-painted at the shop.

MAY 4, 1998
Wimauma, Fla.
The ALF claimed credit for burning down Florida Veal Processors Inc., causing $500,000 in damage.

JUNE 28, 1998
Olympia, Wash.
The ALF and ELF claimed responsibility for an arson at a U.S. Department of Agriculture Damage Control building.

JULY 16, 1998
Paramus, N.J.
The ALF claimed the destruction of a Steven Corn Furs truck.

OCT. 18, 1998
Vail, Colo.
The ELF burned down the Vail Associates ski facility, destroying seven structures valued at more than $12 million.

NOV. 16, 1998
Manalapan, N.J.
A van owned by the Leather and Fur Ranch was firebombed by the ALF.

NOV. 29, 1998
Burns, Ore.
The ALF and the ELF claimed joint responsibility for an arson at the Bureau of Land Management's Wild Horse Corrals.

DEC. 26, 1998
Medford, Ore.
The ELF claimed the $500,000 arson of a U.S. Forest Industries facility.

FEB. 18, 1999
Chicago, Ill.
Unidentified PETA activists were credited for throwing two pies at Procter & Gamble executive John Pepper to protest the company's animal testing.

MARCH 5, 1999
Eugene, Ore.
The "Biotic Baking Brigade" took credit for throwing a banana cream pie in Sierra Club staffer Charlie Raine's face to protest the Club's support of land exchanges between the government and timber companies.

MARCH 11, 1999
Hampton, N.H.

Three Biotic Baking Brigade activists threw pies at University of Wisconsin geneticist Neil First, who was speaking at the University of New Hampshire, to protest genetic engineering at UW. David Pike and Renee Medford were charged with assault.

MARCH 27, 1999
Franklin, N.J.
The ALF firebombed six Big Apple Circus vehicles, destroying two trucks.

APRIL 5, 1999
Minneapolis, Minn.
Laboratories at the University of Minnesota were vandalized and dozens of research animals stolen by the ALF, wrecking research into Alzheimer's and cancer.

MAY 9, 1999
Eugene, Ore.
ALF set a fire that destroyed a two-story office building, a shipping dock and a refrigeration unit at Childer's Meat Co., wreaking about $150,000 in damage.

MAY 10, 1999
Neah Bay, Wash.
Sea Defense Alliance activists Jake Conroy and Josh Harper (who would later work for Stop Huntingdon Animal Cruelty) were charged with felony assault after allegedly throwing ignited smoke canisters at a Makah tribe's whaling support vessel and firing a lighted flare across its bow.

JUNE 25, 1999
Miami, Fla.
The ALF claimed the firebombing of a Worldwide Primates truck.

AUG. 7, 1999
Escanaba, Mich.
ELF arsonists torched two fishing boats at the home of veterinarian James Boydston and spray-painted his garage door with "FUR IS MURDER, ELF."

AUG. 9, 1999
Plymouth, Wis.
Mink feed supplier United Feeds was burned down by ALF at about the same time as an ALF raid and mink release at Gene Myer's Fur Farm, also in the Plymouth area.

AUG. 29, 1999
Orange, Calif.
The ALF claimed an attack on a Bio-Devices Inc., research laboratory that resulted in $250,000 damage and the theft of 46 dogs.

AUG. 31, 1999
Fulton County, Ga.

The ALF burned down a McDonald's restaurant. PETA's Bruce Friedrich announced the crime on AR-News, an online animal rights news service.

SEPT. 23, 1999
Phippsburg, Mass.
The ALF claimed a failed arson at the Phippsburg Sportsmen's Association, where activists turned over coffee pots, left plastic cups on the burners, and turned on a gas line.

OCT. 1999
Various cities
An ALF faction known as the Justice Department took credit for sending over 80 razor blade-laced envelopes, each containing a threatening letter with a picture of a bomb on it, to animal researchers, hunting guides and others in the United States and Canada. An ALF communiqué said some of the razor blades, which were positioned so as to slice open the fingers of anyone opening the envelopes, were coated in rat poison.

OCT. 22, 1999
Warwick, R.I.
The ALF claimed the torching of four Harris Furs vehicles.

NOVEMBER 1, 1999
Seattle, Wash.
Four gasoline bombs were thrown into a Gap clothing store in an attack the FBI attributed to the ALF.

DEC. 4, 1999
Las Vegas, Nev.
PETA activist Dawn Carr hit rodeo showgirl Brandy DeJongh in the face with a pie moments after DeJongh was awarded the Miss Rodeo America 2000 crown.

DEC. 25, 1999
Monmouth, Ore.
The ELF claimed responsibility for burning down logging firm Boise Cascade's regional headquarters.

DEC. 31, 1999
Lansing, Mich.
The ELF used accelerants to destroy $400,000 worth of property at Michigan State University in an action targeting Monsanto's genetically engineered products. The blaze was discovered by a faculty member working late inside the facility.

JAN. 3, 2000
Petaluma, Calif.
The ALF set fire to buildings and trucks at Rancho Veal's meatpacking plant, causing $250,000 in damage.

JAN. 15, 2000
Petaluma, Calif.
The ALF claimed credit for placing five incendiary devices in offices and trucks at a Petaluma Farms chicken farm (which "enslaves chickens for their eggs"). Two trucks were destroyed.

JAN. 23, 2000
Bloomington, Ind.
The ELF claimed credit for torching a house under construction, causing some $200,000 in damage. "No Sprawl, ELF" was painted at the site.

JAN. 24, 2000
Redwood City, Calif.
The ALF claimed credit for attempting to burn down Primate Products, a medical research facility.

MAY 30, 2000
Washington, D.C.
PETA activist Arathi Jayaram was charged with assault after throwing a pie at U.S. Agriculture Secretary Dan Glickman at the National Nutrition Summit.

JULY 2, 2000
North Vernon, Ind.
The ALF took credit for burning a Rose Acre Farm chicken feed truck, causing $100,000 in damage. "Polluter, animal exploiter, your turn to pay," was spray-painted at the scene.

JULY 30, 2000
San Francisco, Calif.
Coalition to Abolish the Fur Trade activist Bhaskar Sinha was charged with battery after threatening rock star Ted Nugent outside a Neiman Marcus department store.

SEPT. 9, 2000
Bloomington, Ind.
In an attack aimed at a highway project, the ELF claimed a minor fire at the Monroe County Republican Party headquarters that was meant as "a reminder to politicians."

NOV. 27, 2000
Boulder, Colo.
The ELF claimed responsibility for torching a $2.5 million Legend Ridge mansion.

DEC. 19, 2000
Miller Place, N.Y.
The ELF claimed credit for burning down a home under construction.

DEC. 29, 2000
Mount Sinai, N.Y.
The ELF took credit for burning down four new homes at Island Estates. Teenagers Jared McIntyre, Matthew Rammelkamp and George Mashkow III pleaded guilty to charges connected to the attack. Fellow teen Connor Cash was later indicted for arson, arson conspiracy and providing material support to terrorists.

JAN. 1, 2001
Glendale, Ore.

The ELF torched the Superior Lumber Co., causing $400,00 in damage. "This year," the ELF said, "we hope to see an escalation in tactics against capitalism."

JAN. 23, 2001
Capitola, Calif.
Peter Schnell and Matthew Whyte, both of the Animal Defense League, were found behind the Capitola City Hall with plastic milk bottles, gasoline and candles. After five containers of gasoline were found in Whyte's car, Schnell told police he was working on a "craft project." Authorities ultimately would sentence Schnell to 24 months and Whyte to 14 months in prison for attempted arson.

FEB. 20, 2001
Visalia, Calif.
The ELF claimed a fire at a research cotton gin owned by Delta & Pine Land, a firm accused of ties to Monsanto's genetically engineered seed program.

MARCH 2, 2001
Douglas County, Ore.
The ELF claimed responsibility for spiking trees at the Umpqua National Forest to prevent a timber sale.

MARCH 30, 2001
Eugene, Ore.
Thirty SUVs at Joe Romania's car dealership were torched, causing about $1 million in damage. The ELF said the attack was in support of Jeff "Free" Luers, who was serving a 23-year prison sentence, in part for torching cars at the same dealership.

APRIL 5, 2001
Arlington, Wash.
The ALF set fire to a National Food Corp. egg farm, causing $1.5 million in damage.

APRIL 15, 2001
Portland, Ore.
The ELF claimed an arson attack, using time-delayed fuses, that caused $210,000 in damage to cement trucks at Ross Island Sand & Gravel.

MAY 21, 2001
Seattle, Wash.
The ALF set fire to the University of Washington's Center for Urban Horticulture, causing $5.6 million in damage and wrecking years of research on genetically altered poplar trees and similar projects.

JUNE 1, 2001
Estacada, Ore.
One logging truck was destroyed and two more damaged during an arson attack on Schoppert Logging trucks by the Cascadia Forest.

JUNE 12, 2001
Tucson, Ariz.

Four under-construction luxury homes were set afire and "CSP," for Coalition to Save the Preserves, was found spray-painted at the site.

JUNE 14, 2001
New York, N.Y.
PETA activists aiming for fur designer Karl Lagerfeld missed and hit designer Calvin Klein with a tofu cream pie. Six members were charged with disorderly conduct and attempted assault.

JULY 2001
Cowlitz County, Wash.
The ELF claimed responsibility for spiking hundreds of trees slated for a timber sale in the Cowlitz Valley.

JULY 4, 2001
Detroit, Mich.
The ELF torched an executive office of logging giant Weyerhauser to protest the company's part in funding Oregon State University and the University of Washington's poplar and cottonwood genetic engineering research.

JULY 24, 2001
Sands Point, N.Y.
The "Pirates for Animal Liberation" claimed responsibility for unsuccessfully trying to sink a Bank of New York employee's 21-foot boat.

SEPT. 8, 2001
Tucson, Ariz.
Saying the attack was meant "as a warning to corporations worldwide," the ALF and ELF claimed joint credit for the $500,000 arson of a McDonald's restaurant.

SEPT. 20, 2001
Alamogordo, N.M.
The ALF claimed a $1 million arson fire at Coulston Foundation's White Sands Research Center. Lab owner Dr. Fred Coulston had earlier had a bomb scare at his home and had also received razor blades in the mail.

OCT. 15, 2001
Susanville, Calif.
The ELF planted four firebombs at a Bureau of Land Management corral, burning down an $85,000 barn.

OCT. 24, 2001
Long Island, N.Y.
The "Special Operations: Huntingdon Life Sciences" cell of the ALF attacked Bank of America offices,

smashing more than 30 windows and later boasting sarcastically that it had "joined the United States in their [sic] noble War Against Terrorism!"

NOV. 5, 2001
Idaho County, Idaho
The ELF claimed the spiking of trees in the Nez Perce National Forest to prevent a timber sale.

NOV. 5, 2001
Houghton, Mich.
After a series of ELF e-mail threats, suspected ELF activists planted incendiary devices at the U.J. Noblet Forestry Building and a U.S. Forest Service laboratory at Michigan Tech University. Security guards disarmed the devices.

NOV. 11, 2001
San Diego, Calif.
The ALF destroyed a contract animal research lab owned by Sierra Biomedical, causing $50,000 in damage.

JAN. 29, 2002
St. Paul, Minn.
The ELF claimed a $250,000 arson at the University of Minnesota's Microbial and Plant Genomics Research Center, which was under construction.

JAN. 29, 2002
Fairfield, Maine
The ELF and ALF jointly claimed the sabotage of a biotech plant being built for Jackson Labs, an animal testing business. Sand and mortar mix were used to wreck construction equipment at the site.

MARCH 24, 2002
Erie, Penn.
Saying it was trying to stop a highway project, the ELF spiked trees and torched a $500,000 construction crane at a bridge worksite.

MAY 3, 2002
Bloomington, Ind.
The ALF claimed a fire that destroyed a Sims Poultry truck.

JULY 10, 2002
Seattle, Wash.
Animal rights activists set off smoke bombs in two downtown buildings, sending 700 office workers fleeing into the streets. The targets were firms insuring Huntingdon Life Sciences, a company that does animal testing.

Security

FBI Targets Domestic Terrorists

**After years of trying to warn the public about the dangers
of ecoterrorism, critics of extremist movements
find themselves winning the war for public opinion.**

BY VALERIE RICHARDSON

Sure, they burn down homes, firebomb universities and terrorize research labs. Even so, for the better part of a decade, the Earth Liberation Front (ELF) and Animal Liberation Front (ALF) were seen not as antisocial thugs but idealistic young kids. After all, the public generally supported their goals—a clean environment and compassion toward animals. Religious fundamentalists and militias were dangerous; groups such as ELF and ALF were well-meaning, even if they sometimes got carried away and torched a ranger station.

Behind the mask:

*Members of ELF and ALF
claimed responsibility for 137
illegal "direct actions" in 2001.*

Then came Sept. 11. For ELF and ALF, that was the day they took joint credit for firebombing a McDonald's in Tucson, Ariz. For the rest of the nation, that was the day that terrorism suddenly ceased being cute.

"The general population is becoming a lot less tolerant toward these groups," says Rep. Scott McInnis (R-Colo.) "The feeling is, if you're going to tolerate this, then why not tolerate al-Qaeda? We need to take away the Robin Hood mystique from these terrorists, which is what they are."

While the nation fights international terrorism overseas, lawmakers such as McInnis have renewed their long-standing campaign to crack down on domestic terrorism, notably ecoterrorism. The FBI now ranks both ALF and ELF as the No. 1 domestic-terrorism threats, surpassing the Timothy McVeigh-style militia extremists who dominated the terrorism scene during much of the 1990s.

"The FBI estimates that the ALF/ELF have committed more than 600 criminal acts in the United States since 1996, resulting in damages in excess of $43 million," said James Jarboe, FBI domestic-terrorism section chief, at a February hearing before the House Resources subcommittee on Forests and Forest Health.

And the threat is growing. Animal and environmental activists are turning increasingly toward vandalism and terrorism to further their causes. "They're all over the place—they've torched so many things, you can't keep track any more," says Ron Arnold, author of *Ecoterror: The Violent Agenda to Save Nature*.

The trend has led to some ominous speculation. "At the rate they're going," adds Mike Burita, spokesman for the Center for Consumer Freedom, "someone's going to get killed."

Still, most Americans have never heard of these groups. Reports of ecoterrorism rarely make it past the local newspaper, and only a handful have received national attention. Chief among these was the October 1998 fire at the Vail, Colo., resort that destroyed four ski lifts and a restaurant at a cost of $12 million.

"Despite the fact that we've been trying to direct attention to the problem, we haven't had much luck," says Nick Nichols, chief executive officer of Nichols Dezenhall, a crisis-management communications firm in Washington whose clients include companies hit by ecoterrorism. "After 9/11, people are more interested in learning about our homegrown terrorists."

The FBI makes a clear distinction between domestic and international terrorism, but longtime foes of ecoterrorism are quick to draw parallels between ALF/ELF and the al-Qaeda network. "The rationalization of ecoterrorists is no different from the al-Qaeda terrorists," said House Resources Committee Chairman James V. Hansen (R-Utah). "Both

---

PR Firm 'Brands' Crisis Management

Spokesmen, logos, jingles, slogans, swooning models and a talking dog or two: This is the typical advertising agency arsenal. Now, add counterterrorism to the list.

Ogilvy Public Relations Worldwide, one of the largest public-relations concerns on the planet, has established "Counter Threat," a new division meant to usher corporate clients into the potential dangers of a post-Sept. 11 world.

"The terrorist attacks have brought home the idea to many companies that they can be seriously affected by things completely beyond their control and out of their own geography," says Kamer Davis, who is coordinating the service from Ogilvy's Washington office.

It is a sobering moment, perhaps, for an industry preoccupied with getting and spending. Ogilvy plans to offer "emergency scenario-based" exercises for employees, crisis counseling and threat assessment of telephones, computer data and Internet resources based on similar work done for federal, state and local agencies. The marker, they believe, is expanding. "The corporate sector can't afford to ignore this anymore," says Davis.

But critics believe Counter Threat is a wily marketing move by Ogilvy, which counts Coca-Cola and drug giant Pfizer as clients. "This is an effort to be taken more seriously, to get really close to clients, right down to their desk drawers," says Richard Linnett, a columnist for *Advertising Age*. "Ogilvy is reinventing some old stuff, but they're getting beyond advertising. Antiterrorism services are another way to tap into more business, to be needed on a very basic level."

Other firms are hopping on the bandwagon. Though it lacks the gutsy cachet of Counter Threat, Ketchum, another global top-10 public-relations agency, established a new "Issues and Crisis Management Network" in January. Indeed, interest in terrorism preparedness is yet another indicator that change is afoot in U.S. advertising since Sept. 11. The collective creative prowess of the nation's biggest agencies shifted into patriotic gear, resulting in a continuing series of uplifting public-service campaigns produced by the Ad Council.

The attacks also inspired Secretary of State Colin L. Powell to appoint advertising expert Charlotte Beers as undersecretary for public diplomacy and public affairs, charged with giving the nation a "brand" with a global image and media message. It is a tricky business, though. The Pentagon's Office of Strategic Information was shut down in a matter of days, after rumors surfaced that the office might peddle disinformation, which the Department of Defense later denied.

Some critics have faulted the State Department for trying to sell the United States as if it were soap, but the "branding" idea has merit, argues Allen Rosenshine, chairman of the advertising agency BBDO Worldwide—as long as it captures "the sense of decency, fairness and opportunity that characterizes our country."

"The usual critics notwithstanding, what makes us good at selling soap can help us sell America," he wrote in the Feb. 18 issue of *Advertising Age*.

JENNIFER HARPER WRITES FOR **Insight**'S SISTER DAILY, THE WASHINGTON TIMES.

---

believe they are the sole proprietor of truth and righteousness. Both believe they have the right to impose their concepts of truth and righteousness on society. Both attack people who they think have violated nature's or God's law."

Some environmental activists seem to invite such comparisons with statements that appear to support the Islamic terrorists who executed the Sept. 11 attacks. "I cheered when the plane hit the Pentagon. Those people are in the business of killing people," said an ELF member in an interview in the February issue of *Details* magazine. "Anyone in their right mind would realize the United States had it coming," added Craig Rosebraugh, a vocal ELF member, in the same interview. In testimony before the domestic-terrorism hearing, Rosebraugh, who testified under subpoena, called the war in Afghanistan "the latest example of U.S.-based terrorism and imperialism" and the legislative and executive branches "the largest group of terrorists and terrorist representatives currently threatening life on this planet."

Efforts to draw similarities between ALF/ELF and the Sept. 11 terrorists have

drawn a sharp rebuke from sympathizers. "What's really scurrilous is that they're all trying to hijack the legitimate fears people have about 9/11," says Ingrid Newkirk, president of People for the Ethical Treatment of Animals (PETA) in Norfolk, Va. "They are absolutely using 9/11 against people who have nothing to do with terrorism, unless you spell it 'terra.'"

David Barbarash, an ALF member who now serves as the group's North American spokesman, says the link is "way off the mark" and inappropriate. "I think 9/11 is being used as a political football by those who want to pursue their own agendas against people who are challenging the practices they defend, like the dairy, meat and fur industries," he says. In two decades of "direct action" against such industries and research labs, his group has never killed or seriously injured anyone, he points out. Indeed, ALF describes itself as waging a "nonviolent campaign," with activists taking precautions not to harm any animal, human or otherwise. "On the one hand, al-Qaeda is killing and maiming thousands of people," says

Barbarash. "The people of the ALF are rescuing and saving lives. There are strict guidelines—we do destroy property, but not lives."

The FBI defines domestic terrorism as "the unlawful use, or threatened use, of violence by a group or individual... committed against persons or property to intimidate or coerce a government, the civilian population or any segment thereof, in furtherance of political or social objectives." Critics note that the "victimless-crime" argument isn't strictly accurate: In the 1998 Vail resort fire set by ELF, for example, a firefighter had to be treated for injuries.

That the harm hasn't been more serious owes more to good fortune than good intentions, says McInnis. "They are lucky so far that they haven't injured anyone, but their luck's going to run out," he says. "It's only a matter of time before someone's injured or killed."

Within the underground world of ALF and ELF, Barbarash's views aren't unusual, but something else about him is: He was captured. Since ALF began

New Weapons in War Against Terror

In James Bond action movies, Agent 007 always visits the laconic "Q." and his lab of white-coated scientists for the latest high-tech gizmos. In the war against terrorism, "Q." comes in the person of Lt. Col. Bill Bass, distributor of the latest inventions from the Defense Advanced Research Projects Agency (DARPA).

In Kandahar, Afghanistan, Bass recently distributed two goodies to the troops—a fourth-generation, task-specific voice and audio language translator, and a miniature water purification unit that is 99.9 percent effective in debugging fluids for drinking.

The Rapid Multilingual Support Unit, better known as the phraselator, is unlike any language translator on the commercial market. First, its language programs, developed at the Massachusetts Institute of Technology, come in Afghanistan's various dialects: Pashto, Dari, Arabic and Urdu (with Tajik and Uzbek in the works). Nine other language programs are available, including Mandarin. Each has about 1,000 phrases the speaker normally would use in specific tasks.

Second, the phraselator is task-specific. For Operation Enduring Freedom, the phrasing categories are force protection and law enforcement, refugee processing and reunification and medical triage. Force-protection and law-enforcement phrases, for example, include "be quiet," "drop the gun" and "hands up." The unit projects the phrases through a built-in speaker, but it can be hooked up to external loudspeakers as well.

Remarkable, the synthesized voice is fluid, full of inflection, rhythm and accent. "It makes sense, I can understand it," says Abdul, an Afghan videographer with an international TV service, who listened to the device. "It's understandable, but it has a northern Pashto accent."

The phraselator, produced for DARPA by Marine Acoustics Inc., weighs just 20 ounces with batteries. It's a bit larger than two Palm Pilots or a handheld video game. It's also fully Windows Pocket PC compliant and can be used to log onto the manufacturer's Website for adding additional phrases and words the operator may need.

The Federal Aviation Administration also is interested in the phraselator, says Bass, and since they are produced through a contractor, the devices eventually will make their way to the commercial market. Berlitz has expressed interest in the gizmo, priced at $1,000 based on a 10,000-unit run.

In six months, a "one-plus-one" phraselator will be available. This more advanced unit will pick up responses, based on keywords, and relay them back to the operator. In a year's time, a full two-way unit will be available, featuring the ability to interpret the semantic meaning of words and phrases voiced by the responder.

Bass also handed out MIOX (micro-oxidation) pen units to soldiers in Kandahar. To avoid getting sick from contaminated water, the user simply pours a sample of the water into the unit, which within 30 to 120 seconds analyzes its content and produces the proper chemicals to neutralize bacteria and other dangerous content. He then pours the agents into the canteen along with the water, and within 15 minutes it's potable. Each pen, with a single analyzation unit and chemical mix, is good for about 300 canteens of water.

"This MIOX pen does everything but desalinate—that comes next," Bass says. "You can fill a canteen with even your urine and it will come out tasting like pure water."

RICHARD TOMKINS WRITES FOR UNITED PRESS INTERNATIONAL.

---

conducting its direct actions in 1979, hundreds of activists have joined the group, but only a couple dozen members in the United States and Canada have ever been apprehended.

Not even ALF and ELF organizers know the identity of all their members, who operate in semiautonomous cells. They receive training from groups such as the Ruckus Society and by reading the how-to manuals available on ALF and ELF Websites. Members also tend to be better educated than the average vandal, meaning that they rarely make rookie mistakes such as leaving fingerprints at the scene.

So confident are ALF and ELF leaders of their secrecy that they actually list their actions on their Websites and publish an annual report of their activities, "like they were IBM," says Nichols. To make matters worse, the attacks have inspired copycats. Residents of Phoenix feared they were under siege by ecoterrorists when eight homes in an upscale

development were torched from April 2000 to January 2001.

A group calling itself the Coalition to Save the Preserves took credit for the arsons. As it turned out, however, the culprit was a 50-year-old unemployed public-relations executive named Mark Warren Sands who lived in the neighborhood and began his life of crime when he found a new home blocking his favorite jogging path.

In addition, ecoterror strikes often are handled by local law enforcement, who have limited resources and whose deputies don't always share vital information with other jurisdictions. To make communications among law enforcement easier, Rep. Darlene Hooley (D-Ore.) has proposed a bill that would create a national clearinghouse on ecoterrorism and bulk up federal assistance at the local level.

The FBI has tried to open the lines of communication with the establishment of joint terrorism task forces, teams that bring local and federal agents together

to brainstorm on domestic-terrorism strikes. Launched in 1999, the agency now has task forces in 44 cities and plans to have one for each of its 56 field offices by 2003.

Despite the elusive nature of its prey, law enforcement can point to some significant arrests:

- In February 2001, one adult and three teen-agers pleaded guilty to a series of arsons committed at a Long Island, N.Y., housing development. One of the teen-agers, Jared McIntyre, said the arsons were committed in solidarity with the ELF movement.

- In January 2001, Frank Ambrose was arrested and charged with timber-spiking, in which spikes are nailed into trees to stop them from being harvested. He is suspected of spiking 150 trees in Indiana state forests, a crime for which ELF took credit.

Prison Industry Goes Global

More than 1,000 illegal immigrants from Afghanistan, Iran, Iraq, Indonesia and other nations are detained in the blistering desert of Australia's Outback. Across the ocean, South African prisoners sleep in newly built cells. Thousands of miles away in Yorkshire, England, 16-year-old violent offenders peer out of small cell windows overlooking the Cheswald River. All have one thing in common: They are watched over by guards of a U.S. company.

Wackenhut Corrections Corp., a Palm Springs, Fla., company, operates 55 prisons, immigration detention centers, juvenile facilities and psychiatric hospitals, with a significant chunk of its business coming from overseas. In the United States, the company operates 36 facilities, including detention centers for the Immigration and Naturalization Service in Queens, N.Y., and Aurora, Colo., and has plans to operate a 1,000-bed prison in Charlotte County, Va., beginning in the fall.

Outside the United States, the company runs 19 facilities, including a maximum-security prison in South Africa and five immigration detention facilities in Australia designed to accommodate the influx of illegal immigrants. In fact, Wackenhut's Australian subsidiary, Australian Correctional Management, operates 10 facilities there under exclusive contracts or licensing agreements with the Department of Immigration and Multicultural and Indigenous Affairs (DIMIA), the Australian immigration agency. The company has exclusive rights to operate three more immigration facilities that are being built as contingencies.

Perhaps most notable of the Wackenhut facilities is the Woomera Immigration and Processing Centre, located in the desert 300 miles from the South Australia capital, Adelaide. It is Australia's largest detention center for illegal immigrants, with 1,200 detainees. (In all, more than 2,700 people from 94 nations are detained in Australia.) The Woomera facility has expanded rapidly since it opened in 1999 as immigrants from oppressive Middle Eastern nations or war-torn countries fled to Australia, most often by boat.

The company has room for growth due to the political stance of Australian Prime Minister John Howard, who was re-elected in November on a strong stand against illegal immigration and support for a policy of indefinite detention for illegal immigrants. Of course, detainees aren't happy with their lot. At Woomera, they reportedly have gone on hunger strikes, some said to sew their mouths shut to protest the government's immigration policies.

Most recently, Wackenhut raised eyebrows when it helped open a new maximum-security prison in South Africa in March. The company entered into a 50-50 partnership with Kensani Corrections Ltd. to build the Kutama-Sinthumule prison under contract from the South African Department of Correctional Services.

The 3,024-bed prison is seen as a risk by some because of the volatile and violent history of South Africa. But analysts say the nation's notoriously high rate of violent crime will ensure the prison will remain full and, therefore, profitable. Furthermore, South Africa is, at least for the time being, stable enough to conduct business.

Meanwhile, the company has moved into other countries through partnerships with international companies and under license agreements or contracts with the national and local governments. In Britain, its joint venture, called Premiere Prison Services, operates seven facilities, including the 524-bed Prison Lowdham Grange, one of the country's largest prisons, located in Nottinghamshire, England.

The company, which began trading on Nasdaq in 1994 and the New York Stock Exchange in 1996, pulled in $562.1 million in 2001, an increase of $27 million over the previous year. Net income also grew from $17 million, or 80 cents per share, in 2000 to $19.4 million, or 92 cents per share.

TIM LEMKE WRITES FOR INSIGHT'S SISTER DAILY, THE WASHINGTON TIMES.

- In November 2000, Justin Samuel was sentenced to two years in prison for releasing minks from a farm in Wisconsin in 1998.
- In June 1997, Douglas Joshua Ellerman pleaded guilty to firebombing a fur breeders' co-op in Sandy, Utah. He was sentenced to seven years in prison. Ellerman said he was a member of ALF.
- In July 1995, Rodney Adam Coronado pleaded guilty to setting fire to an animal-research laboratory at Michigan State University, an attack for which ALF claimed credit. Sentenced to 57 months in prison and ordered to pay restitution of $2 million, he has since been released.

Nevertheless, ELF and ALF claimed 137 direct actions last year in North America, and law enforcement generally has failed to track down the perpetrators of these acts. Police say their job is made harder by the financial support offered these groups by some of the nation's leading foundations. The Turner Foundation contributed $50,000 to the Ruckus Society, which has trained activists from ALF and ELF, before pulling the plug on funding in 1999. "Many of us share their values—we all want to breathe clean air—but there are many ways to go about accomplishing that, and burning down buildings isn't one of them," said foundation President Michael Finley.

Mainstream environmental groups such as the Wilderness Society and Sierra Club have condemned the ecoterrorists' tactics. On the animal-rights front, however, PETA leaders have applauded ALF's actions while insisting that their organization takes no part in them. PETA, which receives grants from the Pond and the Helen Brach foundations, has raised eyebrows by helping pay the legal fees of ALF members. In the case of Coronado, PETA paid more than $45,000 to his legal-defense fund, according to the Center for Consumer Freedom.

What really worries foes of ecoterrorism is the groups' expanding agenda. The latest victims are labs that conduct genetic-engineering research. Last May, the University of Washington Center for Urban Horticulture was burned to the ground because its scientists were attempting to improve the hardiness of urban forests and wetlands. At Michigan State University, a research lab was firebombed after it was found that it was using genetic engineering to grow a sweet potato hardy enough to thrive in the parched soil of famine-stricken Africa. ELF has since taken credit for the December 2000 action.

More recently, ELF has claimed credit for bombing a construction site for a microbial and plant-genomics research center at the University of Minnesota. In its communique, ELF called the lab an attempt "to exploit and control nature to the fullest extent under the guise of progress."

Longtime ecoterror watchers also see a disturbing trend in the level of violence. Both ALF and ELF have their roots in peaceful, nonviolent protest, but later graduated to liberating animals and spiking trees. Arson and vandalism are their latest permutation, but it probably won't be their last, says Arnold, who also is executive vice president of the Center for the Defense of Free Enterprise in Bellevue, Wash.

"ELF and al-Qaeda are fanatics in the same technical sense," Arnold says. "They don't care what their victims think. Al-Qaeda espouses violence, and ELF will get there. It's already there in the United Kingdom."

At the same time, their critics are growing more vocal. Earlier this month, the Competitive Enterprise Institute and Nichols Dezenhall played host to an anti-ecoterrorism conference in Washington aimed at exposing the problem to business leaders and policymakers. Among the panelists was Kelly Stoner, executive director of the Stop Eco-Violence, a 2-month-old Oregon-based group aimed at "turning public apathy into unified outrage." A communications specialist, she says she decided to become involved after the March 2001 bombing of Joe Romania Chevrolet, a Eugene, Ore.-based car dealership. The attack destroyed 35 sport utility vehicles and caused $1 million in damage.

In its communiqué, ELF declared that "gas-guzzling SUVs are at the forefront of this vile imperialist caravan toward self-destruction." But what Stoner saw was the destruction of a family owned business that had contributed to the Eugene economy for 40 years. "They put a real sense of fear in the community," she says. "And there's no telling how far these groups will go."

---

*VALERIE RICHARDSON WRITES FOR **Insight**'S SISTER DAILY, THE WASHINGTON TIMES. LAURA HUDSON CONTRIBUTED TO THIS REPORT.*

Indictment: Smiling face hid hatred

Professor accused of aiding terrorists lived 'a simple life'

By Richard Willing and Deborah Sharp
USA TODAY

TAMPA—U.S. agents listened in as leaders of the terrorist group Palestinian Islamic Jihad discussed a problem during the spring of 1995. That problem, according to court documents, was another PIJ member, Tampa-based computer professor Sammi Amin Al-Arian.

According to allegations in a federal racketeering indictment filed last week, PIJ leaders feared Al-Arian's high public profile was drawing unwanted attention to the group and compromising its mission: to organize suicide bombings to kill Israeli civilians. They said he needed to be "more circumspect," the indictment claims.

It was too late. By then, the American-trained computer engineer had become the Palestinian cause's smiling public face in central Florida, a regular at Middle East studies academic conferences, a source of quotes and quips in accented but Americanized English.

A virulent foe of Israel when before Arabic-speaking groups, Al-Arian appeared soft-spoken, suburban and ordinary to his many American friends.

He has a wife and five handsome kids. He had a good job at the University of South Florida, a resident immigrant's green card and a citizenship application in the works. Al-Arian was the antithesis of the dark image of the Palestinian terrorist.

But the federal government says his loathing of Israel colored al-Arian's violent private side. The 50-count indictment filed Thursday, when he was arrested, charges that Al-Arian was the North American leader of PIJ, a terrorist group that was behind 13 suicide bombings that killed 100 people, including two Americans, from 1992 through 2002.

The indictment says Al-Arian, 45, raided money for the PIJ, made payments to bombers' families, moved the group's money through disguised accounts and recorded wills for at least three bombers.

A bond hearing for Al-Arian that was set for Tuesday has been postponed until March.

The indictment, based on at least 40 wiretaps and raids on Al-Arian's office and home, says he spent a great deal of time fixing problems in a terrorist organization that bordered on the dysfunctional. He refereed factional disputes, struggled to keep costs down, sought alliances with other Palestinian terrorist groups and tried to account for millions of missing dollars, the indictment charges.

"At times, (the indictment) is like *The Sopranos,*," with Al-Arian in the role of the Mob boss, said Walid Phares, a specialist in Middle East terrorist groups at Florida Atlantic University. "It seems as if there were a lot of headaches."

Al-Arian, a Palestinian, was born in Kuwait and raised in a middle-class family in Cairo. He came to the USA in 1978, at 20, and studied at Southern Illinois University and North Carolina State University. By 1986, he had landed a job teaching computer engineering at the University of South Florida, eventually winning tenure.

Al-Arian was active in Palestinian causes from an early date. In 1988 and in 1991, he founded non-profit institutes to sponsor conferences and bring speakers to Tampa and elsewhere.

At a conference in Chicago in 1991, he was videotaped saying Jews were "monkeys and pigs" cursed by God. "Victory to Islam, death to Israel," he said in another speech a year later. "Let us damn America, let us damn Israel, let us damn their allies unto death," he said at another conference about the same time. The statements made in Arabic, weren't publicized until the mid-1990s. By then, Al-Arian had become something of a community activist.

The Rev. Sharon Streater, a member of Tampa's Hillsborough Organization for Progress and Equality, says Al-Arian volunteered on projects such as teaching reading to low-income kids and ridding neighborhoods of prostitution.

"He's very soft-spoken. That's the word I'd use," said Jan Roberts, a community organizer in Tampa who worked with Al-Arian on environmental and human rights causes. "He and his wife always seemed very interested in doing something worthwhile."

Al-Arian and his wife, Nahla, have been married 23 years and have three daughters and two sons. Three are in college or pursuing postgraduate degrees. The family lives in an apartment in a modest, gated complex of three-story buildings near the university. "We live a simple life," said Nahla Al-Arian, 42.

'No way,' wife says of charges

TAMPA—When the father of her five children goes on trial, Nahla Al-Arian will hear him described as the U.S. head of a terrorist group behind scores of Israeli bombings and murders. She won't believe it.

"No way," said Al-Arian, 42. "I know my husband. He would never do anything to hurt people."

Her husband, Sami Al-Arian, 45, is among eight men charged last week with a long-running conspiracy to help fund and support suicide bombers intent on destroying Israel.

His wife was allowed to see him over the weekend, speaking through glass at a jail in Tampa. She took the youngest children: Ali, 12, and Lama, 9. "He told them he was fine," Nahla Al-Arian said. "He wants them to concentrate on their education."

Tuesday, she was at the jail again, joined by some of her husband's supporters, to protest his arrest.

Al-Arian said her husband is being persecuted for his pro-Palestinian beliefs. She said she does not believe he has any ties to terrorist groups.

"Let's pray justice will have its say, and everything will be in the open," she said. "People don't know his sincerity. They think he is some kind of trickster, but it isn't true."

By Deborah Sharp

She says her husband was among the first Muslim leaders to denounce the Sept. 11 attacks. He immediately donated blood and encouraged other community members to do the same. He also organized youngsters at an Islamic school to join a Tampa vigil for Sept. 11 victims.

When his incendiary comments about Jews and Israel became public in 1995, Al-Arian sought to distance himself from them. He said he was not a supporter of PIJ, Hamas or other groups advocating violence against Israel.

Nonetheless, he seemed to find the limelight irresistible. In March 2000, a smiling Al-Arian and his family were photographed with presidential candidate George W. Bush at the Florida Strawberry Festival. Al-Arian told *The Washington Post* that he and his wife later campaigned for Bush among Muslim voters.

In June 2001, Al-Arian was among 160 members of the American Muslim Council who met at the White House with Karl Rove, President Bush's senior adviser. Days later, his son Abdullah, a congressional intern, was ejected from the White House by the Secret Service as a security concern. The agency later termed that a mistake and apologized to the family. Al-Arian's daughter Laila was an intern for USA TODAY's editorial page last summer.

Al-Arian's public image took a hit in September 2001 when he was grilled by Fox News Channel's Bill O'Reilly about past statements regarding Israel and the United States. In the ensuing public furor, Al-Arian was suspended from work with pay.

But even in limbo, his profile remained high. Last November, he spoke to hundreds of anti-war protesters outside Tampa's MacDill Air Force Base.

"To be patriotic is to be able to question, to stand up for the Bill of Rights and the Constitution in times of uncertainty and insecurity," Al-Arian told the crowd.

Privately, the indictment charges, Al-Arian was a critical part of PIJ's leadership.

According to telephone and document intercepts cited, Al-Arian raised funds, encouraged joint bombing operations with the Palestinian terrorist group Hamas and helped pay stipends to the families of dead bombers and PIJ members being held prisoner in the Middle East.

But much of the time, the indictment suggests, Al-Arian had his hands full just keeping the American PIJ branch up and running. Through the 1990s, according to the indictment, he repeatedly stepped in to arrange jobs at the group's Tampa think tanks for visiting radicals, while lobbying group leaders in Damascus, Syria, for back pay for other PIJ members.

In 1997, the Clinton administration declared the PIJ a "foreign terrorist organization." Al-Arian groomed a protégé to take over some of his public functions and was much more careful in what he discussed on the phone, the government says. He used a daughter's e-mail address for some correspondence.

Many of those who know Al-Arian say they have trouble believing the government's charges. Melva Underbakke, who taught with Al-Arian at the University of South Florida, spoke for several longtime Al-Arian friends.

"Just because our federal government is indicting him, it may not necessarily be true," Underbakke says. Al-Arian, "very strongly believes in American values and our system of justice. I only hope he's right."

Intelligence, Terrorism, and Civil Liberties

By Kate Martin

History has repeatedly demonstrated the dangers of allowing governments to secretly collect intelligence on their own people. When government authority extends beyond law enforcement—investigating criminal activity—it has inevitably been followed by abuses. A key lesson learned from the domestic intelligence abuses before the mid-1970s was the necessity for a wall between law enforcement and intelligence in order to protect civil liberties. Careful lines were drawn between law enforcement activities and the previously unchecked secret intelligence agencies to meet the demands of both national security interests and civil liberties.

Terrorist crimes, however, do not fit neatly into the pigeonholes of law enforcement versus intelligence, criminal versus foreign policy matters. Intelligence is an essential tool in combating terrorism and recent events have made only too clear that greater coordination is needed between the intelligence community and the FBI and other law enforcement agencies.

While the terrible attacks of September 11 dramatized the problem of coordination between the CIA and the FBI, the Bush administration's response has been simply to tear down the walls between law enforcement and intelligence activities. This war against terrorism may be the first where intelligence is described as the most important weapon, not in support of battlefield operations in Afghanistan, but inside the United States targeted against Americans.

But what has been missing is any analysis or public discussion of whether the CIA's expanded domestic presence will be an effective counterterrorism measure and if such an expanded role is needed, how to build in safeguards against the recurrence of past abuses.

Distinctions Between Intelligence and Law Enforcement

Secret intelligence agencies, necessary as they are, pose great danger to civil liberties and democracy. By necessity, these agencies must operate in secret, making it difficult to subject them to external oversight. Spying and covert activities overseas by definition violate the laws of the countries in which they occur. The result has been a history of political spying, unlawful disruption and surveillance on the domestic front, and covert actions abroad that for decades, disastrously undermined the building of democratic regimes and the rule of law.

When Congress created the CIA in the 1947 National Security Act (NSA), it drew the lines very sharply between the agency and the FBI in order to protect civil liberties. Thus, it prohibited the CIA from exercising any "police, subpoena, law-enforcement powers, or internal security functions." But by the early 1970s, as documented by the Senate "Church Committee" investigation, both the CIA and the

FBI had embarked on a massive illegal program of political spying and disruption of the civil rights and anti-war movements, to name but a few. In the words of the Church Committee, the intelligence agencies had "adopt[ed] tactics unworthy of a democracy, and occasionally reminiscent of the tactics of totalitarian regimes. We have seen a consistent pattern in which programs initiated with limited goals, such as preventing criminal violence or identifying foreign spies, were expanded to what witnesses have characterized as 'vacuum cleaners,' sweeping in information about lawful activities of American citizens.... Unsavory and vicious tactics have been employed including anonymous attempts to break up marriages, disrupt meetings, ostracize persons from their professions, and provoke target groups into rivalries that might result in deaths. Intelligence agencies have served the political and personal objectives of presidents and other high officials." Overseas, the CIA had acted not only to collect intelligence, but also as the president's secret weapon to carry out covert actions ranging from illegal assassinations to overthrowing democratically elected governments.

The Church Committee found that the CIA had operated with no congressional oversight. Subsequent events show the difficulty of ensuring accountability of secret agencies. Even after enactment of the Intelligence Oversight Act of 1980 requiring the CIA to keep the oversight committees fully and completely informed of its activities, it continued to operate outside the confines of the law. The Reagan White House, for example, used the CIA to end-run legal limits on U.S. support for the Nicaraguan Contras, and CIA officials then lied to Congress about those activities.

One of the key reforms of the 1970s, in addition to the creation of the congressional oversight committees, was the attempt to enforce the original intent of the National Security Act: to create a wall between law enforcement and intelligence agencies and to eject the CIA from domestic activities. That wall has been most visible in the statutory authorities for eavesdropping: Title III governs wiretapping in the investigation of crimes and the 1978 Foreign Intelligence Surveillance Act (FISA) governs wiretapping of agents of a foreign power inside the United States for the purpose of gathering foreign intelligence. The distinction is also mirrored in the Attorney General Guidelines first promulgated by Edward Levi, which in the absence of any statutory charter for FBI investigations, set out the rules for Bureau activities. Those guidelines provide one set of rules for criminal investigations and another for gathering foreign intelligence relating to espionage or international terrorism inside the United States. The rules for gathering foreign intelligence allow the government much wider latitude to gather information about Americans and keep it secret than is allowed under the criminal investigation rules.

Terrorism is both a law enforcement and intelligence matter.

Perhaps the most important protection against domestic abuses by the CIA, however, resides not so much in the Attorney General Guidelines, which have since been weakened, but in the different functions assigned to the CIA and the FBI. The CIA has been confined to gathering foreign intelligence abroad regarding the intentions and capabilities of foreign powers for use by government policymakers. The FBI has been responsible for law enforcement and for counterintelligence activities inside the United States, both counterespionage and the conduct of international terrorism investigations.

This difference in functions has been mirrored in the difference in agency methods. The CIA acts overseas and in secret, those activities are frequently illegal, and it collects information without considering individual privacy, Miranda rights, or evidence admissibility requirements. It is tasked not just with collecting information, but also with covert disruption and prevention. The agency gives the highest priority to protection of its sources and methods. In contrast, the FBI's law enforcement efforts involve the collection of information for use as evidence at trial, and its methods and informants are quite likely to be publicly identified. Perhaps most significantly, and unlike intelligence agencies, law enforcement agencies must always operate within the law.

Terrorism—A Law Enforcement and Intelligence Issue

Terrorism, like espionage and to a lesser extent international narcotics trafficking, is both a law enforcement and intelligence matter. Individuals like Osama bin Laden, while under indictment for the embassy bombings in East Africa, have acted in ways that fit more easily into traditional notions of state rather than individual power. As such, terrorism poses difficult analytical problems concerning the standards for investigation and the protection of intelligence sources and methods consistent with the requirements of due process. Terrorism investigations also stand at the intersection of First and Fourth Amendment concerns. It is crucial to distinguish between those engaged in criminal terrorist activity and those who may share the religious or political beliefs or the ethnic backgrounds of the terrorists, but do not engage in criminal activity.

Since the early 1990s, lawyers from the Department of Justice (DOJ), FBI, and CIA have worked to reconcile protection of intelligence sources and methods with constitutional requirements in criminal prosecutions. The DOJ proudly declared that it had fully respected constitutional requirements in convicting the foreign terrorist Fawaz Yunis, after initially luring him into international waters so that he could be captured for trial in the U.S. The need for reconciling law enforcement requirements and intelligence concerns has increased as Congress has expanded the extraterritorial reach of the U.S. criminal code (without, however, ensuring that con-

stitutional protections accompanied the expansion of U.S. police power).

But instead of carefully considering how to use intelligence while respecting the rule of law, Congress has simply expanded intelligence authorities without enacting safeguards to protect against abuses. In 1994, Congress, in an amendment to FISA, authorized "black bag jobs"—secret searches of Americans' homes and offices—for intelligence purposes, in violation of Fourth Amendment requirements of knock and notice. The 1996 Anti-Terrorism Act allowed the use of secret evidence to deport individuals on the theory that the need to protect intelligence information outweighs an individual's basic due process right to see the evidence against him. Also, in 1996, with virtually no public comment except by the Center for National Security Studies, Congress amended the National Security Act of 1947 to assign the CIA law enforcement responsibilities, for the first time authorizing the CIA to undertake the illegal collection of information overseas for the sole purpose of making a criminal case against a foreigner in a U.S. court. Then in 2000, Congress granted blanket immunity to intelligence officials to violate certain U.S. criminal laws applying to overseas conduct. In none of these cases was there any consideration of the effect that expanding intelligence authorities in these ways would have on promoting the rule of law or respect for human rights.

None of these changes, however, is comparable to the seismic shift in responsibilities between law enforcement and intelligence agencies that has occurred since the September 11 attacks. Most disturbingly, the Bush administration pushed these changes through with no opportunity for careful analysis and public dialogue—the very things needed to find solutions that will be both effective against terrorism and protect constitutional rights.

The Patriot Act

The new anti-terrorism law, the USA Patriot Act (Patriot Act), first expanded the secret surveillance authorities under FISA. Although some changes might have been reasonable to meet recent technological developments, the Patriot Act turned the premise of FISA upside down and eliminated the constitutionally mandated requirement that these extraordinary powers be used only for foreign intelligence purposes, not when the government is seeking to make a criminal case. It then put the director of central intelligence in charge of identifying which Americans to target for these wiretaps and secret searches.

In addition, the Patriot Act requires the Attorney General to turn over to the director of central intelligence all "foreign intelligence information" obtained in any criminal investigation, including grand jury information and wiretap intercepts. The need for law enforcement and intelligence agencies to cooperate and exchange information on terrorism is clear; however, this mandatory sharing is not limited to information related to international terrorism. Instead, the Act requires the DOJ to give the CIA all information relating to any foreigner or to any American's contacts or activities involving any foreign government or organization, without setting any standards or safeguards for using the information. During congressional consideration of the bill, there was no discussion of the existing authority outlined in detailed memoranda by the DOJ's Office of Legal Counsel, which already permitted sharing of grand jury information with the intelligence community in carefully defined circumstances where it is clearly needed. Finally, the Patriot Act simply expanded the definition of terrorism, instead of carefully defining those criminal acts of international terrorism, where the CIA could be usefully involved.

Intelligence Instead of Law Enforcement

Within days of the Patriot Act's enactment, the administration undertook a se-

ries of steps that taken together suggest a deliberate decision to abandon the law enforcement paradigm for government investigations of individuals in the United States and to substitute an intelligence paradigm that seeks to secretly gather all information that might turn out to be useful. There is now reason to worry that the intelligence notion of covert disruption—as distinct from criminal investigation—will again be applied to individuals and groups inside the United States.

The administration has consistently justified its anti-terrorism measures as an intelligence operation designed to prevent further attacks, not to prosecute criminal violations. They have argued that the secret arrests of hundreds of individuals without probable cause and their indefinite detention when charged only with minor immigration violations are an essential piece of a larger intelligence "mosaic." The DOJ has similarly defended its new policy of eavesdropping on the attorney-client communications of detainees as necessary to obtain intelligence information that would not be used in criminal proceedings against the detainee. Additionally, one of the key justifications for the president's extraordinary order authorizing secret military detention and trial of aliens arrested in the United States is the need to protect intelligence sources and methods.

These changes have been made with no public discussion of whether this fundamental shift to an intelligence rather than law enforcement model will in fact be effective in the fight against terrorism. It is not obvious that a dragnet approach to detaining individuals or an intelligence effort to col-

lect all information, relevant or not, will be as effective as a focused law enforcement investigation aimed at identifying, surveilling, and arresting those involved in criminal activity.

We need to be concerned that means and ends have been turned on their head. Intelligence is no longer seen as an important means of protecting liberty and the rule of law, but rather protection of intelligence methods has come to be the justification for limiting liberty and the rule of law. It is crucial that we begin a public discussion about how intelligence can safeguard our lives and liberty without sacrificing our fundamental rights. We must start with the recognition that now that the CIA is involved in the hunt for individuals to be brought to justice, it must plan for the disclosure of its information in court. We must examine whether the need for intelligence outweighs fundamental privacy rights. We have examples in the past, FISA among them, that show that it is possible to reconcile the requirements of secrecy and accountability and civil liberties by taking seriously each of these interests. No less is required if in the long run we expect to be successful in the fight against terrorists who care nothing for either human liberty or individual rights.

Kate Martin is director of the Center for National Security Studies, a nonprofit human rights and civil liberties organization in Washington, D.C., that works to prevent claims of national security from eroding civil liberties or constitutional procedures.

From *Human Rights*, Winter 2002, Vol. 29, No 1, pp. 5-7. © 2002 by ABA Publishing. Reprinted by permission.

UNIT 7
Terrorism and the Media

Unit Selections

Key Points to Consider

- If the media is indeed the "oxygen" of terrorism, should governments attempt to limit media coverage of terrorist incidents? Should the media censor itself? What are the potential benefits and drawbacks of media censorship?

- How has continuing anti-American propaganda shaped public perceptions and undermined U.S. policies in the developing world? What can the United States do to counter the effects of this type of propaganda?

- What factors have contributed to the growth of Islam in urban America? Why are some experts warning of an "Islamic threat in the American underclass"?

- How does the government's public relations campaign, which is designed to garner public support against terrorism, undermine the war against terrorism?

 **Links: www.dushkin.com/online/**
These sites are annotated in the World Wide Web pages.

Institute for Media, Peace and Security
http://www.mediapeace.org

Terrorism, the Media, and the Government: Perspectives, Trends, and Options for Policymakers
http://usinfo.state.gov/topical/pol/terror/crs.htm

The media plays an important role in contemporary international terrorism. Terrorists use the media to transmit their message and to intimidate larger populations. Since the Munich Olympics in 1972, international terrorists have managed to exploit the media to gain access to a global audience. The media provides terrorists with an inexpensive means of publicizing their cause and a forum to attract potential supporters. In this age of increasingly difficult fund-raising, terrorists have become increasingly dependent on accessible media coverage.

As media coverage has become more sophisticated, terrorist organizations have become increasingly conscious of their interactions with the press. Managing public relations, drafting press releases, and arranging interviews have become important functions, often delegated to individuals in the semilegal periphery of the organization.

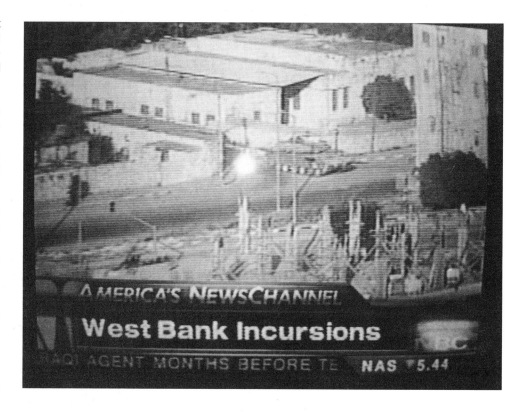

The impact of the increasingly symbiotic relationship between terrorists and media has been two-fold. On the one hand the media has provided terrorists with real-time coverage and immediate 24-hour access to a global public. As long as the explosion is big enough and the devastation horrific enough and there are cameras close by, media coverage of the incident is guaranteed. Holding true to the old axiom "if it bleeds, it leads," the media seems all too willing to provide terrorists with free, unlimited, and at times indiscriminate coverage of their actions.

On the other hand the media also provides terrorists with a means of venting, potentially reducing the number of violent incidents. It subtly influences terrorists to function within certain, albeit extended, boundaries of social norms, as grave violations of these norms could cause unintended or unwanted public backlash and a loss of support. In light of these apparently contradictory tendencies of media coverage as it relates to international terrorism, the debate about media censorship or self-censorship continues.

The four articles in this unit explore the relationship between terrorism and the media. Brigitte Nacos, one of the most well-known experts in the field, provides a well-grounded analysis of the relationship between the media and terrorists who seek to exploit it. While focusing particularly on the potential impact of the Internet, Nacos comes to the broader conclusion that the media will continue to play a crucial role in international terrorism. In the second article "Spin Laden," Philip Taylor argues that we need to better understand the main themes of anti-American propaganda and the perceived image of the United States in the world. "Jihadis in the Hood" focuses on the emergence of an urban counterculture in the United States and the influence that "Islamic hip-hop" music has on inner city youths. Lastly, Jamie Dettmer talks about the potential consequences of the often-criticized symbiotic relationship between terrorists and the press.

Accomplice or Witness?
The Media's Role in Terrorism

"If terrorism is seen as political theater performed for audiences... clearly the mass media plays a crucial role. Without massive news coverage the terrorist act would resemble the proverbial tree falling in the forest."

BRIGITTE L. NACOS

It was the opening day of the World Trade Organization meeting in Seattle, Washington in late 1999. Even before delegates from all over the globe assembled for their first session, violence broke out in the streets near the meeting site. While 40,000 men and women representing various organizations expressed their opposition to WTO policies peacefully, a few dozen masked protesters in fatigues retrieved hammers, M-80 firecrackers, and spray paint from their knapsacks and vandalized brand-name stores such as Starbucks, Nike, FAO Schwarz, and Old Navy. The rampage by self-described "anarchists" and the subsequent "Battle of Seattle" between protesters and police would have amounted to little more than a nuisance without the massive media coverage it received, since only modest property damage and minor injuries were sustained. Indeed, it was not the WTO proceedings inside the convention hall but the violence committed by a small group of people and the overzealous reactions of the security forces that became the major story in the domestic and international media.

Once again the publicity rationale undergirding political violence had worked. Although chiding the "corporate media" for biased reporting, the anarchists (said to share "Unabomber" Ted Kaczynski's antitechnology, anticonsumerism views) recognized the value of nonstop media attention. "The WTO protests are a watershed," they proclaimed on one web site (http://www.chumba.com/_gospel.htm); "after the Battle of Seattle the anarchists will no longer be ignored." Although this may have been an overly optimistic assessment, the violence for political ends had triggered what one might call the calculus of terrorism:

extensive media coverage of an incident that in turn results in public attention, and, most important, reactions by decision-makers (in the wake of the events in Seattle, President Bill Clinton condemned the violence but expressed sympathies for the protesters' environmentalist and labor rights sentiments).

In the latter nineteenth and early twentieth centuries, European and American anarchists resorted to far more lethal acts of violence for reasons quite different from those of their contemporary namesakes. But those who threw bombs into crowded theaters, chambers of deputies, or assassinated prominent political figures also pursued a strategy of "propaganda by deeds" that counted on ample press coverage of their actions and causes. And long before Gutenberg invented the printing press in the fifteenth century, ancient terrorists, such as the Zealots who targeted Roman occupiers in Palestine as well as moderate fellow Jews (66–70 A.D.), and the Assassins, a Shiite sect whose members fought for the purification of Islam (1090–1275 A.D.), preferred to commit their violent acts on holidays and in busy locations to ensure that news of their deeds would spread quickly and widely.

While publicity has been a central goal of most terrorists throughout history, the means of communication have advanced from word-of-mouth accounts by witnesses to news reporting in the print press, radio, newsreel, and eventually television, which has greatly enhanced terrorists' propaganda capabilities. More recently, the World Wide Web has emerged as a new and the perhaps the most potent propaganda vehicle for terrorist groups and "lone wolves" as well as for the advocates of political violence.

PUBLICITY: THE LIFEBLOOD OF TERRORISM?

Terrorism experts, public officials, and even some members of the media have blamed the mass media—especially television—for rewarding terrorist acts with disproportionate coverage that plays into the hands of terrorists. Moreover, since the most gruesome and deadly incidents receive the greatest volume of reporting, media critics have charged that terrorists resort to progressively bloodier violence to satisfy the media's appetite for shocking news. If terrorism is seen as political theater performed for audiences (domestic and international publics, particular groups and individuals, and, of course, political elites), clearly the mass media plays a crucial role. Without massive news coverage the terrorist act would resemble the proverbial tree falling in the forest: if no one learned of an incident, it would be as if it had not occurred. For this reason, media critics have suggested that political violence would radically decline, or even disappear, without the media's eagerness to highlight terrorist acts. Publicity in the form of news coverage is therefore perceived as the lifeblood or, as former British Prime Minister Margaret Thatcher put it, the "oxygen" of terrorism.

Not all experts agree on the centrality of publicity to terrorism. Some cite examples and statistics to establish that terrorists historically have perpetrated violence without claiming responsibility, therefore not advertising their motives. With the World Trade Center bombing in 1993, the Oklahoma City federal building bombing and the sarin gas attacks in the Tokyo subway system in 1995, and the series of major bombings in Saudi Arabia, Tanzania, and Kenya in the late 1990s, this position has gained currency among terrorist scholars. They argue that media coverage and the desire for propaganda cannot be important goals if terrorists do not tell their target audiences who struck and why.

But the idea of a new "terrorism of expression" that does not depend on publicity has weaknesses. Classifying the World Trade Center bombing as a milestone in the short history of so-called faceless or "new" terrorism is inaccurate because those terrorists, in a letter to the March 25, 1993 *New York Times*, did claim responsibility for the bombing and detailed their grievances against the United States.[1]

In other instances, terrorists have left important clues that revealed their grievances and motives. One such case was the Oklahoma City bombing. Obviously trying to avoid arrest, Timothy McVeigh and Terry Nichols did not claim responsibility for the attack. Perhaps they planned to do so at a later date, had they not been arrested so soon after the explosion. Yet by detonating their powerful bomb on the second anniversary of the FBI's ill-fated raid on a group of armed religious extremists, the Branch Davidians, in Waco, Texas, the two ensured that the media would explore the most likely motive—that it was revenge for Waco—and bring it into the public sphere.

McVeigh and Nichols probably never imagined how well the calculus of terror would work for them. As the mass-mediated debate—both in the conventional media and on political talk radio and television programs—linked the bombing of the Murrah Federal Building in Oklahoma City to the fate of the Branch Davidians, public opinion changed radically with respect to the FBI's actions at Waco, which caused the death of more than 80 people. While the vast majority of Americans (73 percent) still approved of the FBI's actions against the Branch Davidians a few days after the blast in Oklahoma City, more Americans (50 percent) criticized than supported (43 percent) the FBI on this issue after several weeks of intensive media reporting. Because of this change in public sentiment, the Oklahoma City bombers achieved that which constant petitions and protests from right-wing circles had not: the United States Congress promptly scheduled and conducted hearings that revisited the Waco case and a similarly controversial incident at Ruby Ridge, Idaho in August 1992 in which the wife and son of Randy Weaver, a right-wing extremist, were killed in a confrontation with FBI agents.

Political violence—especially so-called terrorist spectaculars—always results in widespread news reporting and mass-mediated debates.

Although the linkages among terrorism, media content, effects on public opinion, and decisionmakers are not always as obvious as in the Oklahoma City incident, the calculus of terror has worked well for terrorists and will continue to do so. If nothing else, political violence—especially so-called terrorist spectaculars—always results in widespread news reporting and mass-mediated debates. Even when no "rogue state," group, or lone-wolf extremist such as the Unabomber claims responsibility for violent acts, the fears and anxieties of target societies left in the dark about their attackers can play into the terrorists' design.

Moreover, regardless of whether they claim responsibility, military weak terrorists send forceful messages when they strike powerful countries. In the case of the bombings of the United States embassies in Kenya and Tanzania in 1998, for which no group ever claimed responsibility, the terrorist message again was that even the world's remaining superpower with its vast military and economic superiority is no more than a paper tiger against determined terrorists.[2] And in the case of the 1995 nerve gas attack in the Tokyo subway system, the Aum Shinrikyo sect did not claim responsibility but triggered domestic and international media coverage that sent shockwaves through Japan and the rest of the world, creating a situation that fit well into the cult's end-of-the-world scenarios.

ATTENTION, RECOGNITION, RESPECTABILITY

Most terrorist groups or loners have short- and long-term goals that transcend their publicity objectives. Freeing imprisoned comrades, exacting revenge, or creating fear and confusion are common short-term goals that can be accomplished with a single violent act. The same group or person may also have far a more ambitious long-term goal—regime change or national independence, for example—that will not occur with one bold act of terror. To achieve these ultimate goals, terrorists need the attention of the mass media to manipulate, threaten, intimidate, or co-opt the general public, specific groups and individuals, and government officials. By resorting to more spectacular and brutal acts and thereby heightening the threshold of violence, terrorists and assured of substantial press coverage.

Attention is not the only media-related terrorist goal. Perpetrators of political violence, whether they fight for statehood, a ban on legalized abortions, or animal rights, also want recognition of their grievances, causes, and demands. Finally, many groups strive for respectability and perhaps even a degree of legitimacy in their own society and abroad. If a great deal of political violence is committed to gain attention, recognition, and respectability (and to advance through all of this the perpetrators' short-term and long-term objectives), how are these goals facilitated by the media?

The free press reports, as it should, on terrorism abroad and at home. In the aftermath of major terrorist strikes, the media often provide a vital public service similar to its role in the wake of natural disasters or urban riots. Following the World Trade Center and Oklahoma City bombings, the media—especially local radio, television, and newspapers—were instrumental in helping crisis managers inform the public about emergency phone numbers, traffic restrictions, working schedules, and donations of goods and services. But these exemplary reporting patterns also have another side. Because major terrorist incidents are rich in dramatic, shocking, and tragic human interest aspects, the news media tends to overcover such events. Communication scholar Shanto Iyengar found that between 1981 and 1986 the early evening television news broadcasts of ABC, CBS and NBC carried 2,273 terrorism stories—more than their reports on poverty, crime, unemployment, and racial discrimination combined. Today the traditional news media—television, radio, and print—face stiff competition from the all-news cable channels, such as CNN, MSNBC, and FOX News, and their virtually nonstop coverage of a sensational event. As a result, when terrorists struck in the 1990s, their actions received even more media attention than earlier terrorist violence.

How do terrorists fare in their attempt to win recognition through the media? Early in his career as a mastermind of terrorist acts, George Habash of the Popular Front for the Liberation of Palestine (PFLP) explained the reason for his activities when he said, "We force people to ask what is going on." Yet terrorists also force their target audiences to ask why they are at the receiving end of violence. The media are the most likely sources of this information—often by offering terrorists or their supporters the opportunity to directly communicate their grievances, causes, and objectives. Unwittingly, the mass media thus accommodate terrorists' desire to advertise the reasons behind their violence. As NBC News anchor Tom Brokaw once explained, "I think we have to work harder to put [terrorism] into some kind of political context, however strong or weak that context might be."

Media critics, especially experts on foreign policy and national security matters who have held high government positions and dealt with terrorism, are not persuaded. Former Secretaries of State Henry Kissinger and Alexander Haig and former national security adviser Zbigniew Brzezinski are among those who have repeatedly criticized the media for allowing terrorists to convey their demands and grievances to their target societies—a tendency that often affects and limits government response options.[3]

Finally, it has been suggested that the news media, especially television, enhance terrorists' third publicity goal: to gain respectability. By treating terrorists, their sponsors, and sympathizers as legitimate political actors, the newscasts appear to bestow a degree of respectability on these figures—especially when known terrorists appear with government authorities, ambassadors, and other official personalities. Generally, the news coverage that plays into the respectability objective amounts to about 1 percent of terrorism coverage. But when terrorists and those who speak on their behalf make themselves available to the media during a terrorist situation, more than one-tenth the relevant television coverage tends to fit this category.

COMMUNICATION TECHNOLOGY AND TERRORISM

The proliferation of television and radio channels and, even more important, the vast technological advances in the transmission of news broadcasts, have greatly enhanced terrorists' chances of achieving their media-related goals. Two historical examples illustrate this.

In September 1970, members of the PFLP simultaneously hijacked four New York-bound airliners carrying more than 600 passengers. Eventually, three of the planes were forced to land in a remote region of Jordan, where many of the passengers, mostly Americans and Europeans, were held for about three weeks. While the media in the United States and Europe reported extensively on the hijacking, the reporting paled in comparison to the great attention later hijackings and hostage situations received. The communications technology at the time did not allow instant live transmissions from remote locations. Satellite transmissions were in their early stages and extremely expensive; the live, nonstop reports that have become so common since then were not available. For the PFLP the spectacular hijacking was disappointing. The tense situation did receive media, public, and government attention, but no news organization overcovered the situation and forced President Richard Nixon or European heads of government to act under pressure. More important, the recognition goal was only slightly furthered: the mass public did not gain greater knowledge about the plight of the Palestinians because of the quadruple hijacking episode.

In 1972, during the Olympic Games in Munich, members of Black September, a Palestinian terrorist group, were far more successful in achieving the media-centered goals that had been sought by their PFLP brethren two years earlier. The group killed two Israeli athletes outright and took nine others hostage. As the deadly drama in the Olympic village unfolded, ending with the bloody massacre of the hostages at an airport near Munich during a rescue attempt by German security forces, an estimated 800 million people worldwide witnessed the live nonstop television coverage. In the process many in the global audience learned a considerable amount about Palestinian terrorist groups and their motives for violence. Black September undoubtedly chose Munich at the time of the Olympics because the technology, equipment, and personnel were in place to guarantee a television drama that had never before been witnessed in the global arena.

Nearly two decades later, hand-held cameras and new transmission technologies available to the news media allow terrorists to strike, hold hostages, and establish training camps without sacrificing publicity in the form of television coverage and especially powerful visual images. Yet while they will continue to exploit the traditional media, present and future terrorists are less dependent on the media gatekeepers because of an attractive new medium: the Internet. Web sites, message boards, chat rooms, and e-mail offer new opportunities for terrorists to convey their messages directly to audiences everywhere, including like-minded people and potential new recruits, the traditional media, and the targets of their terrorist deeds and threats.

The possibilities of the Internet were first realized in late 1996, after members of the leftist Túpac Amaru guerrilla group infiltrated and took over the Japanese ambassador's compound in Peru's capital of Lima during a December 17 reception for 600 guests. Terrorism experts knew little or nothing about the small Túpac Amaru Revolutionary Movement, but information on the group was quickly posted on web sites that had been established and updated by members and supporters in North America and Europe, who stayed in touch with the abductors throughout the four-month ordeal (which ended when Peruvian troops stormed the embassy, killing the 14 guerrilla hostage-takers and freeing unharmed 71 of the 72 remaining hostages).

At the beginning of the twenty-first century, most, if not all, organizations perpetrating and advocating terrorism use the Internet in some manner: to communicate with each other, organize actions (often through the use of passwords and encryption to limit access to members and friends), rally supporters and sympathizers, enlist new members, advertise successful actions, honor fallen comrades—especially when they have died during suicide missions—and to convey grievances, threats, and demands to their targets at home and abroad.

According to counterterrorism officials in the United States government, the Saudi expatriate Osama bin Laden and his organization al Qaeda currently represent the greatest terrorist threat to the United States. While bin Laden, who is the FBI's "Most Wanted" fugitive, has repeatedly granted interviews to American and other Western journalists, his views and the full text of his various "fatwas" and declarations are available on many Internet sites. The World Islamic Front Statement of February 23, 1998, which was released on the web by bin Laden and four other leaders, contained the fatwa that proved prophetic less than six months later when more than 300 people were killed and 5,000 injured in the bombing of American embassies in Kenya and Tanzania. That edict—translated into English—remains posted on the Internet (http://www.fas.org/irp/world/para/docs/980223-fatwa.htm).

Domestic groups also use web sites to disseminate and reinforce their agenda, to rally their friends, and to frighten their foes. Even after anti-abortion extremists killed and injured physicians and other workers at abortion clinics, some web sites of militant prolife organizations continued to indoctrinate, if not incite. One site (http://www.operationrescue.org), which displays a running counter of the number of abortions since the *Roe v. Wade* Supreme Court ruling in 1973 and a photo gallery of aborted fetuses, reveals the names of "abortionists" and characterizes First Lady Hillary Rodham Clinton, New York City Major Rudy Giuliani, and others as "baby killers" because of their prochoice positions. The site recently urged supporters to do something against the storefront killing centers on "Main Street," arguing, "If you had a mass murderer/child molester in your community or church, wouldn't you want to know? Join the cry for justice and picket the communities, clubs, churches, and offices of baby killers."

The traditional media may carry excerpts such as this or bin Laden's edicts or describe the positions of these organizations, but web sites provide far more extensive information for the interested public—not only in the wake of a terrorist incident but on a continual basis. The same is true for information that details and condemns violent political deeds and threats.

This leaves a question: If terrorists indeed strike to be heard in the public sphere, will political violence subside or disappear once more people around the globe are connected to the World Wide Web and terrorists can circumvent the traditional media in their quest to communicate messages directly to friends and foes? The answer is that it is not likely in the foreseeable future, even if the Internet community grows more rapidly than predicted. Given the vast number of web sites, an actual act of political violence remains the best bet that the traditional media will report it at great length and in the process whet the public's appetite to obtain more information on the Internet. Just as business-to-consumer and business-to-business Internet companies spend considerable funds to advertise their existence and their services in the traditional media, terrorists, too, need print, radio, and television to draw attention to themselves. After all, without the devastating bombings in Saudi Arabia and East Africa, few people outside the circle of his associates and sympathizers would have had a reason to search the World Wide Web for information on bin Laden; and without the conventional media's generous coverage of the "Battle of Seattle," few people outside the small group of like-minded individuals would be interested in searching the Internet for information on modern-day anarchists in the United States and elsewhere.

Notes

1. The FBI determined that the letter was authentic, and established that it had been written on a typewriter found in the possession of a member of the group that had plotted to bomb the center. The existence of the letter might have escaped some observers and supporters of the expressive terrorism theory because the *Times* delayed publication of the letter until the first suspects had been arrested.

2. Based on several so-called fatwas (religious edicts) that were issued by Saudi-born suspected terrorist Osama bin Laden in the first half of 1998 in which he called on Muslims to kill Americans and their allies—civilian and military—in any country where it is possible to do so. American terrorism experts in the CIA, FBI, and other agencies linked the bombings in Kenya and Tanzania quickly to bin Laden and his organization, al Qaeda (the Base).

3. What amount of news content on terrorist incidents addresses the causes and grievances of terrorists? Studies have found that newspapers in the United States and the United Kingdom typically devote about 10 percent of their terrorism coverage to this particular aspect. I found similar results when analyzing the content of American television news. The point is not that the media are in collusion with terrorists but rather that aggressive reporting in a highly competitive news business facilitates the recognition goal of terrorists who are often as media-savvy as Madison Avenue publicity experts or spin doctors in presidential campaigns.

BRIGITTE L. NACOS is an adjunct associate professor of political science at Columbia University. She is the author of *Terrorism and the Media: From the Iran Hostage Crisis to the Oklahoma City Bombing* (New York: Columbia University Press, 1996) and coauthor, with Lewis J. Edinger, of *From Bonn to Berlin: German Politics in Transition* (New York: Columbia University Press, 1998).

PROPAGANDA WAR AND URBAN MYTHS

'Spin Laden'

In the aftermath of September 11, there was much agonising in the United States as to why the attacks happened, and why the perpetrators appeared to 'hate us so much'. This realisation, in itself, was described in various quarters as a wakeup call for the US and its image in the wider world. Having woken up at last to the need to conduct an information war, and on the principle that it is far better to know your enemy if such a 'war' is to be won, we need to understand the main themes of anti-American propaganda prior to the attacks, not least because they are sufficiently deep-rooted to provide fertile ground today for refutations about America as 'a force for good in the world'.

Philip Taylor

THE PRINCIPAL SOURCE OF ANGER IS, OF COURSE, US support for Israeli 'state-sponsored terrorism' against the Palestinians. Although Bin Laden is a comparatively recent convert to this cause, he fully understands how effectively this resentment can be translated into support for his 'jihad' against the west.

One early manifestation of this occurred in the form of a rumour reported by paknews.com that it was, in fact, the Israeli Secret Service Mossad which was behind the attacks because '4,000 Jews failed to turn up for work at the World Trade Center' on September 11. Another rumour, which went round the world like wildfire on the internet, www.snopes2.com/rumors/cnn.htm, was that the TV footage of celebrating Palestinians on the West Bank was in fact taken during the Gulf War. The Palestinian authorities certainly understood the potentially damaging nature of such imagery—which was in fact recorded the previous day by Reuters news agency—to their cause because similar footage elsewhere in the region was quickly rounded up. Such phenomena appear to flare up like spontaneous combustion, rather than emanate directly from official propaganda sources, they are indicative of deep resentments and have the capacity to become what are often termed urban myths. These are tracked on 'The Rumours of War Page' of www.snopes2.com/rumors/rumors.htm.

Although incidents like these were isolated and relatively minor, the constant repetition of one such celebration on CNN, combined with the rumor about the age of the footage, confirmed suspicions about the station being the 'voice of the US government'. Why some Palestinians would choose to celebrate if four thousand Jews had been absent has yet to be addressed, but Yasser Arafat was quick to be photographed offering blood in support of the World Trade Center and Pentagon victims.

HYPOCRISY AND DUPLICITY

On the Middle Eastern street, CNN is in fact seen to be part of the problem, not the solution. That is because a second main source of grievance about US foreign policy relates to issues of globalisation by which is meant 'American imperialism'. This helps to explain why even Saddam Hussein is regarded as an Arab 'hero'—because he stood up to the west, and survived.

It is not just the presence since the 1991 Gulf War of US troops in the holy Saudi land which also includes Mecca, the growth in the number of McDonalds and accusations of 'coca-colonialism', but it is also the 'cowardly' bombing of Iraq which the western media coverage chose to ignore but which has resulted in the often repeated charge of 'One Million Iraqi children killed'.

A photograph of an American cruise missile bound for Baghdad during Operation Desert Fox with the words

Happy Ramadan chalked on the side is still widely remembered.

The unfortunate initial use of the word crusade by President George Bush and the naming of the 'war' as Operation Infinite Justice—which western leaders have now backtracked from—is seen as further evidence of US hypocrisy, duplicity and selectivity when it comes to dealing with Muslims. Every criminal attack on Muslim citizens or mosques in the US and Europe is reported as further evidence of 'why the US hates Islam'.

How rumours become propaganda would make a fascinating study. Already, patriotic T shirts, 'burn bin Laden' hot sauce, toilet paper and other commercial products are in American shops arising out the desire of individual entrepreneurs to contribute to the war effort—and make some money in the process.

UNCONVINCING

In the Middle East, it is no different and Bin Laden understands this only too well. Every western claim is analysed for the slightest loophole and nowhere is this more apparent than in the deconstruction of so-called western 'evidence' for the involvement of Bin Laden and Al Qaeda. Quite simply, it is found to be unconvincing.

Because many in the west share this view until the complete evidence is released, such democratically expressed doubts are seized upon a further reinforcement for the street level view. Instead, rumours are rife that the United States planned to attack Afghanistan long before September 11 which accordingly provided an 'excuse' or pretext to realise its objectives—and hence the logic of Mossad involvement—and that there have been long-term plans to kill Bin Laden, confirmed now by the CIA brief to assassinate him if possible.

Other stories point to the 'fact' that five of the nineteen named hijackers are still alive, thus discrediting American sources still further. Early on, Mohammed Ata's father was quoted repeatedly as saying that his son was not involved, and American refusal to send any of the hijackers' bodies home is further evidence of 'contempt' for Islamic ways.

It is also pointed out that none of the cell phone messages by doomed passengers to their relatives describe them as Arabs, and that the subsequent discovery of an alleged hijacker's passport in the rubble of the World Trade Center when the black boxes failed to survive, or of Mohammed Ata's suitcase which did not make the first plane, are simply too coincidental to be true: they must be part of a CIA/Mossad 'conspiracy' to discredit Bin laden and justify US actions. Indeed, that is how reports of several 'martyrs' being spotted in Florida strip joints prior to the attacks are also dismissed.

In a sense, it no longer matters whether any of these stories are true or false; it is how western versions of events and news are perceived in many parts of the world. However, all this would seem to be contradicted by a poster that has become popular on the streets of Pakistan that superimposes Bin Laden's photograph over an image of the twin towers being struck. This suggests that some extremists are actually eager to see a connection that others doubt exists at all. In the eyes of the extremists, Bin Laden and the Taliban are not as bad as the west would have them believe.

It is this jumble of apparent contradictions, together with the magnifying—even distorting—lens of television images which western propagandists must now deal. Asking independent western television companies not to run Bin Laden tapes—whether they contain 'coded messages' or not—will not suffice. This merely confirms the 'hypocrisy' of so-called democracies and their claims to value freedom of speech.

PROPAGANDA WEAPON

In a sense, all this highlights one of the fundamental aspects of trying to wage an asymmetrical conflict against a non-state actor. The enemy really only has one weapon with which to fight—propaganda—although to this we should perhaps add terror, surprise and the generation of fear. Starving terrorists of the 'oxygen of publicity'—by taking out Taliban radio stations, by pressurising Muslim governments to moderate their state-controlled media and western media outlets to 'think carefully' about what they show—is only part of strategy needed to wage propaganda war in the information age.

The fact that the western democracies are already on the defensive in this 'war against terror' suggests a failure of their propaganda—but on a much longer timescale dating back well before the twin tower attacks.

PUBLIC DIPLOMACY DOWNGRADED

These resentments have been ignored by the western 'information' services perhaps because since 1999, when the United States Information Agency was absorbed into the State Department, US public diplomacy—for which read counter-propaganda—has been downgraded in significance. Voice of America broadcasts in Arabic were slight compared to the more trusted BBC World Service, which suggests an important role for Britain in the 'perception management' of this information war.

Besides, these public diplomacy programmes have hitherto been directed at elites, rather than at the masses. The hope was that Middle Eastern opinion-makers would pass on the message to their own populations that America was indeed 'a force for good in the world'. Instead all those elites have done is to allow the west to see street-level public opinion in the Muslim world for the first time. That is the real significance of Al Jazeera.

One amusing illustration of cross-cultural miscommunication derived from another poster of Bin Laden which had the character Bert from Sesame Street in the background.

Pakistani protesters had scoured the internet for an image of their hero only to come across a site which transposed the two characters in a 'Bert is Evil' campaign, www.snopes2.com/rumors/bert.htm. As another urban myth circulated, the protesters realised their mistake and airbrushed out the offending, and counter-productive, image.

INFORMATION WAR

But what can be done to counter this propaganda? In early November, it was announced that the Director of Communications in Tony Blair's Downing Street Office, Alistair Campbell, was establishing 'coalition information centres' in Islamabad, London and Washington because of the often repeated assertion that the west was 'losing the propaganda war'. Whether this is in fact the case within Britain and the US is doubtful, as public opinion polls continue to indicate majority support for the military effort. Moderate Islamic opinion remains largely silent. There is some evidence of growing dissent, an inevitable consequence of an air campaign which was bound to cause some 'collateral damage'. Because of the time difference, Al Jazeera images of 'suffering innocent women and children' from the Taliban side—when western journalists are denied, or provided with only limited, access—have been able to frame the daily media agenda in western countries. This has been worrying Campbell and his colleagues.

But urgent attention is really required for the tactical information war at street level Islamic public opinion from the Middle East to Pakistan where western versions of events are simply not believed. Quite simply we need to deploy weapons of mass communication.

We are only just beginning to see some emphasis on US interventions on behalf of Muslim populations in Bosnia, Kosovo and Kuwait, although once again this will only highlight the selective nature of US foreign policy. Hollywood executives have twice visited the White House to discuss themes for incorporation into their movies as part of the wider strategic campaign for 'hearts and minds'. Yet, to be effective, propaganda requires image and reality to go hand in hand, and hence western 'reality' has to prevail not just in the short-term but also over the longer haul.

Philip Taylor is Director of the Institute of Communications Studies, University of Leeds.

Jihadis in the Hood
Race, Urban Islam and the War on Terror

Hisham Aidi

In his classic novel *Mumbo Jumbo*, Ishmael Reed satirizes white America's age-old anxiety about the "infectiousness" of black culture with "Jus Grew," an indefinable, irresistible carrier of "soul" and "blackness" that spreads like a virus contaminating everyone in its wake from New Orleans to New York. Reed suggests that the source of the Jus Grew scourge is a sacred text, which is finally located and destroyed by Abdul Sufi Hamid, "the Brother on the Street." In a turn of events reminiscent of Reed's storyline, commentators are advancing theories warning of a dangerous epidemic spreading through our inner cities today, infecting misguided, disaffected minority youth and turning them into anti-American terrorists. This time, though, the pathogen is Islam, more specifically an insidious mix of radical Islam and black militancy.

Since the capture of John Walker Lindh, the Marin County "black nationalist"-turned-Taliban,[1] and the arrest of would-be terrorist José Padilla, a Brooklyn-born Puerto Rican ex-gang member who encountered Islam while in prison, terrorism experts and columnists have been warning of the "Islamic threat" in the American underclass, and alerting the public that the ghetto and the prison system could very well supply a fifth column to Osama bin Laden and his ilk. Writing in *The Daily News*, black social critic Stanley Crouch reminded us that in 1986, the powerful Chicago street gang al-Rukn—known in the 1970s as the Blackstone Rangers—was arrested en masse for receiving $2.5 million from Libyan strongman Muammar Qaddafi to commit terrorist acts in the US. "We have to realize there is another theater in this unprecedented war, one headquartered in our jails and prisons," Crouch cautioned.

Chuck Colson of the evangelical American Christian Mission, which ministers to inmates around the country, penned a widely circulated article in the *Wall Street Journal* charging that "al-Qaeda training manuals specifically identify America's prisoners as candidates for conversion because they may be 'disenchanted with their country's policies'… As US citizens, they will combine a desire for 'payback' with an ability to blend easily into American culture." Moreover, he wrote, "Saudi money has been funneled into the American Muslim Foundation, which supports prison programs," reiterating that America's "alienated, disenfranchised people are prime targets for radical Islamists who preach a religion of violence, of overcoming oppression by jihad."[2]

Since September 11, more than a few American-born black and Latino jihadis have indeed been discovered behind enemy lines. Before Padilla (Abdallah al-Muhajir), there was Aqil, the troubled Mexican-American youth from San Diego found in an Afghan training camp fraternizing with one of the men accused of killing journalist Daniel Pearl. Aqil, now in custody, is writing a memoir called *My Jihad*. In February, the *New York Times* ran a story about Hiram Torres, a Puerto Rican whose name was found in a bombed-out house in Kabul, on a list of recruits to the Pakistani group Harkat al-Mujahedeen, which has ties to al-Qaeda. Torres, also known as Mohamed Salman, graduated first in his New Jersey high school class and briefly attended Yale, before dropping out and heading to Pakistan in 1998. He has not been heard from since. A June edition of *US News* and *World Report* mentions a group of African-Americans, their whereabouts currently unknown, who studied at a school closely linked to the Kashmiri militia, Lashkar-e Taiba. L'Houssaine Kerchtou, an Algerian government witness, claims to have seen "some black Americans" training at al-Qaeda bases in Sudan and Pakistan.

Earlier this year, the movie *Kandahar* caused an uproar in the American intelligence community because the African-American actor who played a doctor was American fugitive David Belfield. Belfield, who converted to Islam at Howard University in 1970, is wanted for the 1980 murder of Iranian dissident Ali Akbar Tabatabai in Washington. Belfield has lived in Tehran since 1980 and goes by the name of Hassan Tantai.[3] The two most notorious accused terrorists now in US custody are black Europeans, French-Moroccan Zacarias Moussaoui and the English-Jamaican shoe bomber Richard Reid, who were radicalized in the same mosque in the London ghetto of Brixton. Moussaoui's ubiquitous mug shot in orange prison garb, looking like any American inner-city youth with his shaved head and goatee, has intrigued many and unnerved some. "My first thought when I saw his photograph was that I wished he looked more Arabic and less black," wrote Sheryl McCarthy in *Newsday*. "All African-Americans need is for the first guy to be tried on terrorism charges stemming from this tragedy to look like one of our own."

But assessments of an "Islamic threat" in the American ghetto are sensational and ahistorical. As campaigns are introduced to stem the "Islamic tide," there has been little probing of why alienated black and Latino youth might gravitate towards Islamism. There has been no commentary comparable to what British race theorist Paul Gilroy wrote about Richard Reid and the group of Britons held at Guantanamo Bay: "The story of black European involvement in these geopolitical currents is disturbingly connected to the deeper history of immigration and race politics." Reid, in particular, "manifest[s] the uncomfortable truth that British multiculturalism has failed."[4]

For over a century, African-American thinkers—Muslim and non-Muslim—have attempted to harness the black struggle to global Islam, while leaders in the Islamic world have tried to yoke their political causes to African-American liberation. Islamism, in the US context, has come to refer to differing ideologies adopted by Muslim groups to galvanize social movements for "Islamic" political ends—the Nation of Islam's "buy black" campaigns and election boycotts or Harlem's Mosque of Islamic Brotherhood lobbying for benefits and cultural and political rights from the state. Much more rarely, it has included the jihadi strain of Islamism, embraced by foreign-based or foreign-funded Islamist groups (such as al-Rukn) attempting to gain American recruits for armed struggles against "infidel" governments at home and abroad. The rise of Islam and Islamism in American inner cities can be explained as a product of immigration and racial politics, deindustrialization and state withdrawal, and the interwoven cultural forces of black nationalism, Islamism and hip-hop that appeal strongly to disenfanchised black, Latino, Arab and South Asian youth.

Islam in the Trans-Atlantic

The West Indian-born Christian missionary, Edward Blyden, was the first African-American scholar to advocate an alliance between global Islam and pan-Africanism, the system of thought which is considered his intellectual legacy. After studying Arabic in Syria and living in West Africa, Blyden became convinced that Islam was better suited for people of African descent than Christianity, because of what he saw as the lack of racial prejudice, the

doctrine of brotherhood and the value placed on learning in Islam. His seminal tome, *Christianity, Islam and the Negro Race* (1888), laid the groundwork for a pan-Africanism with a strong Islamic cultural and religious undergirding.

Blyden's counterpart in the Arab world was the Sudanese-Egyptian intellectual Duse Muhammad Ali. In 1911, after the First Universal Races Congress held at the University of London, Duse Mohammed launched *The African Times and Orient Review*, a journal championing national liberal struggles and abolitionism "in the four quarters of the earth," and promoting solidarity among "non-whites" around the world. Published in both English and Arabic, the journal was circulated across the Muslim world and African diaspora, running articles by intellectuals from the Middle East to the West Indies (including contributions from Booker T. Washington). Duse would later become mentor to Marcus Garvey when the American black nationalist worked at the *Review* in London in 1913, and would leave his indelible stamp on Garvey's Universal Negro Improvement Association, whose mission "to reclaim the fallen of the race, to administer and assist the needy" would become the social welfare principles animating myriad urban Islamic and African-American movements.[5] In 1926, Duse created the Universal Islamic Society in Detroit, which would influence, if not inspire, Noble Drew Ali's Moorish Science Temple and Fard Muhammad's Temple of Islam, both seen as precursors of the modern-day Nation of Islam (NOI).

Blyden's and Duse's ideas, which underlined universal brotherhood, human rights and "literacy" (i.e., the study of Arabic), had a profound impact on subsequent pan-Africanist and Islamic movements in the US, influencing leaders such as Garvey, Elijah Muhammad and Malcolm X. The latter two inherited an "Arabo-centric" understanding of Islam, viewing the Arabs as God's "chosen people" and Arabic as the language of intellectual jihad—ideas still central to the Nation of Islam today. The NOI's mysterious founder, Fard Muhammad, to whom Elijah Muhammad referred as "God himself," is widely believed to have been an Arab.[6] "Fard was an Arab who loved us so much so as to bring us al-Islam," Minister Louis Farrakhan has said repeatedly. For the past 35 years, Farrakhan's top adviser has been the Palestinian-American Ali Baghdadi, though the two fell out earlier this year when the Minister condemned suicide bombings.[7] In the NOI "typologist" theology, Arabs are seen as a "Sign" of a future people, a people chosen by God to receive the Quran, but who have strayed, and so God has chosen the American Negro, who like the Arab is "despised and rejected" with a "history of ignorance and savagery," to spread Islam in the West.[8]

Malcolm X was probably the most prominent African-American Muslim leader to place the civil rights movement, not just in a pan-Islamic and pan-African context, but within the global struggle for Third World independence. In addition to his historic visit to Mecca, where he would witness "Islamic universalism" and eventually renounce the NOI's race theology, Malcolm X would confer with Egyptian President Gamal Abd al-Nasser and Algerian President Ahmed Ben Bella, leaders of the Arab League and Organization of African Unity, respectively, and consider taking African-American problems to the floor of the UN General Assembly.

When the al-Azhar-educated Warith Deen Muhammad took over the Nation of Islam after the death of his father Elijah in 1975, he renounced his father's race theology and changed his organization's name to the World Community of al-Islam in the West to emphasize the internationalist ties of Muslims over the nationalistic bonds of African-Americans—leading to a split with Minister Farrakhan, who then proceeded to rebuild the NOI in its old image. Arab and Islamic states would persistently woo W. D. Muhammad, apparently eager to gain influence over US foreign policy. "But," lamented one scholar, "he has rejected any lobbying role for himself, along with an unprecedented opportunity to employ the international pressure of Arab states to improve the social conditions of black Americans."[9]

Targeting the Disaffected

Is there any truth to the claim that Muslim states or Islamist groups specifically targeted African-Americans to lobby the US government or to recruit them in wars overseas? *US News and World Report* notes that, just in the 1990s, between 1,000 and 2,000 Americans—of whom "a fair number are African-Americans"—volunteered to fight with Muslim armies in Bosnia, Chechnya, Lebanon and Afghanistan. Many were recruited by radical imams in the US. According to several reports, in the late 1970s the Pakistani imam Sheikh Syed Gilani, now on the run for his alleged role in Daniel Pearl's murder, founded a movement called al-Fuqara (The Poor) with branches in Brooklyn and New Jersey, where he preached to a predominantly African-American constituency. Using his "Soldiers of Allah" video, Gilani recruited fighters for the anti-Soviet jihad in Afghanistan. Likewise, according to the FBI, working out of his "jihad office" in Brooklyn, the blind cleric Sheikh Omar Abd al-Rahman raised millions of dollars for the Afghan resistance and sent 200 volunteers to join the mujahideen.

According to a recent study, Saudi Arabia has historically exerted the strongest influence over the American Muslim community, particularly since the rise of OPEC in 1973.[10] Through the Islamic Society of North America (ISNA), Muslim Student Associations, the Islamic Circle of North America and the Saudi-sponsored World Muslim League, the Saudis have financed summer camps for children, institutes for training imams, speakers' series, the distribution of Islamic literature, mosque-building and proselytizing. In addition, the Saudi embassy, through its control of visas, decides who in the American Muslim community goes on the pilgrimage to Mecca. But there is absolutely no evidence suggesting a connection between this influence and terrorism against the US, as has been alleged by several media outlets.[11]

In the early 1980s, Iran attempted to counter Saudi influence over the American Muslim community and to gain African-American converts to Shiism. On November 17, 1979, Ayatollah Khomeini had ordered the release of 13 African-American hostages, stating that they were "oppressed brothers" who were also victims of American injustice. In 1982, a study commissioned by the Iranian government to appraise the potential for Shiite proselytizing in black America attacked the Nation of Islam and Sunni Muslims for their "insincerity" and argued that Saudi proselytizers were in cahoots with the CIA. The report stated: "Besides being dispirited, the African-American Muslims feel that nobody cares about them. [Everyone] only wants to use them for their own personal reasons as they languish… The majority of African-Americans really want pure Islam. However, until and unless someone is willing, qualified and able to effectively oppose active Saudi oil money…the Islamic movement in America will plod on in a state of abject ineptitude and ineffectiveness."[12] But the Iranian revolution did not have much influence over African-American Muslims, with the notable exception of the aforementioned Belfield.

The majority of African-Americans, and increasingly Latinos, who embrace Islam do not end up wearing military fatigues in the mountains of Central Asia. For most, Islam provides order, meaning and purpose to nihilistic and chaotic lives, but even if most do not gravitate towards radical Islamism, why the attraction to Islam in the first place?

Exiting the West

Many blacks and Latinos in American metropolises live in poverty and feel alienated from the country's liberal political and cultural traditions. Repelled by America's permissive consumerist culture, many search for a faith and culture that provides rules and guidelines for life. Often they are drawn to strands of Christianity that endorse patriarchy, "family values" and abstinence. But many young African-Americans, and increasingly Latinos, reject Christianity, which they see as the faith of a guilty and indifferent establishment. Christian America has failed them, and stripped them of their "ethnic honor." Estranged from the US, and in the case of Latinos, from their parents' homelands, many minority youth search for a sense of community and identity, in a quest that has increasingly led them to the other side of the Atlantic, to the Islamic world. Sunni Islam, the heterodox Nation of Islam and quasi-Muslim movements such as the Five Percenters and Nuwaubians allow for a cultural and spiritual escape from the American social order that often entails a wholesale rejection of Western culture and civilization.

Family breakdown and family values come up often in conversations and sermons at inner-city mosques as explanations for the younger generation's disenchantment with American society and liberalism. The decline of the two-parent household which preoccupies discussion of family values has economic and political roots. In the 1970s and 1980s, the middle classes left for the suburbs, investors relocated and joblessness in urban areas increased rapidly. As one analyst observed, "The labor market conditions which sustained the 'male breadwinner' family have all but vanished." Matrifocal homes arose in its place. The new urban political economy of the 1980s—state withdrawal and capital flight—led to "the creation of a new set of orientations that places less value on marriage and rejects the dominance of men as a standard for a successful husband-wife family."[13] But in the view of many inner-city Muslim leaders, family breakdown and economic dislocation result from racism, Western decadence and immorality—they are the effect of straying from the way of God. Raheem Ocasio, imam of New York's Alianza Islamica, contends: "Latinos in the society at large, due to pressures of modern Western culture are fighting a losing battle to maintain their traditional family structure… Interestingly, the effects of an Islamic lifestyle seem to mitigate the harmful effects of the Western lifestyle and have helped restore and reinforce traditional family values. Latino culture is at its root patriarchal, so Islam's clearly defined roles for men as responsible leaders and providers and women as equally essential and complementary were assimilated. As a result, divorce among Latino Muslim couples is relatively rare."[14]

By embracing Islam, previously invisible, inaudible and disaffected individuals gain a sense of identity and belonging to what they perceive as an organized, militant and glorious civilization that the West takes very seriously. One Chicano ex-convict tried to explain the allure of Islam for Latino inmates, and why Mexican-Americans sympathize with Palestinians: "The old Latin American revolutionaries converted to atheism, but the new faux revolutionary Latino American prisoner can just as easily convert to Islam….There reside in the Latino consciousness at least three historical grudges, three conflicting selves: the Muslim Moor, the Catholic Spanish and the indigenous Indian.… [For the Mexican inmates] the Palestinians had their homeland stolen and were oppressed in much the same way as Mexicans."[15]

"Bringing Allah to Urban Renewal"

In the wretched social and economic conditions of the inner city, and in the face of government apathy, Muslim organizations operating in the ghetto and prisons deliver materially. As in much of the Islamic world, where the state fails to provide basic services and security, Muslim organizations appear, funding community centers, patrolling the streets and organizing people.

As the state withdrew and capital fled from the city in the Reagan-Bush era, social institutions and welfare agencies disappeared, leaving an urban wasteland. Churches have long been the sole institutions in the ghetto, but Islamic institutions have been growing in African-American neighborhoods for the past two decades. In Central Harlem, Brownsville and East New York—areas deprived of job opportunities—dozens of mosques (Sunni, NOI, Five Percenter and Nuwaubian) have arisen, standing cheek by jowl with dozens of churches that try to provide some order and guidance to these neighborhoods. In the ghettoes of Brooklyn and Chicago's Southside and the barrios of East Harlem and East Los Angeles, where aside from a heavy police presence, there is little evidence of government, Muslim groups provide basic services. The Alianza Islamica of New York, headquartered in the South Bronx, offers after-school tutorials, equivalency diploma instruction for high school dropouts, marriage counseling, substance abuse counseling, AIDS awareness campaigns and sensitivity talks on Islam for the NYPD. The Alianza has confronted gangs and drug posses, training young men in martial arts to help clean up the streets of the barrio with little reliance on trigger-happy policemen.

One quasi-Islamic group, the United Nation of Islam, which broke away from Farrakhan's NOI in 1993, has adopted the slogan "Bringing Allah to Urban Renewal" and is resurrecting blighted urban neighborhoods across the country, opening up health clinics, employment centers, restaurants and grocery stores that do not sell red meat, cigarettes or even soda because they're bad for customers' health.[16] The United Nation of Islam does not accept government funds, fearing that federal money would compromise their mission of "Civilization Development." Similarly, the NOI conducts "manhood training" and mentoring programs in inner cities across the country, earning the praise of numerous scholarly reports, which claim that young men who participate in these programs for an extended time show "positive self-conception," improved grades and less involvement in drugs and petty crime.[17]

In addition to delivering basic services, the NOI today tries to provide jobs and housing. The NOI's Los Angeles branch is currently buying up homes for homeless young men (calling them "Houses of Knowledge and Discipline"), building AIDS treatment clinics and starting up a bank specializing in small loans.[18] In 1997, Farrakhan announced a "three-year economic program" aiming to eliminate "unemployment, poor housing and all the other detriments that plague our community."[19] Farrakhan seems to have reverted to the strategies of economic nationalism pursued by Elijah Muhammad. One scholar argues that under Elijah, the NOI was essentially a development organization emphasizing thrift and economic independence among poor black people, with such success that it turned many followers into affluent entrepreneurs. The organization itself evolved into a middle-class establishment, allowing W. D. Muhammad, after his father's death, to shed black nationalist rhetoric and identify with a multiracial *umma*—moves which resonated with his middle-class constituency.[20] In the 1970s, the NOI had owned thousands of acres of farmland, banks, housing complexes, retail and wholesale businesses and a university and was described by C. Eric Lincoln as one of the "most potent economic forces" in black America, but W. D. Muhammad liquidated many of the NOI's assets. When Farrakhan resuscitated the NOI in the 1980s, he revived Elijah's message of black economic empowerment (appealing to many poorer blacks) and began rebuilding the NOI's business empire. According to *Business Week*, in 1995 the NOI owned two thousand acres of farmland in Georgia and Michigan, a produce transport business, a series of restaurants and a media distribution company.

Islam Behind Bars

Over the past 30 years, Islam has become a powerful force in the American prison system. Ever since the Attica prison riots in upstate New York in 1971, when Muslim inmates protected guards from being taken hostage, prison officials have allowed Muslim inmates to practice and proselytize relatively freely. Prior to the rise of Islam, the ideologies with the most currency among minorities in prison were strands of revolutionary Marxism—Maoism and Guevarism—and varieties of black nationalism. According to one report, nowadays one third of the million or more black men in prison are claiming affiliation with the Nation of Islam, Sunni Islam or some quasi-Muslim group, such as the Moorish Science Temple.[21] Mike Tyson, during a stint in prison in the mid-1990s, seems to have combined all three currents, leaving prison as a Muslim convert, Malik Shabbaz, but with Mao and Che Guevara tattoos. "I'm just a dark guy from the den of iniquity," the former heavyweight champion explained to journalists.

The presence of Muslim organizations in prisons has increased in the last decade as the state cut back on prisoner services. In 1988, legislation made drug offenders ineligible for Pell grants; in 1992, this was broadened to include convicts sentenced to death or life-long imprisonment without parole, and in 1994, the law was extended to all remaining state and federal prisoners. In 1994, Congress passed legislation barring inmates from higher education, stating that criminals could not benefit from federal funds, despite overwhelming evidence that prison educational programs not only help maintain order in prison, but prevent recidivism.[22] Legislation also denies welfare payments, veterans' benefits and food stamps to anyone in detention for more than 60 days.

In 1996, the Clinton Administration passed the Work Opportunity and Personal Responsibility Act preventing most ex-convicts from receiving Medicaid, public hous-

ing and Section 8 vouchers. Clinton forbade inmates in 1998 from receiving Social Security benefits, saying that prisoners "collecting Social Security checks" was "fraud and abuse" perpetrated against "working families" who "play by the rules."[23] All these cutbacks affected minorities disproportionately, but African-Americans in particular because of the disproportionately high incarceration rates of African-American men. Disparate treatment by the criminal justice system—which has a devastating effect on the black family, the inner city economy and black political power, since convicts and ex-convicts cannot vote in 39 states—is another powerful factor fueling the resentment of minorities toward the establishment.

In this atmosphere, it is no surprise that Muslim organizations in prisons are gaining popularity. The Nation of Islam provides classes, mentorship programs, study groups and "manhood training" that teaches inmates respect for women, responsible sexual behavior, drug prevention, and life management skills. Mainstream American Muslim organizations also provide myriad services to prisoners. At ISNA's [Islamic Society of North America] First Conference on Islam in American Prisons, Amir Ali of the Institute of Islamic Information and Education described the services and support system that his organization provides to Muslim inmates: regular visits to prisons by evangelists who deliver books and literature, classes in Arabic and Islamic history, correspondence courses in other subjects, 24-hour toll-free phones and collect-calling services for inmates to call families, mentorship programs for new converts and "halfway houses" to help reintegrate Muslim inmates into society after release.

Those who study Islam behind bars cast doubt on the assertions of Colson and Crouch. At ISNA's Third Annual Conference on Islam in American Prisons in July 2002, keynote speaker David Schwartz, who recently retired as religious services administrator for the Federal Bureau of Prisons, strongly rejected the notion that American prisons were a breeding ground for terrorists, and stated that Islam was a positive force in the lives of inmates. Scholar Robert Dannin adds: "Why would a sophisticated international terrorist organization bother with inmates—who are fingerprinted and whose data is in the US criminal justice system?"[24]

Islam and Hip-Hop

> The street life is the only life I know
> I live by the code style it's made PLO
> Iranian thoughts and cover like an Arabian
> Grab a nigga on the spot and put a 9
> to his cranium.
>
> —Method Man, "PLO Style"

"Now that Arabs are the new niggers, will Arab culture become the rage?" asked a columnist for *The Black World Today* some weeks after September 11. Arab culture has not become the rage, but if Rastafarianism and Bob Marley's Third Worldist reggae anthems provided the music and culture of choice for marginalized minority youth two decades ago, in the 1990s "Islamic hip-hop" emerged as the language of disaffected youth throughout the West.

Arabic, Islamic or quasi-Islamic motifs increasingly thread the colorful fabric that is hip-hop, such that for many inner city and suburban youth, rap videos and lyrics provide a regular and intimate exposure to Islam. Many "Old School" fans will recall the video of Eric B and Rakim's "Know the Ledge," which featured images of Khomeini and Muslim congregational prayer, as Rakim flowed: "In control of many, like Ayatollah Khomeini...I'm at war a lot, like Anwar Sadat." Self-proclaimed Muslim rap artists proudly announce their faith and include "Islamic" messages of social justice in their lyrics. Followers of Sunni Islam ("al-Islam" in hip-hop parlance), Q-Tip (Fareed Kamal) and Mos Def are among the most highly acclaimed hip-hop artists, lauded as representatives of hip-hop's school of "Afro-humanism" and positivity. Mos Def, in an interview with Beliefnet, described his mission as a Muslim artist: "It's about speaking out against oppression wherever you can. If that's gonna be in Bosnia or Kosovo or Chechnya or places where Muslims are being persecuted; or if it's gonna be in Sierra Leone or Colombia—you know, if people's basic human rights are being abused and violated, then Islam has an interest in speaking out against it, because we're charged to be the leaders of humanity."[25]

The fluidity and variegated nature of Islam in urban America is seen in the different "Islams" represented in hip-hop, and most poignantly in the friction between Sunni Muslims and Five Percenters. Today most "Islamic" references in hip-hop are to the belief system of the Five Percent Nation, a splinter group of the NOI founded in 1964 by Clarence 13X. The Five Percent Nation (or "The Nation of Gods and Earths") refashioned the teachings of the NOI, rejecting the notion that Fard was Allah and teaching instead that the black man was God and that his proper name is ALLAH (Arm Leg Leg Arm Head). They taught that 85 percent of the masses are ignorant and will never know the truth. Ten percent of the people know the truth but use it to exploit and manipulate the 85 percent; only five percent of humanity know the truth and understand the "true divine nature of the black man who is God or Allah."[26] In Five Percenter theology, Manhattan (particularly Harlem) is known as Mecca, Brooklyn is Medina, Queens is the Desert, the Bronx is Pelan and New Jersey is the New Jerusalem. Five Percenter beliefs have exerted a great influence on hip-hop argot and street slang. The expressions "word is bond," "break it down," "peace," "whassup G" (meaning God, not gangsta) and "represent" all come from Five Percenter ideology.

Orthodox Sunni Muslims see Five Percenters as blasphemous heretics who call themselves "Gods." They accuse Five Percenters of *shirk*, the Arabic word meaning polytheism—the diametrical opposite of the *tawhid* (unitary nature of God) that defined the Prophet Muhammad's revelation. Since Five Percenters often wear skullcaps and women cover their hair, Sunni Muslims will often greet them with *as-salam alaykum* (peace be upon you) to which the Five Percenters respond, "Peace, God." Five Percenters refer to Sunni Muslims as deluded and "soon to be Muslim." In the "ten percent," Five Percenters include the "white devil," as well as orthodox Muslims "who teach that Allah is a spook."

Busta Rhymes, Wu Tang Clan and Mobb Deep are among the most visible Five Percenter rappers. Their lyrics—replete with numerology, cryptic "Islamic" allusions and at times pejorative references to women and whites (as "white devils" or "cave dwellers")—have aroused great interest and controversy. Journalist and former rapper Adisa Banjoko strongly reprimands Five Percenter rappers for their materialism and ignorance: "In hip-hop a lot of us talk about knowledge and the importance of holding on to it, yet under the surface of hip-hop's 'success' runs the thread of ignorance (*jahiliyya*, the Arabic term referring to the pagan age in Arabia before Islam)." Like "the original *jahiliyya* age," hip-hop today is plagued by "*jahili* territorialism and clan affiliation," a "heavy disrespect of women" and a materialism that "borders on *jahili* idol worship."[27] Five Percenter Ibn Dajjal responded angrily to Adisa's criticism: "No amount of *fatwas* or censorship will ever silence the sounds of the NOI and Five Percent *mushrik* (idolater) nations. The group will continue to rise in fame with customers coming from all walks of life: black, white and Bedouin. [F]ar from a masterpiece of style, the book (the Quran) is literally riddled with errors and clumsy style which yield little more than a piece of sacred music.... Maybe there should be a new hip-hop album entitled *Al-Quran Al-Karim Freestyle* by Method Man and Ghostface Killa!"

Though it has nothing to do with the jihadi trend, the language of Islam in the culture of hip-hop does often express anger at government indifference and US foreign policy, and challenge structures of domination. The outspoken rapper Paris, formerly of the NOI, who galled the Establishment with his 1992 single "Bush Killer," has raised eyebrows again with his single "What Would You Do?" (included on his forthcoming LP, "Sonic Jihad") which excoriates the "war on terror" and the USA PATRIOT Act, and implies government involvement in the September 11 attacks. In early 2002, the Brooklyn-based Palestinian-American brothers, the Hammer Bros, "originally from the Holy Land, living in the Belly of the Beast, trying to rise on feet of Yeast," released their pro-*intifada* cut, "Free Palestine," now regularly blared at pro-Palestinian gatherings in New York. One particularly popular and articulate artist is spoken-word poet Suheir Hammad, the Palestinian-American author of *Born Black, Born Palestinian,* on growing up Arab in Sunset Park, Brooklyn. Hammad appeared on HBO's "Def Poetry Jam" some weeks after September 11, and delivered a stirring rendition—to a standing ovation—of her poem, "First Writing

Since," on being an Arab New Yorker with a brother in the US Navy.[28]

"No Real Stake"

Pan-Africanism and pan-Islam were fused together by African-American and Muslim intellectuals over a century ago to fight colonialism, racism and Western domination. Today that resistance strategy has been adopted by tens of thousands of urban youth (judging by NOI rallies in the US and Europe) in the heart of the West. The cultural forces of Islam, black nationalism and hip-hop have converged to create a brazenly political and oppositional counterculture that has a powerful allure. At root, the attraction of African-American, Latino, Arab, South Asian and West Indian youth to Islam, and movements that espouse different brands of political Islam, is evidence of Western states' failure to integrate minority and immigrant communities, and deliver basic life necessities and social welfare benefits—policy failures of which Islamic groups (and right-wing Christian groups) are keenly aware.

Rather than prompt examination of why minority youth, in the ghetto and its appendage institution, the prison, would be attracted to Islam—whether in its apolitical Sunni or Sufi, Five Percenter, overtly political Nation of Islam or jihadi varieties—the cases of Moussaoui, Reid and Padilla have led to arguments about how certain cultures are "unassimilable," hysterical warnings of a "black (or Hispanic) fifth column" and aggressive campaigns to counter Islamic influence in the inner city. Evangelical groups are trying to exclude Islamic institutions from George W. Bush's faith-based development initiative. Jerry Falwell stated that "it is totally inappropriate under any circumstances" to give Federal aid to Muslim groups, because "the Muslim faith teaches hate. Islam should be out the door before they knock. They should not be allowed to dip into the pork barrel."[29] Another Christian effort, Project Joseph, conducts "Muslim awareness seminars" in inner cities across the country, warning that Muslim leaders are exploiting the weakness of black churches, informing African-Americans that conversion to Islam does not imply "recovering their ethnic heritage" and publicly admonishing that "if the conversion rate continues unchanged, Islam could become the dominant religion in black urban areas by the year 2020."[30]

The aspirations of the very poor and disenfranchised in America will continue to overlap with the struggles and hopes of the impoverished masses of the Muslim Third World, who will in turn continue to look towards African-Americans for inspiration and help. Minister Farrakhan's recent "solidarity tour" of Iraq and recent meetings between Al Sharpton and Jesse Jackson and Yasser Arafat show that Muslim causes continue to reverberate in the African-American community. By and large, African-Americans do not seem to share the hostility to Islam which has intensified since September 11. Akbar Muhammad, professor of history at SUNY-Binghamton and son of Elijah Muhammad, wrote in 1985 that because African-Americans have "no real political stake in America, political opposition to the Muslim world is unworthy of serious consideration."[31] These words still hold true for many minorities in post-September 11 America.

Endnotes

1. Many say Lindh was corrupted by reading *The Autobiography of Malcolm X* and his love of hip-hop. See Shelby Steele, "Radical Sheik," *Wall Street Journal*, December 18, 2001. Lindh often posed as black online, going by the names of "Doodoo" and "Prof J." He attacked Zionism, once writing: "Our blackness does not make white people hate us, it is THEIR racism that causes hate… [The N-word] has, for hundreds of years, been a label put on us by Caucasians…and because of the weight it carries with it, I never use it myself." See Clarence Page, "The 'White Negro' Taliban?" *Chicago Tribune*, December 14, 2001.
2. Chuck Colson, "Evangelizing for Evil in Our Prisons," *Wall Street Journal*, June 24, 2002. See also Mark Almond, "Why Terrorists Love Criminals (And Vice Versa): Many a Jihadi Began as a Hood," *Wall Street Journal*, June 19, 2002; Earl Ofari Hutchinson, "Hispanic or African-American Jihad?" *Black World Today*, June 12, 2002; and *Christian Science Monitor*, June 14, 2002.
3. *Guardian*, January 10, 2002.
4. Paul Gilroy, "Dividing into the Tunnel: The Politics of Race Between the Old and New Worlds," *OpenDemocracy*, January 31, 2002. http://www.opendemocracy.net
5. Robert A. Hill, ed. *Marcus Garvey and the Universal Negro Improvement Association Papers*, vol. 3 (Berkeley, CA: University of California Press, 1989), p. 302.
6. Despite Farrakhan's claim to have renounced race theology, *The Final Call* still prints on its back page that "God appeared in the person of W. Fard Muhammad."
7. Ali Baghdadi, "Farrakhan Plans to Meet Sharon," *Media Monitors Network*, April 14, 2002. http://www.mediamonitors.net
8. See Theophus Harold Smith, *Conjuring Culture: Biblical Formations in Black America* (New York: Oxford University Press, 1994).
9. Ernest Allen, Jr. "Minister Louis Farrakhan and the Continuing Evolution of the Nation of Islam," in Amy Alexander, ed. *The Farrakhan Factor* (New York: Grove Press, 1998), p. 73.
10. Robert Dannin, *Black Pilgrimage to Islam* (New York: Oxford University Press, 2002).
11. Gregory Gause, "Be Careful What You Wish For: The Future of US-Saudi Relations," *World Policy Journal* 19/1 (Spring 2002).
12. Muhammad Said, *Questions and Answers About Indigenous US Muslims* (Tehran, 1982). Unpublished manuscript.
13. "In 1993, 27 percent of all children under the age of 18 were living with a single parent. This figure includes 57 percent of all black children, 32 percent of all Hispanic children and 21 percent of all white children." William Julius Wilson, *When Work Disappears: The World of the New Urban Poor* (New York: Alfred A. Knopf, 1996), p. 85. Elsewhere Wilson argues that the sharp increase in black male joblessness since 1970 accounts in large measure for the

rise in the number of single-parent families. Since jobless rates are highest in the inner city, rates of single parent-hood are also highest there.

14. Rahim Ocasio, "Latinos, The Invisible: Islam's Forgotten Multitude," *The Message* (August 1997).
15. *Los Angeles Times*, June 23, 2002.
16. *Christian Science Monitor*, December 1, 1999.
17. Richard Majors and Susan Wiener, *Programs That Serve African-American Youth* (Washington: The Urban Institute, 1995).
18. *Los Angeles Times*, February 13, 2002.
19. *Final Call*, February 11, 1997.
20. Lawrence H. Mamiya, "Minister Louis Farrakhan and the Final Call: Schism in the Muslim Movement," in Earl H. Waugh et al, *The Muslim Community in North America* (Edmonton: University of Alberta Press, 1983).
21. *Newsweek*, October 30, 1995.
22. Josh Page, "Eliminating the Enemy: A Cultural Analysis of the Exclusion of Prisoners from Higher Education" (master's thesis, University of California-Berkeley, 1997).
23. Bill Clinton, radio address, April 25, 1998. Transcript available at http://www.whitehouse.gov.
24. Quoted in Hisham Aidi, "Jihadis in the Cell Block," *Africana.com*, July 22, 2002.
25. Hisham Aidi, "Hip-Hop for the Gods," *Africana.com*, April 31, 2001.
26. Yusuf Nuruddin, "The Five Percenters: A Teenage Nation of Gods and Earths," in Yvonne Haddad et al, *Muslim Communities in North America* (Albany: State University of New York Press, 1994).
27. Adisa Banjoko, "Hip-Hop and the New Age of Ignorance," *FNV Newsletter* (June 2001).
28. The poem appeared in *Middle East Report* 221 (Winter 2001).
29. *Washington Post*, March 8, 2001.
30. *USA Today*, July 19, 2000.
31. Akbar Muhammad, "Interaction between 'Indigenous' and 'Immigrant' Muslims in the United States: Some Positive Trends," *Hijrah* (March/April 1985).

Hisham Aidi, *research fellow at Columbia University's Middle East Institute, works on the university's Islam in New York Project, sponsored by the Ford Foundation. A longer version of this article will appear in Hisham Aidi and Yusuf Nuruddin, eds.,* Islam and Urban Youth Culture.

Supplying Terrorists the 'Oxygen of Publicity'

Jamie Dettmer

Combating terrorism is a desperate undertaking for any democratic government. Fight with merely military might and the struggle can be lost—as the Reagan administration belatedly learned in Central America in the 1980s and the Russians have found in Chechnya.

As every successful antiterrorist expert knows, an essential ingredient in defeating an insurgency or terrorist group must involve mounting an effective, two-pronged, hearts-and-minds strategy that aims, on the one hand, to wean supporters away from the terrorist opponent and, on the other, to maintain the morale and backing of your own people. Repression or overreaction and curtailment of civil liberties risks undermining the hearts-and-minds effort.

The Bush administration did a fine job on the keeping-up-morale front in the immediate aftermath of Sept. 11, steadying jittery Americans and urging them to get back to business. The speedy toppling of the Taliban regime in Afghanistan certainly helped to convince Americans that the Bush administration knew what it was doing and was on the right track.

But in its efforts to ensure the continued support of Americans and to garner backing for proposals such as the establishment of the Department for Homeland Security, the administration risks falling into the trap that other democratic governments fighting terrorism have slipped into to their cost. Bush officials are giving the terrorists what Margaret Thatcher in the 1980s liked to call the "oxygen of publicity."

Thatcher had in mind more the media's role during the troubles in Northern Ireland—troubles which, of course, spilled over to mainland Britain in the form of car-bombings and assassinations. She blamed the media for over-covering the Irish Republican Army (IRA) and other paramilitary groups.

As far as the Iron Lady was concerned, the media and the terrorists became locked in a symbiotic relationship.

The terrorists needed the coverage; reporters and TV producers needed the stories. She had a point. The aim of terrorists is to prompt fear; by closely covering their actions, foiled plots and threats, the media in Britain became a hugely important element in scaring the British public and even in sapping the political will of the British establishment.

But shutting off that oxygen supply can be a tricky thing for a government to pull off. The attempt can lead to a greater enrichment of the terrorist atmosphere, as well as leading to an undermining of the very values a democratic government purports to be defending.

Take the Iron Lady's bid to "suffocate" the IRA by prohibiting British broadcasters from transmitting the voice of paramilitary leaders such as Gerry Adams. The ban, of course, merely prompted the broadcasters to seize on a loophole and guaranteed the Sinn Fein president even more airtime, albeit with a voice-over enunciating his words.

Nowadays, with 24-hour news cycles, cable and satellite TV and editorial standards that allow too much speculation and ill-informed analysis to pass as news, the pernicious side of the media's role in confrontations with terrorists has increased. With its voracious appetite needing to be satisfied, the TV media remain in hyperactive overdrive, giving the impression that the United States is on the brink of turning into a Belfast or a Beirut at the height of their troubles. The public is being scared witless.

But it isn't all the media's fault. In recent weeks, the administration, led by Attorney General John Ashcroft, appears to have done everything it could to ratchet up the scare factor, too. The fanfared disclosure in early June of the May 8 arrest of the feckless terrorist wanna-be Abdullah Al Mujahir, otherwise known as Jose Padilla, is a case in point.

Few experts believe Padilla was anywhere near capable of fulfilling his dirty-bomb mission. Nonetheless, that didn't stop the administration from speaking in apocalyptic terms. The manner of the announcement by a live TV linkup for Ashcroft in Moscow and a star-studded news conference at the Justice Department added massive drama. With the surprising exception of Deputy Defense Secretary Paul Wolfowitz, aides and officials appeared determined to talk up the dirty-bomb threat.

Ashcroft subsequently was criticized for hyping the radioactive menace by the White House (via off-the-record briefings to the press, of course). But the disclosure nonetheless fits into a recent pattern of dramatic statements from senior administration figures that have only added to widespread public alarm.

Vice President Dick Cheney, Defense Secretary Donald Rumsfeld and FBI Director Robert Mueller all have made startling comments of late. All have endorsed the idea that it is inevitable terrorists will get their hands on nuclear weapons. The media, of course, add to the hype.

It is hard not to have sympathy with some Democrats when they argue that the Bush administration seems intent on deflecting attention from the claims of pre-Sept. 11 intelligence lapses and laxity. Others maintain the administration has increased its warnings of future terrorist outrages to help garner support for major measures, such as the establishment of the Department for Homeland Security.

Arguably there is nothing wrong with a massive public-relations effort—the United States needs to prepare to defend itself and to prevent future attacks. But hyping the risks, whatever the motives, remains a dangerous game to play as public fear easily could swing out of control and force the government into more extreme actions at home and abroad. Governments can provide the "oxygen of publicity" for terrorists as well as the media.

JAMIE DETTMER IS A SENIOR EDITOR FOR **INSIGHT**. IN THE 1980S HE COVERED NORTHERN IRELAND FOR THE TIMES OF LONDON.

UNIT 8
Terrorism and Religion

Unit Selections

Key Points to Consider

- What are the characteristics that distinguish doomsday religious movements from other violent groups? Why are they potentially dangerous?

- How should the United States respond to religious terrorism? Can we ultimately win "the hearts and minds of the Middle East"? Defend your answer.

 **Links: www.dushkin.com/online/**
These sites are annotated in the World Wide Web pages.

Coalition for International Justice
http://www.cij.org/index.cfm?fuseaction=homepage

Islam Denounces Terrorism
http://www.islamdenouncesterrorism.com

Over the past decade, the topic of religion has played an increasingly prominent role in discussions of international terrorism. Fears of what some have called the resurgence of fundamentalist Islam have spawned visions of inevitable clashes of civilizations. Even before the events of September 11, the term "religious terrorism" had become a staple in the vocabulary of many U.S. policymakers.

While there is currently no commonly accepted definition of religious terrorism, one should note that in the popular press the term is often used as a euphemism for political violence committed by Muslims. It is naïve to presume that all violence committed by members of a particular religious group is necessarily religious violence. The relationship between religion and political violence is much more complex.

Experts have noted that many of today's religious terrorists were nationalists yesterday and Marxists the day before. Unlike their historical predecessors such as the *Thugs* in India who hunted for sport and killed to sacrifice the blood of their victims to the goddess *Kali*, today's religious terrorists see violence as a means of achieving political, economic, and social objectives. Religion is often seen as a means, rather than an end in itself. In many cases religious ideologies have taken over where other ideologies have failed.

Ideologies are systems of belief that justify behavior. They serve three primary functions: (1) they polarize and mobilize populations toward common objectives, (2) they create a sense of security by providing a system of norms and values, and (3) they provide the basis for the justification and rationalization of human behavior. Ideologies do not necessarily cause violence. They do, however, provide an effective means of polarizing populations and organizing political dissent.

While the emergence of religious ideologies signals an important shift in international terrorism, the role of religion in international terrorism is often exaggerated. Religion is not the cause of contemporary political violence. It does, however, provide an effective means for organizing political dissent. In some parts of the world, political extremists have infiltrated mosques, temples,

and churches and have managed to hijack and pervert the religious doctrine, superimposing their own particular views of the world and encouraging the use of violence.

The first selection, "Doomsday Religious Movements," focuses on millennial groups and the potential threat that they pose to public safety. In the next article, "Understanding the Challenge," Shibley Telhami examines the role of religion in terrorism in his search for effective strategies to address the problem.

Doomsday Religious Movements*

CANADIAN SECURITY
INTELLIGENCE SERVICE

–Report # 2000/03 (December 18, 1999)

This paper uses open sources to examine any topic with the potential to cause threats to public or national security.

Introduction

Often overlooked in the discussion of emerging security intelligence issues is the challenge of contending with religious movements whose defining characteristic is an adherence to non-traditional spiritual belief systems. While only a small fraction of these groups could be considered Doomsday Religious Movements espousing hostile beliefs and having the potential to be violent, the threat they represent is evinced by recent events involving groups such as the American Branch Davidians, as well as Canada's Order of the Solar Temple. Japan's infamous Aum Shinrikyo is a textbook example, where the coupling of apocalyptic beliefs and a charismatic leader fixated on enemies culminated in a nerve-gas attack intended to cause mass casualties in the hope of precipitating a world war and completing its apocalyptic prophecy. By examining the many characteristics of these movements, this paper intends to discuss which types of groups could be prone to violence and which factors indicate a group's move to actualize this violence. The conclusions presented here are solely the result of a review of unclassified information available in the public domain.

Definitions and History

According to relevant literature, "millennialism" is the belief that human suffering will soon be eliminated in an imminent apocalyptic scenario, ensuring that the collective salvation of humanity is accomplished. Millennialism is an enduring pattern in many religious traditions, and it has been reported that 35 percent of Americans believe that the Apocalypse will take place at some point. Cults throughout history have thought that critical dates will bring the fulfillment of their beliefs (e.g. Solar Temple members believe in the supernatural power of solstices and equinoxes). The year 2000 AD as the turning of the

millenium is a central date in the doctrines of many modern cults.

Millennialist beliefs are shared by a variety of groups, but not all foresee a violent turning of the millennium; in fact, many see it as the catalyst for peaceful and harmonious change. Those groups which espouse violence have been called Doomsday Religious Movements in this paper for the purpose of clarity. The approaching year 2000 AD has stimulated millennial anxiety and heightened concern that its unfolding will bring an increase in potential threats by groups that would choose to assert their apocalyptic beliefs through violence.

Characteristics of Doomsday Religious Movements

Although the large number of groups which could be considered a Doomsday Religious Movement presupposes a variety of beliefs, there are some commonalities in both doctrine and action which can be delineated in order to anticipate which groups might pose a physical threat to public safety.

1. *Apocalyptic Beliefs:* Movements often believe in doctrines which are similar to that of mainstream religions, yet the convergence of some of these doctrines expressed through rites helps to shape a violent theological world view characterized by an inherent volatility.

Dualism—The belief that the world is fractured into two opposing camps of Good and Evil, which confers a profound significance on small social and political conflicts as evidence of this great cosmic struggle, and which could precipitate a violent response.

The persecuted chosen—Movements view themselves as prophetic vanguards belonging to a chosen elite but feel persecuted by wicked and tyrannical forces, which push the group to make concrete preparations to defend their sacred status.

Imminence—Because movements believe the apocalypse is unfolding before their very eyes, the "last days" are experienced as psychologically imminent and pressure them to take immediate action to ensure their salvation.

Determinism—Since a group devoutly believes it will be the ultimate winner of the final battle, if it believes a catastrophic scenario is being actualized, the group may feel it has no choice but to try to trigger the apocalypse through violence.

Salvation through conflict / enemy eradication—As salvation depends entirely upon direct participation in the apocalyptic struggle, a group is always on the verge of anticipating confrontation, which justifies action to eliminate evil and eradicate enemies.

2. *Charismatic Leadership:* Millenarian beliefs are associated with volatility when embodied in and disseminated by charismatic leaders who wish to portray themselves as messiahs, identify the millennial destiny of humankind with their own personal evolution and demonize opposition to their personal aggrandizement.

Control over members—Groups monopolize members' daily lives and circumscribe their belief systems within rigid doctrines, insulating them from the influence of broader social constraints. The leader is then well positioned to ask his followers to commit acts they would not normally engage in, albeit violent ones.

Lack of restraint—Leaders believe themselves to be free from religious and social laws, and operate in a social vacuum where there is a relative absence of normal institutionalized restraints to curb their whims. Physical segregation further distances the group from society's mores, where its own social code is established as the basis of all acceptable behaviour. Here authority can be exercised arbitrarily without restraint, a situation that facilitates violence.

Withdrawal and mobilization—While society is often repelled by or hostile to these groups, movements are also often suspicious of others. This tends to lead to their physical, social and psychological withdrawal, intensifying a leader's power and increasing the homogenization and dependency of the followers. When withdrawal is coupled with the group's expectation that it will face hostility and persecution, members often feel they must mobilize for "endtimes" by acquiring weapons and securing defences.

3. *Actions by Authorities:* Violence is often not actualized until the group comes into contact with state authorities, which usually embody all that is evil for the movement and which must be vanquished in order for the apocalyptic scenario to be realized. Action on the part of state agencies will almost always elicit a reaction, which underlines the delicacy with which the situation must be handled.

Lack of comprehension—Authorities often fail to appreciate the leverage they have over doomsday movements, which depend upon them to fulfill their apocalyptic scenarios. Failure to fully comprehend this symbolic role often results in actions that trigger violence.

Unsound negotiation—Should authorities decide to intervene in a crisis situation, negotiators dealing with the movement must understand its belief structure, as ignorance of the minor differences between the beliefs of respective groups can have drastic outcomes.

Hasty action—Hasty actions can directly trigger violence on the part of the group by forcing it to act out its "endtimes" scenario, especially when its grandiose apocalyptic scenario appears discredited under humiliating circumstances.

Spiral of amplification—Sanctions applied by authorities are often interpreted by a movement as hostile to its existence, which reinforces their apocalyptic beliefs and leads to further withdrawal, mobilization and deviant actions, and which in turn elicits heavier sanctions by authorities. This unleashes a spiral of amplification, as each action amplifies each reaction, and the use of violence is facilitated as the group believes that this will ultimately actualize its doomsday scenario.

The presence of these three factors (apocalyptic beliefs, charismatic leadership and actions by authorities), whether inherent to the dynamics of a Doomsday Religious Movement or in response to the actions that it engages in, translates into a predisposition towards violent behaviour.

The Threat to Public Safety

It is difficult to ascertain the potentially violent behaviour and threats to public safety which some movements could represent, since there exists little information about the demographics or attributes of these movements or their members in Canada. This is exacerbated by the ambiguity which surrounds Doomsday Religious Movements: their motives are often not initially comprehensible, their actors not readily identifiable and their methods are difficult to predict. Despite these difficulties, the inherent volatility and unpredictability of some millennialist cults is a cause for concern because any could pose a realistic threat to public safety almost overnight.

1. *Threat to democratic governance:* This threat emerges when movements associate abstract enemies with concrete state entities; when combined with volatile beliefs, this encourages a blatant disregard for the law and overt revolt against the state. The integrity of democratic governance is severely undercut because the methods of these groups end with attacks, subtle or not, on government credibility. A public perception emerges that the government cannot meet its primary raison d'être, namely, the protection of the people.

2. *Weapons Acquisition*

Firearms—In Canada, stricter gun control laws prevent an accumulation of weapons comparable to the US situation, where groups justify the stockpiling of firearms through their interpretation of the US constitutional right to bear arms. However, this does not preclude their acquisition through illegal channels, as demonstrated by the case of the Order of the Solar Temple (see below).

Explosives—The possession of explosives poses an equal, if not greater, threat than do firearms. Given this consideration, it is plausible that a sophisticated bomb-maker could focus on the mass murder of non-group members. Situated in the middle of a continuum of destructive capability, explosives possessed by groups represent mass murder waiting to happen.

Chemical and biological weapons—A still greater threat is the acquisition and use of chemical and biological weapons. It is feared that some doomsday-like groups may have mastered the production of biological agents, while the Aum cult manufactured and deployed chemical weapons. Marking the dawn of a 'New Age,' Aum's vast biological and chemical stockpiles included, respectively, significant amounts of botulinum toxin, one of the most powerful poisons, and hundred of tons of deadly sarin nerve gas ingredients. Although the chances that a group will both acquire and deploy these weapons are slim, the Aum case proves that it is within the range of possible action.

3. Institutional Infiltration

Politics—Bribery has been one costly method of building mainstream political support; the Aum cult allegedly bribed Russian officials in exchange for a series of 'favours'. Another potential threat lies in members who are already involved in the political process; the Solar Temple's roster included the mayor of a Canadian town and a provincial government official. The most direct political linkages concern efforts to exert direct influence over political processes. Both the Aum leader and the head of a Peruvian Doomsday Religious Movement, the Israeli Mission of the New Universal Fact (not associated with the Government of Israel in any way), have campaigned for electoral office.

Business—Businesses owned by groups can both facilitate weapons acquisition and drive membership growth; the Aum cult's multimillion dollar empire financed the purchase of weapons, justified the possession of ingredients for chemical and biological weapons, and provided a legitimate vehicle for widespread recruitment. Also, the position a member occupies in an established enterprise can augment the potential threat; several Solar Temple members were senior employees of a public utility, whose access to sensitive systems could have crippled the provision of a much-needed service.

4. Criminal Activity

Crimes against individuals—Crimes against individuals not affiliated with the state may indirectly enable the above threats. Documented crimes include successful attempts to "silence" opposition from non-and ex-members, while alleged crimes finance weapons acquisition. These acts undermine the state's ability to identify and respond to dangerous groups, where the ultimate costs of such crimes are public safety and, thereby, the legitimacy of government.

Transnational criminal activity—The final category of threats pivots around alleged involvement in transnational crime. The Solar Temple purportedly laundered money and trafficked in arms and illegal drugs, while Aum Shinrikyo allegedly supplied illegal drugs to trans-national organized crime syndicates. If these reports are correct, any possible threats to public safety are magnified.

Identifying the Threat

Doomsday Religious Movements often provide both verbal and tangible early warning signs that are symptomatic of a group's volatility and propensity for violence. The challenge for government and law enforcement is to note those early-warning signs as a group shifts from a 'preoccupation with enemies' to 'enemy eradication', i.e. from belief to action. Such early-warning signs include:

1. *Intensification of illegal activities*—This early-warning sign is most often a noticeable increase in the illegal procurement of weapons, which often attracts the attention of locals, and signals that the group may be making the final preparations for its destiny in the cosmic battle of all time. This occurred at Waco, Texas, before the confrontation with law enforcement agencies unfolded.

2. *Humiliating circumstances*—Should a group be humiliated to the extent that either its leader or apocalyptic scenario appears discredited, for example, if its prophecies fail to actualize by a set date or if group leaders are arrested on minor charges, then it may try to counter this defamation by violently introducing its vision.

3. *Relocation to a rural area*—This indicates both a physical and psychological withdrawal, which usually precipitates the strengthening of group solidarity and increased control over members. A relocation betrays a group's desire to carry out either the defence preparations or violent acts called for by its scripted scenario.

4. *Increasingly violent rhetoric*—This may indicate that the group has reached a level of critical "fervour" and is ready to take the first step towards actualizing its rhetoric and triggering an apocalyptic scenario.

5. *Struggle for leadership*—Owing to the unstable nature of the leadership and the volatility of the group, any situation which threatens the leader's control could result in violence. Examples include the challenging of group beliefs by dissidents and the questioning of the leader's physical health. All of these put the power of the leadership in question, and, by extension, its fundamental apocalyptic vision.

Annex I presents a brief table summarizing the preceding characteristics and serves as a quick reference guide.

A Canadian Example— The Order of the Solar Temple

The Order of the Solar Temple was a group espousing millennialist beliefs which met the preceding criteria of a Doomsday Religious Movement. The Order had members in the US, Quebec, Switzerland and France; in 1994, fifty-four members committed mass suicide. The group was composed of several leaders who were very charismatic and expert public speakers, and who also had aggrandized beliefs about themselves. They believed in an imminent ecological apocalypse, where members were the "chosen ones" to repopulate the earth after its demise, but not before they had been persecuted on the earthly plane by non-believers. Other attributes typical of a Doomsday Religious Movement were the high degree of control exercised over members, the promotion of bigamy within the group, and the physical withdrawal to a rural area. The alleged criminal activities of the Solar Temple (money laundering, drug and arms trafficking) were clear threats to public safety, as was the infiltration of political and business circles by several members.

The Solar Temple mobilized for their coming apocalypse by acquiring weapons and money. This prompted several high-profile investigations and arrests which could have hastened the suicide. This was an early warning sign: a humiliating circumstance running counter to their supposed glorious salvation before the onslaught of the apocalypse. Other events which could have enhanced the feeling of humiliation included: an investigation initiated by the public utility into the Order's infiltration of their company; the near bankruptcy of the Order and the loss of investor capital; then, negative media attention. Finally, other early-warning signs immediately preceded the mass suicide and signalled that their potential for violence could be soon realized: a recent change in leadership; the failing health of one of the leaders; and foreboding, violent statements made by members.

The violence of the incident left 48 people dead in Switzerland and five in Quebec. Had the group believed that its salvation was tied to a direct conflict with the 'enemy' and the leaders opted for 'enemy eradication' rather than escape via mass suicide, the risk to members of the public would have been serious.

Conclusions—Continuing Threats to Canada

The irrationality which underlines the threat posed by Doomsday Religious Movements constitutes a different threat to public safety than that posed by the calculated terrorism traditionally manifested in the last 50 years, usually in support of an identified political cause. One estimation indicates that there are 1,200 active cults throughout the world, and that roughly 400 subscribe to doomsday philosophies which foresee catastrophe on or around the year 2000. While it is not known which cults have the potential for violence, this does not imply that possible threats posed by Doomsday Religious Movements should be ignored, as they can quickly manifest themselves in a variety of forms. Rather, there clearly is a continuing threat potential, given the temporal inaccuracies of the turning of the millennium (various scientific and religious accounts offer competing evidence as to when the new millennium will actually begin) and the tendency for groups to be unpredictable and give early-warning signs of their potential for violence, as well as ambiguities in their structure, dynamics and attributes.

ANNEX I
THE APOCALYPTIC CULT CHECKLIST

Characteristics	Threats	Early Warning Signs
Apocalyptic Beliefs	*Democratic Governance*	
• dualism	*Weapons Acquisition*	
• the persecuted chosen	• firearms	• Intensification of illegal activities
• imminence	• explosives	
• determinism	• chemical/biological weapons	• Humiliating circumstances
• salvation through conflict	*Institutional Infiltration*	• Relocation to a rural area
Charismatic Leadership	• political	• Increasingly violent rhetoric
• control over members	• business	• Struggle for leadership
• lack of restraint	*Criminal Activity*	
• withdrawal	• crimes against individuals	
Actions by Authorities	• transnational crime	
• lack of comprehension		
• unsound negotiation		
• hasty action		
• spiral of amplification		

ANNEX II
REFERENCES AND SUGGESTED READING

Internet Addresses

The Center for Millennial Studies http://www.mille.org/

Cult Awareness and Information Centre http://www.caic.org.au/

AFF http://www.csj.org/

FactNet http://www.factnet.org/

Info-Cult http://www.infocult.org/

Ontario Consultants on Religious Tolerance http://www.religioustolerance.org

Monographs

Bainbridge, William S. (1997). *The Sociology of Religious Movements*. New York: Routledge.

Bromley, David G. & Jeffrey K. Hadden, eds. (1993). *The Handbook of Cults and Sects in America*. Greenwich, CT and London: Association for the Sociology of religion and JAI Press.

Dawson, Lorne L., ed. (1996). *Cults in Context: Readings in the Study of New Religious Movements*. Toronto: Scholar's Press.

Gesy, Lawrence J. (1993). *Destructive Cults and Movements*. Huntington, IN: Our Sunday Visitor, Inc.

Introvigne, Massimo. (1996). *Les Veilleurs de l'Apocalypse: Millénarisme et nouvelles religions au seuil de l'an 2000*. Paris: Claire Vigne.

Kaplan, Jeffrey. (1997). *Radical Religion in America: Millennial Movements from the Far Right to the Children of Noah*. Syracuse, NY: Syracuse University Press.

Lewis, James R. (1998). *The Encyclopedia of Cults, Sects, and New Religions*. Buffalo, NY: Prometheus Books.

Miller, Timothy. (1991). *When Prophets Die: The Postcharismatic Fate of New Religious Movements*. New York: State University of New York Press.

Robbins, Thomas & Susan Palmer, eds. (1997) *Millennium, Messiah, and Mayhem*. New York: Routledge.

Saliba, John A. (1995). *Perspectives on New Religious Movements*. London: Geoffrey Chapman.

Scotland, Nigel. (1995). *Charismatics and the Next Millennium*. Hodder & Stoughton.

Stark, Rodney & William Sims Bainbridge. (1996). *Religion, Deviance, and Social Control*. New York: Routledge.

Storr, Anthony. (1997). *Feet of Clay—Saints, Sinners, and Madmen: A Study of Gurus*. New York: The Free Press.

Strozier, Charles B. (1994). *Apocalypse: On the Psychology of Fundamentalism in America*. Boston: Beacon Press.

Wilson, Bryan & Jamie Cresswell, eds. (1999). *New Religious Movements: Challenge and Response*. London: Routledge.

Understanding the challenge

This article considers the extent to which faith explains the terror the US faced on September 11th, including the use of suicide bombers as an instrument, the extent to which the prevalent anger with the US in the Middle East over policy issues is related to the attacks, why Arab moderate voices have not been louder after the attacks, and what the US can do to reduce both the anger in the region and the chance of anti-US terrorism.

Shibley Telhami

In addressing the challenges posed by the horror that we all faced on September 11th, 2001 and its consequences for the Middle East and US foreign policy, this article will attempt to answer four questions:

- First, what is this terrorism phenomenon, and what is the role of religion in it?
- Second, what is the source of the broader anger at the US in the region?
- Third, where are the moderates in the Middle East today?
- Finally, how can the US win the war on terrorism and help the moderates win against the militants in the region?

THE ROLE OF RELIGION IN TERRORISM

Let us begin by addressing the first question about this horror that the US, and really, the whole international community witnessed, and what we may make of it by asking, who are these people who are willing to commit such horror? And why is it that it has created so much fear not only in the United States, but elsewhere? At one level it is very obvious why. This was a horror on a huge scale: a few individuals with mere knives were able to create so much pain in one day that it shook the international order. The very fact there are people who are capable of it and willing to do it, is itself terrifying.

But I think there was something else frightening, that perhaps is the reason why we tend to look for mysterious answers, and that is that these terrorists seem to come from well-educated families, themselves well-educated, and not only that, they are willing to die, willing to commit suicide in the process, and therefore seem to be insensitive to punishment and reward, therefore irrational by our understanding of rationality, and perhaps even motivated by blind faith that we cannot affect. And so, if there are people we cannot punish and cannot reward, who could be among us, next door, looking like us, and can attack us at any time and create such horror, that is doubly terrifying. Evil

is scary enough, but evil that is also mysterious and irrational is doubly frightening.

I would like to argue, first and foremost, that these perpetrators are evil, but that they are not irrational or mysterious, and that this is not about faith. I know that we have said this, and President George W. Bush has stated that the campaign against terrorism is not a clash of civilizations, but we fall back into looking for religious answers inadvertently, because we just can't figure out why, how, this could happen.

How could people commit suicide in the process of committing horror of this magnitude? Let me first separate analytically, the willingness to commit such acts and the willingness to die. In terms of willingness to commit violence on a large scale for political ends, if you examine the history of violence, political violence, in the world as a whole much as in the Middle East, it has often been carded out by the educated segments in society. The so-called revolutionary movements, whether Marxist, or the Che Guevaras of the world, or the Arab nationalists, or some of the Palestinian secular organizations of the 1950s and 1960s, have often attracted the educated.

That, in a way, is not puzzling because typically the educated segments of society are less accepting of their inferiority in society. Generally, the more educated people are, the less accepting they are of injustice and, more important, the more they understand that they can do something about it. The poor, less educated public may not understand power very well and may be resigned to their fate, but the more educated one is, the more willing one is to seek change, the more understanding one is that one *can* change things.

Now most educated people, fortunately, are moral in the sense that they use their education in a positive way. That's why many intellectual revolutions, positive political movements, are also led by the educated. But the educated have evil among them just as the uneducated have. And those educated evil individuals are more willing to act than the uneducated evil ones.

That is just a fact of life. It is the history of political violence in the world. So it's not a puzzle. It has nothing to do with Islam.

It's not a puzzle historically that the educated would be leaders even in these acts of terror. I mentioned earlier Arab secular movements in the 1950s and 1960s and Palestinian groups such as the Popular Front for the Liberation of Palestine (PFLP), which recently assassinated an Israeli government minister, Rehavam Ze'evi. Those groups, by and large, we should remind ourselves, who were willing to use violence for political ends, were certainly at that time, in the 1950s and 1960s, not driven by Islam at all. They were mostly secular nationalists and, in fact, the PFLP happened to be founded by a Christian physician, George Habash, and it was not unique in its makeup. It attracted a disproportionate percentage of Palestinians to its cause.

In the 1950s and 1960s, the source of violence was seen to be secular nationalism in the region, not Islamic fundamentalism. In fact, there was the opposite perception. There was even a theoretical interpretation in the West that Islam was a passive religion. In fact, unlike what we hear now about the violent nature of Islam, Islam was seen to be the perfect example of Karl Marx's "opiate of the masses," of being an instrument for justifying the status quo. People would refer to the common Arabic phrase *Al-hamdu li-llah*, praise God, as evidence of a Muslim mindset that one accepts one's fate. Fate was the term that we heard in the literature about Islam during that period and clearly that even defined political alliances across the board. That should be a reminder to us all that it is not religion that is at play here. It is not theology. It is something else.

Today, most political militancy in the region—not all, as we were reminded by the PFLP in the Ze'evi case—is carried out by Islamic groups, or groups that are acting in the name of Islam. At the same time, we must remind ourselves that the vast majority of Islamic "fundamentalist" religious groups are not violent. Nonetheless, most violent groups today in the Middle East act in the name of Islam. That is alone an interesting phenomenon.

What explains this? In the Middle East there are political systems that do not allow legitimate political organization for opposition, and there is much despair in the region. There is a felt need for organizing political opposition. This despair is connected to frustration with the political order, the economic order, and foreign policy issues such as the Palestinian question, or the Iraq question. And people cannot affect their lives.

That is why Usama bin Ladin plays to those groups, because what Bin Ladin tries to do is empower people. There is a sense of empowerment. For people who feel they can't make a difference, people who are resigned to their fate, he says: "With a few dozen men and knives, we're able to shake up the world. You can do it." He sends an empowerment message. Certainly that empowerment message scares most people because most people in the region don't want to live in Bin Ladin's world. But it empowers enough people to carry out terror, and we have to recognize that.

When we consider the issue of suicide, we can come up with an even greater link between Islam and this thesis. After all, how could one explain rationally that an individual might be willing to die for the cause? Certainly the justification that is employed is the doctrine of martyrdom, that people are dying

for the promise of the afterlife. And this conception, this notion of martyrdom, seems to be the justification that people use. How could we explain the fact that people are willing to die for a cause, to commit suicide for a cause? And here too, there are a lot of misconceptions.

First, when we look around—if the assumption is that this is a prevalent theological understanding in Islam, that people are mostly looking for the afterlife, not for this life—all we have to do is watch our television screens to see the hundreds of thousands of poor, faithful Afghani civilians who are running away from death to live even if they have to live as refugees. And that should be a reminder of the humanity that transcends religious beliefs. Or, for that matter, look at Bin Ladin's own recruitment tapes. Bin Ladin uses, in his recruitment tapes, pictures of deaths of Muslims elsewhere in order to move his public to act.

It is death that is used to move people to act. Certainly that is not a theological interpretation. It's true that it is used by terrorists for that purpose, but if you look back at the Palestinian groups, the secular Palestinian groups, they were called *fida'iyun*, or fedayeen. Fedayeen are those who sacrificed their lives for the cause. That was the term used, even though they were secular. Whether they were Christian or Muslim, they were called martyrs when they died.

Secondly, we should remember that—in the Middle Eastern context specifically—this phenomenon of martyrdom, this phenomenon of suicide bombings, emerged in Lebanon in the 1980s. And the attackers who used this method were almost entirely Hizballah, and we should remember the common interpretation among some of the Islamic scholars here in the West of that phenomenon: They specifically said this is a function of Shi'i theology, not Sunni theology. There was a great deal of discourse about the Shi'is being the ones who really believe in martyrdom, but not the Sunnis. As it happened, by the end of the 1990s, the Shi'is stopped suicide bombings and the Sunnis started carrying them out. Because *Hamas* is almost entirely Sunni, at least in the Palestinian arena, we are now again linking martyrdom to a broader theological interpretation about Islam.

Third, let us remind ourselves that, although suicide is difficult to explain, not many people are willing to commit it. And those few can be explained by thinking about these groups as cults. There has to be a psychological interpretation, akin to brainwashing, of how these people are persuaded to do it.

From the point of view of the group, suicide is terrifyingly rational, terrifyingly efficient, because if a group is evil and willing to commit mass murder anyway, suicide methods are very effective: because they're very difficult to defend against. But even from the point of view of the losses of the group itself, you lose many fewer people by ordering their individual death than by sending large numbers in guerrilla warfare against superior armies. Guerrilla war would inflict fewer casualties on the enemy, and you would lose more people, so suicide is incredibly efficient, in the thinking of a terrorist group.

So therefore we have to look at this issue a lot more rationally than we have. It is a terrifying method, we should delegitimize it, and certainly Muslims should delegitimize it because it is not a Muslim issue. It is just a horrible method of killing people.

Now let us look at the second question, which is the source of the broader anger at the US in the region.

THE DEMAND SIDE OF TERRORISM

There is no question that Bin Ladin and al-Qa'ida had their own motives for action, and those motives are quite ambitious, pertaining to a broader Islamic state, an intolerant one akin to the Taliban state in Afghanistan, and that they see no room for outsiders or for Israel in their world. That is their vision. But that is not what they argue when they try to sell themselves on tapes. That is not what they argue when they go on television to reach the broader audience. Why? Because they know that vision is at odds with that of the great majority of the people in the region. They can't sell it.

So what do they do? They choose issues over which the public is very angry and that resonate with the public. And there is a lot of anger to be exploited, that is neither the cause of, nor the justification for, the action of the terrorists, but there is a lot of anger there.

And terrorists do exploit anger and despair. They exploit it in very deliberate ways. They exploit it for recruiting members. They exploit it for fundraising. They exploit it for winning a public relations campaign against sitting governments that they want to defeat. And so they clearly use it instrumentally. But why do they use it instrumentally? Because it works. Because there is real anger in the Middle East, there is real despair, and that despair is what I call the demand side of terrorism. That is the despair that is exploited by horrible groups who have different aims from those of the angry publics. You can destroy the supply side of it, but if you keep the demand side of it sitting, other terrorist groups with other ugly aims are going to try to exploit it. And we have to understand that.

And what is the source of this anger in the region that I am talking about? Well, it is certainly not one single issue and certainly not only the Arab-Israeli issue. There is pervasive anger in the region, pervasive despair, and pervasive helplessness. And it is connected to a perception of an economic and political order that is disadvantageous, over which people have no control, and of which the US is seen to be the anchor and, therefore, the target of much of the anger. That is clear. There is economic despair, there is political despair, and there is foreign policy despair. And the US is seen as the anchor of that system.

True as this is, it does not explain the level of anger. One can make similar arguments that there would be anger based on inequality and a sense of American political hegemony in other parts of the Third World, in Latin America, Africa, Asia: but you do not find the same depth of mobilization and anger as you do in the Middle East. The question is why? There is a categorical difference in the magnitude of what we see in the Middle East. Those specific issues that we focus on explain a lot, including the magnitude of the passion. The issues of foreign policy, especially the Arab-Israeli issue, but also the human suffering in Iraq, play into this psychology.

There is a lot of debate about whether the Palestinian issue remains important, or whether this is just an instrument used to incite people. Last summer I conducted a survey in five Arab countries that included Egypt, Saudi Arabia, the United Arab Emirates, Kuwait and Lebanon, and I asked individuals how important the Palestinian issue is to them personally.

In four of these countries, Saudi Arabia, the United Arab Emirates, Lebanon and Kuwait, nearly 60% of the people said that it was the single most important issue to them personally, and in Egypt 79% of the people said it was the single most important issue to them personally.[1] That is astonishing, and it might seem to some to be hypocritical, because how could this be? How could this finding be true in places like Kuwait, where we know there is a lot of resentment toward Palestinians? We know the Kuwaitis do not like Palestinian Authority President Yasir 'Arafat because of his position backing Iraq in the Gulf War. We know they expelled Palestinian workers after the Gulf War. How could this centrality of the Palestinian issue be true in Kuwait? How could this be true in Lebanon?

I think we in the West have misunderstood what this issue means in the region. We think of it in very simplistic terms. This issue is central to the collective consciousness in the region, to the collective Arab and Islamic identity. In the past half century, it has been central to the formation of the collective identity in the same way, I would submit to you, that Israel has become an integral part of contemporary Jewish identity. And thus, when an Arab or a Muslim makes a judgment about the world, subconsciously he or she makes a judgment through the prism of the Palestinian issue. Even if one does not admire Arafat or the Palestinian Authority. It is an instinctive reaction, in the same way that a Jewish person, who does not like Israeli Prime Minister Ariel Sharon in Israel or might even blame him for some of the troubles, will still support Israel if there is a sense of threat to Israel.

There is that instinctive reaction in the Arab world that sees much of the world through this prism. And I do think that we have had a misunderstanding, both about what is happening now and what has happened over the past decade, and it is worth reviewing that misunderstanding. There are people who believe that this attitude is all a product of the media, that this attitude is a function of the "new media" that is broadcasting sensational reports, that is just showing too much blood on television over the past year, especially during the Intifada.

However, my research shows that the "al-Jazeera phenomenon" has nothing to do with this. In Saudi Arabia, for example, those who did not watch the Qatar-based satellite television network al-Jazeera ranked the Palestinian issue higher in their priorities than those who did watch al-Jazeera. And in Egypt, where only about 7% of the people have satellite television, you have the largest share of the public, 79%, saying the Palestinian issue is most important to them.

So it is not the "al-Jazeera phenomenon." In fact, we have to understand that al-Jazeera is a new market-driven phenomenon. They are catering to the market. There is a lot of competition for media in the region. People watch al-Jazeera because of the product it presents, because that's what they want to see. It reflects where they are, rather than makes them what they are. It doesn't explain their identity. It chooses issues that resonate, and that makes it popular.

Why are people dropping other media to watch al-Jazeera, or Middle East Broadcasting (MBC), or other new media? Because these media are providing to the public what it wants. We have a new phenomenon; a market-driven phenomenon. The media, given all the new competition, has to produce what the public wants in order to succeed. In fact, it is no surprise that when you look back only two years, al-Jazeera was the subject of criticism in the Arab world for being too *pro*-Israel, for allowing members of the Knesset to appear on al-Jazeera regularly.

What has changed in the past two years is not al-Jazeera. It is the world. What has changed in the past two years is that there has been a complete transformation of the environment. We had a world in the 1990s that had a seemingly working Israeli-Palestinian peace process. People could point to it, and when a moderate in the Arab world debated an extremist on al-Jazeera or anywhere else, they could not only reject the extremist method, but they could also put forth a positive alternative. They could say look, we have a peace process, peace is around the corner. We're going to have an agreement.

It was a paradigm of peace and prosperity that carried us through the 1990s, and that paradigm collapsed at the end of the decade. Thus the media is a reflection of the public mood. It is not the driver of the public mood. As a consequence of the collapse of the peace process, the moderates have very little to support their position in the battle of ideas, and al-Jazeera is much more reflective of a more militant thread because the militants are on the offensive and the moderates are on the defensive. We will return to this theme later.

A WAR OF IDEAS

Let us move to the question of moderate voices in the Middle East. There is no question in my mind that what we face is not simply an American or global war on terrorism or militancy, but we face a battle for the soul of the Middle East. There is a profound internal battle going on and ultimately, in fact, the outcome of the broader global battle will be a function of what happens in that local battle in the region between moderates and militants.

In my judgment what has transpired in that horror in New York, at the Pentagon and in Pennsylvania is that the vast majority of the moderates—and certainly the elites in the region—were not only horrified by it, but also terrified by the prospect that militants might rule their own world. There is tremendous fear, and there is tremendous apprehension about allowing the militants to take the lead. But we must not forget the other side: there was a huge message of empowerment to those who are inclined to use militant methods because the message was, it works. And those people who want change at almost any price will be mobilized, whether directly by Bin Ladin or as "copycats." That is the fear, that is the horror that we might face because it is too easy, to commit terror, especially if one is willing to die. And we have to remind ourselves of that, that the battle is not just with Bin Ladin and al-Qa'ida. There has to be a battle of ideas.

We in the West, in the United States, cannot wage that war of ideas. For one thing, we would not be trusted. It has to be

waged from within. And the moderates in the region are now on the defensive, for the reasons I described earlier. But in the 1990s, after the Gulf War, they had a vision to offer. It was not a perfect vision, and it had its ups and downs. But it was enough to keep the governing elites in line, trying to put forth an alternate vision to that of the militants. That vision collapsed, leaving the moderates on the defensive.

I have watched many of these media in the past year, not just since September 11th, and I have appeared on much of it. When people discuss issues, the militants ask the moderates: What are you going to do about it? They say, well, we can go back to the peace process. The militants respond: What has that brought you after ten years of promises? What happened to the prosperity that was promised? What happened to the political change that was promised? What happened? And look at the bloodshed that is continuing. And so it is moderates who are on the defensive, and therefore it has become very, very hard to put forth an alternate vision that people are going to buy. We can create one, but we can't lie to the public. We have to have something real to be able to get public trust.

Second, I think that there is a broader phenomenon in the reluctance of moderates to wage their own war of ideas, and that this is not simply absence of courage. I think it is more a phenomenon of this pervasive sense of powerlessness in the region, that reaches into the elite segments. And that pervasive sense of powerlessness is a function, in part, of the historical legacy of self-consciousness of the people in the region, that the entire world order in which they exist has been a creation of imperial powers and continues to be a function of imperial interests.

There is a dominating paradigm that paralyzes thinking, but is also a function of the reality on the ground, that many people have little power to change their own lives in the context of the existing political systems. There is therefore a sense of helplessness and certainly a sense of an inability to wage collective battles. Individual voices are heard, but certainly not collective voices. Ultimately the moderates in the region, those who want a tolerant political system, whatever it is, who want normal lives for their children, who want to be tied to the rest of the world, who are in my judgment a majority, are going to have to find more courage, despite all this weakness.

WHAT THE US CAN DO

What can the US do? We can help, and I want to turn finally to the US role. I do think that US policy right now cannot be oriented at "winning the hearts and minds of the Middle East" in the short term. That is not going to happen. The US has a legacy of decades that is based in part on our policy and in part on impression; it is not going to be able to change the paradigm overnight simply by a charm campaign.

People are not going to trust the message if they don't trust the messenger, especially in the middle of a crisis in which they see that messenger as instrumental. In fact, it might work against us. Moreover, we have seen, for example, high-level Administration officials trying to go on these new Middle Eastern media and say, I'm going to speak to the Arab people directly. Well, the problem is, we have a second handicap here because every single official in the back of their mind is not really speaking to Egyptians, but speaking to Congress, *The Washington Post* and *The New York Times*, because that is the backlash they have to worry about, rather than the backlash in the region. And therefore in the process they reinforce the very paradigm that produces fear in the region. The US cannot do that and succeed.

In my judgment the battle should be waged differently. It should not be seen as a direct battle between the US and the militants. It should be seen as an internal battle within the region between the militants and the moderate elites, and US policy should be oriented toward helping the moderates to win their own battle, empowering them, helping them, assisting them, to win the battle of ideas. The battle of ideas is more important than military battles. And winning that battle entails a number of things that the US can do.

Let me conclude with the two most important issues that I think the US can work on in an effort to convey to the region a sense of mission, a positive vision that we are not only *against* terrorism, but we are also *for* something that the region wants.

The one thing that the terrorists have against them—other than their method—is that they offer no real positive alternative. They only can promise change. And people want change. They are willing to take risks, but they do not have an alternative to provide the public. That is an arena, a vacuum that could be filled by coming up with what we stand for, what people who do not want a world dominated by militants stand for.

And here I think there are two areas where the US can make a difference. One area is the apparent confusion, both here and in the region, about the nature of this campaign against terrorism. We are sending confusing signals. On the one hand we say this is a battle against al-Qa'ida and its allies, and on the other hand we say this is a battle against world terrorism.

Well, those are two separate missions, and we are lumping them together as if they are one and the same. The fears in the region are that this whole campaign is designed to eliminate groups only in the Middle East, to focus on those groups that have to do with Arab and Muslim interests, not the broader international phenomenon. And I think we have to be very clear on our mission.

I think we in the US have two separate missions. The first mission is to defend against and respond to those who attack the United States. That is a right of self-defense of the United States of America. We do not need, if we can show responsibility, any additional international backing or legitimacy. We do not need a coalition for that legally, only instrumentally. In principle, it is an automatic American right to defend itself. And even though many people in the region are critical of the way the response is being conducted, most people understand that what was committed against the US is such a horror that the US certainly has the right to respond.

But the second mission is different because it is not about being attacked. It is about a broader war on terrorism that is much more complicated even in its attainment. We need tre-

mendous international cooperation to succeed, in terms of intelligence, financial cooperation, and more. But more importantly, we cannot singularly define it. We cannot choose which groups we should fight and which we should not. And we should, therefore, send a signal that we will work with international organizations, as we have begun to do with the United Nations, to define what it is that we are against.

The focus should be on anyone targeting civilians deliberately, and that should be a new norm over which we can create a new treaty, through international organizations, that should be universally applicable, in the Middle East and elsewhere. But we should not begin the war by saying, this group now and that group next, because that will play very much into the fears in the region and reinforce them.

Secondly, we must remember the "vision thing." We have to help the moderates rally behind a global vision that would give hope. There is despair in the Middle East. Without hope we are not going to be able to defeat the militants. There are two very important areas where we can do something. One is to create an international forum, that would begin a dialogue about economic change and would signal the commitment of significant resources to help the region develop economically, and with that, politically. We cannot do it overnight, but to begin a process with significant signals of commitment would do a lot to help.

The second is the Arab-Israeli issue. This is a central issue. It is not a sufficient condition for stability in the region. Arab-Israeli peace is not going to be enough. But it is absolutely a necessary condition and unless we have a robust and credible peace process that people can trust, we are not going to buy hope in the short term.

Let me end with the following. I think the biggest campaign, the biggest war in the next months and early years will not be the military campaign, though that will be hard enough. It will be a war of ideas, and it will be much more difficult to wage than the military campaign. And it will require significant resources, much patience, and long deliberation. But we must think again about the sort of danger that we face today, to understand what happened on September 11th as a symptom of the pervasive problem, of a danger that lurks ahead, that is not only a danger to the US, but to the international system and to the Middle East itself. We cannot afford to get it wrong.

NOTE

1. See "Sympathy for Palestinians" by Shibley Telhami, *The Washington Post*, July 25, 2001.

Professor Shibley Telhami is the Sadat Professor of Peace and Development at the University of Maryland. The views expressed by the author do not necessarily reflect the views of the Middle East Institute, which does not take positions on policy issues. This article is based on the keynote address delivered by Professor Telhami at the 55th Annual Conference of the Middle East Institute in October 2001.

UNIT 9
Women and Terrorism

Unit Selections

Key Points to Consider

- What are some major myths concerning the involvement of women in terrorist organizations? Why do women become members of terrorist organizations?

- What motivates young Palestinian women to join organizations such as the al-Aqsa Martyrs Brigade? What impact do role models such as Wafa Idris have on young women?

- What does Robin Morgan mean by "the democratization of fear"? What does she mean by "the democratization of violence"?

 **Links: www.dushkin.com/online/**
These sites are annotated in the World Wide Web pages.

Israel Ministry of Foreign Affairs—The Exploitation of Palestinian Women for Terrorism
http://www.mfa.gov.il/mfa/go.asp?MFAH0Il10

ReliefWeb
http://www.reliefweb.int

Women, Militarism, and Violence
http://www.iwpr.org/pdf/terrorism.pdf

Women are often portrayed as victims rather than perpetrators of political violence. The fact that women played a critical role in the evolution of contemporary international terrorism is too frequently ignored. In the 1970s women like Ulrike Meinhof and Gudrun Ensslin of the German Baader-Meinhof Gang, Mara Cagol of the Red Brigades in Italy, Fusako Shigenobu of the Japanese Red Army, and Leila Khaled of the Palestine Liberation Organization held key leadership roles and significantly influenced the development of modern terrorism.

Today, while often less visible than their male counterparts, women continue to be actively involved in international terrorism. Women like American Lori Berenson, a former anthropology student at MIT, currently in jail in Peru for her involvement with the Tupac Amaru Revolutionary Movement (MRTA), and Wafa Idris, a 28-year-old volunteer medic who became a heroine and role model for a new generation of young Palestinian women after she was the first Palestinian woman to become a suicide bomber, indicate that the involvement of women in international terrorism may again be on the rise.

In the first article in this unit, Rhiannon Talbot tackles existing misconceptions about women involved in international terrorism. In her article she offers an analysis of the roles and motivations of women in terrorist organizations. Talbot argues that, while women involved in terrorism are often subject to existing stereotypes, many have been able to exploit social, economic, and gender biases and have used the perceived "innocence of the female sex" as an effective tool against their opponents. Next, in "Young, Gifted and Ready to Kill," Michael Tierney provides an up-close and personal account of his interview with three Palestinian women who are members of the al-Aqsa Martyrs Brigade and wish to become suicide bombers. Tierney provides a profile of what is believed to be a new generation of suicide bombers.

The final article in this section is "Demon Lover" by Robin Morgan, who recently revised and released her book *Demon Lover: The Roots of Terrorism*. She challenges our perspective of women's involvement in terrorism. She provides psychological and sociological insights into why women choose to support or become involved in violent organizations.

MYTHS IN THE REPRESENTATION OF WOMEN TERRORISTS

RHIANNON TALBOT

... the female murderer has proved herself as easily as deadly as any male and certainly more insidious. Her motives, as a general rule, lack the clearheaded and darkly reasoned purposes of the male. Whim and fancy often rule here. Long-smouldering emotions often burn themselves out only after the victim of the female killer—whether male or female—has been subjected to excruciating agony. Seldom is there the quick, clean stroke of death as with the male.[1]

Such perceptions of women who have murdered appear in both academic and more general media representations of women. The average depiction of women terrorists draws on notions that they are (a) extremist feminists; (b) only bound into terrorism via a relationship with a man; (c) only acting in supporting roles within terrorist organizations; (d) mentally inept; (e) unfeminine in some way; or any combination of the above. The representations of women terrorists within this particular discourse tend to present them as a dichotomy. The identity of a woman terrorist is cut into two mutually exclusive halves; either the "woman" or the "terrorist" is emphasized, but never together. The construction of a "terrorist" is a strongly masculine one, whereas the perception of femininity excludes use of indiscriminate violence. Not surprisingly, when a woman terrorist is represented, her culpability as an empowered female employing traditionally masculine means to achieve her goals very rarely emerges. She is seldom the highly reasoned, non-emotive, political animal that is the picture of her male counterpart; in short, she rarely escapes her sex.

This essay explores the above dichotomy in five parts. First is a contextualization of women's contribution to terrorism globally. Then consideration centers on how criminological explanations inform debates about women terrorists and our understanding of deviant and rebellious women. The main body of the paper offers an analysis of the explanations given for why women become involved in terrorism, including a critique of the separation of the "feminine" from the "terrorist." The fourth section considers the perceptions of women who become involved in terrorism; discussion centers on the role of women as auxiliaries and depictions of terrorists as "unfeminine" women. The concluding section concentrates on female participants' experience with terrorism; it examines what women terrorists do and how they subvert stereotypes to their own advantage, thereby corroborating the existence of the dichotomous representation.

The material herein addresses the scholarly representations that often feed those of popular culture. Academic discourse is regularly presented as a superior form of knowledge. Whenever a terrorist attack or crisis occurs, general media sources frequently turn to academics for guidance in understanding the situation—and its actors. Thus, scholastic constructions of women terrorists can be particularly powerful propaganda tools.

WOMEN WITHIN TERRORIST ORGANIZATIONS

The women who become involved in terrorism around the globe do so for very different reasons; they come from different cultures and have different experiences. Yet in the literature about them one would assume they are a homogeneous group. Historically, women have been very active in the causes they support. From women in Czarist Russia to those who fought for independence in Morocco and Mexico, in almost every rebellion or terrorist campaign women have been present—sometimes in very large numbers. For example, women constituted one-third of the Communist cadre in Korea.[2] Georges-Abeyie has estimated that *20 percent* of all terrorists during the time of his study (1966–1976) were women.[3] The list is extensive and includes, in the US, the Symbionese Liberation Army, Armed Forces of National Liberation, and Weather Underground; in South America, Fuerzas Armed Revolutionaries (Argentina), Montoneros (Argentina), Tupamaros or Movimento de Liberacion (Uruguay); Sandinista, Salvadoran, Zapatista Revolutionary Army (Mexico), Shining Path (Peru); in Europe, the Angry Brigade (UK), Communist

Combatant Cells (Belgium), Direct Action (France), the Provisional Irish Republican Army (UK/Republic of Ireland), the Red Brigades and Prima Linea (Italy), Euzkadita Azkatsuna or ETA (Spain), Movement Two June and the Red Army Faction (Federal Republic of Germany); in the Middle East, HAMAS, Al-Fatah (part of the Palestinian Liberation Organisation), Popular Front for the Liberation of Palestine; in Africa, the Morrocan Liberation Army, the People's Liberation Army of Namibia (SWAPO); in South East Asia, the Liberation Tigers of Tamil Eelam (Sri Lanka), the Communist Party of Nepal, Green Tigers, People's War Group or Naxalites and the United Liberation Front of Assam (India); in the Far East, the Japanese Red Army. This list does not include all of the various number of nationalist struggles around the world, a large number of which have had female input of varying degrees.

Though commentators do on occasion contradict one another, they all agree on one main point: that female involvement in terrorist or revolutionary uprisings can be confirmed throughout history—and women's participation in the modern era is growing. Some maintain that in the past women have predominantly held supportive roles, such as couriers, or assisted in maintenance of safe houses and intelligence gathering. Most assert that even in organizations where females are significant in both their numbers and the contributions they make to the activities and policies of the group, women still wield a much weaker influence than their male colleagues.

Women terrorists do seem to be more attracted to left-wing rather than right-wing groups. In such organizations they are able to gain far more prominence and frequently attain leadership roles.[4] The organizations that follow a Marxist bent employ women as active participants and leaders, even if the societies from which they are drawn do not have strong traditions of female emancipation.[5] Russell and Miller, and Weinberg and Eubank all agree that the women who join terrorist organizations are usually educated, middle class women who are likely to be older than their male comrades when they first come to terrorism.[6] There does, however, seem to be a distinction between social utopia terrorist groups (such as the Red Brigades and Prima Linea) and nationalist revolutionary ones (such as the ETA and the PLO).[7] Women have traditionally been more prominent in the utopian groups than in the nationalists ones; they are likelier to be middle class, educated, and have traditional service sector employment histories before joining than women in nationalist groups.[8]

These distinctions and categorisations, however, are not necessarily reflective of all women terrorists experience. For example, women who join the IRA, like the men, are from predominantly working class backgrounds,[10] they are younger than the usual recruiting age around the world, and they often continue to participate after they have had children. Women play a prominent part in all levels of the organization, more so than for the other nationalist revolutionary groups.[11] The IRA in par-

ticular is keen to be seen to encourage this participation.[12] Moreover, although until 1989 there was only one woman who was represented in the leadership of ETA, Elena Beloki, since September 2000 Spanish Intelligence sources believe that ETA has been headed by María Soledad Iparragirre Genetxea.[13] She is not the only woman commander of a terrorist organisation. Comandante Ramona who is a Tzotzil Indian woman runs the Zapatista Revolutionary Army. Ramona has been largely overlooked in the world media by the balaclava clad and pipe smoking Sub-comandante Marcos.[14] However, the experience of Irish women terrorists is not necessarily typical.

Perhaps the most important distinction that can be made between women terrorists is a political difference between the groups for which they fight. Whereas many of the groups to which they are attracted share Marxist or at least socialist ideology, the political goal of the group often determines the shape of women's involvement. In the socialist utopian groups, feminism is high on the agenda as is the emancipation of all subdued groups within society. In situations where there is a contest over the sovereignty of a group—from colonial independence struggles to ethnic disputes and irredentism—women are often drafted into the conflict, but frequently only as "handmaidens" to help achieve a goal that ignores their own particular social problems.[15] The prolonged nationalist struggles, however, such as those in Ireland, Spain, and the Middle East, have evolved over time, often acquiring a more openly socialist and feminist perspective in order to attract the support of both halves of the society that they claim to represent, and to develop their political legitimacy in the eyes of the world.[16] This social emancipation is only a subsidiary element and is subservient to the needs for national regeneration.

CRIMINOLOGICAL REPRESENTATIONS OF DEVIANT AND REBELLIOUS WOMEN

When any attempt is made to represent or comprehend women who terrorize, it is only reasonable to assume the characterizations might be informed by orthodox criminological views about female criminals. Unfortunately for women terrorists, the majority of criminological works that consider women as a separate category are still steeped in stereotypes and gender roles. In her groundbreaking 1987 work, *Female Crime: The Construction of Women in Criminology*, Ngaire Naffine wrote that

> Criminologists continue to assume that crime for females is a form of expression of gender role. It is associated with legitimate female endeavours to find a mate or sustain a relationship with a man; violent or aggressive crime is avoided because it is inconsistent with the feminine ideal.(62)

Even as recently as 1996 Heindensohn complained about traditional criminology. She argued that its construction of women criminals was dominated by their domestic and sexual roles, that women are commanded "by biological imperatives; they are emotional and irrational."[17] These ideas can be important because, despite their obvious sexist bias, they still reflect underlying assumptions that are brought to bear on women who commit any sort of crime, including terrorism.

These mainstream perceptions of women criminals contour the perceptions of women terrorists through archaic gender roles and construct their behavior with a feminine ideal in mind. As Heidensohn has noted,[18] when women deviate from their designated social role into criminal behavior, they are compared not only against their feminine role but against men as well. The contention is that women terrorists fail to uphold the feminine list of attributes and are thus damned, but they are also compared against male attributes and, if they are seen to possess any (aggression, violence, self-assertion, etc.), then they are similarly condemned. The consequence of this double comparison of women terrorists is a splicing of identity, whereby emphasis is laid either wholly on the feminine or the masculine. If the feminine is the focus, her complicity is minimized through a patronizing assumption of lack of intelligence or a naïveté about her actions. If the masculine is maximized, the result is a diminution of the connection between feminine and terror. Either way, the notion of a woman *as* a terrorist is discarded; she is either a woman *or* a terrorist.

EXPLANATIONS FOR WHY WOMEN BECOME INVOLVED IN TERRORISM

Very rarely are the actions of women terrorists perceived to be coldly reasoned decisions by an intelligent individual with radical views, as male terrorists are increasingly perceived. Georges-Abeyie is one of the few scholars who have attempted to develop a theoretical explanation for women's involvement in terrorism. His article is widely referred to,[19] and the list that he has compiled of the most common explanations contains a range of reasons for women's involvement. The inventory is worth quoting in full, for many of the assertions in it can be observed in the representations of women terrorists elsewhere:

> 1) revolutionary and terrorist activity offers excitement; 2) danger is both an attraction as well as a repellent; 3) terrorist violence is tied to causes which initially may appear legitimate; 4) terrorist organisations provide an opportunity for upward mobility, in leadership and in an active role in formulating the groups' policies, opportunities that are absent or extremely limited in the white male-dominated world of legitimate activity; 5) terrorist organisations offer change and a renunciation of

the current male-dominated chauvinistic mores; 6) the traditional... stereotype of women as weak, supportive, submissive, silent, and of lower intelligence and drive is absent in the philosophies of many terrorist organisations; 7) membership in a terrorist organisation is the natural outgrowth of membership in extreme feminist organisations; 8) women are by nature more violent and dangerous than men, and terrorist organisations provide an outlet for this tendency; 9) women are rejecting stereotypical roles and thus adopting traditional male roles that include revolutionary and terrorist violence; 10) hormonal disturbances, caused by excessive sexual freedom and particularly by having sexual relations before maturity, affect these women; 11) economic, political, and familial liberation due to the trend toward greater justice and equality for women plays a role; 12) a continuation of natural selections, or the survival of the fittest, has an influence;...[20]

The above passage reflects some of the more traditional and conventional notions about women who terrorize. Its assertions are frequently reflected in explanations of why women terrorize.

The most often quoted explanation for the apparent rise in female involvement in terrorism is "feminism." A significant proportion of writers have accorded this reason due space in their annals of discovery about the motivations of women terrorists. Any argument based on this premise relies on the notion that women have only recently become involved in terrorism and similar politically motivated violence.[21] There are two main types of explanations under this heading: first, that there has been direct encouragement from feminist organizations to commit acts of violence, and, second, that the social changes propelled by feminism have led to a suitable environment in which women can terrorize.

The notion of a direct encouragement from feminist organizations involves some divergent ideas. First, women become involved in terror through membership in an extremist feminist organization; membership in a radical feminist organization acts as a conduit to participation in terrorism. Two prominent examples of women who have become involved in terrorism in this way are Astrid Proll of the RAF and Susanna Ronconi, co-founder of Prima Linea. The second notion is that these organizations directly encourage women to commit violence. There are a couple of examples of militant feminist movements that have sponsored terrorist crimes, including Red Zora[22] and the Society for Cutting Up Men (SCUM).[23] There seems to be little way of proving how vital a motivational factor feminism is, but in the interviews conducted by MacDonald, and Neuburger and Valentini, direct encouragement of this nature does not seem to be a causal factor cited by the women.[24]

The indirect link between female emancipation and an increased incidence of female involvement in terrorism appears more plausible and widespread. MacDonald found that both an Interior Ministry official and the head of the country's anti-terrorism squad attributed female involvement in terrorism to social changes made in the wake of feminism:

German women are more liberated and more self-aware than Italian and French women; the Italians still have the image of the woman as the mamma. One could say that the emancipation of women is not so advanced in France, Italy and Britain as it is in Germany and that is why there are fewer women terrorists in those countries.[25]

Conversely, Georges-Abeyie argues that it is not just the increased but frustrated desires of women that lead them into terrorism; for women to become terrorists the society in which they live must be experiencing dramatic economic change.[26] Although we can accept that a society in flux will produce more violent or criminal women, to reduce the analysis of change solely to economics is both restrictive and unreflective of women's global involvement in terrorism.

The supposition that women who terrorize are liberated from the traditional mores of their society is particularly Western. To this day Leila Khaled refuses to describe herself as a feminist, yet she led a group of men to hijack a plane in 1969.[27] Although scholars acknowledge that women terrorists also emerge from countries that do not have a strong feminist tradition,[28] the majority of academic work on terrorism assumes that developing feminism will inevitably lead to increased instances of female terrorism.[29]

Feminism and female emancipation and empowerment as a motivation for women terrorists is a powerful and difficult to dislodge premise. Georges-Abeyie asserts that, "female input in terrorist acts is tied in part to feminist demands and practices."[30] Weinberg and Eubank clearly state that the feminist issue was the attracting or repelling factor for women becoming embroiled in terrorism.[31] Weinberg and Eubank make the further claim that feminism was central to the women's involvement.[32] On the contrary, women did not see themselves in such narrow fields. Astrid Proll described their groups as "well armed social workers"[33] and Mara Aldrovandi stated, "We cannot make a woman's island within the Communist revolution."[34] Feminist writers are quick to point out that feminism is not as popular a motive as the stereotype would indicate.[35] The equating of female terrorism with the "excesses of women's lib"[36] and female emancipation stresses that the cause of violence can be traced back ultimately to womanly concerns (feminism), and thereby emphasizes the femaleness of the actors involved to the detriment of the terrorist image:

No one who understands the feminist movement, or who knows the soul of a real woman would make the mistake of supposing that the modern woman is fighting because she wants to be a man. That idea is the invention of the masculine intelligence.[37]

This line of representation stems from an assumption that women become drawn into terrorism because of the men in their lives; their fathers, husbands, brothers, or boyfriends persuade or coerce them into joining the organizations to which they belong. This assumption is a conventional criminological explanation. It is both a persuasive and very pervasive argument; many authors and even law enforcers[38] attempting to explain women's embroilment in terrorism cite it as an antecedent. Weinberg and Eubank argue that because there are so many marital relationships within the terrorist organizations in the survey, it must be the women who were drawn in by their men.[39] Even the feminist study by Collen Laur reached a similar conclusion[40] to that of the group that won.[41]

If, however, one turns to research asking women themselves why they became involved, one finds that most women are indignant at the suggestion that involvement in terrorism is a passive act. In the interviews that MacDonald conducted for her research, she asked a number of her interviewees whether they thought this analysis accurate; virtually all disagreed. For example, she cites the indignation of the women of ETA at the suggestion,[42] and Leila Khaled's experience as an unmarried Palestinian woman who had to sneak out of her house at night to attend PLO meetings because of her family's disapproval of her involvement. When Susanna Ronconi had to choose between her lover Sergio Segio, and Prima Linea,[43] she chose loyalty to the group.[44]

From the social utopian fighters to the territorial nationalists, the only real evidence that can be found of women being dragged into terrorist organizations at the behest of their men is in right-wing organizations, which by definition are reluctant to allow women strong leadership roles because such permission would undermine the political/social objectives of those groups. Women were known to have made important contributions to some of the neo-Nazi organizations in Germany, but their activities there subscribe to gender stereotypes more easily than those of other women terrorists. Sibylle Vorderbrugge served eight years of a life sentence for a double murder, bomb attacks, arson, and membership in an illegal neo-Nazi organization. In a series of interviews she minimized her complicity by claiming that she did it for the love of Manfred Roeder, the leader of the group that she joined. She claimed that "it was as if I was blind."[45] However, in recent years women's participation in right wing terror movements might be developing. Fagen notes the previous scarcity of women in right wing underground movements. She argues, however, that because of their exclusion from the hierarchies of most right wing groups in the mid 1990s women right wing extremists in Norway developed their own all-woman group. Moreover, she contends that:

"The creation of women's groups has also led to more women becoming attracted to the movement. And, more than before, they seem to be remaining with it."[46]

Fagen's research seems to indicate that in contemporary right wing groups women are not drawn in by men but actually by other women. Female membership of a right wing organisation, however, remains unusual as is being drawn into any terrorism by relationships with men.

The pervasiveness of this illusory stereotype, however, might be due to an enduring construction of conventional womanhood being defined only in reference to men. The belief that women enter the realm of the terrorist only at the behest of men supports the depiction of women as a disempowered entity whose destiny and action are not wholly theirs to control. This conviction in turn identifies and contains women terrorists as women first and terrorists second, continuing the separation of terror from the female.[47]

PERCEPTIONS ABOUT WOMEN WHO TERRORIZE

The perception of women terrorists as "unfeminine" is partly an explanation, the only one to be discussed not wholly stressing the essential "womanliness" of female terrorists. It makes its case by contrasting the women terrorists with the male-defined ideal of womanhood. Women involved in politically or criminally deviant activities, the modern female terrorist especially, are depicted as unsexed and "unnatural."[48] The most obvious and the least subtle way that portrayal works is by describing women terrorists as physically resembling males.

In her research MacDonald came across explanations for women terrorists that stemmed from "mad, to bad to hairy."[49] In his article Georges-Abeyie writes of women terrorists displaying male personality and physical traits.[50] These women are often described as so unattractive that they would only find a mate through their involvement in a male dominated world:

> … women who lack the characteristics and traits that society considers appropriate—gentleness, passivity, non-violent personalities, seductiveness, physically attractive faces and figures— may seek success in some non-feminine realm, by displaying aggression, unadorned faces and bodies, toughness, or other masculine qualities.[51]

One only has to survey most of the photographs of women who have committed terrorist crimes to plainly see the fallacy of the argument. Nevertheless, it persists.

The contemporary interpretation of this representation is that the women within armed subversion become androgynous, cutting their hair short and looking boyish.[52] Though this assertion was made in the Italian context, it falters in other spheres. In the 1980s ETA devised a system of sleeping cells where the activists would live a routine life of marriage, work, and children—which they would leave only for a brief time to carry out an attack and then return to their families. If all women activists had been markedly androgynous, they would not have blended so well into their communities.[53]

This early perception has altered slightly; now it would appear that women terrorists are perceived not as masculine but rather as failing to display traditional feminine traits—a subtle but important distinction. For example, very few people would accept that a woman terrorist is hairier than a "normal" woman. It is much easier to believe that they are "unnatural" and unfeminine, for example, without maternal instincts. Although many women involved in terrorism refrain from having children, or like Gudrun Ensslin and Ulrike Meinhof give up their children to go underground, this is not universally true nor is it justifiable to assume that these women do not have any "natural" maternal instincts.

Although Collen Laur[54] and the women of ETA have highlighted the fact that children and armed subversion do not mix,[55] some active women do have children and many have maternal feelings. Even Nash, from whose work the opening quote was taken, has acknowledged that most women criminals, even terrorists, have retained their motherly instincts.[56] Some women imprisoned for life in Northern Ireland have children.[57] Some women have expressed regret at not having children, and a strong theme across the experience of women terrorists is that they envisage their organization in a maternal-sacrificial complex.[58] The women of the Intifada,[59] most of whom have a number of children, have described similar maternal feelings toward the PLO. Children and terrorism may not be a common combination, but they are not mutually exclusive, and the rarity of the combination is not proof of women terrorists lack of feminine maternal feelings. The persistent, surviving image of the female *terrorist* as unwomanly or unnatural distances her from "real" women, which in turn strengthens her dichotomous representation.

One of the most deeply rooted myths about women who become involved in armed rebellion is that they act only in supporting roles. A pervasive image of women in the Irish conflict, for example, is of housewives banging bin lids to warn male fighters of approaching soldiers. Russell and Miller are exponents of the well-worn assumption that,

> with few exceptions, the role of these women was confined to intelligence collection, operations as couriers, duties as nurses and medical personnel, and in the maintenance of safe houses for terrorists sought by police and for the storage of weapons, propaganda, false documentation, funds, and other supplies.[60]

Georges-Abeyie's and Vetter and Perlstein's work on women terrorists states that women have held predominantly non-combative supporting roles.[61] The work by Weinberg and Eubank offers a typical example of this misinterpretation. They acknowledge that there were well over three hundred militarily active Italian women terrorists but still assert that these women overwhelmingly belong to the category of supporters.[62]

However, the delineation of women exclusively as auxiliaries is rapidly becoming a redundant notion. This is not to say that women never act as auxiliaries.[63] But women have long fulfilled active service duties in terrorist organizations. For example, the first known woman to fall in armed Palestinian rebellion was Fatmeh Ghazzal in 1936.[64] Women fought in the 1910 revolutionary uprising in Mexico,[65] as they also did in the armed insurrection in Morocco.[66] As Russell and Miller point out, women often serve in active roles for practical and political reasons; they are not suspected by virtue of their gender.[67] As de Cataldo Neuburger and Valentini, Preteet, and Baker have all discovered by talking to the activists themselves, women have entered the battle zones.

The enduring construction of women as auxiliaries to the "real" male terrorist, despite the substantial evidence to the contrary, continues the separation of female from terrorist. The insinuation is that even when women are involved they would only fulfill appropriately feminine supportive roles—not combat duties. Defining women involved in terrorism as auxiliaries consolidates the construction of the "essential nature of womanhood" as non-combative, non-violent. Thus the myth of the woman terrorist as auxiliary reflects how the enduring representations of women involved in armed struggle have been contorted to perpetuate an ideal of the feminine woman.

BEYOND THE GENDERED THRESHOLD

Once women have been perceived as crossing the line between the "woman" and the "terrorist," representations of them alter. Now the emphasis is on the "terrorist" who lacks all feminine traits, which highlights the distance between "real" feminine women and terrorists. Consequently, when the woman's culpability as a killer is accepted, her femininity is denied and she is perceived as being far more ruthless than her male counterpart.

MacDonald was able to talk to some of the male law enforcers who dealt with members of the RAF. Their insights into the nature of the women who terrorize are very informative. Dedication to the cause was the overriding description male officers pronounced over women terrorists,[68] and it is one that is to be found in most of the literature pertaining to the women. de Cataldo Neuburger and Valentini's research was originally inspired by the persistent refusal of women terrorists, unlike men, to take up the benefits of the Italian penitents law, a refusal reflecting the women's greater fealty to the groups with which they were involved. Laur and MacDonald argue that the greater

obstacles that women must overcome before joining explains their greater commitment to the cause:

> Women seem to believe their commitment to terrorism is stronger than males because of deeper "soul-searching" and emotive determination to achieve the goal of the movement.[69]

Christian Lochte, Chief of the Hamburg Office for the Protection of the Constitution, offers two additional reasons for women's stronger dedication than that of the men they fight with. First, the women are emotionally rather than intellectually driven, and emotional instinct is "an easier and readier motive for killing than a set of political beliefs."[70] Second, their involvement comes from a deep-seated desire to change society for the better.[71] This second notion has been perpetuated by women themselves—from Astrid Proll's description of women terrorists as social workers with guns to Gudrun Ensslin's lawyer, Professor Heinitz, at her arson trial in October 1968; Heinitz argued that Ensslin's actions were motivated by her misplaced conscience over the Vietnam war.[72]

Despite the altruistic motivations ascribed to female violence, society appears to be more fearful of women who cross the social threshold and kill for political beliefs than they are of men who do so. Collen Laur asserts that

> many police officers attest to similar experiences [that women can be ruthless and murderous]. Numerous accounts of terrorist incidents support the belief that the gender traditionally viewed as the weaker, less violent sex is stronger and more sadistically violent in her terrorist activities.[73]

MacDonald argues that women are more feared as terrorists than men because of the maternal-sacrificial complex; a woman terrorist views her cause like a surrogate child.[74] de Cataldo Neuburger and Valentini also explore this concept. Both MacDonald and de Cataldo Neuburger agree than an essentially feminine trait makes women terrorists much more dedicated to the cause than men—and thus are more ruthless and deadly. MacDonald uses the analogy of a lioness and her cubs.[75]

Susanna Ronconi, co-founder of Prima Linea, points out that violence is linked to maternity in another way: "It is the woman who gives life; it is the woman who also takes life."[76] Others have also made this connection. Reverend William McCrae, MP, has said that he found it hard to comprehend that notion. Such women terrorists, he insists, must be "twisted and warped by hate."[77] This link might explain society's awe and dread of women who resort to violence outside the sanctioned act of protecting their children from danger. The thought of those who bring forth life actually destroying it is disturbing. This maternal-violence link—coupled with social repugnance of female violence—creates an image both gendered and terrifying; thus it is an image frequently ignored in representations of women terrorists.

WOMEN'S EXPERIENCES AS ACTIVE TERRORISTS

Once women have stepped across the threshold into the world of armed insurrection and subversion, macho interpretations can be vitally important to them and their organizations' survival. The women who terrorize manipulate such representations to their own advantage. They subvert the stereotypes of both women and women terrorists as a tool against their enemies, playing on the masculine interpretations and representations of them to confuse and confound. This section discusses how female terrorists have manipulated such persistent imagery as part of their armory. One of the consequences of manipulating stereotypes is that women then have difficulty breaking from them within their organizations; hence rendering combat is a masculine-gendered enterprise. The male representations and images of women terrorists are vital in analyzing these experiences.[78]

Women in terrorism have deployed assumptions of the "innocence of the female sex" in order to disguise their activities from the security forces. For example, during the Moroccan rebellion against the French, many Moroccan women who had already adopted European-style dress reverted back to their traditional clothes to use the voluminous clothing to hide weapons. The traditional female outdoor wear in Morocco is a cumbersome garment that exposes only one eye. But, by the time of the war of independence, this female form of dress had been widely discarded for less cumbersome attire. Women fighters, however, began to wear traditional dress once again because they could conceal much more beneath the extra weight of material. French soldiers believed that the terrorists were more traditional than other women and thus could not possibly belong to the revolt. Thus, soldiers interpreted the women's activities in accordance with gender boundaries;[79] gender parameters were being subverted and defiled by the women to attain their goal.

During her residence in the West Bank, MacDonald witnessed how an old woman urging on stone throwers was ignored by soldiers; "the age-old deception that a woman is by her sex innocent, had come to her aid."[80] MacDonald also recalls how teenage girls reported that the soldiers thought it was more important to catch the boy stone-throwers and petrol bombers.[81] During the Intifada the girls of the Shehab carried the illegal leaflets and flags because the Israeli soldiers chased the boys. In the 1970s women smuggled bombs into a fortified Belfast city center by placing them underneath the babies in their prams. In the 1980s the women of ETA successfully avoided the worst legal penalties by claiming ignorance or a necessary submission to their male partners.[82]

The success of this "female-equals-innocent" stratagem is not as simplistic as it might seem. In Palestinian refugee camps and occupied territories, security forces are mindful that it is usually the women who carry the weapons beneath their clothing; but officials are afraid to search or manhandle women because of cultural taboos and the furor they will create among Muslim men as a result of touching Muslim women.[83] The Spanish authorities, now well aware that women are involved in terrorism, still believe the myth of the masculine revolutionary and remain unable to conceive of well-dressed feminine-looking women being involved in mass murder:

> Even today, they [women of ETA] claimed, the police are still unable to accept that "certain kinds" of women could be members of an ETA cell embarking on an action. The secret, apparently, is to dress very elegantly and to wear lots of make-up in order to appear middle-class and respectable.... Several actions have been carried out by very elegant women.[84]

Even when the authorities do know that women are involved in the violence, they are reluctant to use the same degree of retribution against them that is routinely directed against men.[85] Israeli soldiers have been ordered not to shoot at women participants in riots.[86] Collen Laur claims that in her research she uncovered a reluctance on the part of the security services to treat women terrorists with an equitable level of violence dispensed to their male colleagues,[87] a situation confirming that women are deemed innocent by virtue of their sex. All of this manipulation is only possible because of the entrenched nature of representations of women terrorists. Because the representation of the woman terrorist remains connected with feminine categories, authorities assume that "real" women would not stoop to indiscriminate political violence; hence the role of female is distanced from the role of terrorist.

Many women terrorists resist any representation of themselves as masculine; others argue that through membership in an illegal violent organization they do in some way lose an essential part of their character as women. Italian women, in particular, have argued that their needs as women were subsumed under the masculine role of combatant.[88] They seem to suggest that the terrorist role cannot be filled by women as women, and that despite their involvement in all levels of activity it is the men who actually dictate the parameters of the military theatre.

Though this perception can be validated in a comparison with the early RAF and Robin Morgan's analysis of her experience as a member of the Weather Underground,[89] the correlation is most acute when looking at ETA, HAMAS, the PLO, and the IRA, in which the highest echelons of power are still usually filled by men. Women generally agree that the cause has politicized them, but the combat is conducted as a masculine enterprise.[90] It would be erroneous to argue that women fight only for causes defined by men or that they wish to be men; it is just that their own female viewpoint is often swamped by the masculine prerogative of the fight.[91] This is a result of the overwhelming stereotyped representation of women terrorists that cannot conceive of a female form of politicized violence—even within the organizations themselves.

CONCLUSIONS

This study was inspired by several questions: what are the representations of women terrorists, and how far do these representations differ from women's own experiences as terrorists? The first question was answered in three ways. First, women are seen to be involved in terrorism because of feminist ideology or because they are dependent on men. Second, women terrorists are perceived as unfeminine and subordinate to men in the organizations. Third, perceptions about women once they have been categorized as a militarily active terrorist were considered. The second question about women's experiences was addressed by reviewing women's own accounts of their involvement and comparing such accounts to representations of them.

Discrepancies between the experiences of women terrorists and representations of such experiences are based on more than simple gender discriminations or bias. All of the descriptions seem to point toward an effort to separate concepts of womanhood from those of terrorism. For example, the explanation of feminism stresses the "femaleness" of the concerns that inspire women to join and thereby minimizes their political motivation; more encompassing aspirations such as irredentism or independent sovereignty are denied to them. Defining women as auxiliaries and their entry as dependent on their menfolk also reduces the importance of their contribution and their culpability; such explanations separate women from "real" terrorists who kill innocents in cold blood. The tag of unfemininity and the assumptions brought to bear on women who are classed as cold-blooded killers further this separation of "real" women from "real" terrorists.

The absence of female models for rebellion, as discussed earlier in this article, results in women's actions being judged against the male example. As there are no alternative models of violent rebellion for society to interpret female terrorism, if women are to be conceived as subversives by their society, they must conform to this male model and defeminize themselves; they must leave their womanhood behind them.[92] This construction of women terrorists as in some way masculine has been seen throughout their representations. This masculinization of women terrorists occurs in different ways; first, through descriptions of women having more body hair and displaying male personality traits (competitiveness, aggression) as defined by men; second, through a systematic denial of maternal instincts

in the representations of them; finally, the equation of feminism with armed subversion appears in the subtle insinuation that women who terrorize are not feminine, not real women. Other themes inherent in the representations of women terrorists also subtly imply that females who terrorize must conform to masculine norms. The assumptions that by virtue of their sex women are innocent, that it is their men who draw them into the underground world, and that all have moral motivation for their actions certify that these females are feminine women.

Many models for male rebellion have been developed against which female subversive activities are constructed by society. The rebel woman cannot hope to be judged against feminine structures of armed rebellion—for they do not exist. As the main perpetrators of crime, men are the standard. When women are conceived as equal with men in revolt, they are thus conceptualized in the standard terms, a male archetype not a female one. By emphasizing the masculine terrorist, commentators draw attention from the gendered part of the identity of a woman *as* a terrorist; the gaze of the onlooker is fixed on the "terrorist" half of the image to the depreciation of the "woman." When the reverse occurs, and emphasis is placed on the feminine, the identity of the "woman" is severed from that of the "terrorist," and her agency as a terrorist is minimized. It is as if the two halves are mutually exclusive in attempts to depict a woman terrorist. By splicing the identity of the "woman terrorist" in half in representations of her and by predominately focusing on the feminine at the expense of the combatant, commentators reduce the culpability of the women involved. They thus sustain the association of the "male" with "terrorist." The question still remains: why is there no model for female rebellion?

Representations of women are intimately intertwined with their cultural symbolism. In times of conflict the sexes are often understood as the exemplification of "gender specific virtues,"[93] such as masculine assertion and feminine nurturing. Terrorism is a situation of conflict even if only a few individuals are perpetrating the violence; thus these gender-specific virtues are associated with the actors involved. This, however, does not explain all of the representations nor does it explain why women are conceived as being *more lethal* once they have become terrorist killers. Yuval-Davies'[94] assertion that women are the symbolic embodiment of the culture of their society might provide some insights into this absence of a modal. She argues that women collectively uphold important moral, cultural, and social identities of the group.[95] Thus, when women are involved with terrorism (rebellion), the connotations associated with their contribution are quite different from those of men—provided women are perceived to be "real" women *and* "real" terrorists. If women indeed are the predominate cultural symbol of their group or nation, when they become involved in terrorism the focus of the conflict is warped to include a cultural burden that is distinct and absent from most discourse about male terrorism. This cultural struggle exists on a very different plane from the political, and in this multi-cultural world it produces neither heroes nor easily identified positions of right and wrong aspirations, thus increasing the complexity in our already multifarious responses to terrorism."

Notes

1. J.R. Nash, *Look for the Woman: A Narrative Encyclopaedia of Female Prisoners, Kidnappers, Thieves, Extortionists, Terrorists, Swindlers and Spies from Elizabethan Times to the Present* (London, 1981), vi.

2. See Kim Hyun Hee, *The Tears of My Soul* (New York, 1993). From the scant published statistical accounts of women's presence within terrorist organizations and the roles that they maintain, some distinct trends have been claimed to be observed: feminist inspiration for women's involvement, female terrorists continuing subservience to men in their organizations, and women filling only supporting roles. Most of these types of publications are based purely on official records and thus include no ingredient of the participants' impressions about their experiences. This has led to some fundamental contradictions between the claims made in the works of this nature and others that commence from a more personal account and are based on trends gathered from the stories of the actors involved.

3. D.E. Georges-Abeyie, "Women as Terrorists," in L.Z. Freedman and Y. Alexander (eds.), *Perspectives on Terrorism* (Wilmington, DE, 1983), 60. In more recent times, there are numerous organizations that have committed acts of warfare of a terrorist or guerrilla nature globally, which count on a large roll call of women. Claims of objective "truth" or knowledge drawn from statistics alone must be treated with caution, but a review of the general position of women globally as can be gleaned from such reports will be of use in understanding the importance, or not, of women terrorists.

4. Examples include Ulrike Meinhof and Gudrun Ensslin in the RAF, and Susanna Ronconi in Prima Linea.

5. Countries such as Ireland, Italy, and Spain all have strong female involvement in terrorism, but these are still arguably quite traditional and conservative countries.

6. L. Weinberg and W.L. Eubank, "Italian Women Terrorists," in *Terrorism an International Journal* 9 (1987), 258–59; and C.A. Russell and B.H. Miller, "Profile of a Terrorist," in Freedman and Alexander, op. cit., 54.

7. Though many groups do hold Marxist ideas as a strong component of their ideology, nationalists tend to view social awareness as part of their wider plans for developing freedom for their people. Utopian terrorists consider their ideology as the cause for which they are fighting.

8. The assertion is only true if the Irish Catholics, the Basque separatists, the PLO, and the nationalists of East, South, and Central Africa are ignored. Perhaps one ought to add those in South America as well.

9. The Irish National Liberation Army and the Real IRA, whose co-founder and co-head of operations is reputed to be Bernadette Sans-McKevit.

10. The conflict in the north of Ireland is perhaps unique in the world, whereby the majority of its terrorist leaders are drawn from the working classes.

11. See M. McGuire, *To Take Arms: My Year with the IRA Provisionals* (New York, 1973); and E. Fairweather, R. McDonough, and M. McFadyean, *Only the Rivers Run Free, Northern Ireland; The Women's War* (London, 1984), 242.

12. It is, however, unclear whether women hold seats on the Army Council of the Provisional IRA.

13. Daly, E, "Eta women Emerge as Top Guns Terror War", *The Observer*, 24th September 2000. Guardian Unlimitd; Special Reports. http://guardian.co.uk/spain/article/0,2763,372380,00.htm 10th June 2001.

14. Perez, M U, & Casrellanos, L, "DO NOT LEAVE US ALONE! Interview with Comandante Ramona," translated by Judith and Time Richards, *Double Journal*, Monday 7th March 1994, p.2.

15. For example, the women of the Mexican and Moroccan revolutions.

16. In particular, the United Nations.

17. F. Heindensohn, "Women and Crime," in *Women in Society: A Feminist List*, ed. Jo Campling (Macmillan Press, 1996), 115.

18. Ibid., 112–15.

19. See, for example, H.J. Vetter and G.R. Perlstein, *Perspectives on Terrorism* (Wadsworth, CA, 1991); Weinberg and Eubank, op cit.

20. Georges-Abeyie, op. cit., 77.

21. Many women have been intimately involved in most anti-colonial struggles of the last century. Although many of these women did not fight in the name of feminism they often believed that their emancipation would flow through their country's emancipation, but they frequently found themselves in more restrictive societies after independence had been won.

22. This German organization grew out of an earlier one called the Militant Black Panther Aunties. They murdered a 61-year-old politician, Heinz Karry, in 1981, and bombed the marriage bureaux in 1983, holiday agencies, and the Philippines Embassy in Bonn for complicity in the sex trade.

23. This was an American group that was established by Valerie Solanas, the woman who shot Andy Warhol. Its activities were more centered on propaganda than murder; she advocated the action that they on the whole did not commit.

24. E. MacDonald, *Shoot the Women First* (London: Fourth Estate, Ltd., 1991), 21; Valentini, op. cit., 105.

25. MacDonald, op. cit., 201.

26. Georges-Abeyie, op. cit., 83.

27. Not a period noted for feminist liberation in the Palestinian refugee camps.

28. Georges-Abeyie, op. cit., 75.

29. See, for example, Vetter and Perlstein, op. cit., 110.

30. Georges-Abeyie, op. cit., 82.

31. Weinberg and Eubank, op. cit., 243.

32. They conveniently ignore the fact that this assertion contradicts their other claim that women become embroiled in terrorism only at the behest of their menfolk.

33. MacDonald, op. cit., 64.

34. L. de Cataldo Neuburger and T. Valentini, *Women and Terrorism* (London, 1992), 105.

35. Collen Laur, op. cit., 112; Fairweather, op. cit.

36. Quoted by a German Interior Ministry official in Mac-Donald, op. cit., 6.

37. Anne B. Hamman, "Professor Beyer and the Woman Question," *Educational Review* 47 (1914), 296, quoted in de Cataldo Neuburger and Valentini, op. cit., 92.

38. See, for example, E. MacDonald, D.E. Georges-Abeyie, and S. Aust, *The Baader-Meinhof Group: The Inside Story of a Phenomenon,* trans. by Anthea Bell (London, 1985); L. de Cataldo Neuburger and J. Becker, *Hitler's Children: The Story of the Baader-Meinhof Terrorist Gang* (3rd ed.) (London, 1989).

39. Weinberg and Eubank, op. cit., 255.

40. "Unlike most female terrorists, and in support of the stereotype, Italian female terrorists were often motivated by males to join the organisation" (Laur, op. cit., 71).

41. MacDonald, op. cit., 192.

42. Ibid., 20.

43. Segio and Ronconi were lovers and co-founders of Prima Linea. When Segio became disillusioned with the extreme left and the armed struggle, he tried to persuade Ronconi to leave the organization with him. She refused and thus had to choose the organization and armed struggle over her lover.

44. MacDonald, op. cit., 192.

45. Ibid., 221.

46. Fagen, K, 'The Emergence of an All-Female Group in Norway's Rightist Underground' *Terrorism and Political Violence*, Vol. 9 Autumn 1997, No. 3, p. 122–164. p. 157.

47. That is despite its being a direct contradiction of the argument that women are there because of an excess of feminism, which is inexplicably but conveniently ignored.

48. de Cataldo Neuburger and Valentini, op. cit., 33.

49. E. MacDonald, op. cit., 3.

50. "…they [women terrorists] exhibit masculine body types and psychological profiles…." (Georges-Abeyie, op. cit., 78).

51. Ibid., 82.

52. de Cataldo Neuburger and Valentini, op. cit., 95.

53. Perhaps the perception of these women is contoured by what we expect them to be.

54. Collen Laur, op. cit., 13.

55. MacDonald, op. cit., 40.

56. Nash, op. cit., viii.

57. Examples from the early 1990s include Patricia More (three children and a life sentence), Karen Quinn (three children and a nine-year sentence), and Teresa Brown (three children and a five-year term).

58. de Cataldo Neuburger and Valentini, op. cit., 77.

59. Quoting Aida, a mother of four who lives in the West Bank, "You see the Intifada is my son. I would drown without it" (MacDonald, op. cit., 83).

60. Russell and Miller, op. cit., 49. Their study reviewed only the years 1966–1976, which could explain their findings.

61. Georges-Abeyie, op. cit., 81; Vetter and Perlstein, op. cit., 108.

62. Weinberg and Eubank, op. cit., 257.

63. Fairweather, op. cit., 242.

64. J. Preteet, *Gender in Crisis: Women and the Palestinian Resistance Movement* (New York, 1991).

65. S. Soto, *Emergence of the Modern Mexican Woman: Her Participation in Revolution and Struggle for Equality, 1910–1940* (Denver, CO, 1990).

66. A. Baker, *Voices of Resistance: Oral Histories of Moroccan Women* (New York, 1998), 3.

67. Russell and Miller, op. cit., 50.

68. MacDonald, op. cit., 222.

69. Collen Laur, op. cit., 72; MacDonald, op. cit., 133–32.

70. MacDonald, op. cit., 237.

71. Ibid., 179.

72. see Aust, op. cit., and Becker, op. cit., 67–68.

73. Collen Laur, op. cit., 24.

74. MacDonald, op. cit., 237.

75. Ibid., 236.

76. MacDonald, op. cit., 235.

77. Ibid., 133.

78. As Skarpec argues, perhaps the reason why there have been so few reported cases of female serial killers is because the police have simply not looked for women as suspects. There is an analogy with women terrorists here. C. Skarpec, "The female serial killer: An evolving criminality," in H. Birch, ed. *Moving Targets: Women, Murder and Representation* (Virago Press, Ltd., 1993), 265.

79. Baker, op. cit., 166; see also B. Aretxaga, *Shattering Silence: Women, Nationalism and Political Subjectivity in Northern Ireland* (Princeton, 1997), 66.

80. MacDonald, op. cit., 83.

81. That is despite the fact that the PLO released propaganda films of young women bombers disguising bombs by strapping them to their bodies before planting them (ibid., 85).

82. Ibid., 31.

83. Ibid., 73.

84. Ibid., 32.

85. The experiences of those in the IRA and ETA might dispute this contention.

86. MacDonald, op. cit., 75.

87. Collen Laur, op. cit., 35. This is not the typical experience of women in the IRA or ETA.

88. de Cataldo Neuburger and Valentini, op. cit., 18.

89. R. Morgan, *The Demon Lover: On the Sexuality of Terrorism* (London, 1989).

90. This is also true when the women are caught and imprisoned; for some women, the most defeminizing experience of all is prison. See Fairweather, op. cit., 237; A Maguire (with Jim Gallagher), *Why Me? One Woman's Fight for Justice and Dignity* (London, 1994).

91. Anne B. Hamman, "Professor Beyer and the Woman Question," *Educational Review* 47 (1914), 296 (qtd. in de Cataldo Neuburger and Valentini. op. cit., 92).

92. Morgan, op. cit.

93. L. Dowler, "'And They Think I'm Just a Nice Old Lady': Women and War in Belfast, Northern Ireland," *Gender, Place and Culture* 5:2 (1998).

94. "A figure of a woman, often a mother, symbolises in many cultures the spirit of the collectively, whether it is Mother Russia, Mother Ireland or Mother India" (Yuval-Davis, op. cit., 45).

95. See also Aretxaga, op. cit.

YOUNG, GIFTED AND READY TO KILL

**In a dingy room in Lebanon, three women dream of martyrdom.
Within months, days or even hours, they could get the call to die.
This is the new generation of suicide bombers**

Michael Tierney

Abstract

Al-Aqsa Martyrs Brigade, which the US Government recently added to its list of Foreign Terrorist Organisations, has taken part in at least ten suicide attacks. In May this year a suicide bomber killed himself and two Israelis, in the town of Petah Tikva, near Tel Aviv, and the Brigades claimed responsibility for the attack. Subsequent reports in the Israeli media claimed that Israeli security forces had focused on Maqdah in its hunt for a culprit expressing hostile intentions towards Lebanon and the Palestinian refugee camps. Around this time Ariel Sharon's media adviser stated that following the questioning of senior Fatah operatives, it was revealed that Maqdah "directed and financed major attacks against Israeli citizens during the course of the current wave of Palestinian violence."

Despite years of negotiation with the Israelis, he says, the only thing that will allow the Palestinians to return to their former home is resistance. "The intifada will grant us the right to return." At least 1,471 Palestinians and 564 Israelis have been killed since Palestinians began an uprising for independence in September 2000 after peace talks stalled. Once seen as an aberration, the suicide bomber is now almost commonplace: it has proved the most effective weapon in the Palestinian arsenal having killed around 250 Israelis in two years. In response to such actions Israel reoccupied West Bank cities last month. Generally, extreme acts of violence have not formed part of the lexicon of Palestinian women's struggle but since the beginning of the second intifada in September 2000 there have been four female suicide bombers, all trained by al-Aqsa. The granite certainties of suicide bombing have made Maqdah something of a cult hero among the refugees in Ain al-Hilweh.

More than an hour passes before Maqdah tells us to travel to the Badaweh refugee camp in the north of Lebanon where we are to meet [Iman], [Halima] and [Maha]. Two hours later, past the cityscape of Beirut, we arrive in the camp. Step into any refugee camp in Lebanon and you can see much of what you want to know about this conflict. The voice of Maqdah echoes in voices everywhere: that when [Yasser Arafat] accepted the Oslo accords he abdicated his responsibilities to the 1948 refugees, especially in Lebanon. The people here are in exile from exile. They are second-class Palestinians dreaming of a homeland they have never even set foot in.

A pretty, curly-haired girl, who looks about seven, is peek-a-booing round the corner, hands over her eyes and laughing. I tease her back and she is gently pleased by the game. Then she puffs the trigger of an imaginary gun in my direction and I turn away in mock horror, clutching at the invisible bullet in my chest.

Beside her, assuming the shape of an invincible bandit, is a toothless man with a machine gun slung across his shoulders. He is peering into another room where three young women dressed in material that looks like billowing black sails, stand around a table. One has light-purple san-

dals, another scrubbed nails, while the third wears the faint smell of sweet perfume.

The young women in the room, their eyes moving awkwardly between a small canvas of skin, have a magnetic lure as they fidget and whisper and twist. Two of them have explosives, probably triacetone-triperoxide, strapped to their bodies while the other wields a cumbersome rifle. Despite their obvious immaturity they are potent, volatile and assured.

The little olive-skinned girl, smiling and starry-eyed, is edging closer to the room, offering a hiccup of colour and softness to the air. A squat table bulges with a mosaic of violence and rhetoric: hand grenades, a rocket launcher, a pristine copy of the Koran and some ammunition. Behind it, on the wall, are posters of child victims of the Israeli-Palestinian conflict. The solid black mass of teenagers is standing around the table; they are five feet tall and anxious. One of them is whispering and delicately fixing her friend's veil.

The mock gunfight over, we are ushered into yet another room where we are given orange juice, water, coffee and cola. The air is thick with humidity. We finish our drinks and step towards the young women, a gunman with shaking hands at our side. Each of the girls has dark, almond-shaped eyes that trade delicate, giggling smiles. The three girls refuse to give their names but I will call them Iman, Halima and Maha. They are volunteers of the al-Aqsa Martyrs Brigade, a militant group that is part of Palestinian leader Yasser Arafat's Fatah movement. In days, weeks or months one or all of them will strap explosives to their girlish frames and blow up themselves—and their victims—in a bloody show of defiance against Israel.

It has taken more than three months of preparation to wend our way through the arabesque maze of Beirut's military factions—Hamas, Hezbollah, Islamic Jihad and the al-Aqsa Martyrs Brigade—and finally meet Iman, Halima and Maha. But such is the volatility of camp life that the obstacles of the last few days almost proved insurmountable following the murder, in mid-July, of three Lebanese soldiers by a Palestinian from the Ain al-Hilweh Palestinian city refugee camp, in southern Lebanon. The Lebanese army tightened its siege of the camp where we had arranged to meet with Mounir Maqdah, a former commander in Yasser Arafat's elite Force 17 and new a senior commander of the al-Aqsa Martyrs Brigade.

Lebanese authorities are not allowed into the country's Palestinian refugee camps so in a bid to solve the crisis without bloodshed a security committee representing major Palestinian factions—Fatah, Palestinian Liberation Front, Saiqa, Hamas, Palestinian Struggle and Popular Committees—was set up to pressure anyone who knew the whereabouts of the alleged killer. Effectively this meant no one was getting in or out of the camp. After a few days of negotiation Maqdah was in the custody of the Lebanese army and he finally agreed to see me.

Driving into the camp past the Lebanese military checkpoint we are met with stares and much document checking. Once through we pass a maze of alleyways, a throng of shouting people, a fusion of Koranic verses and fiery rhetoric. We are meeting at the headquarters of Fatah, amid overcrowded cinderblock houses and rubbish-strewn streets, in a courtyard bustling with chickens and dusky, clapped out Mercedes. Young men in combat fatigues mill around, hands clasped around Kalishnikovs and AK-47 assault rifles. These days Maqdah grants few public appearances, preferring to spend his time embroiled in military affairs; he is in constant touch with leaders of the Palestine intifada by phone and internet. There is a palpable tension of mistrust in the air, tempered only by suspicion and caution.

Al-Aqsa Martyrs Brigade, which the US Government recently added to its list of Foreign Terrorist Organisations, has taken part in at least ten suicide attacks. In May this year a suicide bomber killed himself and two Israelis, in the town of Petah Tikva, near Tel Aviv, and the Brigades claimed responsibility for the attack. Subsequent reports in the Israeli media claimed that Israeli security forces had focused on Maqdah in its hunt for a culprit expressing hostile intentions toward Lebanon and Fatah operatives, it was revealed that Maqdah "directed and financed major attacks against Israeli citizens during the course of the current wave of Palestinian violence."

Later, when I speak with Israeli government spokesman Daniel Seaman, he confirms Maqdah is considered a risk to the security and the citizens of Israel. "He is relatively secure in Lebanon because in the meantime we are honouring the commitments of the UN resolutions and we are not taking any activities in south Lebanon unless in self-defence. But if he plays with fire he will get burned. He is someone we are aware of and we'd like to make it clear to him he is not in a profession that he can retire from."

Mounir Maqdah is a tall 42-year-old, beguilingly cinematic, with an alligator's smile and eyes that appear stripped of any illusions about what decency there may be left in human nature. He was born in the one-and-a-half kilometre area of Ain al-Hilweh and has a wife and six children aged from eight to 21. Involved with the military groups since he was 12 he seems intense but is by no means unpleasant. His carefully considered uniform of crumpled military fatigues and the small weapon he has at his side brings to mind the Che Guevera-style Arab nationalist era of Beirut from years gone by. His "true home," he says, is in Gabsiyeh, from which his family fled in 1948, when Israel declared itself a state.

On March 28, 2000, Jordan's State Security Court indicted Maqdah on charges of providing military training to a group of Osama bin Laden's followers who planned to carry out attacks in the Kingdom. He denied the charges but told United Press International that if bin Laden had attempted "to liberate the holy city of Jerusalem, I would have been honoured to co-ordinate with them." In September 2001 Maqdah was convicted in absentia and sentenced to death.

Despite years of negotiation with the Israelis, he says, the only thing that will allow the Palestinians to return to their home is resistance. "The intifada will grant us the right to return." At least 1,471 Palestinians and 564 Israelis have been killed since Palestinians began an uprising for independence in September 2000 after peace talks stalled. Once seen as an aberration, the suicide bomber is now almost commonplace: It has proved the most effective weapon in the Palestinian arsenal having killed around 250 Israelis in two years. In response to such actions Israel reoccupied West Bank cities last month. Generally, extreme acts of violence have not formed part of the lexicon of Palestinian women's struggle but since the beginning of the second intifada in September 2000 there have been four female suicide bombers, all trained by al-Aqsa. The granite certainties of suicide bombing have made Maqdah something of a cult hero among the refugees in Ain al-Hilweh.

The brigades began as an offshoot of Fatah, the secular Palestinian nationalist movement led by Arafat. When Israel and the PLO signed a peace deal in 1993, Arafat renounced terrorism and founded a new, Palestinian-led administration in the West Bank and Gaza Strip. Maqdah believes the Oslo accords failed to fulfil the minimum aspirations of Palestinians in the diaspora and Arafat deserted his people and became part of the occupation. It has fallen, he says, to the Brigades to achieve the legitimate aims of the Fatah movement. "Every time we show our identity cards we remember Palestine," he says. "Every time we walk through the cramped streets we remember Palestine and every time one of us dies in these conditions we remember Palestine. They can kill everything in our minds but not our dreams of Palestine."

Every so often he raises a hand and flicks an order, requesting a mobile telephone or a drink of water, like an insecure bureaucrat from a local municipality. Maqdah insists that when a man or woman volunteers to become a martyr it is not difficult to get them into the West Bank to begin their mission. "We can arrange it, we have our ways. It is harder to go to Tel Aviv, of course, but not the West Bank. It's not complicated."

Typically, a volunteer female suicide bomber will train for between two weeks and two months, depending on the woman involved and her maturity. Previously the suicide bomber fitted a stereotype: male, unmarried, immature, under-educated, aged between 17 to 23 and fanatically religious. Today the martyr has evolved: he has become she. With al-Aqsa they are usually aged between 18 and 25, are female, intelligent and less inclined to be swayed by the promise to males of a Paradise of 70 virgins.

On January 27, this year, Wafa Idris, 28, started the new trend of suicide bombers by killing an 81-year-old man and wounding about 40 more people in Jerusalem. The following month Darin Abu Aysheh, 21, who was studying English at university, struck at a roadblock. On March 29, Ayat Akhras, 18, killed herself, a guard and a 17-year-old girl outside a Jerusalem supermarket. The most recent was the deadliest. On April 12 Andaleeb Takafka exploded herself at a bus stop in Jerusalem—104 people were injured and six Israelis died. "If they are needed we will send them," continues Maqdah. "They need to have a strong and mature mind to carry out their operation. We do not accept everyone who comes to us. The volunteer will be told about her operation maybe one day before or one hour before. She will know when she knows."

Maqdah has two daughters aged 18 and 21 and insists he would have no problems if one of them wanted to volunteer. "I would accept," he says, "because she can make her own choice." Some days earlier I spoke with Usama Hamdan, a representative of the Muslim fundamentalist group Hamas, at his office in the suburb of Haret Hreik. Hamas, he told me, do not accept women as "martyrs" from a religious standpoint, believing they have a more positive role than a military one. The ideology of the al-Aqsa Martyrs Brigade, however, is rooted in Palestinian nationalism, not political Islam. While al-Aqsa commit the same sort of suicide bombings associated with Hamas and Palestinian Islamic Jihad, members draw their inspiration from Hezbollah, the Shiite Lebanese militia whose attacks drove Israel out of its self-declared security zone in southern Lebanon in 2000.

"Darin Abu Aysheh, who blew herself up [in Jerusalem]," says Hamdan, "had firstly gone to Hamas to offer herself as a volunteer but was rejected." Al-Aqsa was happy to accept her. "We are more open religiously," states Maqdah, "unlike Hamas. This is the strongest weapon we have against Israel. We mourn the loss of our women, but we know if we cannot stomach casualties we cannot exist in the Middle East. We will continue with attacks despite Israel's military offensive and the world's condemnation against them. What do we have to lose?"

More than an hour passes before Maqdah tells us to travel to the Badaweh refugee camp in the north of Lebanon where we are to meet Iman, Halima and Maha. Two hours later, past the cityscape of Beirut, we arrive in the camp. Step into any refugee camp in Lebanon and you can see much of what you want to know about this conflict. The voice of Maqdah echoes in voices everywhere: that when Arafat accepted the Oslo accords he abdicated his responsibilities to the 1948 refugees, especially in Lebanon. The people here are in exile from exile. They are second-class Palestinians dreaming of a homeland they have never even set foot in.

Decades after they fled to Lebanon the Palestinians in the 11 refugee camps are still a foreign presence. They have neither home, money, nor identity since they or their parents fled during Israel's War of Independence in 1948 and the Six Day War in 1967. Although there are no accurate statistics there are around 350,000 registered refugees, all rejected by their reluctant host Lebanon as permanent residents and largely forgotten by Arafat, who has little time and money to champion their cause.

Palestinians are barred from many professions, including medicine, law and engineering and they enjoy no political rights in the country. In the camps there are no telephone lines, and barely any electricity with most people living around open sewers. The affairs of the camps remain under the control of local activists because the Lebanese government fear taking responsibility for the Palestinians. In the camps Palestinian children role-play martyrdom where they lie in the dirt and pretend they have been buried in a shallow grave.

Iman tugs at her hijab and examines her rifle. Her olive skin is luminous in the hazy light of the room. Her clothes are deceptive and misleading, hiding as they do the severity of her proposed actions. She is 17 years old with a kind voice and a shy and hopeless look in her eyes. She scratches at her arm. Iman would like to study to be a doctor and help her people but, as a refugee, she is excluded from doing so.

She lives in Badaweh with her parents and brother but her future is measured by the vagaries of politics. When she's serious her whole body nods. When she's angry her arms quickly rise. She doesn't understand why Western girls her age are only interested in pop music. She confesses that she is a little afraid to die but she is ready to become a martyr because it is, she believes, the only way to resist occupation by Israel and what she sees as the American support of Israel. "I am a little afraid but I am more afraid of what I see when I watch what they do against my people," she says. "This encourages me to do the operating against Israel." There is an injured quality to her voice when I suggest she might be too young to be a volunteer. "What Israel do against my people means I am not too young to become a martyr. I want to give freedom for my people." Do her parents know? "My mother knows and has given me encouragement for my operation."

The three girls believe it is their duty to volunteer for their country and they cannot watch what is happening in "occupied Palestine" and expect someone else to do this for them. What al-Aqsa have managed to do is turn themselves into a group less dependent on a mass army of hardened fighters into an organisation of ordinary people ready to replenish the ranks. Politics is the girls' regular conversation in school and each of them can list "martyrs" they admire. All three mention Mohammed Daragmeh, who was 19 when he killed nine people and injured more than 50 at a bar mitzvah, in the name of al-Aqsa Martyrs Brigade.

The practice of suicide bombing is alarming for the astonishing momentum that it has visited upon Israel. Each mission involves a great deal of support including drivers, explosive experts, scouts and guerillas. Mostly made from triacetone-triperoxide, usually in rented apartments and garages, the bombmakers combine acetone and phosphate with water. The mixture is left out to dry before a grinder breaks it down into powder form. From here the material is packed into pipes and strapped to the waist of the bomber. The way a woman dresses makes it much easier to carry out such missions.

Families of suicide bombers now receive more than double the financial compensation than do the families of those killed by other means. Most bombers' survivors receive a permanent pension of $300–600 per month in addition to health care and the education of bombers' children. The Iraqi President Saddam Hussein has offered to pay around $25,000 to the family of each Palestinian suicide bomber.

Halima, who is 18, shares Iman's ambition to train as a doctor. She has, she says, changed dramatically in the last year. Since Israel's two-week assault on the Jenin refugee camp—Palestinians claimed hundreds were killed, Israel claimed it was around 50—she has become much more militant. "I could die at any time so I will die for my people," she says. "I watch what is happening to my people on television and that is enough persuasion for me." Does she

watch what is happening to Israeli people too? Her head rears back; she struggles for an answer.

Maha, who is 17, has set her steely heart on becoming a poet and would love to put her dreams onto paper, telling "heroic stories of the struggle of my people." When I ask how she feels about the prospect of killing innocent civilians, Iman interrupts saying that Israel also kills innocent Palestinians, so she does not worry about this. "They are killing us also." All these women seem familiar—intelligent, forceful, naive and energetic—but are eminently unknowable. Yet they are at the cusp of their lives—the age of potential. They have formed the habits and preferences they will keep most of their days. If it weren't for the confines of the camp they would be delighting in the all-consuming nature of their teenage lives. Maha continues answering questions with aplomb, well versed in rhetoric. Yet I find the honesty of her answer to my last question unsettling. What will she miss most if she carries out her mission? Maha thinks a while. "I will miss poetry." What about your family? "They will accept what I am going to do. There is no need to miss them. I will be in a better place."

Halima blinks a hundred times as she struggles with her veil and lifts her hand to her head for the umpteenth time. Her hazel eyes, deeply politicised by violence, television images and poverty, are heavy. For the most part I have become used to looking at them this way and feel less complicit because of it. She tosses her head into the air and makes a tsk sound. Halima's veil slips briefly from her eyes to reveal a petite, childish face with a girlish gap between her teeth. She offers a look so withering it might break her and I turn away, embarrassed.

Five minutes later I watch the three teenagers as they are escorted away by their minders, and feel empty at the thought of what we have discussed and what might happen in the future. I walk outside sucking on the thin air. The pretty, olive-skinned girl is still peek-a-booing from the courtyard. She puts her hands in the air in surrender. I want to save her but I can't. Instead I pull the trigger on my imaginary gun. The invisible bullet fires straight through her heart. In a few years she'll probably be dead.

Killing for the cause

The first suicide bombing in the history of the Israeli-Palestinian conflict ripped through a West Bank cafe on April 16, 1993. Sahar Tamam Nabulsi, 22, acting on behalf of Hamas, drove into two buses, killing himself and wounding eight Israelis.

The aim of suicide bombing is to sacrifice one's life while attempting to destroy a target for the sake of a political goal. This type of attack was first witnessed in the 1980s in Lebanon, Kuwait and Sri Lanka. The Tamil Tigers in Sri Lanka have launched roughly 200 suicide attacks, killing hundreds of people.

By the 1990s it had spread to Israel, Pakistan, Argentina, Panama, Turkey, Croatia and Kenya. During the Israeli occupation of southern Lebanon, which ended in May 2000, Hezbollah used women suicide bombers for the first time, although this practice was later stopped.

Initially suicide bombers targetted their opponent's political and military infrastructure, but the focus has shifted to attacking civilians.

In 1993 there were 13 suicide attacks on Israel and the figure gradually decreased until there were none in 1999. Since the Palestinian uprising against Israeli occupation in the West Bank and Gaza Strip began in September 2000, however, the numbers have increased significantly. In 2000 there were four, while the following year there were 36. Prior to the most recent attack in Jerusalem, on July 31, when a Hamas suicide bomber struck at a Hebrew University killing himself, at least seven other people and wounding around 80, there had been 43 suicide bombings.

The first female attack was carried out on January 27, 2002, by Wafa Idris, 28, a divorced ambulance worker from the Ramallah refugee camp. She killed an 81-year-old man and wounded about 40 more people in Jerusalem. The following month Darin Abu Aysheh, 21, who was studying English at university, struck at a roadblock. On March 29, Ayat Akhras, 18, was just months away from graduation and then marriage when she killed herself, a guard and a 17-year-old girl outside a Jerusalem supermarket. On April 12 Andaleeb Takafka blew herself up at a bus stop in Jerusalem killing six Israelis.

All the women killed themselves on behalf of the al-Aqsa Martyrs Brigade. This year the brigade's attacks have killed more Israelis than those of Hamas. The al-Aqsa Martyrs Brigade believes that suicide bombing will inflict much more pain on the Israelis than guerilla warfare, eventually hastening an end to occupation.

Demon Lover

When Robin Morgan first published her award-winning feminist book on terrorists and terrorism in 1989, it seemed a frighteningly on-target description of a world coming into being. Now, we're living it.

BY ROBIN MORGAN

Look closely at her.

She crosses a city street, juggling her briefcase and her sack of groceries. Or she walks down a dirt road, balancing a basket on her head. Or she hurries toward her locked car, pulling a small child along with her. Or she trudges home from the fields, the baby strapped to her back.

Suddenly there are footsteps behind her. Heavy, rapid. A man's footsteps. She knows this immediately, just as she knows that she must not look around. She quickens her pace in time to the quickening of her pulse. She is afraid. He could be a rapist. He could be a soldier, a harasser, a robber, a killer. He could be none of these. He could be a man in a hurry. He could be a man merely walking at his normal pace. But she fears him. She fears him because he is a man. She has reason to fear.

She does not feel the same way—on city street or dirt road, in parking lot or field—if she hears a woman's footsteps behind her. It is the footstep of a man she fears. This moment she shares with every human being who is female. This is the democratization of fear.

The majority of terrorists—and those against whom they are rebelling—are men. The explosions going off today worldwide have been smoldering on a long sexual and emotional fuse. The terrorist has been the subliminal idol of an androcentric cultural heritage from prebiblical times to the present. His mystique is the latest version of the Demon Lover.

He evokes pity because he lives in death. He emanates sexual power because he represents obliteration. He excites the thrill of fear. He is the essential challenge to tenderness. He is at once a hero of risk and an antihero of mortality.

He glares out from reviewing stands, where the passing troops salute him. He straps a hundred pounds of weaponry to this body, larger than life on the film screen. He peers down from huge glorious-leader posters, and confers with himself at summit meetings. He is a living weapon. Whatever he does at first appalls, then becomes faddish. We are told that women lust to have him. We are told that men lust to be him. We have, all of us, invoked him for centuries. Now he has become Everyman. This is the democratization of violence.

Now look closely at him. He hurries through the airports to catch his plane. Or he pedals his bicycle, basket laden with books, to the university. Or he mounts the steps of his embassy on official business. Or he snaps a fresh roll of film into his camera and starts out on assignment. Suddenly there are footsteps behind him. Heavy, rapid. A man's footsteps. In the split second before he turns around, he knows he's afraid. He tells himself he has no reason to fear. But he fears. He does not feel the same way if he hears a woman's footsteps behind him.

It is possible that terrorism attracts so much attention today because men, as well as being its main perpetrators, are also among its victims? If men are now

afraid in daily circumstances, why then the situation must be taken seriously, attention must be paid.

Men of the State-that-is [the Establishment] and men of the State-that-would-be ["rebels" or "terrorists"] share a peculiar intoxication. It permits them to call up armies, attach electrodes to living flesh, justify the invention, testing, and stockpiling of world-destroying weapons; it also permits them to "kneecap" informers with electric drills, purge "incorrect" colleagues by literal crucifixion, and eventually to consider the political reasons for doing these things as secondary or irrelevant, the mere doing them as creative acts. Such men suffer from a lack of ambivalence.

A lack of ambivalence cannot tolerate complexity or compassion. Indeed, the State-that-is trains its sons in this lack. Sometimes the sons fight for the State and sometimes they fight against it, but either way they reinforce it.

Here are two brief histories of men suffering from a lack of ambivalence—two U. S. veterans of the (undeclared) Vietnam war:

The first man is named Dennis John Malvasi. He was born in 1950, his mother's seventh child. She had her first baby at age 15 and bore 12 children by three different men. Until age 14, Dennis lived in a Catholic orphanage; then he came home to Brooklyn, New York, to a slum neighborhood of racial warfare between whites, blacks, and Hispanics. He enlisted in the Marines at age 17 (faking parental consent), was shipped to Vietnam, and conducted 505 patrols, 214 ambushes, and eight extensive sweep-and-clear operations around Da Nang. He took heavy fire and relished it: "I felt really alive, really wanted. The baddest people I knew were in front and they came shooting at me. I felt kind of honored." After his discharge in 1970, he became an itinerant actor on Manhattan's Lower East Side, was involved in street crime, charged with assault, sentenced, put on probation, arrested again, and wound up serving two years in jail. When he was released, he drifted through various odd jobs—as mailroom clerk, paramedic, licensed pyrotechnician. He joined the Vietnam Veterans Ensemble Theater Company, but persisted in shady extralegal activities. He became a fugitive in 1985 on a six-weapons felony charge. "Stuff like that doesn't bother me," he said. "Actually, I don't feel good unless I have someone hunting me down. It makes me feel alive. It makes me feel wanted." He became involved in a Roman Catholic cult with a particular dedication to Saint Benedict and a fanatic aversion to abortion. In February 1987, after a two-year manhunt involving 300 federal agents and city detectives and a public appeal by Cardinal O'Connor, Archbishop of the New York Catholic Diocese, Dennis John Malvasi turned himself in to stand trial on the charge of bombing the Manhattan Women's Medical Center (December 10, 1985), the Eastern Women's Center (October 29, 1986), the Queens Women's Medical Office (November 11, 1986), and a Planned Parenthood center (December 14, 1986). The bomb in the last attack—made with 15 sticks of dynamite and a sophisticated assembly of blasting cap, timer, and battery—was defused at the last minute, but was potent enough to have collapsed the entire facade of the building and to have broken windows blocks away. Tucked in with the dynamite was a medal of Saint Benedict. Malvasi spoke of abortions as "kills," in Vietnam troop parlance, and was indignant that "when I came back from Vietnam they called me a baby-killer." His defense hinged on whether his wartime experience "warped him to the point of insanity." He pleaded guilty and was sentenced to seven years, a reduced sentence

because of his promise to Cardinal O'Connor "not to take part in bombings again."

The second man was a Vietnam hero who could display six rows of ribbons on his chest. He was called "the ultimate marine [who] wants to step forward and take the spears in his own chest." He was bitter after Vietnam; a fellow platoon leader recalled his "clear feeling was that we were winning but the press was portraying our victories as defeats." He came home to teach war at Quantico, Virginia, in the Marine Corps officers' training school, and began to "act out"— he taught classes dressed in jungle fatigues and battle paint, and he accidentally injured a student by spraying a room with blanks from an assault rifle. He was transferred to Okinawa to direct a marine training camp. There he was known as the workaholic who hand hung a banner over his quarters reading LEAD, FOLLOW, OR GET THE HELL OUT OF THE WAY. Back in the U. S. in 1974, he apparently suffered some sort of breakdown and spent three weeks recovering at Bethesda Naval Hospital. Unconfirmed marine lore claims that a fellow officer found him running naked through the streets of his suburban neighborhood, waving a .45 pistol and screaming, "I'm no good, I'm no good." In 1981 he was given full security clearance to join the staff of the National Security Council of the White House of the United States. The name of this lieutenant colonel is Oliver North.

A lack of ambivalence must be trained into a man. Can it ever be trained out of him? The war toy, the rigid penetrating missiles, the dynamite and the blasting cap—these are at first only symbols of the message he must learn, fetishes of the ecstasy he is promised. But he must become them before he is rewarded with what the lack of ambivalence promises him: a frenzy, an excitement, an exhilaration—an orgasmic thrill in violent domination with which, he is taught, no act of lovemaking could possibly compete.

This is the transition of identity that makes possible (and inevitable) acts of terror. If manhood is perceived as localized in a hardened penis, and if the penis is perceived as a weapon, then manhood

itself is the means by which male human beings must (and do) make of themselves weapons.

If one is a weapon, how can god not be wrathful?

If one is a weapon, how can power not mean dominance?

If one is a weapon, what is one to do with oneself but kill or be killed?

If one is a weapon, how can sex not be murderous and murder not be sexual?

If one is a weapon, how can women be other than targets?

If one is a weapon, how can death not bring ecstasy?

Contrarily, if one sees a human body that can dance, can laugh, can kiss, sing, sleep and wake, can touch and be touched—a miracle—and finds that such a human being believes himself a weapon, how can one not try to stop him? How can one not try to stop him by thinking love will release him from the weapon of himself?

Because women are the other side of the story.

On April 17, 1986, there was an attempt to plant a high-powered plastique bomb aboard an El Al jet bound for Tel Aviv from London's Heathrow Airport. The explosives were found in the carry-on bag of a 32-year-old chambermaid named Anne Marion Murphy. She went into shock. The bag had been given to her—packed with "surprise gifts" to open when she landed in Israel—by her lover, the man she thought was going to marry her, a 31-year-old Jordanian-born Libyan, Nezar Nawaf Mansur Hindawi. He had said he would meet her in Israel in a few days.

She was pregnant with his child.

He was already married. He had deserted his Polish wife and their four-year-old daughter, but had never been formally divorced. His brother, it appeared, had been involved in an earlier bombing of a West German discotheque. The brother too, had a girlfriend, a German woman, and she too was stunned; Heiderose Pohmer, age 30, described her lover as "completely unpolitical, a gentle lover, and an excellent cook." She worked as a cleaning woman in a nursing home. The brothers came from a family that had lived in various parts of the Middle East, had fled Palestine when Israel was declared a state, and had settled in Bakura, in northern Jordan. There, their home was destroyed by an Israeli raid—which in turn was a retaliation for guerilla attacks on Israel—which in turn were retaliation for…which in turn… which in turn…

Are further details necessary? Surely we can fill them in by now. They sicken us with familiarity, these details—of hatred, grief, revenge. What we don't know, we can imagine.

In the Demon Lover's world, the elite are those who claim to fight and sacrifice on behalf of those beneath them; to confront on your own behalf means the humiliation of acknowledging your own oppression, as well as the risk of being accused of selfishness. So she who lies in terror's arms clutches for another bond of reassurance, and it is waiting to curl and knot around her loins: charisma. The men will initiate her and she will be (al-most) one of them; other women will look upon her with awe. The charisma attaches because of her intensifying proximity to death: she becomes even more of a treasure to him, since she will be lost to him and since he loves only what he can lose or kill. How well this skein meets now around her throat with another—her well-fostered nurturant "mothering instinct" that longs to interpose her between death and others. And the final bond, pure satin steel the color of blood ruby is knotted tight around her heart: it is, in almost every case, her own personal passion for an individual man.

From Marx to Ortega, they have used her and acknowledge it. They have made it plain: they need women. They cannot do it without women.

If they cannot do it without us, then what will happen if we turn from them, turn to our own definitions, means, and energies?

Such a message of selfhood and sisterhood is more than terrifying. It takes time for that message to filter through the thick hangings that curtain terror's bed, time we have less of each day. The women there are literally in terror of hearing it. The women there lie, not fully living yet undead as Dracula's legion of brides, in the Demon Lover's embrace, trusting him, trusting his love, trusting his promise of immortality, trusting their own lies that they have chosen this. And somewhere, in the deepest recesses of her soul, each one suspects otherwise.

Robin Morgan was editor in chief of Ms. *from 1990 to 1993. The Demon Lover* has just been republished, updated with a new introduction and afterword, in paperback by Washington Square Press. Her latest books include A Hot January: Poems, *and* Saturday's Child: A Memoir *(both from W. W. Norton).*

UNIT 10
Countering Terrorism

Unit Selections

Key Points to Consider

- What role do global politics play in our war against terrorism? Is a political strategy based on democratic principles, tolerance, and social justice an alternative to military action? Defend your answer.

- How does the lack of effective interagency cooperation inhibit contemporary efforts to counter international terrorism? Will the creation of a Homeland Security Agency resolve these problems?

- Has counterterrorism become the new organizing principle for U.S. foreign policy? What are the short-term and long-term implications of a sustained campaign against international terrorism?

 **Links: www.dushkin.com/online/**
These sites are annotated in the World Wide Web pages.

Counter-Terrorism Page
http://counterterrorism.com
Index of Heritage Library
http://www.heritage.org/index.cfm

Since the failed mission to rescue U.S. hostages held at the U.S. embassy in Iran in April 1980, the U.S. government has attempted to develop a cohesive policy for countering terrorism. While initial steps toward such a policy were taken in the Ronald Reagan and George H.W. Bush administrations, a relatively cohesive counterterrorism policy did not emerge until after the first attack on the World Trade Center in 1993. In the wake of the attack, the Clinton administration developed a series of initiatives that later merged into a four-track policy. Economic isolation, multilateral cooperation, resource allocation, and retaliation became key elements in the Clinton administration's antiterrorism policy.

The economic isolation of states supporting international terrorism has been a key theme in U.S. policy since the 1980s. While initially targeting only states, this policy was expanded in 1995 to target organizations and groups in the United States that raise funds to support international terrorism. The freezing of assets and the disruption of financial networks became important policy objectives during the Clinton administration.

U.S. efforts to formally enlist multinational cooperation in its fight against international terrorism can be traced to the Halifax summit of the G-8 in 1995. At the summit the United States launched a series of initiatives to codify G-8 cooperation in response to terrorist incidents. A series of joint declarations and international agreements resulting from the continuation of these efforts form the political and legal framework for the current cooperation in the "war on terrorism."

One of the more controversial aspects of U.S. policy, prior to the attacks of September 11, has been the ever-increasing allocation of new resources. Since the Oklahoma City bombing in 1995, the U.S. government has allocated billions of dollars in additional funds to combat terrorism. It has continually expanded FBI investigative capabilities, provided billions to enhance airport security, and invested heavily in training and equipment designed to enhance national and local disaster response capabilities. According to some estimates the U.S. government currently spends in excess of $30 billion annually to combat international terrorism.

Since Ronald Reagan ordered the bombing of Libya in response to an attack on La Belle Discotek in Berlin in the 1980s, retaliation has become an important part of U.S. policy to combat terrorism. Military attacks against Iraq after the discovery of a plot to assassinate former President George Bush in Kuwait in 1993 and retaliatory strikes against a Sudanese chemical factory and terrorist training camps in Afghanistan, after the bombings of U.S. embassies in Nairobi, Kenya, and Dar es Salaam, Tanzania, indicate a willingness to continue to employ this tactic as part of an overall strategy for combating terrorism.

It appears that the current George W. Bush's administration's efforts on terrorism are an expansion of the above-noted policy. President Bush has extended ongoing efforts to eco-

nomically isolate state sponsors and significantly increased the number of groups subject to investigation and seizure of assets. He has continued to seek the cooperation of allies, significantly increased U.S. counterterrorism spending, and elevated U.S. efforts to retaliate against terrorists by declaring war on terrorism.

The articles in this unit explore potential alternatives in countering terrorism. Victor Bulmer-Thomas argues against a unilateral U.S. response. He asserts that good intelligence, effective law enforcement, and political initiatives that undermine terrorist support are essential to ending the cycle of violence. Seymour Hersh's article "Missed Messages" highlights past failings of the U.S. intelligence community. He argues that a "chronic inability to synthesize intelligence reports, draw conclusions, and work with other agencies" has hampered U.S. intelligence efforts. Finally, James Steinberg examines the limits of "counterterrorism as an organizing principle for U.S. foreign policy." He argues that the United States must not lose sight of "broader national interests."

Targeting Terrorism

The end of the Cold War in the 1980s left the United States as the only military superpower. Then the economic boom in the '90s established it as the primary beneficiary of globalisation. While espousing globalisation, Washington has been able to defend a traditional view of national sovereignty that has emphasised its ability to shape events without paying too much attention to the opinion of others. The new Bush administration reasserted the tradition of unilateralism in foreign policy, reminding other countries that the United States needs them less than they need it.

Victor Bulmer-Thomas

THE EXTENSION OF US POWER AROUND THE GLOBE MAY have made enemies, but foreign states have been powerless to protest. One by one hostile states have been forced to recognise its overwhelming military, political and economic power. And unlike the Roman Empire 1500 years ago, Washington has not faced barbarous hordes intent on destroying it. On the contrary, it is confronted by millions of economic migrants with a desire only to share the fruits of globalisation.

The inability of other nations to challenge US dominance perhaps lulled the authorities into a false sense of complacency. Having shifted policy in many parts of the world after the Cold War, it now espouses support for democratic governments, respect for human rights and recognition of individual liberties. Admittedly the Bush administration has distanced itself from a number of international treaties, but why should anyone hate the United States? Yet its policies are deeply unpopular in many parts of the world and non-state actors—arguably with the occasional connivance of states—have been prepared to use force against symbols of its power.

JUST AS VULNERABLE

As little as a decade ago, terrorism was almost unknown in the United States. Officials had been assassinated by terrorists beyond its borders, overseas military installations had been the object of attacks and embassies had frequently been under assault. Yet most citizens felt safe on the assumption either that terrorists would never dare operate on US soil or that the intelligence services were sufficiently effective to foil any such plot.

Terrorism in the United States is therefore relatively new. The first attempt to blow up the World Trade Center in 1993 was largely unsuccessful. The Oklahoma bombing was a much greater tragedy, but responsibility was laid at the door of Timothy McVeigh, acting largely on his own and with no apparent international links. There was a widespread feeling that terrorism was something that happened outside the United States even if the targets could be US citizens.

All that changed with the tragic events in New York and Washington. The United States, it would seem, is just as vulnerable to attack as other countries—if not more so. The only military superpower, blessed with abundant counter-espionage and intelligence resources, was unable to protect its citizens from an enemy prepared to sacrifice its life in pursuit of its objectives.

PREPARING THE GROUND

Terrorism demands a response and the US administration has had to grapple with this new security threat. Its first response was to define the terrorist attack as an act of war. This is understandable and has been well received by the people of the United States, but it is not necessarily correct. Wars are normally declared between states. Those instigated by non-state actors are usually civil wars. At the very least a declaration of war requires an identifiable enemy.

The second response was to make clear that there would be no distinction between those who committed these atrocities and those who harbour and finance them. Again, this is understandable and it is right that terrorists should not feel that there are any safe havens. Yet it is very difficult to make such a link. When Irish Republican Army (IRA) terrorists fled across the border from Northern Ireland into the Republic of Ireland in the 1970s, the British government respected the sovereignty of a foreign state despite suspicions that the Irish intelligence services were not doing all that they could to bring them to justice. Similarly, London has tried unsuccessfully for years to prevent the IRA raising finance from supporters in the United States.

The third response was to win international support for its campaign. The UN Security Council issued a strong condemnation of the attacks on September 11 and called on the international community to do everything necessary to prevent and suppress terror. On the same day NATO's North Atlantic Council for the first time in its fifty-two year history invoked article 5 of its treaty to assert that, if it was established that the attack was directed from abroad, then it should be regarded as an armed attack on all the alliance members.

With these three responses, the ground has been prepared for international action designed to destroy the terrorists and the organisations responsible. Other countries are now involved not only symbolically, but also perhaps in providing military support. The US has made it clear that this is a new kind of war that demands a different response. There can be no prevarication and foreign states must demonstrate tangibly their opposition to terror.

Can this strategy succeed? Terrorism is now a global threat and demands an international response. A US-led campaign to eradicate it must stand a better chance of success than one led by other countries. Its defeat would be a major victory for all who believe in the rule of law, making the world a safer and better place.

Yet it is not so simple. Terrorism is rarely mindless. It is usually carried out by individuals who believe passionately in their cause, some of whom are prepared to die for it. An eradication campaign will not necessarily remove the causes of terrorism and retaliation may simply extend rather than end the cycle of violence.

The omens are not good. US retaliation for the bombing of its embassies in East Africa in 1998 was both ineffective and, it would now appear, counterproductive. Israel's relentless campaign against Palestinian terrorist organisations has led to a deterioration in the Middle East security situation. Attempts by Russia to crush its opponents in Chechnya have not ended terror attacks on Russian citizens.

MEANS BEFORE ENDS

The first problem with the American strategy is that the means—military retaliation—was chosen before the ends were defined. Yet if the target is those responsible for the New York and Washington tragedies, the correct response must first be the international criminal judicial process. Although the International Criminal Court has not yet been established and is opposed by the Bush administration, there are still ways of bringing criminals to justice as the trial of Slobodan Milosevic has shown.

If, on the other hand, the target is the network of terrorism linked to the fugitive Osama Bin Laden, retaliation is unlikely to be effective in dismantling those operations located in Europe and North America. Finally, if the objective is an end to all international terrorism, then the sad truth is that retaliation will be no more effective than crop-spraying is in the war on drugs.

Secondly, we still do not know the precise motives for the atrocities against the United States, but this is surely relevant in designing an appropriate response. Since these were suicide attacks, it is safe to assume that they were not carried out by Latin American guerrilla organisations, drug traffickers or anti-globalisation protesters. Indeed, only two groups have used suicide attacks: Islamic militant organisations and the Tamil Tigers in Sri Lanka. Since the United States is only marginally involved in the Sri Lankan situation, it seems inevitable that Islamic mil-

itants are responsible and this has been underlined by what we already know about the suspects.

Islamic militants' hatred for the United States has many causes, but the principal ones remain US policies in the Middle East and the presence of its troops on the Arabian peninsula. The policy towards Iraq of sanctions and bombing is deeply offensive to many. The continued isolation of Iran and Libya looks increasingly anachronistic. And the territorial dispute between Israel and the Palestinians, in which the US is far from neutral, is a cancer at the heart of the international system. Yet without a settlement of these Middle East disputes, retaliation against terror will not end the cycle of violence; it will simply increase the supply of martyrs.

ENDING THE CYCLE

Terrorism is not inevitable and it is not a new phenomenon, even if the scale of the tragedy in the United States breaks new ground. The cycle of terror can be ended either because the organisations behind it implode—the Baader-Meinhof gang in West Germany—or because intelligence leads to the arrest and conviction of the main actors—the Medellin drug cartel in Colombia—or because political initiatives render terror activities inappropriate—the Provisional IRA in Northern Ireland. Force alone will not end a terror campaign.

The British have been the victims of such attacks for many years and many lives have been lost. Canary Wharf, the British equivalent of the twin towers in New York, has been a target. The British government learnt early on that terrorism could not be defeated without international cooperation. However, they also discovered that it required a political response. Unpalatable though it seemed at the time, negotiating with erstwhile terrorists has brought substantial dividends in ending the cycle of violence.

The United States currently occupies the high moral ground. The attack on its citizens has rightly been condemned in the strongest possible form by all responsible people. If the US authorities are able to identify those still alive that had some hand in these terrible acts, they will have the support of virtually all states to bring them to justice. Similarly, if the US leads an international alliance designed to defeat terrorism through superior intelligence, it will rightly be applauded. Last, but not least, new political initiatives in the Middle East could cut the ground from under the terrorists' feet.

Military force is not the answer. As the world's only superpower, the United States is constantly asked to mediate between warring parties. It is difficult to advocate moderation or restraint for others if the United States does not lead by example. The thirst for revenge is understandable, but it is rarely effective. This is a time for reflection to ensure that the response to the tragedy in the United States really does have a chance of bringing to an end the curse of global terrorism.

Professor Victor Bulmer-Thomas is Director of Chatham House.

From *The World Today*, October 2001, pp. 8-10. © 2001 by The World Today. Reprinted by permission.

ANNALS OF NATIONAL SECURITY

MISSED MESSAGES

Why the government didn't know what it knew.

BY SEYMOUR M. HERSH

On September 23rd, twelve days after the terror attacks on America, Secretary of State Colin Powell told a Sunday-morning television-news show that the Bush Administration planned to publish a white paper that would prove to the world that Osama bin Laden and his Al Qaeda organization were responsible for the hijackings. "We are putting all of the information that we have together, the intelligence information, the information being generated by the F.B.I. and other law-enforcement agencies," Powell said. The information that the White House had available, we now know, included a top-secret briefing, given to President Bush on August 6th, documenting what was known about Al Qaeda's determination to attack American targets. The briefing, prepared by the C.I.A. at the President's request, was reportedly entitled "Bin Laden Determined to Strike in U.S." It warned that Al Qaeda hoped to "bring the fight to America." Despite Powell's declaration, the Administration never released the white paper. And in October, when the evidence of bin Laden's involvement was made public, by proxy—by the British Prime Minister, Tony Blair—there was no mention of the pre-attack warnings. In fact, the white paper stated, incorrectly, that no such information had been available before the attacks: "After 11 September we learned that, not long before, Bin Laden had indicated he was about to launch a major attack on America."

It is now clear that the White House, for its own reasons, chose to keep secret the extent of the intelligence that was available before and immediately after September 11th. In addition to the August briefing, there was a prescient memorandum sent in July to F.B.I. headquarters from the Phoenix office warning of the danger posed by Middle Eastern students at American flight schools (Robert Mueller, the F.B.I. director, did not see the memo until a few days after September 11th), and there was what Condoleezza Rice, the President's national-security adviser, called "a lot of chatter in the system." Congressional hearings will almost certainly take place in the next few months, given the conviction of Democratic Party leaders that they finally have a viable political issue.

What the President knew and when he knew it may not be the relevant question, however. No one in Washington seriously contends that the President or any of his senior advisers had any reason to suspect that terrorists were about to fly hijacked airplanes into buildings. A more useful question concerns the degree to which Al Qaeda owed its success to the weakness of the F.B.I. and the agency's chronic inability to synthesize intelligence reports, draw conclusions, and work with other agencies. These failings, it turns out, were evident long before George Bush took office.

Neither the F.B.I. nor America's other intelligence agencies have effectively addressed what may be the most important challenge of September 11th: How does an open society deal with warnings of future terrorism? The Al Qaeda terrorists were there to be seen, but there was no system for seeing them.

Several weeks before the attacks, the actor James Woods was in the first-class section of a cross-country flight to Los Angeles. Four of his fellow-passengers were well-dressed men who appeared to be Middle Eastern and were obviously travelling together. "I watch people like a moviemaker," Woods told me. "As in that scene in 'Annie Hall'"—where Woody Allen and Diane Keaton are sitting on a bench in Central Park speculating on the personal lives of passers-by. "I thought these guys were either terrorists or F.B.I. guys," Woods went on. "The guys were in synch—dressed alike. They didn't have a drink and were not talking to the stewardess. None of them had a carry-on or a newspaper. Nothing.

"Imagine you're at a live-music event at a small night club and you're standing behind the singer. Everybody is clapping, going along, enjoying the show— and there's four guys paying no attention. What are they doing here?" Woods concluded that the men were "casing" the plane. He said that his concern led him to hang on to his cutlery after lunch. He shared his worries with a flight attendant. "I said, 'I think this plane is going to be hijacked.' I told her, 'I know how serious it is to say this,' and asked to speak to the captain." The flight attendant, too, was concerned. The plane's first officer came over immediately and assured Woods that he and the captain would keep the door to the cockpit locked. The remainder of the trip was bumpy but uneventful, and Woods recalled laughingly telling his agent, who asked about the flight, "Aside from the terrorists and the turbulence, it was fine."

Woods said that the flight attendant told him that she would file a report about the suspicious passengers. If she did, her report probably ended up in a regional Federal Aviation Authority office in Tulsa, or perhaps Dallas, according to Clark Onstad, the former chief counsel of the F.A.A., and disappeared in the bureaucracy. "If you ever walked into one of these offices, you'd see that they have no secretaries," Onstad told me. "These guys are buried under a mountain of paper, and the odds of this"—a report about suspicious passengers—"coming up to a higher level are very low." Even today, eight months after the hijacking, Onstad said, the question "Where would you effectively report something like this so that it would get attention?" has no practical answer.

Throughout the spring and early summer of 2001, intelligence agencies flooded the government with warnings of possible terrorist attacks against American targets, including commercial aircraft, by Al Qaeda and other groups. The warnings were vague but sufficiently alarming to prompt the F.A.A. to issue four information circulars, or I.C.s, to the commercial airline industry between June 22nd and July 31st, warning of possible terrorism. One circular, from late July, noted, according to Condoleezza Rice, that there was "no specific target, no credible info of attack to U.S. civil-aviation interests, but terror groups are known to be planning and training for hijackings, and we ask you therefore to use caution."

For years, however, the airlines had essentially disregarded the F.A.A.'s information circulars. "I.C.s don't require special measures," a former high-level F.A.A. official told me. "To get the airlines to react, you have to send a Security Directive"—a high-priority message that, under F.A.A. regulations, mandates an immediate response. Without a directive, the American airline industry was operating in a business-as-usual manner when Woods noticed the suspicious passengers on his flight.

On the evening of September 11th, Woods telephoned the Los Angeles office of the F.B.I. and told a special agent about the encounter. In an interview on Fox Television in February, Woods described being awakened at six-forty-five the next morning by a telephone call from the agent. "I said, 'I'll get ready and I'll come down to the federal building,'" Woods recounted. "He said, 'That's O.K. We're outside your house.'" By then, Woods told me, he was no longer certain of the date of his trip. "The first thing I said is 'I'm not sure which flight it was on.'" But he had a vivid memory of the men's faces. When he was shown photographs, Woods thought he recognized two of the hijackers—Hamza Alghamdi, who flew on United Airlines Flight 175, which struck the south tower of the World Trade Center, and Khalid Almihdhar, who was on American Airlines Flight 77, which struck the Pentagon. One of the men stood out because of his "pointy hair," Woods told me, and the other looked like one of the characters in the movie version of John le Carré's "The Little Drummer Girl."

A senior F.B.I. official told me that the bureau had subsequently investigated Woods's story but had not been able to find evidence of the hijackers on the flight Woods thought he had taken. "We don't know for sure," the official said.

Woods's flight was not the only one the F.B.I. looked into after September 11th. The bureau found other evidence that the terrorists from the four different planes had flown together earlier, in various combinations, to "check out flights," as one agent put it. The F.B.I. now thinks that the hijackers flew on perhaps a dozen flights, together and separately, in the summer of 2001.

The hijackers' decision to risk flying together calls into question much of the conventional wisdom about September 11th. The F.B.I. and the C.I.A. have repeatedly characterized the Al Qaeda terrorists as brilliant professionals—what I. C. Smith, who retired in 1998, after a twenty-five-year career at the F.B.I., much of it in counterintelligence, calls "the superman scenario." In a rare public appearance, at Duke University in April, James Pavitt, the C.I.A.'s deputy director for operations—the agency's top spymaster—said of Al Qaeda:

> The terror cells that we're going up against are typically small and all terrorist personnel… were carefully screened. The number of personnel who know vital information, targets, timing, the exact methods to be used had to be smaller still.… Against that degree of control, that kind of compartmentation, that depth of discipline and fanaticism, I personally doubt—and I draw again upon my thirty years of experience in this business—that anything short of one of the knowledgeable inner-circle personnel or hijackers turning himself in to us would have given us sufficient foreknowledge to have prevented the horrendous slaughter that took place on the eleventh.

The point of operating in cells is to insure that if one person is caught he can expose only those in his own cell, because he knows nothing of the others. The entire operation is not put at risk. The Al Qaeda terrorists seem to have violated a fundamental rule of clandestine operations. Far from working independently and maintaining rigid communications security, the terrorists, as late as last summer, apparently mingled openly and had not yet decided which flights to target. The planning for September 11th appears to have been far more ad hoc than was at first assumed.

A senior F.B.I. official insisted to me that the September 11th attacks were "carefully orchestrated and well planned," but he agreed that serious and potentially fatal errors were made by the terrorists. Another official said, "We early on thought that people on flight one did not know anything about flights two, three, and four, but we did find that there was cross-pollination in travel and coördination. If they're so good, why did they intermingle?" A third F.B.I. official said, "Are they ten feet tall? They're not."

The fact that the terrorists managed to bring down the World Trade Center may simply mean that seizing an airplane was easier than the American public has been led to believe. The real message of missed opportunities like the Woods flight may be that, even at a time when America's intelligence agencies had raised an alarm, chatter remained chatter—diffuse noise. There were no mechanisms to either dispose of leads, warnings, and suspicious incidents or effectively translate them into a plan for preventing Al Qaeda from attacking.

By 1990, in the wake of the terrorist bombing of Pan Am Flight 103, congressional committees had concluded that the F.A.A. needed more immediate access to current intelligence, and urged that an F.A.A. security official be assigned to the relevant offices in the C.I.A., the F.B.I., and the State Department. Leo Boivin, who was the agency's primary security analyst at the time, told me, "I started the program. Getting into the C.I.A. and State was no problem, but the F.B.I. effectively said no—that it wasn't going to happen. The bureau didn't want anybody in there, and we couldn't fight the bureau." In 1996, after the crash of T.W.A. Flight 800, a commission directed by Vice-President Al Gore also called for closer liaison. This time, according to Boivin, who retired last August, the F.B.I. refused to give the F.A.A. security officer a building pass that would permit unfettered access to F.B.I. headquarters. "The problem with the intelligence community is that you didn't know what you didn't know," Boivin said. "'If there is a problem,' the bureau would say, 'we'll tell you about it.'" The difficulties continued after September 11th. Boivin said that the F.B.I. sought to get rid of the F.A.A.'s liaison man at headquarters, because, in Boivin's words, "he was seen as too pushy about trying to get information." (An F.B.I. spokesman, when asked for comment, said, "Both before September 11th and after September 11th, the bureau shared information with our law-enforcement partners to the fullest extent possible.")

The airlines, always eager to trim operating expenses, successfully lobbied against many of the safety provisions recommended by the Gore commission, such as more stringent security checks on airline employees and tighter screening of passenger baggage. William Webster, the former F.B.I. director, served as the airlines' lobbyist. "The airlines never wanted to spend a lot of money on security," said David Plavin, who was on the Gore commission and is the president of Airports Council International, the lobbying arm of the nation's more than five hundred commercial airports. "They were always concerned that the government would stick them with the bill." Much of that worry, Plavin told me, was alleviated after September 11th with the passage of legislation creating the Transportation Security Administration, which puts the responsibility for security on the federal government, but the new legislation won't solve the most serious problem: bureaucratic infighting. "More than half a dozen federal agencies are involved in airline travel, and their inability to work with each other is notorious," Plavin said. "Protecting their own turf is what matters."

In the late nineteen-nineties, the C.I.A. obtained reliable information indicating that an Al Qaeda network based in northern Germany had penetrated airport security in Amsterdam and was planning to attack American passenger planes by planting bombs in the cargo, a former security official told me. The intelligence was good enough to warrant the dissemination of an F.A.A. Security Directive, and the C.I.A., working with German police, planned a series of successful preëmptive raids. "The Germans rousted a lot of people," the former official said. The F.A.A. and the C.I.A. worked closely together and the incident was kept secret. "While the threat was on, the F.A.A. was getting two or three C.I.A. briefings a day," the former official said. In contrast, in operations in which the F.B.I. took the lead, "the F.A.A. got nothing. The F.B.I. people said, 'If there is a threat, we'll tell you, but we're not going to tell you what's going on in the investigations.' The F.A.A. told them that it had much more information about threats in Hamburg and Beirut than in Detroit, and they said, 'That's the way it is.' They'd come and give a dog-and-pony show."

Long before September 11th, the American intelligence community had a significant amount of information about specific terrorist threats to commercial airline travel in America, including the possibility that a plane could be used as a weapon. In 1994, an Algerian terrorist group hijacked an Air France airliner and threatened to crash it into the Eiffel Tower. In 1995, police in Manila broke up a terrorist operation that was planning to plant bombs with timing devices on as many as twelve American airliners. They also found information that led to the arrest of Ramzi Ahmed Yousef, who directed the 1993 bombing of the World Trade Center. Abdul Hakim Murad, one of Yousef's collaborators, told the Philippine police and, later, U.S. intelligence officers that he had earned his pilot's license in an American flight school and had been planning to seize a small plane, fill it with explosives, and fly it into C.I.A. headquarters. Murad confessed, according to an account published last December in the Washington *Post*, that he had gone to the American flight school "in preparation for a suicide mission." In 1996, the F.B.I. director, Louis Freeh, asked officials in Qatar—a nation suspected of harboring Al Qaeda terrorists—for help in apprehending another alleged accomplice of Yousef, Khalid Shaikh Mohammed, who was then believed to be in Qatar. One of Freeh's diplomatic notes stated that Mohammed was involved in a conspiracy to "bomb U.S. airliners" and was also believed to be "in the process of manufacturing an explosive device."

In late December of 1999, a group of Al Qaeda terrorists armed with knives hijacked an Indian airliner and diverted it to Kandahar, Afghanistan. The hijackers maintained control of the passengers and crew by cutting the throat of a young passenger and letting the victim bleed to death, a tactic that the September 11th terrorists are believed to have used on flight attendants. (Shortly after the Indian hijacking, the F.B.I. opened a liaison office in New Delhi, and has since worked closely with Indian security officials.) The F.A.A., in its annual report for the year 2000, warned that bin Laden and Al Qaeda posed "a significant threat to civil aviation." The F.A.A. had earlier noted, according to the *Times*, that there was a specific report from an exiled Islamic leader in Britain alleging that bin Laden was planning to "bring down an airliner, or hijack an airliner to humiliate the United States."

The attendance of potential terrorists at flight-training schools in America is not a new phenomenon, either. As early as 1975, according to an unpublished Senate Foreign Relations

Committee document, Raymond Winall, then the F.B.I.'s assistant director for intelligence, revealed that a suspected member of Black September, the Palestinian terrorist group responsible for the deaths of eleven Israeli athletes at the 1972 Olympics in Munich, had explained his presence in the United States by telling the F.B.I. that he had been admitted for pilot training—the same explanation for the presence here of a number of the September 11th terrorists. The suspect was indicted but fled the country before he could be arraigned. Since then, according to Bill Carroll, a former district director for the Immigration and Naturalization Service, thousands of young Middle Easterners have obtained visas to enroll in flight-instruction programs.

In recent interviews, three senior F.B.I. officials in charge of responding to terrorism threats did not defend the bureau's past performance, and acknowledged that many of the long-standing complaints had merit. But they insisted that, since September 11th, many things had been done right. The F.B.I. had invested enormous resources in tracking the terrorists' travel activities, and much progress had been made in disrupting the international flow of money to Al Qaeda. The officials admitted that there are still questions about the reliability of some of the information that was collected in the days immediately after September 11th. One unresolved mystery is how many of the nineteen hijackers understood that the mission called for the immolation of all aboard.

The officials maintained that they have correctly established the true identity of all nineteen, by consulting records and going back to their countries of origin. There are, however, lingering questions about at least eight of them. For example, the F.B.I. has identified one of the hijackers aboard United Airlines Flight 77, which crashed into the Pentagon, as Nawaf Alhazmi. A Maryland motel he had checked into under this name had a record of a New York driver's license number and a Manhattan address he had given. But the address turned out to be a hotel, which reported that it had no record of him. And the New York Department of Motor Vehicles said that the number was invalid, and that it had never issued a license to anyone named Nawaf Alhazmi. Similarly, Waleed Alshehri, who was aboard American Airlines Flight 11, was identified by the F.B.I. as a college graduate from Florida whose father was a Saudi diplomat. And yet, last fall, the diplomat told a Saudi Arabian newspaper that his son was still alive and working as a pilot for Saudi Arabian Airlines.

The prevalence of identity theft has also complicated matters. There are an estimated seven hundred and fifty thousand cases of stolen identity in the United States every year, according to Rob Douglas, a leading privacy expert. Saudi newspapers eventually reported that at least four men with the same names as those listed by the F.B.I. as hijackers had been victims of passport theft. A hijacker identified as Abdulaziz Alomari, who also was aboard Flight 11, was reported by the *Rocky Mountain News* to have the same name as a graduate of the University of Colorado, a man who did not resemble a photograph of the hijacker. That Alomari had been stopped by the Denver police several times for minor offenses while attending college

and had given three different birth dates. One of the dates matches the birth date used by the hijacker. Investigators subsequently learned that in 1995 the Colorado student had reported a theft in his apartment; among the items stolen was his passport.

Another hijacker, who used the name Saeed Alghamdi and was aboard Flight 93, was reported last fall by *Newsday* to have taken the Social Security number of a Vermont woman who had been dead since 1965. The name is a common one in Saudi Arabia. At least four other men with that name have shown up on records at the flight school in Florida where Alghamdi was said by the F.B.I. to have trained. The school reported that it had trained more than sixteen hundred students with the first name Saeed and more than two hundred with the surname Alghamdi. Social Security officials also said that six of the nineteen hijackers were using identity cards belonging to other people.

In April, police in Milan raided the apartment of Essid Sami Ben Khemais, the alleged head of an extremist group based in Italy that has been linked to Al Qaeda. A prosecutor's affidavit, the Baltimore *Sun* reported, described what was found: a cache of forged Tunisian and Yemeni passports, Italian identity cards, and photocopies of German driver's licenses. The prosecutor wrote, "One of the most essential illegal activities of the group is the procurement and use of false documents… to guarantee a new identity to the 'brothers' who must hide or escape investigation." The prosecutor further said that the police had recorded telephone conversations in which Khemais discussed with Al Qaeda members the mechanics of falsifying documents.

The complaints about the F.B.I. are well known to the Senate Judiciary Committee, whose chairman, Patrick Leahy, of Vermont, has been urging extensive reform of the bureau for years. "These are not problems of money," Leahy said last July, during confirmation hearings on the appointment of Robert Mueller as the new F.B.I. director. "We have poured a lot of money into the F.B.I. It is a management problem."

The F.B.I.'s computer systems have been in disarray for more than a decade, making it difficult, if not impossible, for analysts and agents to correlate and interpret intelligence. The F.B.I.'s technological weakness also hinders its ability to solve crimes. In March, for example, Leahy's committee was told that photographs of the nineteen suspected hijackers could not be sent electronically in the days immediately after September 11th to the F.B.I. office in Tampa, Florida, because the F.B.I.'s computer systems weren't compatible. Robert Chiradio, the special agent in charge, explained at a hearing that "we don't have the ability to put any scanning or multimedia" into F.B.I. computer systems. The photographs had "to be put on a CD-ROM and mailed to me."

Part of the problem, former F.B.I. agents have told me, is the long-standing practice by the F.B.I. leadership of "reprogramming" funds intended for computer upgrading. I. C. Smith, who was in charge of the F.B.I.'s budget for national-security programs, told me that his department was "constantly raiding the technical programs" to make up for shortfalls in other areas—such as, in one case, the travel budget.

Mueller, who had been on the job for only a week before September 11th, acknowledged in a speech in April that many of the desktop computers at the F.B.I. were discards from other federal agencies that "we take as upgrades." He went on, "We have systems that cannot talk with other bureau systems, much less with other federal agencies. We're working to create a database… that we can use to share information and intelligence with the outside world. We hope to test it later next year"—that is, sometime in 2003.

Clearly, the agents in the field and their superiors at F.B.I. headquarters did not have the optimal tools to cope with the complex world of Middle Eastern terrorism—and the outpouring of intelligence data and warnings about activities inside the United States. (They were not alone. The C.I.A. and other intelligence agencies also contributed to the failure that led to September 11th.) The F.B.I. also found it extremely difficult to field undercover operatives inside the Islamic fundamentalist movement. The situation remains the same today, intelligence officials told me. "They're incapable of it," one former intelligence official said, referring to the F.B.I.'s lack of experience in covert operations. "This is much scarier than the C.I.A.'s inability to penetrate overseas. We don't have eyes and ears in the Muslim communities. We're naked here."

In a recent conversation, a senior F.B.I. official acknowledged that there had been "no breakthrough" inside the government, in terms of establishing how the September 11th suicide teams were organized and how they operated. America's war in Afghanistan, despite success in driving Al Qaeda from its bases there, has yet to produce significant information about the planning and execution of the attacks. U.S. forces are known to have captured thousands of pages of documents and computer hard drives from Al Qaeda redoubts, but so far none of this material—which remains highly classified—has enabled the Justice Department to broaden its understanding of how the attack occurred, or even to bring an indictment of a conspirator. The government's only criminal proceeding filed thus far is against Zacarias Moussaoui, a French citizen who was already in jail on September 11th, on immigration charges. "It's kind of obvious that we haven't wrapped anything up," a C.I.A. consultant told me.

One senior F.B.I. official argued, however, that the intensive American bombing campaign in Afghanistan and the dramatically improved coördination with international police forces and intelligence agencies have led to a serious degradation of Al Qaeda's command and control, and, he said, "the over-all structure of Al Qaeda has been disrupted." Referring to the heavy satellite monitoring of the many training camps operated by Al Qaeda and other terrorist groups in Afghanistan, he said, "For years, we watched the graduating classes every year at the University of Terrorism." What's left, he went on, are "those fleas—the graduates of the training classes who are spread out in the world. We are going to have problems with them for years to come. Could there be a flea who strikes this week in Kansas City? Absolutely."

In Senate testimony in May, Robert Mueller emphasized how difficult it would have been to thwart the September 11th attacks, noting that fifty million people entered and left the United States in August, 2001. "The terrorists took advantage of America's strengths and used them against us," he said. "And as long as we continue to treasure our freedoms we always will run some risk of future attacks."

"These guys were not superhuman," I. C. Smith noted, "but they were playing in a system that was more inept than they were. If you go back to the aircraft hijackings of the early nineteen-seventies, I can't recall a single instance where we caught a guy"—in advance—"who really intended to hijack a plane." But men like Mueller, Smith added, "can't afford to say that the terrorists stumbled through this."

Mueller has one of the most difficult jobs in government today. He is trying to reorganize a bureaucracy that has resisted changes—and outsiders—for decades. He does not praise the old days, and the old ways of doing business, in his public statements. "We must refocus our mission and our priorities," he told the Senate Judiciary Committee in May. "We must improve how we hire, manage, and train our workforce, collaborate with others, and manage, analyze, share, and protect our information." He added, "I am more impatient than most, but we must do these things right, not simply fast."

Mueller's insistence on centralizing decision-making and control of counterterrorism operations at F.B.I. headquarters has provoked discord in some of the F.B.I.'s fifty-six bureaus across the nation. Senior officers with specialized expertise were reassigned to counterterrorism duty after September 11th, and many still find their new jobs bewildering.

Increasingly, the divisions are becoming public. Last week, a letter of complaint sent to the House and Senate intelligence committees by the F.B.I.'s general counsel in Minneapolis was leaked to the press. It accused F.B.I. headquarters of obstructing the local inquiry into Zacarias Moussaoui and accused Mueller personally of misrepresenting the bureau's handling of the case. Mueller quickly announced that he had referred the matter to the Justice Department for investigation. A Senate aide told me that Mueller's willingness to air the problems—even at the risk of adverse publicity—had won him few friends inside the Bush Administration. "He's had his hand slapped by the Justice Department," the official said, "and he's having problems with the White House."

Mueller does have the support, thus far, of the often skeptical Senate Judiciary Committee. The committee, under Senator Leahy, began extensive oversight hearings into the F.B.I. last year—the first comprehensive hearings in two decades. "He inherited a mess," Leahy said. "The F.B.I. has improved since the days of J. Edgar Hoover. It doesn't go around blackmailing members of Congress anymore. But it still has a 'We don't make mistakes or admit mistakes' culture." Mueller seems to be committed to changing that attitude, Leahy told me. "I have confidence in him, and it will continue as long as we see a bureau that really wants to correct its mistakes. Mueller's best defense—and his best offense—is to be as forthcoming with

Congress as possible." The Senator added, "White Houses come and go, but he has a ten-year tenure."

Since the hijackings, the F.B.I. and the C.I.A. have gone to great lengths to improve coöperation, and C.I.A. personnel are assigned to F.B.I. offices. In some basic ways, however, the F.B.I. still doesn't work. The bureau, one of Mueller's aides said, is undergoing an enormous and painful change in its day-to-day approach to investigations. "The mission now is not just to put handcuffs on people and throw them into jail but to stop acts of terrorism in the future. A lot of people here are not prepared to radically change their way of doing business, and it's frustrating for many agents, with their black-and-white way of looking at the world. The F.B.I.'s priority now is to get information to prevent the next event—even if it means we lose the case." The transition will lead to many forced early retirements. "There hasn't been time to build up a cadre of people with the right skills," the aide said. One inevitable problem is that the most significant of Mueller's changes—such as the recruitment and hiring of experts in foreign languages, area studies, and computer technology—will not pay dividends for years.

A longtime clandestine C.I.A. operative was skeptical about the rival agency's ability to transform itself. "They're cops," he said of the F.B.I. agents. "They spent their careers trying to catch bank robbers while we spent ours trying to rob banks."

The Administration did not respond passively to the recent wave of media reports of warnings gone unheeded. It went on the offensive. Vice-President Dick Cheney warned against "incendiary rhetoric," and said that the criticism from Democrats about the missed messages was "thoroughly irresponsible of national leaders in a time of war." Other Cabinet members issued dire public warnings of increased terrorism threats—based not on specific information but on more "chatter," in various corners of the Islamic world. In earlier interviews with me, senior F.B.I. counterterrorism officials had made a point of criticizing such vague warnings. "Is there some C.Y.A."—cover your ass—"involved when officials talk about threats to power supplies, or banks, or malls?" one senior F.B.I. official asked. "Of course there is."

"Puffing up the threat because of a political interest is a disservice," the official added. When such threats are unfulfilled, the result is that "the country lowers its guard. And that kind of flippancy is what we don't need now. The American people are going back to sleep."

Another F.B.I. official depicted the question of when to warn the public as a "lose-lose" situation. "Say we get a report that three Al Qaeda guys are driving up from Mexico to blow up an unspecified mall in Dallas," the official said. "What do you want to be told?" He added, "We know the power of the people. Do we want you calling us if your neighbor is turning in to his driveway at two in the morning?" The bureau responded to three hundred calls about suspicious packages between January 1st and September 10th of 2001. After September 11th, the official said, "we received fifty-four thousand calls and physically responded to fourteen thousand of them." Even now, according to another official, scores of tips arrive every day from overseas, many of them relayed by C.I.A. sources that are known to pay for such information. "And the C.I.A. is happy to forward them to us," he noted. "Then it's not the C.I.A.'s problem."

Stories of supposed terrorist sightings have also become common inside the airline industry—a part of its post-September 11th folklore. One widely repeated tale involves a stewardess who flew with a man dressed as a captain—he had hitched a ride, as crew members often do—whom she later recognized as Mohammed Atta. Many in the industry, it seems, know someone who knows someone who saw one or another of the September 11th terrorists in captains' uniforms in cockpit jumpseats.

There also has been a series of jarring alerts from federal health agencies and the Office of Homeland Security depicting the far-reaching threat posed by biological warfare or the possible use of fissile materials by Al Qaeda. One public-health official who has participated in Homeland Security discussions described the group as being overwhelmed by the potential threat to America's water supply, electrical grids, oil depots, and even the wholesale processing of milk. "Where do we start?" he said. "So many threats. We're like deer in the headlights."

"Traditionally, when Americans have had a war, they go and find the enemy, defeat it on the battlefield, and come home to replant," a senior F.B.I. official said. The war against terrorism is a long-term struggle and has no borders. "We need maturity when it comes to protecting our society," the official went on. "We shouldn't profoundly change our system, but we need a balance. Democracy is a messy business." Meanwhile, the terrorists won't go away. Another senior F.B.I. official said, "They'd like nothing better than to regroup and come back."

Counterterrorism

A New Organizing Principle for American National Security?

by James Steinberg

In his address to Congress nine days after the September 11 attacks, President Bush declared war on global terrorism and announced his intent to deploy "every resource at our command" to defeat terrorist networks and to treat states that harbor and support terrorism as "hostile regimes." The speech appeared to presage a political reorientation of U.S. foreign and security policy on a scale not seen since the early days of the Cold War, comparable in scope to the Truman Doctrine and the adoption of the strategy of containment in the late 1940s.

The experience of the Cold War illustrates the potentially far-reaching consequences for foreign (and domestic) policy of a decision to make antiterrorism the organizing principle for U.S. international relations and domestic security. During the Cold War, the United States defined its relations with other countries through the benchmark of who was with us and who against us in the struggle against communism and the Soviet Union. We built alliances with democracies and authoritarian governments alike if they shared our commitment. We organized our military forces and doctrine to shape that struggle. We intervened politically and militarily based on a perception of how regional conflicts and national governments would affect the East-West balance.

We helped reconstruct Europe and Japan and provided foreign aid based on those same criteria. We supported a defense-industrial establishment to assure the wherewithal to sustain our technological edge. We even sent a man to the moon to demonstrate the superiority of Western democracy over Soviet totalitarianism and the command economy.

To the extent that counterterrorism becomes a comparable, new organizing principle, it will have similarly widespread consequences for a broad range of U.S. policies. Nearly nine months after the September 11 attacks, it is now possible to see the extent—and the limits—of counterterrorism as an organizing principle for U.S. foreign policy.

New Friends

The clearest impact of this strategic shift can be seen in the reorientation of U.S. relations with key international partners, particularly in connection with the military operations in Afghanistan. Perhaps the most dramatic illustration is Pakistan. Just before September 11, U.S. relations with Pakistan had sunk to unprecedented lows. Pakistan's nuclear weapons program had led to strict sanctions; formerly close military ties had been cut off; and further sanctions had been imposed when General Pervez Musharraf ousted the elected government of Nawaz Sharif in 1999. Pakistani support for Islamic militants in Kashmir threatened to land Pakistan on the U.S. terrorism list, and persistent economic mismanagement imperiled Pakistan's relationship with the International Monetary Fund.

What a difference a day makes. Following the September 11 attacks and Musharraf's decision to provide political and military support to the U.S. effort to oust the Taliban, Musharraf became a welcome interlocutor, and a meeting was arranged with President Bush in New York. Sanctions were quickly lifted, and new aid totaling $1 billion was offered along with promises of more debt relief. In the war against terrorism, Pakistan is once again a U.S. ally.

Similar though less dramatic changes have marked U.S. relations with Central Asian countries. Although Washington had begun to develop ties with former Soviet states in the 1990s, serious concerns about repressive regimes, lack of democracy, and corruption were a brake on moves to further deepen the relationship. Yet, as Uzbekistan and Tajikistan opened their territory to stationing U.S. forces, the Bush administration began to be more forthcoming, both in economic and military assistance and in political support, to these new partners.

Other adversaries-turned-friends include Yemen, seen before September 11 as noncooperative in investigating the bombing of the USS Cole in 2000, and Sudan, long the object of U.S. criticism for a broad range of policies. No doubt wishing to avoid the Taliban's fate, both governments have shown new zeal in counterterrorism cooperation with Washington.

For the United States and India, September 11 has strengthened ties that had already begun to improve with President Clinton's visit in 2000. The U.S. military action in Afghanistan ousted India's nemesis, the Taliban, which had supported Islamic militants in Kashmir. And India's positive disposition has been further enhanced by the U.S. decision to resume military sales, which had been cut off for decades.

Even before September 11, Russian testiness about missile defense, proliferation, and its military operations in Chechnya had been easing with the budding personal tie between Presidents Bush and Putin. But the courtship blossomed into a full-blown romance when Putin was the first to call Bush after the attacks, offering not only political support, but invaluable intelligence cooperation and the benefit of Russia's own difficult experience in Afghanistan. In return, Washington has softened its rhetoric on Chechnya, shown new flexibility in discussing arms control and Russia's entry into the World Trade Organization, and become more forthcoming on Russia-NATO ties—although taking care not to appear to give Russia a veto over NATO military decisions.

U.S.-China relations too have felt the transformative winds of September 11. Relations had warmed considerably from the early days of the Bush administration—when the new team had spoken of China as a strategic competitor. But following the World Trade Center and Pentagon attacks, China supported the United States in the Security Council, and while not exactly endorsing the military effort in Afghanistan, conspicuously refrained from attacking it. And the United States reciprocated. During President Bush's trip to Shanghai for the APEC summit in October, the dialogue with President Jiang steered clear of blunt talk that might have been anticipated just a few months earlier. Bush avoided public confrontations on the familiar sources of disagreement—from Tibet to Taiwan to proliferation—and the largely cooperative tone continued during Bush's second visit to China in February.

The search for new partners in the fight against terrorism found support in unexpected quarters. For example, the Bush administration found a new predicate for seeking to improve its relations with a frequent nemesis—President Mahatir of Malaysia, whose own struggle with Islamic extremists in his country put Malaysia "on our side" in the counterterrorism campaign.

In the first weeks following September 11, it even appeared briefly that the new counterterrorism paradigm might portend a new opportunity for rapprochement between the United States and Iran. Although U.S.-Iran relations were confrontational on the eve of the attacks, in their immediate aftermath President Mohammad Khatami strongly stated his sympathy for the victims and, even more notably, granted the United States overflight rights for humanitarian and search-and-rescue operations in Afghanistan. But the honeymoon proved short-lived. Intelligence reports linked Iran to arms sales to the Palestinian Authority and to ongoing support for terrorist groups in the Middle East. The administration claimed that Iran was undermining Hamid Karzai's interim government in Afghanistan. Iran soon found itself on the "axis of evil"—"against us" in the new bipolar geopolitics of counterterrorism.

Old Friends

September 11 was also consequential for America's traditional partners worldwide. Europe's initial response was overwhelming sympathy: even the traditionally skeptical French press declared, "We are all Americans." NATO allies invoked for the first time the "Article 5" guarantee to come to the aid of any alliance member who was attacked; they conducted sweeping raids on suspected al Qaeda members throughout Europe.

But some Europeans felt slighted that the United States did not make greater use of the NATO military apparatus in Afghanistan or act quickly to incorporate other European military forces into Operation Enduring Freedom. Those who had hoped that Washington would turn away from what they feared was excessive unilateralism were initially comforted by the U.S. approach to Afghanistan (including securing a United Nations Security Council resolution), but disquiet grew as the rhetoric shifted to the axis of evil and the focus appeared to shift from stabilizing Afghanistan to overthrowing Saddam Hussein.

U.S.-Japan relations also received a boost. Determined, after the shock of September 11, to demonstrate that Japan could provide not just financial support, but meaningful operational assistance to the military effort in Afghanistan, Prime Minister Koizumi won approval for changes in the interpretation of Japan's constitution that permitted Japan to deploy forces to the Indian Ocean. Although the Diet imposed some restrictions, such as a time limit on the deployment, the policy change was momentous. And in a sign of the broad effect of September 11, it received a muted reaction in both Beijing and Seoul.

By contrast, U.S.-South Korean relations, already rocked by disagreements over what strategy to pursue toward North Korea, were further troubled by Bush's decision to include North Korea as the eastern wing of the axis of evil. Although the move appeared again to distance the United States from President Kim Dae Jung's sunshine policy, its long-term impact is uncertain. Despite the rhetoric, the Bush administration continued to advocate dialogue with North Korea, and coming elections in South Korea could bring to power a government more in tune with Washington.

The Middle East: Testing Ground for the New Paradigm

In perhaps no corner of the world does the counterterrorism paradigm have the potential to transform U.S. policy more than in the Middle East, where relations with traditional Arab partners Saudi Arabia and Egypt are now in question. For many in the United States, both in and out of government, the rise of al Qaeda can be directly linked to the policies of the Saudi government—suppressing dissent at home but supporting fundamentalism abroad, with deadly consequences for the United States. Tensions were exacerbated by a perception that the Saudi and Egyptian governments failed to speak out forcefully against the attacks, tolerated (if not encouraged) anti-Americanism in their state-sponsored media, and offered only lukewarm military support for the operation in Afghanistan. Some members of Congress have proposed cutting U.S. aid to Egypt and withdrawing U.S. military forces from Saudi Arabia.

The Middle East has also demonstrated the tensions inherent in a single-minded application of counterterrorism as an organizing principle. As the suicide bombings against Israel intensified through last fall and winter, the government of Ariel Sharon sought to wrap its forceful response in the mantle of Bush's categorical language against those who harbor terrorism—and for a time, the Bush administration largely adopted a similar view, ostracizing Yasser Arafat and placing the onus on the Palestinian Authority to halt the violence. But it became apparent, during Vice President Cheney's trip to the Middle East in March, that the deepening violence had become a major obstacle to the administration's strategy to remove Saddam Hussein. Thus, as Israel accelerated its military moves following the Passover suicide bombings, the administration was finally forced to call for limits on Israel's use of force and defend Arafat's continued involvement in the peace process. In short, the administration came to realize that it had to juggle multiple objectives and interests, not all of which could fit into the "with us or against us" mantra of the counterterrorism paradigm. But critics of this shift denounced it as a betrayal of "moral clarity" in the campaign against terrorism.

The administration's efforts to calm the Israeli-Palestinian conflict were motivated in part by its own plans for "regime change" in Iraq. Although the nexus between Iraq and al Qaeda remains in dispute, Iraq's robust weapons of mass destruction program is universally acknowledged—as is the possibility that Iraq might share its know-how with terrorists. But, as Cheney learned during his trip, Arab willingness to support Bush's counterterrorism agenda on Iraq depends on U.S. willingness to address the Arab priority—the Palestinian issue.

New Priorities

September 11 has also changed American priorities. Just a month before the attacks, President Bush welcomed Mexican President Vicente Fox to Washington, proclaiming the bond with Mexico to be our nation's most important relationship. Today, the two countries are focusing not on deeper integration, but on how to secure the U.S. border.

During the presidential campaign of 2000, candidate Bush denounced the Clinton administration's preoccupation with "nation building." But after the Afghan military operation, President Bush committed the United States to "helping to build an Afghanistan that is free from this evil and is a better place in which to live," citing the post–World War II examples of the Marshall Plan in Europe and the reconstruction of Japan.

Similarly, Bush initially placed little emphasis on foreign aid as a tool of foreign policy. But the need to win friends who felt the administration was doing too little to address the "root causes" of terrorism prompted Bush to double aid spending for 2003.

Perhaps the biggest question mark about the impact of September 11 concerns the U.S. balance between unilateralism and multilateralism. Before September 11, concern was growing abroad about the administration's preference for unilateral action and its skepticism about international institutions and treaties—from the Kyoto Climate Change Protocol, to the Comprehensive Test Ban Treaty, to the International Criminal Court, to the Anti-Ballistic Missile Treaty. But after the attacks, perceptions began to shift, as the administration patiently assembled an international coalition before launching a military attack on Afghanistan. Secretary Powell famously observed, "We're so multilateral it keeps me up 24 hours a day checking on everybody." How significant the change is may become clearer as the administration develops its strategy toward Iraq— in particular, whether it attempts to build an international coalition focusing on Iraq's noncompliance with Security Council resolutions on eliminating weapons of mass destruction before using force to overthrow Saddam Hussein.

A Sustainable Focus?

The U.S. campaign against terrorism will be a long one. Terrorism is the most serious threat to the safety of Americans today, and the growing proliferation of weapons of mass destruction makes the threat likely to become all the more dangerous. But terrorism is not the only peril. As the administration has recognized, some governments pose a threat to our interests whether or not they are aligned with terrorists. Other transnational threats include organized crime, drug trafficking, and proliferation of weapons of mass destruction, as well as risks posed to the stability of the international financial and trading systems, to resources like energy and water, and to global environment and health. A sustainable counterterrorism strategy must recognize that there is no one-size-fits-all approach to counterterrorism and that the effort must be integrated into a larger strategy that allows the United States to reap the benefits and counter the dangers of our increasingly interdependent world.

What, in practical terms, does this mean to the United States? Allies and partners are crucial in the fight against terrorism. However powerful the United States may be, it will need to rely on others to carry out this multifaceted challenge. To sustain those partnerships, the United States must be prepared both to consult meaningfully (not just to inform) and to be responsive to other nations' priorities. While it will always be possible to cobble together coalitions of convenience, durable alliances provide special advantages—reliability, habits of cooperation, and shared outlooks.

By building on the international support it gained in the wake of September 11, the United States has a unique opportunity to revive ties with traditional friends and build new relationships with former adversaries. If the administration can capitalize on its successful coalition-building effort for the Afghan war, we could see the emergence of a new, more constructive set of relationships among most, if not all, global actors.

The counterterrorism campaign has both a short-term and a long-term dimension. To thwart the immediate threat, the emphasis must necessarily be on law enforcement, intelligence, and, occasionally, military tools. But in the long run, terrorist networks will reconstitute themselves unless we make it harder for them to recruit new members and sustain their activities. This means helping to build stable, prosperous, democratic societies in countries that have seen too little of all three, particularly in the Arab world, Africa, and parts of Central, South, and Southeast Asia.

No single approach will fit all circumstances. Different terrorist groups pose different challenges and require different tools, even as we categorically condemn their methods. The threat posed by al Qaeda differs from the threat posed by the Irish Republican Army or even by the bloody suicide killers of the Tamil Tigers. Often a political approach will be necessary to separate terrorists from publics with political grievances as a parallel track to counterterrorism.

Washington must not lose sight of broader U.S. interests. The administration's decision to boost foreign aid represented a sound recognition that poverty, ignorance, and disease threaten our interests. So does excessive reliance on partnerships of convenience with countries that don't share our values. During the Cold War, from Iran to Latin America, we discovered the long-term costs of relationships of short-term expediency.

Finally, it is essential to maintain the vitality of key international institutions. Granted, these institutions pose constraints, but they also provide important leverage and burden sharing. As we have learned in the Balkans and in Afghanistan, there are many tasks the United States doesn't want to take on alone (or at all). Organizations like the UN or the Organization for Security and Cooperation in Europe can provide an important alternative.

By placing counterterrorism in the framework of securing our broader national interests, the United States will not only be more effective in reducing the long-term threat from terrorists, but will also help assure that the fight against terrorism does not inadvertently weaken our overall security and prosperity.

James Steinberg is vice president and director of the Brookings Foreign Policy Studies Program.

UNIT 11
Future Threats

Unit Selections

Key Points to Consider

- Has the use of biological agents by terrorists become more likely? Is the public health system in the United States prepared to handle such an emergency?

- Describe the difference between terrorism and principled civil disobedience as clarified by Don Whipple.

- What makes the United States particularly vulnerable to cyberterrorism? What are potential consequences of attacks against the critical infrastructure of the United States?

- Why will terrorism continue to grow in the twenty-first century? What factors suggest the continued development of more destructive forms of terrorism? What are the implications for future policy?

 **Links: www.dushkin.com/online/**
These sites are annotated in the World Wide Web pages.

Centers for Disease Control and Prevention—Bioterrorism
http://www.bt.cdc.gov

Nuclear Terrorism
http://www.nci.org/nci/nci-nt.htm

Terrorism Files
http://www.terrorismfiles.org

The devastating attacks on the World Trade Center and the Pentagon have spawned wild speculation and apocalyptic predictions concerning the future of U.S. security. The general theme of the articles in this unit gives the reader a realistic sense of what may be. The tragedy of September 11 and the subsequent anthrax attacks have fueled fears and have led to an exaggeration of terrorist capabilities. It is only natural for these fears to lead to visions of future catastrophe and carnage. The existence of terrorism cannot be ignored. The U.S. government and the media, however, continue to project images of terrorists as almost superhuman, often endowing them with capabilities far beyond their actual reach. The articles in this unit, rather than furthering myths and fears, seek to educate the reader about how some believe the future of terrorism may look. As terrorism continues to be a top priority in public policy and government spending, difficult choices must be made. As policymakers attempt to find ways to reassure a concerned public, choices between spending for security today and preparing for the threats of the future have become increasingly difficult.

Terrorism will, undoubtedly, remain a major policy issue for the United States well into the twenty-first century. Opinions as to what future perpetrators will look like and what methods they will pursue continue to vary. Some argue that the traditional methods of terrorism, such as bombing, kidnapping, and hostage-taking, will continue to dominate the new millennium. Others warn that weapons of mass destruction or weapons of mass

disruption, such as biological and chemical weapons or even nuclear or radiological weapons, will be the weapons of choice for terrorists in the future.

"Waiting for Bioterror" examines the U.S. government's preparedness for and response capability to biological attacks. Katherine Eban argues that there are problems with the public health system which, if left uncorrected, will leave the United States vulnerable. Then, Don Whipple describes the environmental movement in terms of acts of principled civil disobedience rather than terror. Barton Gellman's article addresses the

possibilities that our nation's critical infrastructure may be vulnerable to new forms of terrorism. He argues that a combination of cyberterrorism and traditional physical attacks poses a new and grave risk to U.S. security. Finally, Virginia Gewin, in "Agriculture Shock," highlights the potential economic and physical consequences of an attack on plants and animals. She argues that the threats posed to plant and animal health and the wide-ranging ramifications that would arise from such a terrorist attack are often overlooked in discussions of future terrorist threats.

WAITING FOR BIOTERROR

IS OUR PUBLIC HEALTH SYSTEM READY?

By KATHERINE EBAN

Just before the July 4 holiday this past summer, as National Guardsmen with sniffer dogs monitored the nation's bridges and airports, Jerome Hauer, an assistant secretary at the Health and Human Services Department, dispatched a technician to Atlanta to set up a satellite phone for the new director of the Centers for Disease Control.

If smallpox broke out, if phones failed, if the federal government had to oversee mass vaccination of an urban center, Hauer would have a way to communicate with the CDC director, who since last fall has worked with him on health crises, particularly bioterror. It was one of many precautions that might make the difference between a manageable event and full-scale disaster.

But at the same time, an attempt at crisis management of a more immediate kind was unfolding 2,500 miles to the west. As the FBI chased reports of potential new threats, including a possible attack on Las Vegas, Dr. John Fildes, the medical director of Nevada's only top-level trauma center, watched helplessly as a real medical disaster developed, one that had nothing and everything to do with the problems that Hauer was working to solve.

Faced with a dramatic spike in the cost of their malpractice insurance, fifty-seven of the fifty-eight orthopedic surgeons at University Medical Center in Las Vegas resigned, forcing the state's only trauma center that could treat it all—from car crash, burn and gunshot victims to potential bioterror casualties—to close for ten days.

With Las Vegas a potential target, a quarter-million tourists at the gaming tables and the closest high-level trauma center 300 miles away, the crisis barely registered in the federal government. Nevada's Office of Emergency Management called to inquire about a backup plan, which, as Dr. Fildes later recounted, was to dissolve the county's trauma system, send patients to less prepared hospitals and take the critically injured to Los Angeles or Salt Lake City, both about eighty minutes by helicopter.

During that anxious week Hauer's satellite phone and Fildes's resignation letters formed two bookends of the nation's disaster planning. Hauer—whose Office of the Assistant Secretary for Public Health Emergency Preparedness (ASPHEP) was created by the department Secretary, Tommy Thompson, after the anthrax attacks—can get a last-minute satellite phone, a crack staff and even the ear of President Bush on public health concerns.

The recent flurry of concern has not begun to address our greatest vulnerability: the decrepit state of our healthcare system.

But Fildes, whose trauma center is the third-busiest in the nation and serves a 10,000-square-mile area, struggles to keep his staff intact and the doors of his center open. And this is in a state with no appointed health director, few mental health facilities, no extra room in its hospitals and the nation's only metropolitan area, Las Vegas, without a public health laboratory within 100 miles. In the event of a public health disaster, like the bioterror attack, Fildes says, "we're prepared to do our best. And I hope our best is good enough."

A Public Health 'Train Wreck'

On taking office, President Bush eliminated the health position from the National Security Council, arguing that health, while in the national interest, was not a national security concern. In the wake of the anthrax attacks last year, he changed his tune, declaring, "We have fought the causes and consequences of disease throughout history and must continue to do so with every available means." Next year's budget for biodefense is up 319 percent, to $5.9 billion. States, newly flush with $1.1 billion in biodefense funds, have gone on shopping sprees for emergency equipment like gas masks, hazmat suits and Geiger counters. Newly drafted to fight the war on bioterror, doctors and public health officials are now deemed vital to national security, and their hospitals are even under threat, according to an alert released in mid-November by the FBI.

And yet this flurry of interest and concern has not begun to address America's greatest public health vulnerability: the decrepit and deteriorating state of our healthcare system. In states from Nevada to Georgia, dozens of health officials and doctors told *The Nation* that anemic state funding, overcrowding and staff shortages may be greater problems in responding to bioterror than lack of equipment or specific training. "We don't have enough ER capacity in this country to get through tonight's 911 calls," said Dr. Arthur Kellerman, chairman of the emergency medicine department at the Emory University School of Medicine in Atlanta. Two decades of managed care and government cuts have left a depleted system with too few hospitals, overburdened staff, declining access for patients, rising emergency-room visits and an increasing number of uninsured. The resulting strain is practically Kafkaesque: How do you find enough nurses to staff enough hospital beds to move enough emergency-room patients upstairs so that ambulances with new patients can stop circling the block?

The infusion of cash for bioterror defense without consideration of these fundamental problems is like "building walls in a bog," where they are sure to sink, said Dr. Jeffrey Koplan, the recently departed head of the CDC.

Between 1980 and 2000, the number of hospitals declined by 900 because of declining payments and increased demands for efficiency, according to the American Hospital Association, leaving almost four-fifths of urban hospitals experiencing serious emergency-room overcrowding. Burnout and low pay have left 15 percent of the nation's nursing jobs unfilled, and the staffing shortage has led to a drop in the number of hospital beds by one-fifth; in Boston by one-third, according to the Center for Studying Health System Change in Washington.

Meanwhile, emergency room visits increased by 5 million last year, according to the American College of Emergency Physicians. One in eight urban hospitals diverts or turns away new emergency patients one-fifth of the time because of overcrowding, the American Hospital Association reports. And the costs of health insurance and medical malpractice premiums continue to soar.

In public health, chronic underfunding has closed training programs and depleted expertise. According to a recent CDC report, 78 percent of the nation's public health officials lack advanced training and more than half have no basic health training at all. During the anthrax crisis inexperienced technicians in the New York City public health laboratory failed to turn on an exhaust fan while testing anthrax samples and accidentally contaminated the laboratory.

A government study of rural preparedness this past April found that only 20 percent of the nation's 3,000 local public health departments have a plan in place to respond to bioterror. Thirteen states have had no epidemiologists on payroll, said Dr. Elin Gursky, senior fellow for biodefense and public health programs at the ANSER Institute for Homeland Security. Meanwhile, 18 percent of jobs in the nation's public health labs are open, and the salaries create little hope of filling them. One state posted the starting salary for the director of its public health laboratory program—a PhD position—at $38,500, said Scott Becker, executive director of the Association of Public Health Laboratories. Becker calls the combination of state cuts and workforce shortages a "train wreck."

Amid this crisis, clinicians have a new mandate: to be able to fight a war on two fronts simultaneously. They must care for the normal volume of patients and track the usual infectious diseases while being able to treat mass casualties of a terrorist event. They now have some money for the high-concept disaster, but with many states in dire financial straits, there is less money than ever for the slow-motion meltdown of the healthcare system, in which 41 million Americans lack health insurance. In the event of a smallpox attack, the tendency of the uninsured to delay seeking treatment could be catastrophic.

Hauer hopes that the "dual use" of federal resources could herald a golden age in public health, with tools for tracking anthrax or smallpox being used also to combat West Nile virus or outbreaks from contaminated food. But politicians of all stripes continue to propose beefing up biodefense in isolation from more systemic problems. In October, Al Gore argued in a speech that the problem of the uninsured should take "a back seat" temporarily to the more urgent matter of biodefense. And Bush has proposed shifting key public health and biodefense functions into his proposed Department of Homeland Security, a move likely to weaken daily public health work like disease surveillance and prevention, according to the General Accounting Office. A bipartisan report recently issued by the Council on Foreign Relations warned that America remains dangerously unprepared for a terrorist attack, with its emergency responders untrained and its public health systems depleted.

The solution, say doctors, is to tackle the systemic and not just the boutique problems. "If you have a health system that is chaotic and has no leadership and is not worried about tuberculosis and West Nile and just worried about these rare entities, you'll never be prepared," said Dr. Lewis Goldfrank, director of emergency medicine at Bellevue Hospital Center in New York City. "To be useful, money has to be earmarked for public health generally, so that it will prepare you for terrorism or naturally occurring events."

President Bush strongly resisted federalizing airport security until it became clear as day that private security companies and their minimum-wage workers would continue to let a flow of box cutters, knives and handguns through the metal detectors. Some clinicians now say that the specter of bioterror raises a similar question, which almost nobody in Washington has yet begun to address: Has healthcare become so vital to national security that it must be centralized, with the federal government guaranteeing basic healthcare for everyone?

"Forget about paying for the smallpox vaccine," said Dr. Carlos del Rio, chief of medicine at Atlanta's Grady Memorial Hospital. "Who's going to pay for the complications of the vaccine? With what money? We haven't even addressed that. As you look at bioterror issues, it's forcing us to look at our healthcare delivery."

Crisis Management in Crisis

Hauer spends much of his time in a windowless set of offices within the vast Health and Human Services Department, trouble-shooting the medical consequences of a hypothetical dirty bomb or intentional smallpox outbreak. He must also navigate the knotted bureaucracy of forty federal agencies that respond to terrorism, twenty of which play some role in bioterror response, and guide the states through infrastructure problems so severe they boggle the mind. His tactic at a meeting in Washington this August with state emergency managers was to put the fear of God into them. In the event of mass vaccinations for smallpox, the logistics are "very daunting," he told the small and sleepy group in a conference room at the Mayflower Hotel. "They will fall on emergency management, and the health departments will turn to you and say, 'You need to open 200 vaccination centers.'"

This seemed to focus the group. Before Hauer got up, these local and regional representatives had been talking about lessons learned from managing hurricanes and the best kinds of handheld chemical-weapons detectors.

Tommy Thompson created Hauer's office after the CDC, then his lead agency on bioterror, appeared to bungle the anthrax response and the Administration found itself in a scientific and logistical quagmire. Some officials claimed the White House muzzled the CDC. Others accused the CDC of sloth and bad science for failing to realize quickly that anthrax spores can leak from taped envelopes. Hauer seemed like a good choice to find a way out of this mess: He had developed the nation's first bioterrorism response plan as director of New York City's Office of Emergency Management under Mayor Rudolph Giuliani.

Hauer told the group that his office had moved $1.1 billion to the states in ninety days and was now doing audits, offering technical assistance and helping to stage drills.

But it was the nitty-gritty of mass vaccination that really quieted the room. Training a vaccinator usually takes two hours, though it can be done in fifteen minutes; for every million people vaccinated, about two will die; the vaccinators need to be federally insured because of liability; and all those vaccinated must keep the vaccination site unexposed to others for up to twenty-one days. Who would pay the salaries of contract workers on their days off?

Few emergency managers seemed to have considered such problems. Most were still immersed in competing disaster plans and state budget battles, coping with teetering local health departments and venders hawking "equipment that will detect the landing of Martians ten miles away in a windstorm," as James O'Brien, emergency manager for Clark County, Nevada, put it.

Hauer returned that afternoon to just such a morass: figuring out how to create a unified command for the national capital area, encompassing Maryland, Virginia and the District of Columbia, seventeen jurisdictions over 3,000 square miles, with embassies, consulates, the World Bank and the International Monetary Fund. He had assigned this problem to a team from the Office of Emergency Response (OER), the federal office under ASPHEP that coordinates medical resources during disasters, who arrived at his office to report their progress.

Each state, unsurprisingly, wanted to be the lead responder, and the team recommended that Hauer try to break the logjam and give direction. He poured over the list of those invited to a coordinating committee meeting—twenty-nine people from twenty-nine different agencies—and concluded, "We need to come away with plans, not some loosie-goosie love fest where everyone pats each other on the back and jerks each other off."

The OER team trooped out with its marching orders and the next meeting began. The CEO of the New York Blood Center, Dr. Robert Jones, with a DC consultant in tow, came to ask for money to expand the center's program of making umbilical cord (placental) blood, used for patients exposed to massive radiation. Jones said the center already had about 18,000 units of cord blood stored in "bioarchive freezers" on First Avenue in Manhattan.

"You might want to think about storing it away from Manhattan," said Hauer, suggesting the obvious, as he got out a little booklet and looked up a one-kiloton nuclear bomb. "You'd need 20,000 to 40,000 units" to begin treating a city of people, said Hauer. "What's the lead time for getting it into a patient?"

Jones, who had never met Hauer before, seemed surprised to be taken so seriously and to be crunching numbers about three minutes into the conversation. Hauer, wanting to stockpile cord blood, seemed surprised that Jones had not brought a written proposal with a dollar amount. This was no time to be coy about asking for money.

Suddenly Hauer's secure phone rang and the room fell silent. "This is Jerry Hauer," he said. "You have the wrong number."

Leaving Las Vegas—in the Lurch

In Las Vegas, a gaming town with an appetite for risk, little by way of a medical infrastructure ever developed. With the population exploding and 6,000 families a month moving into the Las Vegas area in Clark County, population 1.4 million, it is also dramatically short on hospitals. By a thumbnail calculation—for every 100,000 people you need 200 beds—the county, which has eleven hospitals, is 600 beds short, said Dr. John Ellerton, chief of staff at University Medical Center, where the trauma center closed.

Even if you build more hospitals, how would you staff them? The state ranks fiftieth in its nurse-to-patient ratio, and because of the malpractice crisis, ninety of the state's 2,000 doctors have closed their practices and another eighty-three said they have considered leaving, according to Lawrence Matheis, executive director of the Nevada State Medical Association. The overcrowded emergency rooms are closed to new patients 40 percent of the time. Paramedics often drive and drive, waiting for an open emergency room. In turn, patients can wait four hours for an X-ray, three for a lab test. "There is no surge capacity, minimal staffing, minimal equipment," said Dr. Donald Kwalick, chief health officer of Clark County. "Every hospital bed in this county is full every day."

Last year Nevadans began to lose their cool as the medical system disintegrated. Then came the anthrax crisis.

At times, the populace and even the doctors have seemed strangely indifferent. One night this summer an ambulance crew from the private company American Medical Response got called to a casino, and as they wheeled a stretcher amid the gaming tables, not a single patron looked up. Their patient: a man with a possible heart attack slumped over a slot machine. "The purity of our devotion to individual liberties tends to diminish our security and humane concern," said Matheis.

The September 11 attacks did not entirely transform this mindset. Since 1998 the city had been included on a federal government list of 120 cities that should prepare for possible attack. Eleven of the world's thirteen largest hotels, one with more than 5,000 rooms, are here. But this August, even the president of the state's medical association, Dr. Robert Schreck, said he worried little about terrorism. Al Qaeda's intent is "to kill capitalism," he said, sipping wine in the lobby of the elaborate Venetian Hotel, home to a massive casino and dozens of stores. "Why would they hit us?"

But last year Nevadans began to lose their cool as the medical system disintegrated. As malpractice insurance premiums skyrocketed, about thirty of Clark County's ninety-three obstetricians closed down their practices. Insurers, trying to reduce risk by limiting the remaining obstetricians to 125 deliveries a year, left thousands of pregnant women to hunt for doctors, some by desperately rifling through the Yellow Pages under "D." This year, the last pediatric cardiac surgery practice packed up and left the state.

Not surprisingly, Nevada was also unprepared for the anthrax crisis. Last October, when Microsoft's Reno office got suspicious powder in the mail that initially tested positive, an "outbreak of hysteria" ensued, said Matheis. The Clark County health district got 1,200 phone calls reporting everything from sugar to chalk dust, and investigated 500 of them with its skeletal staff. The state had no stockpiled antibiotics, and without a lab in Clark County, samples were shipped 500 miles north to Reno for testing.

The new federal money for bioterror preparedness, $10.5 million for Nevada alone, will help enormously. Of that, more than $2 million will go to building a public health laboratory in Las Vegas. But the money will do nothing to solve the problems of staff shortages and soaring medical malpractice premiums that forced the trauma center to close in July.

By July 4, the city of Las Vegas awoke to maximum fear of terror and a minimal medical system, with the trauma center closed for a second day. Governor Kenny Guinn had called an emergency session of the legislature and vowed to make sure that doctors did not abandon the state. An official at the nearby Nellis Air Force Base called the chief of orthopedics, Dr. Anthony Serfustini, asking what to do in the event of injuries. The lanky surgeon said that he reminded the man, You're the Air Force. You can fly your pilots to San Bernardino.

The community's medical infrastructure had declined to a level not seen in twenty-five years, said Dr. Fildes. And on July 4, the inevitable happened. Jim Lawson, 59, a grandfather of nine, was extracted from his mangled car and rushed to a nearby hospital—one with a nervous staff and little up-to-date trauma training—and died about an hour later. His daughter, Mary Rasar, said that she believes the trauma center, had it been open, could have saved him.

Atlanta's Health Emergency

On September 11, 2001, Dr. Arthur Kellerman was in Washington waiting to testify before Congress about the consequences of uninsurance when a plane struck the Pentagon, across the street from his hotel room. He immediately called back to Grady Memorial Hospital in Atlanta, where he oversees the emergency room residents, and got a disturbing report.

While Atlanta appeared to be safe from terrorism, the emergency room had twenty-five admitted patients waiting for hospital beds, the intensive-care area was packed and the staff had shut the emergency room to new patients. Worse, every emergency room in central Atlanta had declared saturation at the same time. None were taking new patients, and loaded ambulances were circling the block. If attacks had occurred in Atlanta that morning, "there was no way on God's earth we could have absorbed more patients," said Kellerman. Since then, all the Atlanta-area hospitals have gone on simultaneous diversion numerous times, leaving "nowhere to put casualties."

Despite all the effort to gear up for biological terror, the problem of overcrowded and understaffed emergency rooms—where terror's victims would be treated—has received only spotty attention. *U.S. News & World Report* featured the problem as a cover story, "Code Blue: Crisis in the E.R.," but it ran on September 10, 2001. A month after the attacks, Representative Henry Waxman prepared a report on ambulance diversions and their effect on disaster preparedness, finding a problem in thirty-two states. In at least nine states, every hospital in a local area had diverted ambulances simultaneously on a number of occasions, causing harm or even death to some patients. In Atlanta, one diverted patient was admitted only after he slipped into respiratory arrest while in the idling ambulance. The report quoted an editorial from the *St. Louis Post-Dispatch* last year:

> A word to the wise: Try not to get sick between 5 p.m. and midnight, when hospitals are most likely to go on diversion. Try not to get sick or injured at all in St. Louis or Kansas City, where diversions are most frequent. And if you're unlucky enough to end up in the back of an ambulance diverted from one E.R. to another, use the extra time to pray.

In Washington, Hauer has directed each region to identify 500 extra beds that can be "surged" or put into use quickly, which has led a number of states to identify armories, school auditoriums, stadiums and hotels that can be used as MASH hospitals. But no bubble tent can replace a hospital bed, with a full complement of services readily available within the "golden hour" so crucial to treating trauma patients, said Kellerman. And no proposal exists to address the problem as a systemic one, in which a shortage of nurses and cutbacks in reimbursement have made it impossible for hospitals to staff enough beds.

Without a solution in sight, Grady Memorial uses a makeshift system, parking admitted patients on stretchers in the hallways beneath handwritten numbers that run from 1 to 30. With the crisis deepening, more numbers—1a, 1b, 1c, for example, seventeen additional spaces in all—have been squeezed between the initial numbers up and down the hall. The other night Kellerman had fifty patients lined up waiting for rooms. "These are not disaster scenarios," he said. "This is Friday night. Wednesday afternoon."

September 11's Hard Lessons

New York City, with sixty-four hospitals, more than any other in the country, was probably the best prepared for a mass-casualty incident. Except that on September 11, most of the victims were dead. Within minutes, the Bellevue emergency room was crowded with hundreds of doctors, each bed with its own team of specialists, from surgeons and psychiatrists to gynecologists. "The entire physician and nursing force of the hospital just came down at once," said Dr. Brian Wexler, a third-year emergency medicine resident. At Long Island College Hospital in Brooklyn, Dr. Lewis Kohl, chairman of emergency medicine, said that by noon, he had a doctor and a nurse for each available bed and could have tripled that number. Doctors from all over the country at a defibrillation conference in downtown Brooklyn were begging to work, "I spent most of the day sending volunteers away," he recalled.

Tragically, so many people died that doctors had little to do. But the people who answered phones, counseled the distraught or drew blood from volunteers were overrun. A web-based patient locator system cobbled together by the Greater New York Hospital Association got 2 million hits within days from frantic relatives. Beth Israel Medical Center ran out of social workers, psychologists and psychiatrists to answer calls. "I answered the phone for half an hour and said, 'I'm not qualified to do this,'" said Lisa Hogarty, vice president of facility management for Continuum Health Partners, which runs Beth Israel.

If anything, New York learned that targeted improvements, such as the creation of regional bioterror treatment centers, will not work. Susan Waltman, senior vice president of the Greater New York Hospital Association, told a CDC advisory committee in June that on September 11, 7,200 people, many covered in debris, wound up at 100 different hospitals, jumping on trains, boats and subways, or walking, to get away from downtown Manhattan. Now imagine if the debris had been tainted with some infectious biological agent. "You can't put the concentration of knowledge or staffing or supplies in regional centers," she said, "because you can't control where patients go."

The anthrax attacks, when they came, were a wake-up call of the worst kind. Baffled government officials with minimal scientific knowledge attributed the outbreak initially to farm visits, then contaminated water and finally to a fine, weaponized anthrax that had been sent through the mail. With no clear chain of communication or command for testing the samples, reporting the results, advising the medical community or informing the public, samples vanished into dozens of laboratories. Conference calls between officials from different local, state and federal agencies were required to track them down, said those involved with the investigation. Testing methods were not standardized, with the Environmental Protection Agency, the postal service, the CDC, the FBI and the Defense Department all swabbing desktops and mailrooms using different methods and different kits, some of which had never been evaluated before. "A lot of those specimens that were said to be positive were not," said

Dr. Philip Brachman, an anthrax expert and professor at the Rollins School of Public Health at Emory University.

For three weeks, from the initial outbreak on October 4, 2001, Americans seeking clear information from the CDC were out of luck. Until October 20, the agency's website still featured diabetes awareness month instead of the anthrax attacks. Dr. David Fleming, the CDC's deputy director for science and public health, said that while the CDC did respond quickly and accurately, "we were too focused on getting the public health job done, and we were not proactive in getting our message out."

But it wasn't just the CDC. Few officials nationwide knew what to do. In New York, police were marching into the city's public health laboratory carrying furniture and computers they suspected of being tainted, recalled Dr. David Perlin, scientific director of the Public Health Research Institute, an advanced microbiology center then located a few floors above the city lab. Since those terrible days, the CDC under new director Dr. Julie Gerberding has made a great effort to establish its leadership and develop emergency response systems. "We have the people, we have the plans and now we have the practice," Gerberding, a microbiologist and veteran of the anthrax investigation, declared this September 11. "We're building our knowledge and capacity every day to assure that CDC and our partners are ready to respond to any terrorist event."

After September 11, however, such confident talk rings a little hollow. This past September the CDC laid out a radical plan for vaccinating much of the country within a week in the event of a smallpox attack. Medical experts greeted the plan as unrealistic and almost impossible to execute, given that disasters inevitably depart from plans to address them. They are pressing for the pre-vaccination of critical healthcare workers, and a decision on this is soon to be announced.

Preparing for the Worst

Past a strip mall outside Washington, and down a nondescript road, the federal OEP keeps a warehouse of equipment that can all but navigate the end of civilization. It has the world's most sophisticated portable morgue units, each one able to support numerous autopsies. Another pile of boxes unfolds to become a full operating theater that can support open-heart surgery, if need be.

All this equipment can function during "catastrophic infrastructure failure," said Gary Moore, deputy director of the agency. And all of it can be loaded onto a C-5 transport plane and flown anywhere in the world. The federal government has massive resources—twelve fifty-ton pallets of drugs called the National Pharmaceutical Stockpile, which can get anywhere in the country in seven to twelve hours. After the New York City laboratory became contaminated, the Defense Department flew in six tons of laboratory equipment and turned a two-person testing operation into ten laboratories with three evidence rooms, a command center and seventy-five lab technicians operating around the clock.

This monumental surge capacity is crucial to preparedness. So are supplies. Dr. Kohl at Long Island College Hospital, who describes himself as a "paranoid of very long standing," feels ready. He's got a padlocked room full of gas masks, Geiger counters and Tyvek suits of varying thicknesses, most purchased after the anthrax attacks. Pulling one off the shelf, he declared confidently, "You could put this on and hang out in a bucket of Sarin."

But none of this can replace the simple stuff: hospital beds, trained people, fax machines, an infrastructure adequate for everyday use. Indeed, as states slash their public health and medical budgets, the opposite may be happening: We are building high-tech defenses on an ever-weakening infrastructure. In Colorado, for example, Governor Bill Owens cut all state funding for local public health departments in part because the federal government was supplying new funds. Public health officials there suddenly have federal money to hire bioterror experts but not enough state money to keep their offices open. While the Larimer County health department got $100,000 in targeted federal money, it lost $700,000 in state funds and fifteen staff positions. A spokesman for Governor Owens did not return calls seeking comment. States across the country are making similar cuts, said Dr. Gursky of the ANSER Institute, their weakened staffs left to prepare for bioterror while everyday health threats continue unchecked.

From her office window, Dr. Ruth Berkelman, director of Emory's Center for Public Health Preparedness, can see the new, $193 million infectious-disease laboratory rising on the CDC's forty-six-acre campus. While the new laboratory and information systems are needed, she says, if we detect smallpox, it's going to be because some doctor in an emergency room gets worried and "picks up the telephone."

Katherine Eban, an investigative journalist who covers medicine and public health for national magazines, lives in Brooklyn. Research support was provided by the Investigative Fund of the Nation Institute.

Blue Planet:
Ecoterrorism redefined

By Dan Whipple
UPI Science News

In this Sept. 11 week, it is useful to examine the word "terrorism"—especially the inflation of definition that has accompanied it.

In the spring of 1981, I sat in the Cowboy Bar in Jackson, Wyo., interviewing Howie Wolke, a longtime friend and an environmental activist in the Rocky Mountain region.

The Cowboy Bar is the sort of place tourists think of as a Western bar. It is narrow and dark and has those slatted swinging doors through which the bartenders throw out the drunks in movies. Most of the light comes from rectangular faux-Tiffany Budweiser lamps hanging above the pool tables. Top-notch country music bands entertain in the evenings, while beautiful women in tight blue jeans dance the Cotton-Eyed Joe.

The bar runs nearly the length of one wall, the barstools in front of it are saddles—a tip-off the place really is not a Western bar. Saddles make excessively uncomfortable seats. Few cowboys will sit in one unless they are being paid to do it.

In any case, neither Howie nor I was a cowboy. He recently had left his job as a regional representative for the environmental group Friends of the Earth. Now he was working for the bar—as a bouncer. I was a journalist at the High Country News, a bi-weekly that covered environmental issues in the Rocky Mountain region.

This interview with Howie, and another guy whose name I've forgotten—a Vietnam War veteran with an encyclopedic knowledge of explosives—concerned what we then called "ecotage," the destruction of property of companies that were, in the opinion of some people, degrading the wilderness.

The second fellow—let's call him Steve because I really can't remember his name—had described it this way: "The legal process isn't working. There's a lot of money against the environmental movement and there's a lot of

propaganda that the average environmentalist is a bleeding heart. As more conventional and legal methods of saving planet Earth are failing, it becomes necessary to force the issue."

A group had organized in the Jackson area to sabotage efforts to explore for oil and gas in the Bridger-Teton Mountains, a major petroleum play just south of Yellowstone National Park. The kind of activities they did, by today's terror standards, seem pretty juvenile: pouring sugar into vehicle fuel tanks, cutting up seismic cable, pulling up survey stakes. Most of these things had been described in Edward Abbey's classic novel, "The Monkey Wrench Gang," so it's often called "monkeywrenching."

Howie and Steve had organized a group that went around spreading ecoterror into the hearts of the corporate interests they saw as threatening the mountains ringing the Cowboy Bar. I pressed Howie for the name of the group, since that's the kind of detail that makes up a good story. He hemmed. He hawed. Finally he said, "I can't tell you. We might want to use it for something else."

The name of their group was *Earth First!*—exclamation theirs.

In 1986, Howie was arrested for pulling up survey stakes for a road being built by Chevron Oil into the Grayback Ridge roadless area in the B-T. He pleaded the felony down to a misdemeanor, but was given the maximum sentence—six months in the county jail.

It was the kind of activity that would warrant the equivalent of a parking ticket—10 days, suspended, say—if it had not been a political act. Howie Wolke was, essentially, a political prisoner.

The monkeywrenching in Jackson continued. In fact, the Chevron road was disrupted again later by a group calling itself "Barmaids for Howie." I never did learn what happened to Steve.

As an environmental journalist, I occasionally receive "communiqués" from a group called the Earth Liberation Front, an "underground" organization that commits acts of sabotage ostensibly in pursuit of pro-environmental goals. Because their actions are illegal, ELF doesn't send e-mail, it sends communiqués—to make them sound more like the free French underground, I suppose.

In a recent "urgent news advisory," ELF claimed credit—if that's the appropriate word—for breaking two plate glass windows at a Detroit-area McDonald's, setting fire to eight Ford Expeditions at a Detroit dealership and starting a fire at a Weyerhaeuser office in Washington state someplace—the details were a little vague.

Ecoterrorism has come a long way since Howie pulled up Chevron's survey stakes. Earth First! is still around, although Howie quit in 1990. "It had become militant vegan feminist witches for wilderness," he said recently. "People wanted to talk about tree-spiking and bombing, not ecosystems."

Earth First! is practically mainstream.

Earth Liberation Front's best-known action was the arson of a restaurant atop the Vail ski area in Colorado. ELF was founded in 1992 in Brighton, England, by some disgruntled Earth First! activists. Despite a bonfire of publicity, and apocalyptic warnings from property rights activists and congressional committees, the list of ELF's "accomplishments" is small: Two "actions" in 1996, three in 1997, eight in 1998, three in 1999, nine in 2000 and four in 2001.

Having pulled up a few survey stakes myself, I'm not in a position to take the high moral ground. But is it terrorism? Is even burning a restaurant—and we all know how tough it is to find a good restaurant—on the same level as blowing up the Alfred P. Murrah Building in Oklahoma City, Okla., or leveling the World Trade Center?

There is an enormous difference between principled civil disobedience—including monkeywrenching—and murder. The word "terrorism" has been thrown around too loosely.

I hadn't talked to Howie in many years—he's now a successful wilderness outfitter in Montana—so I called him to find out if his views had changed since we sat around that day at the Cowboy Bar.

"My perspective on non-legal protests really hasn't changed fundamentally since the early days of Earth First!" he said. "I think that civil disobedience has always occupied an essential role in American politics—and I fear the day where it no longer does so. We should all fear that day, even people who may vehemently disagree with the goals of a particular nonviolent civil disobedience protest."

Given the country's mood post-Sept. 11, Howie said, "There is more danger that we are losing our tolerance of people who are on the legal fringe in terms of the way they protest. I think it is more important than ever—especially given the U.S.A. Patriot Act—for Americans to really look at the essential role that nonviolent civil disobedient protest has played in social change, from the Boston Tea Party to the Underground Railroad to the Civil Rights Movement to the anti-war movement."

Even the conjunction of the ecological with civil disobedience in America is old. Henry David Thoreau, America's first environmentalist and the author of "Walden," declined to pay his poll tax as a protest against slavery. In his 1849 essay, "On the Duty of Civil Disobedience," he wrote: "Even voting for the right thing is doing nothing for it. It is only expressing to men feebly your desire that it should prevail. A wise man will not leave the right to the mercy of chance, nor wish it to prevail through the power of the majority."

The Cyber-Terror Threat

Al Qaeda is working on computer-generated attacks, experts warn

By Barton Gellman
Washington Post Staff Writer

Late last fall, Detective Chris Hsiung of the Mountain View, Calif., police department began investigating a suspicious pattern of surveillance against Silicon Valley computers. From the Middle East and South Asia, unknown browsers were exploring the digital systems used to manage Bay Area utilities and government offices. Hsiung, a specialist in high-technology crime, alerted the FBI's San Francisco computer intrusion squad.

Working with experts at the Lawrence Livermore National Laboratory, the FBI traced trails of a broader reconnaissance. A forensic summary of the investigation, prepared in the Defense Department, said the bureau found "multiple casings of sites" nationwide. Routed through telecommunications switches in Saudi Arabia, Indonesia and Pakistan, the visitors studied emergency telephone systems, electrical generation and transmission, water storage and distribution, nuclear power plants and gas facilities.

Some of the problems suggested planning for a conventional attack, U.S. officials say. But others homed in on a class of digital devices that allow remote control of services such as fire dispatch and of equipment such as pipelines. More information about those devices—and how to program them—turned up on al Qaeda computers seized this year, according to law enforcement and national security officials.

Unsettling signs of al Qaeda's aims and skills in cyberspace have led some government experts to conclude that terrorists are at the threshold of using the Internet as a direct instrument of bloodshed. The new threat bears little resemblance to familiar financial disruptions by hackers responsible for viruses and worms. It comes instead at the meeting points of computers and the physical structures they control.

U.S. analysts believe that by disabling or taking command of the floodgates in a dam, for example, or of substations handling 300,000 volts of electric power, an intruder could use virtual tools to destroy real-world lives and property. They surmise, with limited evidence, that al Qaeda aims to employ those techniques in synchrony with "kinetic weapons" such as explosives.

"The event I fear most is a physical attack in conjunction with a successful cyber-attack on the responders' 911 system or on the power grid," Ronald Dick, director of the FBI's National Infrastructure Protection Center, told a closed gathering of corporate security executives hosted by Infraguard in Niagara Falls on June 12.

In an interview, Dick said those additions to a conventional al Qaeda attack might mean that "the first responders couldn't get there... and water didn't flow, hospitals didn't have power. Is that an unreasonable scenario? Not in this world. And that keeps me awake at night."

Regarded until recently as remote, the risks of cyber-terrorism now command urgent White House attention. Discovery of one acute vulnerability—in a data transmission standard known as ASN.1, short for Abstract Syntax Notification—rushed government experts to the Oval Office on Feb. 7 to brief President Bush. The security flaw, according to a subsequent written assessment by the FBI, could have been exploited to bring down telephone networks and halt "all control information exchanged between ground and aircraft flight control systems."

Officials say Osama bin Laden's operatives have nothing like the proficiency in information war of the most sophisticated nations. But al Qaeda is now judged to be considerably more capable than analysts believed a year ago. And its intentions are unrelentingly aimed at inflicting catastrophic harm.

One al Qaeda laptop found in Afghanistan, sources say, had made multiple visits to a French site run by the Societe Anonyme, or Anonymous Society. The site offers a two-volume, online "Sabotage Handbook" with sections on tools of the trade, planning a hit, switch gear and instrumentation, anti-surveillance methods and advanced techniques. In Islamic chat rooms, other computers linked to al Qaeda had access to "cracking" tools used to search out networked computers, scan for security flaws and exploit them to gain entry—or full command.

Most significantly, perhaps, U.S. investigators have found evidence in the logs that mark a browser's path through the Internet that al Qaeda operators spent time on sites that offer software and programming instructions for the digital switches that run power, water, transport and communications grids. In some interrogations, the most recent of which was reported to policymakers two weeks ago, al Qaeda prisoners have described intentions, in general terms, to use those tools.

SPECIALIZED DIGITAL DEVICES ARE USED BY THE millions as the brains of American "critical infrastructure"—a term defined by federal directive to mean industrial sectors that are "essential to the minimum operations of the economy and government."

The devices are called distributed control systems, or DCS, and supervisory control and data acquisition, or SCADA, systems. The simplest ones collect measurements, throw railway switches, close circuit-breakers or adjust valves in the pipes that carry water, oil and gas. More complicated versions sift incoming data, govern multiple devices and cover a broader area.

What is new and dangerous is that most of these devices are now being connected to the Internet—some of them, according to classified "Red Team" intrusion exercises, in ways that their owners do not suspect.

Because the digital controls were not designed with public access in mind, they typically lack even rudimentary security, having fewer safeguards than the purchase of flowers online. Much of the technical information required to penetrate these systems is widely discussed in the public forums of the affected industries, and specialists say the security flaws are well known to potential attackers.

Until recently, says Director John Tritak of the Commerce Department's Critical Infrastructure Assurance Office, many government and corporate officials regarded hackers mainly as a menace to their e-mail.

"There's this view that the problems of cyberspace originate, reside and remain in cyberspace," Tritak says. "Bad ones and zeroes hurt good ones and zeros, and it sort of stays there.... The point we're making is that increasingly we are relying on 21st century technology and information networks to run physical assets." Digital controls are so pervasive, he says, that terrorists might use them to cause damage on a scale that otherwise would

"not be available except through a very systematic and comprehensive physical attack."

The 13 agencies and offices of the U.S. intelligence community have not reached consensus on the scale or imminence of this threat, according to participants in and close observers of the discussion. The Defense Department, which concentrates on information war with nations, is most skeptical of al Qaeda's interest and prowess in cyberspace.

"DCS and SCADA systems might be accessible to bits and bytes," Assistant Security of Defense John P. Stenbit said in an interview. But al Qaeda prefers simple, reliable plans and would not allow the success of a large-scale attack "to be dependent on some sophisticated, tricky cyber thing to work."

"We're thinking more in physical terms—biological agents, isotopes in explosions, other analogies to the fully loaded airplane," he says. "That's more what I'm worried about. When I think of cyber, I think of it as ancillary to one of those."

WHITE HOUSE AND FBI ANALYSTS, AS WELL AS officials in the Energy and Commerce departments with more direct responsibility for the civilian infrastructure, describe the threat in more robust terms.

"We were underestimating the amount of attention [al Qaeda was] paying to the Internet," says Roger Cressey, a longtime counterterrorism official who became chief of staff of the President's Critical Infrastructure Protection Board in October. "Now we know they see it as a potential attack vehicle. Al Qaeda spent more time mapping our vulnerabilities in cyberspace than we previously thought. An attack is a question of when, not if."

Ron Ross, who heads a new "information assurance" partnership between the National Security Agency and the National Institute of Standards and Technology, reminded the Infraguard delegates in Niagara Falls that, after the Sept. 11 attacks, air traffic controllers brought down every commercial plane in the air. "If there had been a cyber-attack at the same time that prevented them from doing that," he said, "the magnitude of the event could have been much greater."

"It's not science fiction," Ross said in an interview. "A cyber-attack can be launched with fairly limited resources."

U.S. Intelligence agencies have upgraded their warnings about al Qaeda's use of cyberspace. Just over a year ago, a National Intelligence Estimate on the threat to U.S. information systems gave prominence to China, Russia and other nations. It judged al Qaeda operatives as "less developed in their network capabilities" than many individual hackers and "likely to pose only a limited cyber-threat," according to an authoritative description of its contents.

In February, the CIA issued a revised Directorate of Intelligence Memorandum. According to officials who read it, the new memo said al Qaeda had "far more interest" in cyber-terrorism than previously believed and contemplated the use of hackers for hire to speed the acquisition of capabilities.

"I don't think they are capable of bringing a major segment of this country to its knees using cyber-attack alone," says an official representing the current consensus, but "they would be able to conduct an integrated attack using a combination of physical and cyber resources and get an amplification of consequences."

Counterterrorism analysts have known for years that al Qaeda prepares for attacks with elaborate "targeting packages" of photographs and notes. But, in January, U.S. forces in Kabul, Afghanistan, found something new.

A computer seized at an al Qaeda office contained models of a dam, made with structural architecture and engineering software, that enabled the planners to simulate its catastrophic failure. Bush administration officials, who discussed the find, declined to say whether they had identified a specific dam as a target.

The FBI reported that the computer had been running Microstran, an advanced tool for analyzing steel and concrete structures; Autocad 2000, which manipulates technical drawings in two or three dimensions; and software "used to identify and classify soils," which would assist in predicting the course of a wall of water surging downstream.

To destroy a dam physically would require "tons of explosives," Assistant Attorney General Michael Chertoff said a year ago. To breach it from cyberspace is not out of the question. In 1998, a 12-year-old hacker, exploring on a lark, broke into the computer system that runs Arizona's Roosevelt Dam. He did not know or care, but federal authorities say he had complete command of the SCADA system controlling the dam's massive floodgates.

Roosevelt Dam holds back as much as 1.5 million acre-feet of water, or 489 trillion gallons. That volume could theoretically cover the city of Phoenix, down river, to a height of five feet. In practice, that could not happen. Before the water reached the Arizona capital, the rampant Salt River would spend most of itself in a flood plain encompassing the cities of Mesa and Tempe—with a combined population of nearly a million.

IN QUEENSLAND, AUSTRALIA, ON APRIL 23, 2000, police stopped a car on the road to Deception Bay and found a stolen computer and radio transmitter inside. Using commercially available technology, Vitek Boden, 48, had turned his vehicle into a pirate command center for sewage treatment along Australia's Sunshine coast.

Boden's arrest solved a mystery that had troubled the Maroochy Shire wastewater system for two months. Somehow the system was leaking hundreds of thousands of gallons of putrid sludge into parks, rivers and the manicured grounds of a Hyatt Regency hotel. Janelle Bryand of the Australian Environmental Protection Agency says "marine life died, the creek water turned black and the stench was unbearable for residents." Until Boden's capture—during his 46th successful intrusion—the utility's managers did not know why.

Specialists in cyber-terrorism have studied Boden's case because it is the only one known in which someone used a digital control system deliberately to cause harm. Details of Boden's intrusion, not disclosed before, show how easily Boden broke in—and how restrained he was with his power.

Boden had quit his job at Hunter Watertech, the supplier of Maroochy Shire's remote control and telemetry equipment. Evidence at his trial suggested that he was angling for a consulting contract to solve the problems he had caused.

To sabotage the system, he set the software on his laptop to identify itself as "pumping station 4," then suppressed all alarms. Paul Chisholm, Hunter Watertech's chief executive, said in an interview two weeks ago that Boden "was the central control system" during his intrusions, with unlimited command of 300 SCADA nodes governing sewage and drinking water alike. "He could have done anything he liked to the fresh water," Chisholm says.

Like thousands of utilities around the world, Maroochy Shire allowed technicians operating remotely to manipulate its digital controls. Boden learned how to use those controls as an insider, but the software he used conforms to international standards and the manuals are available on the Web. He faced virtually no obstacles to breaking in.

Nearly identical systems run oil and gas utilities and many manufacturing plants. But their most dangerous use is in the generation, transmission and distribution of electrical power, because electricity has no substitute and every other key infrastructure depends on it.

Massoud Amin, a mathematician directing new security efforts in the industry, describes the North American power grid as "the most complex machine ever built." Commerce Department, participants say, government and industry scientists agreed that they have no idea how the grid would respond to a cyber-attack.

What they do know is that "Red Teams" of mock intruders from the Energy Department's four national laboratories have devised what one government document listed as "eight scenarios for SCADA attack on an electrical power grid"—and all of them work. Eighteen such exercises have been conducted to date against large regional utilities, and Richard A. Clarke, Bush's cyber-security adviser, says the intruders "have always, always succeeded."

Joseph M. Weiss of KEMA Consulting, a leading expert in control system security, reported at two recent industry conferences that intruders were "able to assemble a detailed map" of each system and "intercepted and changed" SCADA commands without detection.

"What the labs do is look at simple, easy things I can do to get in" with tools commonly available on the Internet, Weiss said in an interview. "In most of these cases, they are not using anything that a hacker couldn't have access to."

Rise in Computer Hackings

The number of reported computer hackings began growing sharply in the late 1990s.

Number of reported cyber incidents
United States, in thousands*

Industry and nondefense governmnent: **52,658**

Defense: **40,076**

2,340

225

'94 '95 '96 '97 '98 '99 '00 '01

* Includes probes, illicit entries and attacks aimed at causing damage or taking control.

SOURCE: Defense Department

THE WASHINGTON POST

The U.S. government may never have fought a war with so little power in the battlefield. That became clear again on Feb. 7, when Clarke and his vice chairman at the critical infrastructure board, Howard A. Schmidt, arrived in the Oval Office.

They told the president that researchers in Finland had identified a serious security hole in the Internet's standard language for routing data through switches. A government threat team found implications—for air traffic control and civilian and military phone links among others—that were more serious still.

"We've got troops on the ground in Afghanistan and we've got communication systems that we all depend on that, at that time, were vulnerable," Schmidt recalls.

Bush ordered the Pentagon and key federal agencies to patch their systems. But most of the vulnerable networks were not government-owned. Since Feb. 12, "Those who have the fix in their power are in the private sector," Schmidt says. Asked about progress, he says: "I don't know that we'd ever get to 100 percent."

Frustrated at the pace of repairs, Clarke traveled to San Jose on Feb. 19 and accused industry leaders of spending more on coffee than on information security. "You will be hacked," he told them. "What's more, you deserve to be hacked."

Tritak, at the Commerce Department, appealed to patriotism. Speaking of al Qaeda, he said: "When you've got people who are saying, 'We're coming after your economy,' everyone has a responsibility to do their bit to safeguard against it."

New public-private partnerships are helping, but the government case remains a tough sell. Alan Paller, director of research at the SANS Institute in Bethesda, Md., says not even banks and brokerages, considered the most security-conscious businesses, tell the government when their systems are attacked. Sources say the government did not learn crucial details about September's Nimda worm, which caused an estimated $530 million in damage, until the stricken companies began firing their security executives.

Experts say public companies worry about the loss of customer confidence and the legal liability to shareholders or security vendors when they report flaws.

The FBI is having even less success with its "key asset initiative," an attempt to identify the most dangerous points of vulnerability in 5,700 companies deemed essential to national security.

"What we really want to drill down to, eventually, is not the companies but the actual things themselves, the actual switches… that are vital to [a firm's] continued operations," Dick says. He acknowledges a rocky start: "For them to tell us where their crown jewels are is not reasonable until you've built up trust."

Michehl R. Gent, president of the North American Electric Reliability Council, said in May that it will not happen. "We're not going to build such a list.… We have no confidence that the government can keep that a secret."

Bush has launched a top-priority research program at the Livermore, Sandia and Los Alamos labs to improve safeguards in the estimated 3 million SCADA systems in use. But many of the systems rely on instantaneous responses and cannot tolerate authentication delays. And the devices deployed now lack the memory and bandwidth to use techniques such as "integrity checks" that are standard elsewhere.

In a book-length Electricity Infrastructure Security Assessment, the industry concluded on Jan. 7 that "it may not be possible to provide sufficient security when using the Internet for power system control." Power companies, it said, will probably have to build a parallel private network for themselves.

FOR FEAR OF TERRORIST INFILTRATION, CLARKE'S critical infrastructure board and Tom Ridge's homeland security office are now exploring whether private companies would consider telling the government the names of employees with access to sensitive sites.

"Obviously, the ability to check intelligence records from the terrorist standpoint would be the goal," Dick says.

There is no precedent for that. The FBI screens bank employees but has no statutory authority in other industries. Using classified intelligence databases, such as the Visa Viper list of suspected terrorists, would mean the results could not be shared with the employers. Bobby Gillham, manager of global security at oil giant Conoco Inc., says he doubts his industry would go along with that.

"You have Privacy Act concerns," he said in an interview. "And just to get feedback that there's nothing here, or there's something here but we can't share it with you, doesn't do us a lot of good. Most of our companies would not [remove an employee] in a frivolous way, on a wink."

Exasperated by companies seeking proof that they are targets, Clarke has stopped talking about threats at all.

"It doesn't matter whether it's al Qaeda or a nation-state or the teenage kid up the street," he says. "Who does the damage to you is far less important than the fact that damage can be done. You've got to focus on your vulnerability… and not wait for the FBI to tell you that al Qaeda has you in its sights."

Washington Post staff researcher Robert Thomason contributed to this report.

Agriculture shock

Fears about terrorism usually centre on nuclear or biological weapons.
But attackers could cause huge economic damage by spreading plant or animal diseases.
Virginia Gewin asks how this threat is being confronted.

The statistics on the 2001 outbreak of foot-and-mouth disease (FMD) in Britain make for disturbing reading. Four million cattle were culled to contain the disease, and estimates of the cost to the British economy—primarily to the agriculture and tourism industries—run as high as £30 billion (US$48 billion).

The outbreak was unintentional, probably the result of illegal imports of infected meat being fed to pigs. But it can also be seen as an expensive warning. Although smallpox and anthrax receive the bulk of government and media attention when it comes to assessing the risk of bioterrorism, a deliberate attack on agriculture could disrupt trade and cripple agricultural industries. The risk of human fatalities or a serious food shortage is low, but few events would cause more economic damage than attacking the food supply. "The British FMD epidemic has given a blueprint to any terrorist," says Martin Hugh-Jones, a veterinary epidemiologist at Louisiana State University in Baton Rouge.

If such an attack seems unlikely, it is worth noting that agricultural bioweapons have been used before. During the First World War, German agents infected Allied horses with the bacterium *Burkholderia mallei,* which causes glanders—a disease that can kill horses and can also infect humans. And Simon Whitby, a peace-studies researcher at the University of Bradford, UK, says that any country that has studied biological weapons, including the United States and Russia, will have looked at plant and animal diseases. Iraq, for example, is known to have weaponized wheat pathogens.

The main effects of any new attack are likely to be economic. The World Trade Organization lists few reasons for refusing to import crops and animals, but the presence of disease is one of them. Such bans can have rapid and severe consequences. When karnal bunt, a fungal disease of wheat, was found in northern Texas in 2001, over 25 countries banned wheat imports from the four infected counties within a single day. The estimated loss of revenue was $27 million.

Agriculture is also now more open to attack, as a result of large-scale methods such as the use of factory farms and monoculture cropping systems. "There is a vulnerability. It isn't anyone's fault, it's just how agriculture has evolved," says Jim Cook, a plant pathologist at Washington State University in Pullman. And although the ease with which a pathogen could be introduced is the root of the problem, weaknesses in the systems used to detect an outbreak could exacerbate any damage.

On the alert

Thankfully, the threat is now receiving attention. Funding in the United States has increased since the attacks on 11 September 2001—President George W. Bush's proposed budget for the 2003 financial year includes an extra $146 million to protect agriculture and the food supply, including money for monitoring animal health and for setting up a coordinated system to respond to disease outbreaks. And last September, the US National Academy of Sciences released *Countering Agricultural Bioterrorism,* a report detailing the problems that it says need to be addressed, from better diagnosis to improved communication between those who monitor potential outbreaks.

In Europe, defences are being boosted in response to an increase in the number of diseases that the continent's agriculture is expected to be exposed to, whether through increased trade or the possibility of climate change. "We have to be prepared to fight diseases that we didn't have to fight before," says Alex Thiermann of the Paris-based World Organization for Animal Health (OIE). Britain's FMD epidemic has also given a new urgency to research on diagnostic tools and vaccines, as well as encouraging countries to coordinate their plans for responding to future outbreaks.

Of all the lines of defence, rapid detection is considered most important. In many agricultural settings, surveillance systems usually rely on a farmer or local-government agent noticing something unusual. But the clinical symptoms of some diseases appear days after infection. With animals kept so closely confined, entire farms can rapidly become infected before anyone is aware of the problem. "Animals are kept in perfect environmental conditions for spread," says Larry Madden, a plant pathologist at Ohio State University in Columbus. It is not uncommon, for instance, to find

5,000 animals on 20 hectares of land in a typical US dairy operation. Rapid and extensive movement of animals between farms, slaughterhouses and markets also accentuates the problem. FMD, for example, had spread across Britain before it was detected.

The backbone of the global disease-detection system is the chain of 156 reference laboratories and collaborating centres run by the OIE, which analyse samples taken from animals that are thought to be infected. In the United States, the laboratory responsible for diagnosing exotic diseases is the Plum Island Animal Disease Center in New York, run by the US Department of Agriculture (USDA). It currently conducts fewer than 1,000 tests every year for FMD, each of which is sent to the lab. But an outbreak of FMD would require it to run tens of thousands of tests. And the quicker it could deliver the results, the sooner vets working in the field could decide what action to take.

'Pen-side' tests could help to speed up the process. Researchers at Britain's Institute for Animal Health in Pirbright, Surrey, for example, have adapted the laboratory procedure used to check for the presence of the FMD virus so that fieldworkers can perform the test by applying a treated paper to a tissue sample from a live animal. By monitoring the change in colour of the paper, the researcher can determine whether the antigens are present in about 10 minutes. The test has its drawbacks: false negatives can occur at rates of 10–20% when only small amounts of the FMD virus are present, and a cell-culture test is needed to confirm results that prove negative for the virus. But it could yet be a useful aid when time is short, and it is expected to undergo field trials in the next few months. "Those kits are extremely valuable if we have to make quick decisions," says Thiermann.

Another quick, but more sensitive, approach to FMD testing is being explored at Plum Island and Pirbright. Researchers have been evaluating field versions of a method for detecting viral RNA using the polymerase chain reaction (PCR), a common tool used to copy lengths of genetic material. Pirbright officials say they have a fully automated version of the test that could readily be established in a mobile lab should the need arise.

Below the radar

Early detection of crop pathogens is also vital. The United States has more than four million square kilometres of farmland, much of it in remote areas where surveillance is virtually non-existent. Crop diseases can go unnoticed for a long time, during which they are continually spreading. It is estimated that the plum pox virus, discovered in Pennsylvania fields three years ago, was present for six to eight years before it was detected. In the past, a disease sample might have awaited identification until it eventually found its way to the often solitary plant clinician in the agricultural department of the local university.

The USDA is now attempting to improve this situation. Training modules are being developed for 'first responders', such as the farmers and crop consultants who are likely to be the first to notice a problem. And of the $43 million allocated to agricultural-bioterrorism preparedness in the 2002 budget, $20 million is earmarked to establish a network of diagnostic labs for plant and animal pathogens. Five new regional centres are currently being set up at universities around the country, with the goal of providing rapid and accurate diagnosis of disease threats. Many existing labs will also get much-needed improvements. For example, the Great Plains Diagnostic Network at Kansas State University in Manhattan couldn't even run tests involving PCR until the recent funding arrived.

Once diagnoses have been made at the regional centres, all of the relevant information will be transferred to the National Agricultural Pest Information System, a database maintained at Purdue University in West Lafayette, Indiana.

To treat an infection once it has been detected, better knowledge of the pathogen involved is often required. Gaps in our understanding are being filled by new genomic sequences of animal and plant pathogens. In September 2002, for example, scientists at The Institute for Genomic Research (TIGR) in Rockville, Maryland, sequenced the genome of *Brucella suis* (V. G. DelVecchio *et al. Proc. Natl Acad. Sci. USA* **99,** 443–448; 2002), a pathogen that is considered a likely bioterrorism agent—the US military itself weaponized the bug in the 1950s. *B. suis* primarily affects animals, but can cause a debilitating disease in humans that can be lethal to people with weakened immune systems.

Surprisingly, the genome of this bacterium suggests that animal and plant pathogens are not as different as was once thought (see I. T. Paulsen *et al. Proc. Natl Acad. Sci. USA* **99,** 13148–13153; 2002). Many of the genes that control the metabolism of *B. suis* are also found in the plant pathogen *Agrobacterium tumefaciens,* as well as in *Mesorhizobium loti,* a soil bacterium that forms a symbiotic relationship with plants. By investigating these links, TIGR researchers hope to reveal how *B. suis* survives outside its host, and thus generate new leads for tackling the pathogen.

Progress with plant diseases has been less impressive. As of September 2002, less than 6% of microbial genomes that had been sequenced and made publicly available belonged to plant-associated microbes. Animal pathogens are generally viruses or bacteria, but over three-quarters of plant pathogens are fungi, which have much larger genomes. "Compared to human and animal pathogens, plant pathogens are definitely behind," says Jacqueline Fletcher, president of the American Phytopathological Society.

Things are set to improve, albeit slowly. The US Department of Energy's Joint Genome Initiative announced in October that it will sequence two species of *Phytophthora,* a genus of fungus that is responsible for diseases as varied as sudden oak death syndrome and potato blight. What's more, a joint USDA and National Science Foundation programme has funded the sequencing of *Fusarium graminearum,* a fungus that causes disease in wheat and barley.

Forensic studies of deliberately caused outbreaks could also benefit from sequence data. Take the investigation of the US anthrax attacks, for example. Scientists had already sequenced the type of anthrax used—the Ames strain—and so were able to whittle down the number of possible places from which the bug could have been obtained. If sequences of different strains of other pathogens were available, investigators could eliminate many dead ends, as well as gaining incriminating evidence. "One of the differences is to be able to trace back and be able to get enough evidence to bring a case against the perpetrator," says Cook.

Take the strain

But realizing these ambitions will take hard work. Fourteen more strains of anthrax are being sequenced, and for other pathogens, many strains will also have to be sequenced if genomic databases are to be of any forensic use. Several researchers have called for the creation of a database of pathogen genomes, which could be used to investigate outbreaks of animal diseases, but it will take many years to gather enough information to respond to the range of possible bioterrorism agents.

More immediate improvements to our defences could come from new vaccines that are currently under development. Vaccines are an important means for dealing with animal disease, but existing versions are plagued with problems. FMD vaccines, for example, struggle to cope with different strains of the pathogen. "No single vaccine can bring immunity to more than a few of strains," says Mark Wheelis, a bioterrorism expert at the University of California, Davis. Immunity is also often short-lived, and vac-

cinated animals cannot be distinguished from infected ones—and so are impossible to sell—because a weakened version of the live virus is used in the vaccine.

A new class of vaccines could counter some of these problems. Rather than using a version of the live virus, researchers are creating deleted, or 'subunit', vaccines, in which some genes have been removed. Proteins that are not crucial for antibody production, for example, can be removed from the vaccine. The treatment still prompts the production of the antibodies that protect against the virus, but vaccinated animals do not produce antibodies against the missing protein, and so can be distinguished from infected animals. Subunit vaccines have already been developed for Aujeszky's disease in pigs and bovine respiratory disease in cattle, and several groups are working on one for FMD.

Prepare for the worst

Like most recent developments, the vaccine work is driven by the need to contain an accidental outbreak of disease. But should countries be preparing specifically for a deliberate pathogen release? An intentional release could cause even more damage than an accident. The perpetrator could choose to release several highly virulent pathogens simultaneously in remote areas, for example. Authorities in the United States and Europe say that they are considering specific anti-terrorism measures, but many

of the steps, taken so far, such as the development of better diagnostic networks, tie in with conventional strategies for tackling plant and animal disease.

Given the scale of damage that a deliberate pathogen release could cause, some researchers say that stronger measures are needed. But others question this argument. In the bag of terrorist tricks, agricultural bioterrorism is the wild card, and some experts feel that is unlikely to appeal to terrorists. "People attracted to terrorism wouldn't be as attracted to this," says Rocco Casagrande, who studies biological-agent detectors at Surface Logix in Brighton, Massachusetts. "Most terrorists are urban. They want a big bang. Killing cows or pigs is not a big bang," agrees Hugh-Jones.

But others warn that different approaches are likely to be used in future terrorist attacks. Whitby, for example, says that he and his colleagues consider an attack on agriculture to be the most likely form of biological terrorism that we're going to see. Predicting the behaviour of terrorists is, of course, notoriously difficult. But if economic damage is the aim, agricultural bioterrorism is certainly a viable threat. The size of that threat may be hard to define, but the financial scars left by Britain's FMD outbreak show just how serious it could be.

Virginia Gewin is a freelance writer in Corvallis, Oregon.

UNIT 12
Trends and Projections

Unit Selections

Key Points to Consider

- How do the new weapons of mass disruption differ from weapons of mass destruction? Which of these weapons is more likely to be used by terrorists in the future?

- What are the most important elements that must be considered when developing an effective policy framework to ensure future security?

- How does the belief in Samuel Huntington's 1993 prediction of an "inevitable clash of civilizations" affect future U.S. policy? Can we prevent Huntington's thesis from becoming a self-fulfilling prophecy? Explain.

 **Links: www.dushkin.com/online/**
These sites are annotated in the World Wide Web pages.

The Brown Daily Herald—Future Terrorism Will Not Be Prevented by Retaliation
http://www.browndailyherald.com/stories.asp?dbversion=2&storyID=4961
Eliminate the Tools of Future Terrorism
http://backfromthebrink.org/newsroom/gorbachevv2.html

Experts believe that there are certain trends that will characterize international terrorism in the coming years. Some scholars predict that the continuing rise of religions extremists will give rise to a new generation of violent, anti-American terrorists. Others warn of a rejuvenation of left-wing terrorism in Europe. Most believe that the tactics employed by terrorists will be more complex. Future terrorism will cause more casualties and will involve the use of weapons of mass destruction.

The first article in this unit "The Rise of Complex Terrorism," by Thomas Homer-Dixon, focuses on future tactics and targets of international terrorism. Homer-Dixon believes that terrorism is gradually becoming more complex. Increased American reliance on information systems and technology has made the United States vulnerable to attack. As more and more businesses rely on technology, targeted cyber attacks could send the American economy into chaos. The resulting massive economic damage could significantly undermine the U.S. economy and inhibit a quick recovery after an attack.

Harlan Ullman, in "Defusing Dangers to U.S. Security," argues that the United States has not faced up to the realities of the world. This article outlines five major outstanding issues that the Bush administration must resolve in order to ensure the nation's security.

Finally, in "The Clash of Ignorance," Edward Said takes issue with Samuel Huntington's famed thesis. In 1993 Huntington claimed that future conflicts would arise from clashes between cultures rather than ideologies or economics. Said, critical of Huntington's ideas, argues that this is an oversimplification. He maintains that Huntington's populist thesis serves as an excuse for many in the West to remain selectively ignorant of cultures unlike their own. Addressing this cultural ignorance is the first step in understanding and combating international terrorism. Broad generalizations, political arrogance, cultural elitism, and ignorance may undermine our chances for success in the war on terrorism and, more important, may undermine our chance for peaceful coexistence in the future.

THE RISE OF
Complex
TERRORISM

Modern societies face a cruel paradox: Fast—paced technological and economic innovations may deliver unrivalled prosperity, but the} also render rich nations vulnerable to crippling, unanticipated attacks. By relying on intricate networks and concentrating vital assets in small geographic clusters, advanced Western nations only amplify the destructive power of terrorists-and the psychological and financial damage they can inflict.

By Thomas Homer-Dixon

It's 4 a.m. on a sweltering summer night in July 2003. Across much of the United States, power plants are working full tilt to generate electricity for millions of air conditioners that are keeping a ferocious heat wave at bay. The electricity grid in California has repeatedly buckled under the strain, with rotating blackouts from San Diego to Santa Rosa.

In different parts of the state, half a dozen small groups of men and women gather. Each travels in a rented minivan to its prearranged destination—for some, a location outside one of the hundreds of electrical substations dotting the state; for others, a spot upwind from key, high-voltage transmission lines. The groups unload their equipment from the vans. Those outside the substations put together simple mortars made from materials bought at local hardware stores, while those near the transmission lines use helium to inflate weather balloons with long silvery tails. At a precisely coordinated moment, the homemade mortars are fired, sending showers of aluminum chaff over the substations. The balloons are released and drift into the transmission lines.

Simultaneously, other groups are doing the same thing along the Eastern Seaboard and in the South and Southwest. A national electrical system already under immense strain is massively short-circuited, causing a cascade of power failures across the country. Traffic lights shut off. Water and sewage systems are disabled. Communications systems break down. The financial system and national economy come screeching to a halt.

Sound far-fetched? Perhaps it would have before September 11, 2001, but certainly not now. We've realized, belatedly, that our societies are wide-open targets for terrorists. We're easy prey because of two key trends: First, the growing technological capacity of small groups and individuals to destroy things and people; and, second, the increasing vulnerability of our economic and technological systems to carefully aimed attacks. While commentators have devoted considerable ink and airtime to the first of these trends, they've paid far less attention to the second, and they've virtually ignored their combined effect. Together, these two trends facilitate a new and sinister kind of mass violence—a "complex terrorism" that threatens modern, high-tech societies in the world's most developed nations.

Our fevered, Hollywood-conditioned imaginations encourage us to focus on the sensational possibility of nuclear or biological attacks—attacks that might kill tens of thousands of people in a single strike. These threats certainly deserve attention, but not to the neglect of the likelier and ultimately deadlier disruptions that could result from the clever exploitation by terrorists of our societies' new and growing complexities.

WEAPONS OF MASS DISRUPTION

The steady increase in the destructive capacity of small groups and individuals is driven largely by three technological advances: more powerful weapons, the dramatic progress in communications and information processing, and more abundant opportunities to divert nonweapon technologies to destructive ends.

Consider first the advances in weapons technology. Over the last century, progress in materials engineering, the chemistry of explosives, and miniaturization of electronics has brought steady improvement in all key weapons characteristics, including accuracy, destructive power, range, portability, ruggedness, ease-of-use, and affordability. Improvements in light weapons are particularly relevant to trends in terrorism and violence by small groups, where the devices of choice include rocket-propelled grenade launchers, machine guns, light mortars, land mines, and cheap assault rifles such as the famed AK-47. The effects of improvements in these weapons are particularly noticeable in developing countries. A few decades ago, a small band of terrorists or insurgents attacking a rural village might have used bolt-action rifles, which take precious time to reload. Today, cheap assault rifles multiply the possible casualties resulting from such an attack. As technological change makes it easier to kill, societies are more likely to become locked into perpetual cycles of attack and counterattack that render any normal trajectory of political and economic development impossible.

Meanwhile, new communications technologies—from satellite phones to the Internet—allow violent groups to marshal resources and coordinate activities around the planet. Transnational terrorist organizations can use the Internet to share information on weapons and recruiting tactics, arrange surreptitious fund transfers across borders, and plan attacks. These new technologies can also dramatically enhance the reach and power of age-old procedures. Take the ancient *hawala* system of moving money between countries, widely used in Middle Eastern and Asian societies. The system, which relies on brokers linked together by clan-based networks of trust, has become faster and more effective through the use of the Internet.

Information-processing technologies have also boosted the power of terrorists by allowing them to hide or encrypt their messages. The power of a modern laptop computer today is comparable to the computational power available in the entire U.S. Defense Department in the mid-1960s. Terrorists can use this power to run widely available state-of-the-art encryption software. Sometimes less advanced computer technologies are just as effective. For instance, individuals can use a method called steganography ("hidden writing") to embed messages into digital photographs or music clips. Posted on publicly available Web sites, the photos or clips are downloaded by collaborators as necessary. (This technique was reportedly used by recently arrested terrorists when they planned to blow up the U.S. Embassy in Paris.) At latest count, 140 easy-to-use steganography tools were available on the Internet. Many other off-the-shelf technologies—such as spread-spectrum" radios that randomly switch their broadcasting and receiving signals—allow terrorists to obscure their messages and make themselves invisible.

High-tech societies are filled with super-charged devices packed with energy, combustibles, and poisons, giving terrorists ample opportunities to divert such non-weapon technologies to destructive ends.

The Web also provides access to critical information. The September 11 terrorists could have found there all the details they needed about the floor plans and design characteristics of the World Trade Center and about how demolition experts use progressive collapse to destroy large buildings. The Web also makes available sets of instructions—or "technical ingenuity"—needed to combine readily available materials in destructive ways. Practically anything an extremist wants to know about kidnapping, bomb making, and assassination is now available online. One somewhat facetious example: It's possible to convert everyday materials into potentially destructive devices like the "potato cannon." With a barrel and combustion chamber fashioned from common plastic pipe, and with propane as an explosive propellant, a well-made cannon can hurl a homely spud hundreds of meters-or throw chaff onto electrical substations. A quick search of the Web reveals dozens of sites giving instructions on how to make one.

Finally, modern, high-tech societies are filled with supercharged devices packed with energy, combustibles, and poisons, giving terrorists ample opportunities to divert such nonweapon technologies to destructive ends. To cause horrendous damage, all terrorists must do is figure out how to release this power and let it run wild or, as they did on September 11, take control of this power and retarget it. Indeed, the assaults on New York City and the Pentagon were not low-tech affairs, as is often argued. True, the terrorists used simple box cutters to hijack the planes, but the box cutters were no more than the "keys" that allowed the terrorists to convert a high-tech means of transport into a high-tech weapon of mass destruction. Once the hijackers had used these keys to access and turn on their weapon, they were able to deliver a kiloton of explosive power into the World Trade Center with deadly accuracy.

HIGH-TECH HUBRIS

The vulnerability of advanced nations stems not only from the greater destructive capacities of terrorists, but also from the increased vulnerability of the West's economic and technological systems. This additional vulnerability is the product of two key social and technological developments: first, the growing complexity and interconnectedness of our modern societies; and second, the increasing geographic concentration of wealth, human capital, knowledge, and communication links.

Consider the first of these developments. All human societies encompass a multitude of economic and technological systems. We can think of these systems as networks—that is, as sets of nodes and links among those nodes. The U.S. economy consists of numerous nodes, including corporations, factories, and urban centers; it also consists of links among these nodes, such as highways, rail lines, electrical grids, and fiber-optic cables. As societies modernize and become richer, their networks become more complex and interconnected. The number of nodes increases, as does the density of links among the nodes and the speed at which materials, energy, and information are pushed along these links. Moreover, the nodes themselves become more complex as the people who create, operate, and manage them strive for better performance. (For instance, a manufacturing company might improve efficiency by adopting more intricate inventory-control methods.)

Complex and interconnected networks sometimes have features that make their behavior unstable and unpredictable. In particular, they can have feedback loops that produce vicious cycles. A good example is a stock market crash, in which selling drives down prices, which begets more selling. Networks can also be tightly coupled, which means that links among the nodes are short, therefore making it more likely that problems with one node will spread to others. When drivers tailgate at high speeds on freeways, they create a tightly coupled system: A mistake by one driver, or a sudden shock coming from outside the system, such as a deer running across the road, can cause a chain reaction of cars piling onto each other. We've seen such knock-on effects in the U.S. electrical, telephone, and air traffic systems, when a failure in one part of the network has sometimes produced a cascade of failures across the country. Finally, in part because of feedbacks and tight coupling, networks often exhibit nonlinear behavior, meaning that a small shock or perturbation to the network produces a disproportionately large disruption.

Terrorists and other malicious individuals can magnify their own disruptive power by exploiting these features of complex and interconnected networks. Consider the archetypal lone, nerdy high-school kid hacking away at his computer in his parents' basement who can create a computer virus that produces chaos in global communications and data systems. But there's much more to worry about than just the proliferation of computer viruses. A special investigative commission set up in 1997 by then U.S. President Bill Clinton reported that "growing complexity and interdependence, especially in the energy and communications infrastructures, create an increased possibility that a rather minor and routine disturbance can cascade into a regional outage." The commission continued: "We are convinced that our vulnerabilities are increasing steadily, that the means to exploit those weaknesses are readily available and that the costs [of launching an attack] continue to drop."

Terrorists must be clever to exploit these weaknesses. They must attack the right nodes in the right networks. If they don't, the damage will remain isolated and the overall network will be resilient. Much depends upon the network's level of redundancy—that is, on the degree to which the damaged node's functions can be offloaded to undamaged nodes. As terrorists come to recognize the importance of redundancy, their ability to disable complex networks will improve. Langdon Winner, a theorist of politics and technology, provides the first rule of modern terrorism: "Find the critical but nonredundant parts of the system and sabotage … them according to your purposes." Winner concludes that "the science of complexity awaits a Machiavelli or Clausewitz to make the full range of possibilities clear."

The range of possible terrorist attacks has expanded due to a second source of organizational vulnerability in modern economies—the rising concentration of high-value assets in geographically small locations. Advanced societies concentrate valuable things and people in order to achieve economies of scale. Companies in capital-intensive industries can usually reduce the per-unit cost of their goods by building larger production facilities. Moreover, placing expensive equipment and highly skilled people in a single location provides easier access, more efficiencies, and synergies that constitute an important source of wealth. That is why we build places like the World Trade Center.

In so doing, however, we also create extraordinarily attractive targets for terrorists, who realize they can cause a huge amount of damage in a single strike. On September 11, a building complex that took seven years to construct collapsed in 90 minutes, obliterating 10 million square feet of office space and exacting at least $30 billion in direct costs. A major telephone switching office was destroyed, another heavily damaged, and important cellular antennas on top of the towers were lost. Key transit lines through southern Manhattan were buried under rubble. Ironically, even a secret office of the U.S. Central Intelligence Agency was destroyed in the attack, temporarily disrupting normal intelligence operations.

Yet despite the horrific damage to the area's infrastructure and New York City's economy, the attack did not cause catastrophic failures in U.S. financial, economic, or communications networks. As it turned out, the World Trade Center was not a critical, nonredundant node. At least it wasn't critical in the way most people (including, probably, the terrorists) would have thought. Many of the financial firms in the destroyed buildings had made contingency plans for disaster by setting up alternate facilities for data, information, and computer equipment in remote locations. Though the NASDAQ headquarters was demolished, for instance, the exchange's data centers in Connecticut and Maryland remained linked to trading companies through two separate connections that passed through 20 switching centers. NASDAQ officials later claimed that their system was so robust that they could have restarted trading only a few hours after the attack. Some World Trade Center firms had made advanced arrangements with companies specializing in providing emergency relocation facilities in New Jersey and elsewhere. Because of all this proactive planning—and the network redundancy it produced—the September 11 attacks caused remarkably little direct disruption to the U.S. financial system (despite the unprecedented closure of the stock market for several days).

To maximize their psychological impact, the perpetrators of complex terrorism will carry out their attacks in audacious, unexpected, and even bizarre manners—using methods that are, ideally, unimaginably cruel.

But when we look back years from now, we may recognize that the attacks had a critical effect on another kind of network that we've created among ourselves: a tightly coupled, very unstable, and highly nonlinear psychological network. We're all nodes in this particular network, and the links among us consist of Internet connections, satellite signals, fiber-optic cables, talk radio, and 24-hour television news. In the minutes following the attack, coverage of the story flashed across this network. People then stayed in front of their televisions for hours on end; they viewed and reviewed the awful video clips on the CNN Web site; they plugged phone lines checking on friends and relatives; and they sent each other millions upon millions of e-mail messages—so many, in fact, that the Internet was noticeably slower for days afterwards.

Along these links, from TV and radio stations to their audiences, and especially from person to person through the Internet, flowed raw emotion: grief, anger, horror, disbelief, fear, and hatred. It was as if we'd all been wired into one immense, convulsing, and reverberating neural network. Indeed, the biggest impact of the September 11

attacks wasn't the direct disruption of financial, economic, communications, or transportation networks—physical stuff, all. Rather, by working through the network we've created within and among our heads, the attacks had their biggest impact on our collective psychology and our subjective feelings of security and safety. This network acts like a huge megaphone, vastly amplifying the emotional impact of terrorism.

To maximize this impact, the perpetrators of complex terrorism will carry out their attacks in audacious, unexpected, and even bizarre manners—using methods that are, ideally, unimaginably cruel. By so doing, they will create the impression that anything is possible, which further magnifies fear. From this perspective, the World Trade Center represented an ideal target, because the Twin Towers were an icon of the magnificence and boldness of American capitalism. When they collapsed like a house of cards, in about 15 seconds each, it suggested that American capitalism was a house of cards, too. How could anything so solid and powerful and so much a part of American identity vanish so quickly? And the use of passenger airplanes made matters worse by exploiting our worst fears of flying.

Unfortunately, this emotional response has had huge, real-world consequences. Scared, insecure, grief-stricken people aren't ebullient consumers. They behave cautiously and save more. Consumer demand drops, corporate investment falls, and economic growth slows. In the end, via the multiplier effect of our technology-amplified emotional response, the September 11 terrorists may have achieved an economic impact far greater than they ever dreamed possible. The total cost of lost economic growth and decreased equity value around the world could exceed a trillion dollars. Since the cost of carrying out the attack itself was probably only a few hundred thousand dollars, we're looking at an economic multiplier of over a millionfold.

THE WEAKEST LINKS

Complex terrorism operates like jujitsu—it redirects the energies of our intricate societies against us. Once the basic logic of complex terrorism is understood (and the events of September 11 prove that terrorists are beginning to understand it), we can quickly identify dozens of relatively simple ways to bring modern, high-tech societies to their knees.

How would a Clausewitz of terrorism proceed? He would pinpoint the critical complex networks upon which modern societies depend. They include networks for producing and distributing energy, information, water, and food; the highways, railways, and airports that make up our transportation grid; and our healthcare system. Of these, the vulnerability of the food system is particularly alarming [see "Feeding Frenzies"]. However, terrorism experts have paid the most attention to the energy and information networks, mainly because they so clearly underpin the vitality of modern economies.

The energy system—which comprises everything from the national network of gas pipelines to the electricity grid—is replete with high-value nodes like oil refineries, tank farms, and electrical substations. At times of peak energy demand, this network (and in particular, the electricity grid) is very tightly coupled. The loss of one link in the grid means that the electricity it carries must be off-loaded to other links. If other links are already operating near capacity, the additional load can cause them to fail, too, thus displacing their energy to yet other links. We saw this kind of breakdown in August 1996, when the failure of the Big Eddy transmission line in northern Oregon caused overloading on a string of transmission lines down the West Coast of the United States, triggering blackouts that affected 4 million people in nine states.

Large gas pipelines, many of which run near or even through urban areas, have huge explosive potential; attacks on them could have the twin effect of producing great local damage and wider disruptions in energy supply.

Substations are clear targets because they represent key nodes linked to many other parts of the electrical network. Substations and high-voltage transmission lines are also "soft" targets, since they can be fairly easily disabled or destroyed. Tens of thousands of miles of transmission lines are strung across North America, often in locations so remote that the lines are almost impossible to protect, but they are nonetheless accessible by four-wheel drive. Transmission towers can be brought down with well-placed explosive charges. Imagine a carefully planned sequence of attacks on these lines, with emergency crews and investigators dashing from one remote attack site to another, constantly off-balance and unable to regain control. Detailed maps of locations of substations and transmission lines for much of North America are easily available on the Web. Not even all the police and military personnel in the United States would suffice to provide even rudimentary protection to this immense network.

The energy system also provides countless opportunities for turning supposedly benign technology to destructive ends. For instance, large gas pipelines, many of which run near or even through urban areas, have huge explosive potential; attacks on them could have the twin effect of producing great local damage and wider disruptions in energy supply. And the radioactive waste pools associated with most nuclear reactors are perhaps the most lethal targets in the national energy-supply system.

If the waste in these facilities were dispersed into the environment, the results could be catastrophic. Fortunately, such attacks would be technically difficult.

Even beyond energy networks, opportunities to release the destructive power of benign technologies abound. Chemical plants are especially tempting targets, because they are packed with toxins and flammable, even explosive, materials. Security at such facilities is often lax: An April 1999 study of chemical plants in Nevada and West Virginia by the U.S. Agency for Toxic Substances and Disease Registry concluded that security ranged from "fair to very poor" and that oversights were linked to "complacency and lack of awareness of the threat." And every day, trains carrying tens of thousands of tons of toxic material course along transport corridors throughout the United States. All a terrorist needs is inside knowledge that a chemical-laden train is traveling through an urban area at a specific time, and a well-placed object (like a piece of rail) on the track could cause a wreck, a chemical release, and a mass evacuation. A derailment of such a train at a nonredundant link in the transport system—such as an important tunnel or bridge—could be particularly potent. (In fact, when the U.S. bombing campaign in Afghanistan began on October 7, 2001, the U.S. railroad industry declared a three-day moratorium on transporting dangerous chemicals.) Recent accidents in Switzerland and Baltimore, Maryland, make clear that rail and highway tunnels are vulnerable because they are choke points for transportation networks and because it's extraordinarily hard to extinguish explosions and fires inside them.

Modern communications networks also are susceptible to terrorist attacks. Although the Internet was originally designed to keep working even if large chunks of the network were lost (as might happen in a nuclear war, for instance), today's Internet displays some striking vulnerabilities. One of the most significant is the system of computers-called "routers" and "root servers"—that directs traffic around the Net. Routers represent critical nodes in the network and depend on each other for details on where to send packets of information. A software error in one router, or its malicious reprogramming by a hacker, can lead to errors throughout the Internet. Hackers could also exploit new peer-to-peer software (such as the information-transfer tool Gnutella) to distribute throughout the Internet millions of "sleeper" viruses programmed to attack specific machines or the network itself at a predetermined date.

The U.S. government is aware of many of these threats and of the specific vulnerability of complex networks, especially information networks. President George W. Bush has appointed Richard Clarke, a career civil servant and senior advisor to the National Security Council on counterterrorism, as his cyberspace security czar, reporting both to Director of Homeland Security Tom Ridge and National Security Advisor Condoleezza Rice. In addition, the U.S. Senate recently considered new legislation

Feeding Frenzies

Shorting out electrical grids or causing train derailments would be small-scale sabotage compared with terrorist attacks that intentionally exploit psychological vulnerabilities. One key vulnerability is our fear for our health—an attack that exploits this fear would foster widespread panic. Probably the easiest way to strike at the health of an industrialized nation is through its food-supply system.

Modern food-supply systems display many key features that a prospective terrorist would seek in a complex network and are thus highly vulnerable to attack. Such systems are tightly coupled, and they have many nodes—including huge factory farms and food-processing plants—with multiple connections to other nodes.

Attackers could break into grain silos to deposit small amounts of contaminants, which would then diffuse throughout the food system.

The recent foot-and-mouth disease crisis in the United Kingdom provided dramatic evidence of these characteristics. By the time veterinarians found the disease, it had already spread throughout Great Britain. As in the United States, the drive for economic efficiencies in the British farming sector has produced a highly integrated system in which foods move briskly from farm to table. It has also led to economic concentration, with a few immense abattoirs scattered across the land replacing the country's many small slaughterhouses. Foot-and-mouth disease spread rapidly in large part because infected animals were shipped from farms to these distant abattoirs.

Given these characteristics, foot-and-mouth disease seems a useful vector for a terrorist attack. The virus is endemic in much of the world and thus easy to obtain. Terrorists could contaminate 20 or 30 large livestock-farms or ranches across the United States, allowing the disease to spread through the network, as it did in Great Britain. Such an attack would probably bring the U.S. cattle, sheep, and pig industries to a halt in a matter of weeks, costing the economy tens of billions of dollars.

Despite the potential economic impact of such an attack, however, it wouldn't have the huge psychological effect that terrorists value, because foot-and-mouth disease rarely affects humans. Far more dramatic would be the poisoning of our food supply. Here the possibilities are legion. For instance, grain storage and transportation networks in the United States are easily accessible; unprotected grain silos dot the countryside and railway cars filled with grain often sit for long periods on railway sidings. Attackers could break into these silos and grain cars to deposit small amounts of contaminants, which would then diffuse through the food system.

Polychlorinated biphenyls (PCBs)—easily found in the oil in old electrical transformers—are a particularly potent group of contaminants, in part because they contain trace amounts of dioxins. These chemicals are both carcinogenic and neurotoxic; they also disrupt the human endocrine system. Children in particular are vulnerable. Imagine the public hysteria if, several weeks after grain silos and railway cars had been laced with PCBs and the poison had spread throughout the food network, terrorists publicly suggested that health authorities test food products for PCB contamination. (U.S. federal food inspectors might detect the PGBs on their own, but the inspection system is stretched very thin and contamination could easily be missed.) At that point, millions of people could have already eaten the products.

Such a contamination scenario is not in the realm of science fiction or conspiracy theories. In January 1999, 500 tons of animal feed in Belgium were accidentally contaminated with approximately 50 kilograms of PGBs from transformer oil. Some 10 million people in Belgium, the Netherlands, France, and Germany subsequently ate the contaminated food products. This single incident may in time cause up to 8,000 cases of cancer.

—T.H.D.

(the Critical Infrastructure Information Security Act) addressing a major obstacle to improved security of critical networks: the understandable reluctance of firms to share proprietary information about networks they have built or manage. The act would enable the sharing of sensitive infrastructure information between the federal government and private sector and within the private sector itself. In his opening remarks to introduce the act on September 25, 2001, Republican Sen. Bob Bennett of Utah clearly recognized that we face a new kind of threat. "The American economy is a highly interdependent system of systems, with physical and cyber components," he declared. "Security in a networked world must be a shared responsibility."

PREPARING FOR THE UNKNOWN

Shortly following the September 11 attacks, the U.S. Army enlisted the help of some of Hollywood's top action screenwriters and directors—including the writers of *Die Hard* and *McGyver*—to conjure up possible scenarios for future terrorist attacks. Yet no one can possibly imagine in advance all the novel opportunities for terrorism provided by our technological and economic systems. We've made these critical systems so complex that they are replete with vulnerabilities that are very hard to anticipate, because we don't even know how to ask the right questions. We can think of these possibilities as "exploitable unknown unknowns." Terrorists can make connections between components of complex systems—such as between passenger airliners and skyscrapers—that few, if any, people have anticipated. Complex terrorism is particularly effective if its goal is not a specific strategic or political end, but simply the creation of widespread fear, panic, and economic disruption. This more general objective grants terrorists much more latitude in their choice of targets. More likely than not, the next major attack will come in a form as unexpected as we witnessed on September 11.

What should we do to lessen the risk of complex terrorism, beyond the conventional counter terrorism strategies already being implemented by the United States and other nations? First, we must acknowledge our own limitations. Little can be done, for instance, about terrorists' inexorably rising capacity for violence. This trend results from deep technological forces that can't be stopped without producing major disruptions elsewhere in our economies and societies. However, we can take steps to reduce the vulnerabilities related to our complex economies and technologies. We can do so by loosening the couplings in our economic and technological networks, building into these networks various buffering capacities, introducing "circuit breakers" that interrupt dangerous feedbacks, and dispersing high-value assets so that they are less concentrated and thus less inviting targets.

These prescriptions will mean different things for different networks. In the energy sector, loosening coupling might mean greater use of decentralized, local energy production and alternative energy sources (like small-scale solar power) that make individual users more independent of the electricity grid. Similarly, in food production, loosening coupling could entail increased autonomy of local and regional food-production networks so that when one network is attacked the damage doesn't cascade into others. In many industries, increasing buffering would involve moving away from just-in-time production processes. Firms would need to increase inventories of feedstocks and parts so production can continue even when the supply of these essential inputs is interrupted. Clearly this policy would reduce economic efficiency, but the extra security of more stable and resilient production networks could far outweigh this cost.

Circuit breakers would prove particularly useful in situations where crowd behavior and panic can get out of control. They have already been implemented on the New York Stock Exchange: Trading halts if the market plunges more than a certain percentage in a particular period of time. In the case of terrorism, one of the factors heightening public anxiety is the incessant barrage of sensational reporting and commentary by 24-hour news TV. As is true for the stock exchange, there might be a role for an independent, industry-based monitoring body here, a body that could intervene with broadcasters at critical moments, or at least provide vital counsel, to manage the flow and content of information. In an emergency, for instance, all broadcasters might present exactly the same information (vetted by the monitoring body and stated deliberately and calmly) so that competition among broadcasters doesn't encourage sensationalized treatment. If the monitoring body were under the strict authority of the broadcasters themselves, the broadcasters would—collectively—retain complete control over the content of the message, and the procedure would not involve government encroachment on freedom of speech.

If terrorist attacks continue, economic forces alone will likely encourage the dispersal of high-value assets. Insurance costs could become unsupportable for businesses and industries located in vulnerable zones. In 20 to 30 years, we may be astonished at the folly of housing so much value in the exquisitely fragile buildings of the World Trade Center. Again, dispersal may entail substantial economic costs, because we'll lose economies of scale and opportunities for synergy.

Yet we have to recognize that we face new circumstances. Past policies are inadequate. The advantage in this war has shifted toward terrorists. Our increased vulnerability—and our newfound recognition of that vulnerability—makes us more risk-averse, while terrorists have become more powerful and more tolerant of risk. (The September 11 attackers, for instance, had an extremely high tolerance for risk, because they were ready and willing to die.) As a result, terrorists have significant leverage to hurt us. Their capacity to exploit this leverage depends on their ability to understand the complex systems that we depend on so critically. Our capacity to defend ourselves depends on that same understanding.

Thomas Homer-Dixon is associate professor of political science and director of the Centre for the Study of Peace and Conflict at the University of Toronto. He is the author of, most recently, The Ingenuity Gap: How Can We Solve the Problems of the Future? *(New York: Alfred A. Knopf, 2000).*

Reproduced with permission from *Foreign Policy*, No. 128, January/February 2002, pp. 52-62. © 2002 by the Carnegie Endowment for International Peace.

Defusing Dangers to U.S. Security

by Harlan Ullman

September 11 is a date that "changed America forever," or so goes conventional wisdom. In fact, the horror of that day really showed how the world had changed. The consequence was that the United States was no longer safe, secure, and insulated from the violence and terror that were commonplace around the world.

On that day, 19 men armed with box cutters and loyal to a cause, not a country, turned commercial airliners into flying bombs and in a matter of moments did far more physical, psychic, and economic damage to the United States than did the tens of thousands of Soviet nuclear weapons aimed at us during the Cold War.

Sadly, in the year and a half since, despite much rhetoric and breast-beating, the United States has still not faced up to the realities of this changed world. Indeed, it is very possible that the danger is the most serious the country has faced since the Civil War. Understanding how we arrived at this point is critical to seeing the way ahead and the means of defusing the dangers that threaten our security.

Every major war creates legacies, or pieces of "unfinished business," often with profound consequences. From World War I came fascism, communism, and World War II. From that war emerged the Cold War and the Gulf War in 1991. It is from them that five major pieces of business remain unfinished. Unless or until we deal with each, the safety of the United States is in grave jeopardy. President George W. Bush must confront these legacies, ironically inherited from the days when his father, George H.W. Bush, was president.

FREEDOM AND SECURITY

The first piece of unfinished business is the most serious. The attacks of September 11 were directed against the basic nature of American society—its openness, freedom, and complete accessibility. As security becomes more important, its needs inherently conflict with freedom. By exploiting that tension, those wishing this nation harm can do fundamental damage even without killing a single American. It is the basis of our political system that is the target. How we deal with this potential weakness and vulnerability may prove the most difficult challenge the nation has faced since 1861.

The second piece is the inherent vulnerability to disruption of the U.S. infrastructure; that is, our networks for commerce, communications, banking, power, food, emergency services, and the rest of the sinews upon which our way of life depend. There are no means for protecting all or even much of this infrastructure for an extended period.

Third, the country's national security organization was designed for an era that no longer exists—the Cold War. The Commission on National Security Strategy/Twenty-first Century, cochaired by former Senators Gary Hart and Warren Rudman, called this structure "dysfunctional." The commission study, released in February 2001, predicted that a major terrorist attack, possibly with weapons of mass destruction, would occur within 25 years. Unfortunately, these events took place less than eight months later. Both senators went on to serve on another commission, reporting in October 2002 that America was "still unprepared... and still in danger."

Fourth, the chief danger to the United States emanates from the "crescent of crisis," the region bounded in the west by the Arab-Israeli-Palestinian conflict, extending through the Middle East and Persian Gulf to the Bay of Bengal and east to the Straits of Malacca. Egypt, Saudi Arabia, Iraq, Iran, India, Pakistan, and Indonesia are key states in which extremism abounds. Osama bin Laden and al Qaeda are the current enemies. However, as long as the causes that breed this extremism exist, then the United States will be at great risk.

The final piece of unfinished business is the need to construct a strategic framework to replace that of the Cold War. The United States has not yet been able to weave together NATO, the European Union, Russia, China, and other key states in some form of partnership or relationship to deal with these new dangers.

What Needs Updating

⊃ The attacks of September 11 were directed against the basic nature of American society—its openness, freedom, and complete accessibility.

⊃ The terrorist attacks revealed the inherent vulnerability of the U.S. infrastructure.

⊃ Our national security organization is designed for an era that no longer exists—the Cold War.

⊃ The chief danger to the United States emanates from the "crescent of crisis," stretching from Israel to Indonesia.

⊃ The most important piece of unfinished business is the need to reconstruct a strategic framework.

President Bush has defined the danger as terrorism and declared a global war against it, in the form of al Qaeda. But what motivates al Qaeda and bin Laden, arousing in his followers a commitment to die in the process? The answer is not unique to today: it is the basis for extremism, whether manifested in the Crusades or the extremist movements of the late nineteenth and twentieth centuries. The danger is the intent to foment political change by using terror.

Bin Laden has done that with ruthless cunning. Drawing on a psychotic interpretation of Islam, he believes Western and American infidels have violated holy Saudi soil by their presence. Seizing on Israel, bin Laden has added the plight of the Palestinians to his list of grievances. His aim is to achieve some form of fundamentalist Islamic regime throughout the crescent of crisis, buttressed with Saudi oil money and made powerful by Pakistan's nuclear weapons.

This scheme need not involve one large or several integrated states but rather a loose collection of countries with fundamentalist regimes all loyal to an extremist interpretation of Islam. Terror is the tactic and tool. Saudi Arabia and Pakistan are the long-term prizes, and the United States is the immediate target. Hence, attacks such as September 11 must be expected. Sadly, bin Laden and his followers discovered that the target in America, to use Bill Clinton's favorite phrase, "is the economy, stupid!" Disruption of our economy will be a principal aim.

WHAT CAN BE DONE?

As this goes to press, the United States may well be at war against Iraq. However odious Saddam Hussein may be, Iraq is incidental to the larger danger of extremism. Hence, another Gulf War will dilute our attention from the main event.

Here is what we must do to deal with the five pieces of unfinished business. The crucial test is that in the process of protecting ourselves, we do not do grave damage to our freedom. We need to work within the framework of the Constitution, our laws, and the fundamental constraints imposed by checks and balances. Only by reestablishing trust and confidence is that possible. This is not something that can be done through laws, campaign promises, or fancy slogans.

Three domestic deficits arising from this unfinished business must be corrected: deficits in the rationality of the political process, in our security structure, and in our ability to attract the best and brightest to public service.

To attack the first deficit, Congress and the executive branch must be able to function with little or no partisanship when it comes to defending and protecting the nation. This was the case during World War II and the Cold War. It is not today.

Congress should create a committee for national security and defense that directly relates with the president's National Security Council. This committee would have the authority to set policy for Congress in conjunction with the NSC, thereby removing many of the current bureaucratic logjams.

Next, the National Security Act of 1947 must be revised to restructure the country's organization in line with the twenty-first century—not the Cold War. The old structure is vertical, with responsibilities neatly divided among diplomacy (State Department), military force (Defense Department), intelligence (CIA), and other agencies. This was fine when there was a seemingly monolithic, single threat such as the Soviet Union.

Today, the dangers of terror and extremism are horizontal, cutting across many government agencies and branches. For example, law enforcement and intelligence are no longer separable when it comes to terror. The consular service, responsible for granting visas to foreign nationals, is as much the first line of defense as were U.S. forces stationed in Germany and Japan during the Cold War. The National Security Act does not recognize these realities.

DEFUSING EXTREMISM

The revised act should take into account homeland security and break down these bureaucratic barriers. One model is Great Britain, where MI-5 is responsible for domestic intelligence, MI-6 takes care of foreign intelligence, and Scotland Yard performs the principal law enforcement tasks. Given the extraordinary difficulty in establishing a new cabinet position for homeland security, changing the law will be harder. But if it is not done, we will never be secure.

Regarding personnel, tens if not hundreds of thousands will be needed as homeland security becomes a higher priority. Incentives are crucial. One means of attracting good people would be to expand the four military service academies to national security schools and double their enrollment. Not all graduates would have to serve on active duty, though they would have a period of mandatory government service in national security billets.

Without closing these domestic deficits, the nation cannot possibly hope to become safer or more secure. Internationally, the challenge is at least as great. To deal with the crescent of crisis, a new and expanded form of the Marshall Plan, which rebuilt Europe and Japan after World War II, is crucial. A newer version should focus on reducing or eliminating the causes of extremism, which vary greatly from state to state.

For example, until the Arab-Israeli Palestinian conflict is resolved, the roots of extremism will flourish. The only workable solution is extraordinarily difficult. We need some form of international force on the ground to keep the peace. It would have to start small, perhaps in Gaza or a tiny slice of the West Bank. However, unless such a force is put in place and underwritten with economic resources, there will never be peace.

In Pakistan, such a plan would have to cope with the poverty that forces thousands of youth to enter *madrassas* for food, clothing, and shelter. These schools, virulently anti-Western and anti-American, teach the most extreme forms of Islam.

Finally, a new strategic framework is essential. A starting point is preventing the use and spread of weapons of mass destruction, nuclear weapons in particular. The United States should convene a series of strategic stability talks among the known nuclear states (United States, United Kingdom, France, Russia, China, India, and Pakistan) and include Israel and North Korea. We need to ensure these weapons will never be used and reduce them to the lowest possible number. From this framework, other vital issues can be added and membership shaped accordingly.

September 11 and what it means will require a fundamental change in how the nation goes about protecting and defending itself. If we fail to face up to these challenges and complete these pieces of unfinished business, neither we nor our children will be safe and secure.

Harlan Ullman is a senior associate in the International Security Program at the Center for Strategic and International Studies in Washington, D.C.

THE CLASH OF IGNORANCE

EDWARD W. SAID

Samuel Huntington's article "The Clash of Civilizations?" appeared in the Summer 1993 issue of *Foreign Affairs*, where it immediately attracted a surprising amount of attention and reaction. Because the article was intended to supply Americans with an original thesis about "a new phase" in world politics after the end of the cold war, Huntington's terms of argument seemed compellingly large, bold, even visionary. He very clearly had his eye on rivals in the policy-making ranks, theorists such as Francis Fukuyama and his "end of history" ideas, as well as the legions who had celebrated the onset of globalism, tribalism and the dissipation of the state. But they, he allowed, had understood only some aspects of this new period. He was about to announce the "crucial, indeed a central, aspect" of what "global politics is likely to be in the coming years." Unhesitatingly he pressed on:

"It is my hypothesis that the fundamental source of conflict in this new world will not be primarily ideological or primarily economic. The great divisions among humankind and the dominating source of conflict will be cultural. Nation states will remain the most powerful actors in world affairs, but the principal conflicts of global politics will occur between nations and groups of different civilizations. The clash of civilizations will dominate global politics. The fault lines between civilizations will be the battle lines of the future."

Most of the argument in the pages that followed relied on a vague notion of something Huntington called "civilization identity" and "the interactions among seven or eight [sic] major civilizations," of which the conflict between two of them, Islam and the West, gets the lion's share of his attention. In this belligerent kind of thought, he relies heavily on a 1990 article by the veteran Orientalist Bernard Lewis, whose ideological colors are manifest in its title, "The Roots of Muslim Rage." In both articles, the personification of enormous entities called "the West" and "Islam" is recklessly affirmed, as if hugely complicated matters like identity and culture existed in a cartoonlike world where Popeye and Bluto bash each other mercilessly, with one always more virtuous pugilist getting the upper hand over his adversary. Certainly neither Huntington nor Lewis has much time to spare for the internal dynamics and plurality of every civilization, or for the fact that the major contest in most modern cultures concerns the definition or interpretation of each culture, or for the unattractive possibility that a great deal of demagogy and downright ignorance is involved in presuming to speak for a whole religion or civilization. No, the West is the West, and Islam Islam.

The challenge for Western policy-makers, says Huntington, is to make sure that the West gets stronger and fends off all the others, Islam in particular. More troubling is Huntington's assumption that his perspective, which is to survey the entire world from a perch outside all ordinary attachments and hidden loyalties, is the correct one, as if everyone else were scurrying around looking for the answers that he has already found. In fact, Huntington is an ideologist, someone who wants to make "civilizations" and "identities" into what they are not: shut-down, sealed-off entities that have been purged of the myriad currents and counter-currents that animate human history, and that over centuries have made it possible for that history not only to contain wars of religion and imperial conquest but also to be one of exchange, cross-fertilization and sharing. This far less visible history is ignored in the rush to highlight the ludicrously compressed and constricted warfare that "the clash of civilizations" argues is the reality. When he published his book by the same title in 1996, Huntington tried to give his argument a little more subtlety and many, many more footnotes; all he did, however, was confuse himself and demonstrate what a clumsy writer and inelegant thinker he was.

The basic paradigm of West versus the rest (the cold war opposition reformulated) remained untouched, and this is what has persisted, often insidiously and implicitly, in discussion since the terrible events of September 11. The carefully planned and horrendous, pathologically motivated suicide attack and mass slaughter by a small group of deranged militants has been turned into proof of Huntington's thesis. Instead of seeing it for what it is—the capture of big ideas (I use the word loosely) by a tiny band of crazed fanatics for criminal purposes—international luminaries from former Pakistani Prime Minister Benazir Bhutto to Italian Prime Minister Silvio Berlusconi have pontificated about Islam's troubles, and in the latter's case have used Huntington's ideas to rant on about the West's superiority, how "we" have Mozart and Michelangelo and they don't. (Berlusconi has since made a half-hearted apology for his insult to "Islam.")

> *Labels like Islam and the West mislead and confuse the mind, which is trying to make sense of a disorderly reality.*

But why not instead see parallels, admittedly less spectacular in their destructiveness, for Osama bin Laden and his followers in cults like the Branch Davidians or the disciples of the Rev. Jim Jones at Guyana or the Japanese Aum Shinrikyo? Even the normally sober British weekly *The Economist*, in its issue of September 22–28, can't resist reaching for the vast generalization, praising Huntington extravagantly for his "cruel and sweeping, but nonetheless acute" observations about Islam. "Today," the journal says with unseemly solemnity, Huntington writes that "the world's billion or so Muslims are 'convinced of the superiority of their culture, and obsessed with the inferiority of their power.'" Did he canvas 100 Indonesians, 200 Moroccans, 500 Egyptians and fifty Bosnians? Even if he did, what sort of sample is that?

Uncountable are the editorials in every American and European newspaper and magazine of note adding to this vocabulary of gigantism and apocalypse, each use of which is plainly designed not to edify but to inflame the reader's indignant passion as a member of the "West," and what we need to do. Churchillian rhetoric is used inappropriately by self-appointed combatants in the West's, and especially America's, war against its haters, despoilers, destroyers, with scant attention to complex histories that defy such reductiveness and have seeped from one territory into another, in the process overriding the boundaries that are supposed to separate us all into divided armed camps.

This is the problem with unedifying labels like Islam and the West: They mislead and confuse the mind, which is trying to make sense of a disorderly reality that won't be pigeonholed or strapped down as easily as all that. I re-

member interrupting a man who, after a lecture I had given at a West Bank university in 1994, rose from the audience and started to attack my ideas as "Western," as opposed to the strict Islamic ones he espoused. "Why are you wearing a suit and tie?" was the first retort that came to mind. "They're Western too." He sat down with an embarrassed smile on his face, but I recalled the incident when information on the September 11 terrorists started to come in: how they had mastered all the technical details required to inflict their homicidal evil on the World Trade Center, the Pentagon and the aircraft they had commandeered. Where does one draw the line between "Western" technology and, as Berlusconi declared, "Islam's" inability to be a part of "modernity"?

One cannot easily do so, of course. How finally inadequate are the labels, generalizations and cultural assertions. At some level, for instance, primitive passions and sophisticated know-how converge in ways that give the lie to a fortified boundary not only between "West" and "Islam" but also between past and present, us and them, to say nothing of the very concepts of identity and nationality about which there is unending disagreement and debate. A unilateral decision made to draw lines in the sand, to undertake crusades, to oppose their evil with our good, to extirpate terrorism and, in Paul Wolfowitz's nihilistic vocabulary, to end nations entirely, doesn't make the supposed entities any easier to see; rather, it speaks to how much simpler it is to make bellicose statements for the purpose of mobilizing collective passions than to reflect, examine, sort out what it is we are dealing with in reality, the interconnectedness of innumerable lives, "ours" as well as "theirs."

In a remarkable series of three articles published between January and March 1999 in *Dawn*, Pakistan's most respected weekly, the late Eqbal Ahmad, writing for a Muslim audience, analyzed what he called the roots of the religious right, coming down very harshly on the mutilations of Islam by absolutists and fanatical tyrants whose obsession with regulating personal behavior promotes "an Islamic order reduced to a penal code, stripped of its humanism, aesthetics, intellectual quests, and spiritual devotion." And this "entails an absolute assertion of one, generally de-contextualized, aspect of religion and a total disregard of another. The phenomenon distorts religion, debases tradition, and twists the political process wherever it unfolds." As a timely instance of this debasement, Ahmad proceeds first to present the rich, complex, pluralist meaning of the word *jihad* and then goes on to show that in the word's current confinement to indiscriminate war against presumed enemies, it is impossible "to recognize the Islamic—religion, society, culture, history or politics—as lived and experienced by Muslims through the ages." The modern Islamists, Ahmad concludes, are "concerned with power, not with the soul; with the mobilization of people for political purposes rather than with sharing and alleviating their sufferings and aspirations. Theirs is a very limited and time-bound political agenda." What has made matters worse is that similar distortions and zealotry occur in the "Jewish" and "Christian" universes of discourse.

The 'Clash of Civilizations' thesis is better for reinforcing self-pride than for a critical understanding of the interdependence of our time.

It was Conrad, more powerfully than any of his readers at the end of the nineteenth century could have imagined, who understood that the distinctions between civilized London and "the heart of darkness" quickly collapsed in extreme situations, and that the heights of European civilization could instantaneously fall into the most barbarous practices without preparation or transition. And it was Conrad also, in *The Secret Agent* (1907), who described terrorism's affinity for abstractions like "pure science" (and by extension for "Islam" or "the West"), as well as the terrorist's ultimate moral degradation.

For there are closer ties between apparently warring civilizations than most of us would like to believe; both Freud and Nietzsche showed how the traffic across carefully maintained, even policed boundaries moves with often terrifying ease. But then such fluid ideas, full of ambiguity and skepticism about notions that we hold on to, scarcely furnish us with suitable, practical guidelines for situations such as the one we face now. Hence the altogether more reassuring battle orders (a crusade, good versus evil, freedom against fear, etc.) drawn out of Huntington's alleged opposition between Islam and the West, from which official discourse drew its vocabulary in the first days after the September 11 attacks. There's since been a noticeable de-escalation in that discourse, but to judge from the steady amount of hate speech and actions, plus reports of law enforcement efforts directed against Arabs, Muslims and Indians all over the country, the paradigm stays on.

One further reason for its persistence is the increased presence of Muslims all over Europe and the United States. Think of the populations today of France, Italy, Germany, Spain, Britain, America, even Sweden, and you must concede that Islam is no longer on the fringes of the West but at its center. But what is so threatening about that presence? Buried in the collective culture are memories of the first great Arab-Islamic conquests, which began in the seventh century and which, as the celebrated Belgian historian Henri Pirenne wrote in his landmark book *Mohammed and Charlemagne* (1939), shattered once and for all the ancient unity of the Mediterranean, destroyed the Christian-Roman synthesis and gave rise to a new civilization dominated by northern powers (Germany and Carolingian France) whose mission, he seemed to be saying, is to resume defense of the "West" against its historical-cultural enemies. What Pierenne left out, alas, is that in the creation of this new line of defense the West drew on the humanism, science, philosophy, sociology and historiography of Islam, which had already interposed itself between Charlemagne's world and classical antiquity. Islam is inside from the start, as even Dante, great enemy of Mohammed, had to concede when he placed the Prophet at the very heart of his *Inferno*.

Then there is the persisting legacy of monotheism itself, the Abrahamic religions, as Louis Massignon aptly called them. Beginning with Judaism and Christianity, each is a successor haunted by what came before; for Muslims, Islam fulfills and ends the line of prophecy. There is still no decent history or demystification of the many-sided contest among these three followers—not one of them by any means a monolithic, unified camp—of the most jealous of all gods, even though the bloody modern convergence on Palestine furnishes a rich secular instance of what has been so tragically irreconcilable about them. Not surprisingly, then, Muslims and Christians speak readily of crusades and *jihads*, both of them eliding the Judaic presence with often sublime insouciance. Such an agenda, says Eqbal Ahmad, is "very reassuring to the men and women who are stranded in the middle of the ford, between the deep waters of tradition and modernity."

But we are all swimming in those waters, Westerners and Muslims and others alike. And since the waters are part of the ocean of history, trying to plow or divide them with barriers is futile. These are tense times, but it is better to think in terms of powerful and powerless communities, the secular politics of reason and ignorance, and universal principles of justice and injustice, than to wander off in search of vast abstractions that may give momentary satisfaction but little self-knowledge or informed analysis. "The Clash of Civilizations" thesis is a gimmick like "The War of the Worlds," better for reinforcing defensive self-pride than for critical understanding of the bewildering interdependence of our time.

Edward W. Said, University Professor of English and Comparative Literature at Columbia University, is the author of more than twenty books, the most recent of which is Power, Politics, and Culture *(Pantheon). Copyright Edward W. Said, 2001.*

Index

Index

Test Your Knowledge Form

We encourage you to photocopy and use this page as a tool to assess how the articles in *Annual Editions* expand on the information in your textbook. By reflecting on the articles you will gain enhanced text information. You can also access this useful form on a product's book support Web site at *http://www.dushkin.com/online/*.

NAME: _____   DATE: _____

TITLE AND NUMBER OF ARTICLE: _____

BRIEFLY STATE THE MAIN IDEA OF THIS ARTICLE:

_____

LIST THREE IMPORTANT FACTS THAT THE AUTHOR USES TO SUPPORT THE MAIN IDEA:

_____

WHAT INFORMATION OR IDEAS DISCUSSED IN THIS ARTICLE ARE ALSO DISCUSSED IN YOUR TEXTBOOK OR OTHER READINGS THAT YOU HAVE DONE? LIST THE TEXTBOOK CHAPTERS AND PAGE NUMBERS:

_____

LIST ANY EXAMPLES OF BIAS OR FAULTY REASONING THAT YOU FOUND IN THE ARTICLE:

_____

LIST ANY NEW TERMS/CONCEPTS THAT WERE DISCUSSED IN THE ARTICLE, AND WRITE A SHORT DEFINITION:

We Want Your Advice

ANNUAL EDITIONS revisions depend on two major opinion sources: one is our Advisory Board, listed in the front of this volume, which works with us in scanning the thousands of articles published in the public press each year; the other is you—the person actually using the book. Please help us and the users of the next edition by completing the prepaid article rating form on this page and returning it to us. Thank you for your help!

ANNUAL EDITIONS: Violence and Terrorism 04/05

ARTICLE RATING FORM

Here is an opportunity for you to have direct input into the next revision of this volume.
We would like you to rate each of the articles listed below, using the following scale:

1. **Excellent: should definitely be retained**
2. **Above average: should probably be retained**
3. **Below average: should probably be deleted**
4. **Poor: should definitely be deleted**

Your ratings will play a vital part in the next revision.
Please mail this prepaid form to us as soon as possible.
Thanks for your help!

RATING	ARTICLE	RATING	ARTICLE
	1. Inside Terrorism		34. The Cyber-Terror Threat
	2. Terror as a Strategy of Psychological Warfare		35. Agriculture Shock
	3. Current and Future Trends in Domestic and International Terrorism: Implications for Democratic Government and the International Community		36. The Rise of Complex Terrorism
			37. Defusing Dangers to U.S. Security
			38. The Clash of Ignorance
	4. Ghosts of Our Past		
	5. The Terrorist Mentality		
	6. The Pentagon's New Map		
	7. The Terrorist Notebooks		
	8. Hostage, Inc.		
	9. Inside Suicide, Inc.		
	10. Overview of State-Sponsored Terrorism		
	11. Remarks to the United Nations Security Council		
	12. Osama bin Laden's "Business" in Sudan		
	13. Extremist Groups in Egypt		
	14. Colombia and the United States: From Counternarcotics to Counterterrorism		
	15. "Déjà Vu All Over Again?" Why Dialogue Won't Solve the Kashmir Dispute		
	16. From Push to Shove		
	17. FBI Targets Domestic Terrorists		
	18. Indictment: Smiling Face Hid Hatred		
	19. Intelligence, Terrorism, and Civil Liberties		
	20. Accomplice or Witness? The Media's Role in Terrorism		
	21. 'Spin Laden'		
	22. Jihadis in the Hood: Race, Urban Islam and the War on Terror		
	23. Supplying Terrorists the 'Oxygen of Publicity'		
	24. Doomsday Religious Movements		
	25. Understanding the Challenge		
	26. Myths in the Representation of Women Terrorists		
	27. Young, Gifted and Ready to Kill		
	28. Demon Lover		
	29. Targeting Terrorism		
	30. Missed Messages		
	31. Counterterrorism		
	32. Waiting for Bioterror		
	33. Blue Planet: Ecoterrorism Redefined		

(Continued on next page)

NO POSTAGE
NECESSARY
IF MAILED
IN THE
UNITED STATES

BUSINESS REPLY MAIL
FIRST-CLASS MAIL PERMIT NO. 84 GUILFORD CT

POSTAGE WILL BE PAID BY ADDRESSEE

McGraw-Hill/Dushkin
530 Old Whitfield Street
Guilford, Ct 06437-9989

Illoullooloololloolldloldlolddooldd

ABOUT YOU

Name _____   Date _____

Are you a teacher? ☐   A student? ☐
Your school's name _____

Department _____

Address _____ City _____ State _____ Zip _____

School telephone # _____

YOUR COMMENTS ARE IMPORTANT TO US!

Please fill in the following information:
For which course did you use this book?
_____

Did you use a text with this ANNUAL EDITION? ☐ yes ☐ no
What was the title of the text?
_____

What are your general reactions to the *Annual Editions* concept?
_____

Have you read any pertinent articles recently that you think should be included in the next edition? Explain.
_____

Are there any articles that you feel should be replaced in the next edition? Why?
_____

Are there any World Wide Web sites that you feel should be included in the next edition? Please annotate.
_____

May we contact you for editorial input? ☐ yes ☐ no
May we quote your comments? ☐ yes ☐ no